THE
YOUTH
DEVELOPMENT
HANDBOOK

COMING OF AGE IN AMERICAN COMMUNITIES

EDITORS

STEPHEN F. HAMILTON
CORNELL UNIVERSITY

MARY AGNES HAMILTON
CORNELL UNIVERSITY

SAGE Publications
International Educational and Professional Publisher
Thousand Oaks ■ London ■ New Delhi

For information:

Sage Publications, Inc.
2455 Teller Road
Thousand Oaks, California 91320
E-mail: order@sagepub.com

Sage Publications Ltd.
6 Bonhill Street
London EC2A 4PU
United Kingdom

Sage Publications India Pvt. Ltd.
B-42, Panchsheel Enclave
Post Box 4109
New Delhi 110 017 India

Printed in the United States of America

Library of Congress Cataloging-in-Publication Data

Library of Congress Cataloging-in-Publication Data

The youth development handbook: Coming of age in American communities / edited by Stephen F. Hamilton and Mary Agnes Hamilton.
    p. cm.
Includes bibliographical references and index.
ISBN 0-7619-2634-8
ISBN 0-7619-8872-6
    1. Youth—Services for—United States. 2. Social work with youth—United States. I. Hamilton, Stephen F. II. Hamilton, Mary Agnes.
HV1431.Y6876 2004
362.71—dc21
                              2003013110

This book is printed on acid-free paper.

03   04   05   06   10   9   8   7   6   5   4   3   2   1

Acquisitions Editor:	James Brace-Thompson
Editorial Assistant:	Karen Ehrmann
Production Editor:	Denise Santoyo
Copy Editor:	Carla Freeman
Typesetter:	C&M Digitals (P) Ltd.
Indexer:	Teri Greenberg
Cover Designer:	Sandy Sauvajot/Janet Foulger

THE
YOUTH
DEVELOPMENT
HANDBOOK

To Urie Bronfenbrenner, colleague, friend, and mentor.

Contents

Foreword

This excellent volume contains within its two covers a wealth of practical information for practitioners who work with adolescents as they go through their daunting voyage toward adulthood.

Surfers spend their lives searching for the perfect wave. So, one might say, do youth development experts. They continually refine their insights—based on research, interaction with the field, and good sense—to produce better guidance and materials to help those on the front line. This book constitutes a good-sized step forward in stating the art. It's not the "perfect" wave, but we're coming along.

The task is so complicated. There are the challenges of being there for individual young people—by definition different for each person but presenting at the same time universal commonalities and commonalities of group cultures and problem sets. There are challenges of program design, differing by objective, age of the young people served, location, and a host of other variables. There are challenges of empowerment and efficacy, of how to maximize the number of young people who participate successfully in the economy and in the workings of the civil society. There are challenges of community building, seeing programs in terms of what they will contribute to and how they will draw from the context in which they are nested. There are challenges of relationship to and interaction with a host of broader societal institutions, including schools, the labor market, the health care system, law enforcement, and child protection services. There are challenges of being relevant to and responsive to structural issues of discrimination, whether based on race, ethnicity, gender, religion, disability, or sexual orientation.

This book covers many of these bases, constructively and usefully.

I am particularly concerned about a dimension of isolation and even denial in youth development practice. One might say that youth development work comes in two flavors: being there for all young people as they move toward adulthood, and being there for those who are at particular risk of falling by the wayside. The deck is so stacked against those in the second group, for a whole host of reasons. And yet I don't see great emphasis in the literature or, more important, in much of the practice, on taking on the racism and the economic stratification and the lousy schools and the recalcitrant employers and the awful juvenile and criminal justice and child welfare systems, and all the rest of it. But maybe the point of youth development work is to be the infantry, the people on the front line who do the one-on-one work that is a vital part of the answer, and maybe the only one that works in an immediate sense. Maybe taking on the big stuff is somebody else's responsibility.

But I keep thinking that more is possible—that, even with the fact that there are only 24 hours in the day, youth development as a field could encompass more explicitly attention to and connection to fighting against the larger forces that are stacking the deck against too many young people in America. Heaven knows, we need it. The people in Washington are openly and ostentatiously cutting taxes to make the rich richer and to make it impossible for our country to find the money to do something about the long list of real national needs that we have. We need—desperately need—people, especially young people, to take up the in-our-face challenge that has been placed before us. There's nothing secret going on here, no backroom deal, no silent coup. The whole thing is right there—blatant, unmistakable.

So if this foreword serves any purpose other than to praise this valuable book, my purpose is to challenge all of us to step up our game, and, even more important, to challenge all of the young people with whom we work to play to the hilt their role as citizens and participants in the American community. That, in the end, is the only way we're going to have even a fair shot at making youth development into the force that it ought to be in fulfilling America's promise.

—*Peter Edelman,*
Georgetown University

Preface

Our purpose in editing this volume is to give youth workers and others who wish to promote youth development in communities access to a rapidly growing body of knowledge. We hope the readers will be encouraged to build connections among settings or contexts for youth development to build a system within their communitites so that all youth may thrive. The aim of the book is to stimulate and inspire. It is not a "How-to" guide.

The term *youth development* and the ideas and practices associated with it have emerged from the field of youth work, but they have extended beyond practice to influence local, state, and national decision makers in the public and private sectors. Recently, youth development has become a focus for research. This sequence is important. The youth development movement began with professionals and volunteers engaged day-to-day with young people in their communities, in Boys and Girls Clubs, parks and recreation programs, faith groups, families, essentially in settings or contexts other than schools. Recognizing the primacy of practitioners in the field, our intention is to support them by providing a compact and readable set of essays summarizing current theory and research in the field, illustrated by examples of good practice.

Youth development is not unique in arising from practice. Practice seldom follows theory in lockstep. Rather, the two advance reciprocally as knowledge from each domain influences the other. We emphasize theory and research in this volume, with the goal of illuminating, extending, and challenging practice, not as something temporally prior and superior to practice that practitioners should regard as the received truth. We hope readers will not only use the theory and research and the case illustrations, learn from them, and appeal to them for external validation but also challenge, refine, correct, and enlarge them to continue the evolution of the field.

The literature on youth development has grown rapidly, especially in the past decade. Enough written material can now be found both in print and on the Web to confuse any reader. One source of confusion is the different ways in which the term is used; another source of confusion is with the number of related terms—especially *positive youth development* and *community youth development*. In addition, writers emphasize different aspects of the topic, according to their varying perspectives and purposes: internal and external assets, resilience, prevention, and youth empowerment. But writers also disagree about some of the major tenets of the field, which is inevitable when a field encompasses so much.

The first chapter addresses the question of what we think youth development is and how it happens. Chapters in Part I describe how different contexts or settings contribute to youth development. They capture much of what we know about those contexts and how each may support youth development. These chapters are organized around people and activities that influence youth development. We emphasize contexts or settings because that reflects the way many people who work with youth identify themselves. The contexts within which development takes place are interrelated. Descriptions of exemplary programs in each chapter illustrate the kinds of issues people face in these environments as they implement the principles of youth development.

Some chapters refer to physical locations (schools, neighborhoods), others to moveable contexts (family, peer group), and some may overlap (peers congregate in schools and neighborhoods). One, the popular media culture, is a context only in an abstract way. But it is too pervasive and powerful an influence to neglect.

Although we hope each chapter will contain material that is valuable to all readers, we recognize that someone who is experienced in working with youth, for example, in a faith-based organization, might find little new in the few pages that can be devoted to that topic. Those pages may be more valuable for a reader familiar with community development who can gain a clearer understanding of how faith-based organizations might contribute to a youth initiative.

Our subtitle intentionally pays homage to Margaret Mead, whose book *Coming of Age in Samoa* (1928/1970) taught us that many of the youth issues we think of as being biologically programmed result instead from the interaction of biology with society: "Adolescence is not necessarily a time of stress and strain, but that cultural conditions make it so" (p. 170). Adolescence, in other words, is not inherently a tumultuous stage of life that youth and adults simply have to suffer through. This insight offers hope that we can make our communities more caring and supportive places where all youth can come of age as engaged and respected members, fully human though rapidly gaining competence. The ideas, findings, and examples contained in these pages can help us fulfill that hope.

Reference

Mead, M. (1928/1970). *Coming of age in Samoa.* Ann Arbor, MI: Morrow (Laurel Edition).

Acknowledgments

T he idea for this book arose from a seminar on youth development led by Stephen Hamilton at Cornell University in the spring of 2001. Regular participants, several of whom are authors of chapters, included Frank Barry, Catherine Bradshaw, Meghan Butryn, Amanda Carreiro, Charlotte Coffman, Aram DeKoven, Jutta Dotterweich, Marcia Eames-Sheavley, Doug Elliott, Steve Goggin, Héléne Grégoire, Mary Agnes Hamilton, Charlie Izzo, Cathann Kress, Jane Powers, Geoffrey Ream, Nancy Schaff, Chrissie Schelhas-Miller, Ray Swisher, Sue Travis, Janis Whitlock, Jerry Ziegler, and David Zielinski.

As the semester drew to a close, we began to discuss the idea of an edited book to share with practitioners some of what we had learned by reading, discussing, and writing about the literature of the field. Janis Whitlock was heavily involved in the first several iterations of a plan for such a book and in drafting a paper on principles now discussed in Chapter 1; we are grateful for her contributions. Rich Lerner urged us to proceed with the idea and generously referred us to Jim Brace-Thompson at Sage, who embraced the plan and encouraged our continued refinements of it. We appreciate the assistance of Karen Ehrmann, Carla Freeman, and Denise Santoyo in preparing the manuscript for publication.

Cathann Kress alerted us to a survey of youth workers that led us to limit both the number and the length of the chapters. Many colleagues nominated outstanding youth programs and organizations throughout the country that we contacted for telephone interviews seeking advice about our plans for the volume and how they might use it. We appreciate both the nominations and the advice. Catherine Bradshaw helped with these interviews. Several themes came through clearly. Respondents said they would like to read about principles and research related to best practices (and we learned about some of those practices as they described their own programs). They said they could use a resource for training staff, informing their boards, and as background for planning and proposals. Several made the point that they could learn how youth development works in contexts other than the one in which they worked and how to collaborate more effectively across contexts. We have tried to respond to these recommendations by providing recent research findings along with rich illustrations of youth and adults engaged in activities in various settings. Trying to shape the book in this mold, we asked the chapter authors to write in an engaging style and to work within the framework we set. We appreciate their patience through multiple revisions.

We have learned from youth who have shared parts of their lives with us over the years: youth apprentices, volunteers, and interns we have interviewed and observed and the caring and committed adults who worked with them; Cornell students who have assisted with a series of research projects; our students at Farquhar Middle School, George Wythe High School, and Phelps Vocational High School; and the denizens of the Belmont Youth Center.

Colleagues too numerous to mention have challenged and instructed us, both in our professional lives and as community volunteers. Through Cornell Cooperative Extension's 4-H Youth Development program, we have experienced the complexity of creating opportunities for youth. Participation in New York State's Youth Development Team and in the Assets Coming Together for Youth initiative were major motivations for this book. Serving as board members made us aware of the range of people and organizations supporting youth in our community, the resource constraints they face, and their potential power.

Nicole Yohalem worked closely with us on the first chapter and also in planning for the book and providing resource information. We appreciate her great ideas, positive outlook, and hard work. Our three sons, Pete, Joey, and Ben, deserve thanks as well for teaching us, with untiring patience, wit, and ingenuity, about today's youth, who they are, who they can become and how, and for reminding us of how much more we have to learn. We trust that their youthful vitality will endure as they emerge into adulthood.

Introduction

WHAT IS YOUTH DEVELOPMENT?

1

Principles for
Youth Development

Stephen F. Hamilton,
Mary Agnes Hamilton, and Karen Pittman

The term *youth development* is used in at least three different ways, referring to a natural *process* of development, *principles*, and *practices*. All three are important, and they are logically related.[1]

1. *A natural process.* Youth development has traditionally and is still most widely used to mean a natural process: the growing capacity of a young person to understand and act on the environment. In this usage, it is identical to child or adolescent development. Human development is the natural unfolding of the potential inherent in the human organism in relation to the challenges and supports of the physical and social environment. Development lasts as long as life. Optimal development in youth enables individuals to lead a healthy, satisfying, and productive life, as youth and later as adults, because they gain the competence to earn a living, to engage in civic activities, to nurture others, and to participate in social relations and cultural activities. *Youth* sometimes includes childhood and adolescence, but the field of youth development emphasizes adolescence, roughly the second decade of life. This age range is the primary target of this book. Both heredity and environment influence the natural unfolding. People can actively shape their own development

through the choices they make and interpretations they place on their experiences.

2. *Principles.* In the 1990s, the term *youth development* came to be applied to a set of principles, a philosophy or approach emphasizing active support for the growing capacity of young people by individuals, organizations, and institutions, especially at the community level. The youth development approach is rooted in a commitment to enabling all young people to thrive. This simple statement combines two principles: universality or inclusiveness (all youth) and a positive orientation building on strengths (thriving). Youth development arose as a counterbalance to the emphasis in problem prevention and treatment programs on categorizing youth according to their deficits and trying to remedy them. The contrast between a youth development approach and approaches designed to prevent or treat specific kinds of problems among groups of youth identified as being at high risk is somewhat analogous to that between public health and medical treatment (see Chapter 5 on health care). As in the health field, sharp debates and rivalries are often dulled in practice, where, in reality, a blend of both approaches is needed. If all youth are to thrive, some of them need prevention and treatment. Additional principles will be discussed below, notably that youth development occurs in the context of healthy relationships and challenging activities that endure and change over time and that youth are fully engaged participants, not just recipients.

3. *Practices.* The third use of the term youth development is to describe a range of practices in programs, organizations, and initiatives. Youth development in this sense refers to the application of the principles (Number 2) to a planned set of practices, or activities, that foster the developmental process (Number 1) in young people. The distinction between principles and practices is especially useful when considering the various settings or contexts in which young people spend time, which is the theme of Part I in this volume. Development takes place in families, neighborhoods, youth organizations, faith-based organizations, schools, and a multitude of other places, including cyberspace. Although the specific practices that adults use to create and sustain such opportunities differ across settings, the principles are consistent.

In our terminology, programs, organizations, and initiatives are sequentially larger aggregations of practices. A program may be short-term or long-term. It may involve large or small numbers of youth. It is usually embedded in or sponsored by an organization. An organization is more enduring and has multiple components. Organizations typically engage youth in a range of different programs. For example, a youth in the East Oakland Youth Development Center (see Chapter 2 on youth organizations) might enroll in their arts, employment, and/or physical development programs. By *initiative,* we mean a multifaceted collaborative effort to enlist the broadest possible set of people and organizations in making communities more conducive to youth development. Two initiatives, Beacons and New Futures Initiatives, are treated in the chapter on communities.

Youth development has also gained prominence as a movement (Pittman, Irby, & Ferber, 2000) serving as a unifying theme for a wide range of discussions and actions aimed at shaping policy as well as practice. *Policy,* a fourth "P," refers to a course of action adopted by an organization, especially a government. Youth development principles have informed policy at all levels of government (local, state, and national) and in a variety of different sectors or departments that include a focus on young people. We treat the policy arena throughout the volume because it is relevant to all chapters.

We turn now to youth development as a process, followed by a discussion of the theoretical basis for some of the key youth development principles. We address practices only briefly in this introduction, because the chapters in Part I illustrate effective youth development practices across the range of settings youth inhabit.

The Process and Goals of Youth Development

Development is a process, not a goal. People continue to develop throughout their lifetimes. Therefore, promoting youth development is an enduring, overarching purpose, not a goal that is ever finally achieved. John Dewey (1938) captured this quality by noting that the purpose of development is to enable a person to continue to develop. Viewing development in this way complicates the identification of goals. Rather than setting out concise measurable behaviors, developmental goals identify domains for growth. Progress, as opposed to attainment, is the key (Kohlberg & Mayer, 1972).

This circular quality of development makes it difficult to separate *goals* from *methods for achieving goals.* Goals and methods, ends and means, and process and product are intertwined. Because goal setting is such an important part of program planning, we will refer to developmental goals, recognizing that even though such goals are not always amenable to measurable outcomes or behavioral objectives, they can provide a helpful framework to guide action.

Human qualities that we wish to promote can be described in multiple ways. A simple formulation is that development leads to the "Five Cs": competence, character, connections, confidence, and contribution (listed as caring and/or compassion in other formulations) (Pittman, Irby, Tolman, Yohalem, & Ferber, 2002). *Competence* includes knowledge and skills that enable a person to function more effectively to understand and act on the environment. Competence enables a person to accomplish what he or she intends, provided external circumstances are favorable, or to adapt to circumstances to achieve as much as possible. *Character* is what makes a person intend to do what is just, right, and good. *Connections* refer to social relations, especially with adults, but also with peers and with younger children. *Confidence* is the assuredness a person needs to act effectively. It enables a person to demonstrate and build competence and character in challenging situations. *Contribution* means that a person uses these other attributes not only for self-centered purposes but also to give to others.

Notice that none of these developmental goals has an upper limit. One is never perfectly competent or of such high character that no further progress is needed. However, it is possible to get out of balance, especially with connections and confidence. We denigrate as a "social butterfly" a person who cares too much about superficial connections, especially when that person seems to sacrifice character, adopting whatever opinions or behaviors are popular. When confidence outruns competence, danger looms. We think of the "Five Cs" as logically linked. Competence and character are central. Young people gain competence and character by being connected with others, especially caring adults, and their competence and character in turn help them form new connections. Confidence flows from competence, and the two mutually reinforce each other. Finally, contributions demonstrate one's character and provide an outlet for competence. (These connections are discussed further in the chapter on work and service.)

The "Five Cs" briefly summarize the goals of youth development. They are useful as a quick mental checklist when thinking about what a particular program, organization, or initiative offers to youth. They can provide a focus for community-wide initiatives. However, each is broad enough to pose challenges when it comes to designing and evaluating programs. Programs might try to enhance the competence of young people in a multitude of ways and across a range of contexts or settings, making it difficult to know when progress occurs and what led to it. For program-planning purposes, a longer, finer-grained analysis of the goals of development is needed.

The Committee on Community-Level Programs for Youth, convened by the National Research Council and Institute of Medicine of the National

Table 1.1   Personal and Social Assets That Facilitate Positive Youth
Development

Physical Development

- Good health habits
- Good health risk management skills

Intellectual Development

- Knowledge of essential life skills
- Knowledge of essential vocational skills
- School success
- Rational habits of mind—critical thinking and reasoning skills
- In-depth knowledge of more than one culture
- Good decision-making skills
- Knowledge of skills needed to navigate through multiple cultural contexts

Psychological and Emotional Development

- Good mental health, including positive self-regard
- Good emotional self-regulation skills
- Good coping skills
- Good conflict resolution skills
- Mastery motivation and positive achievement motivation
- Confidence in one's personal efficacy
- "Planfulness"—planning for the future and future life events
- Sense of personal autonomy/responsibility for self
- Optimism coupled with realism
- Coherent and positive personal and social identity
- Prosocial and culturally sensitive values
- Spirituality or a sense of a "larger" purpose in life
- Strong moral character
- A commitment to good use of time

Social Development

- Connectedness—perceived good relationships and trust with parents, peers, and some other adults
- Sense of social place/integration—being connected and valued by larger social networks
- Attachment to prosocial/conventional institutions, such as school, church, nonschool youth programs

(Continued)

Table 1.1 (Continued)

- Ability to navigate in multiple cultural contexts
- Commitment to civic engagement

SOURCE: National Research Council and Institute of Medicine (2002, Box 3-1, pp. 74-75). Reprinted with permission from Community Programs to Promote Youth Development. ©2002 by the National Academy of Sciences, courtesy of the National Academies Press, Washington, DC.

Academy of Sciences, has provided an authoritative summation of the critical domains of youth development, adopting the terminology of *personal and social assets* (See Table 1.1). They categorized these assets as physical, intellectual, psychological and emotional, and social development.[2]

Note that the term *asset* allows for the same ambiguity we have attributed to developmental goals. Assets are both desirable in themselves (think of cash and real estate) and useful in obtaining other desirable things that may themselves also be assets (buying artwork with cash, using real estate to secure a loan).

If one adds *promote* or *increase* to each of the assets listed in the box, they serve well as a list of goals for youth development. The formulation by the Committee on Community-Level Programs for Youth of the key domains of youth development and the implied goals associated with each has several strengths. First, it represents a distillation of available research by distinguished scholars on the qualities of people who succeed by most standards. Second, it provides far more specific targets for youth development than the preceding abbreviated sets of goals. This fuller compilation aids both the design of programs and their evaluation. Third, this list is detailed enough that it distinguishes among and explicates some goals that are at best implicit in the briefer lists, notably, physical and mental health; knowledge, skills, and values that open one to multiple cultures; emotional self-regulation; and spirituality.

On the other hand, a long, detailed set of goals may not necessarily help rally large numbers of people behind a community initiative or serve as a quick reminder of what programs are trying to accomplish. Thus, choosing which list of developmental goals to use depends on how it will be used rather than which one is "correct." The point of presenting both the "Five Cs" and the personal and social assets identified by the Committee on Community-Level Programs for Youth is precisely that they do not conflict.

The second expands on and adds detail to the first. The longer list can provide a framework for helping different youth development programs and organizations identify both their unique contributions and the goals they share with others.

The term *developmental assets* is most closely associated with the Search Institute (Benson, 1997), a not-for-profit organization that conducts research and provides materials, training, and technical assistance to youth organizations and communities. As pioneers in the youth development movement, the Search Institute found that they could motivate community-wide initiatives around 40 developmental assets (see Table 1.2). Half are external assets that exist to varying degrees in the settings young people inhabit and the people with whom they interact, including family support, safety, adult role models, and creative activities. The other 20 are internal assets that are attributes of young people themselves, such as school engagement, honesty, interpersonal competence, and sense of purpose.

Comparing the Search Institute's list of internal assets with the list produced by the Committee on Community-Level Programs for Youth shows substantial overlap, especially when minor differences in wording are considered. The Committee's list, as noted, has the authority of its eminent members and the National Academy of Sciences behind it, along with substantial documentation. The Search Institute has produced a volume substantiating its 40 assets with research, as well (Scales & Leffert, 1999). Therefore, youth development advocates may use either list with confidence. Although we believe a short list, especially the "Five Cs," may be most effective for rallying community support, the Search Institute has infused its 40 assets into community-wide initiatives. In one community, for example, a grocery store printed the list on shopping bags to remind citizens of what their youth need.

The 40-asset framework is useful in illustrating the circular nature of developmental goals. The research cited indicates that "the more of these assets young people have, the less likely they are to engage in risky behavior . . . and the more likely they are to engage in positive behaviors" (Scales & Leffert, 1999, p. 7). But is it helpful to learn that youth who are more engaged in school get better grades? Are these really two different things, one an input and the other an output? They appear to be reciprocally related: Students who do better in school are likely to feel more engaged. Distinguishing between what is cause and what is effect muddies discussions about outcomes, which makes goal setting difficult. Perhaps part of the appeal of the asset construct is precisely that we value assets for themselves as well as for their correlation with other desired behaviors and states.

Principles for Promoting Youth Development

Calling attention to the usage of the term *youth development* to designate a set of principles is easier than stating those principles precisely. To gain widespread support, any set of principles must be rather broad; specificity is likely to create disagreement. Moreover, as a term spreads, it acquires new meanings, not all of which are universally accepted or even compatible. The youth development principles we find most central and most useful for present purposes are those stated at the beginning of this chapter: the emphasis on a positive approach and universality, or the goal of all youth thriving; the importance of healthy relationships and challenging activities that endure and change over time; and engaging young people as participants, not merely recipients. Others would add to or restate some of the items on this list, but we believe it captures most of what is critical. The following pages provide a theoretical basis for these principles.

All Youth Thrive

The positive orientation is best understood in contrast to what has been the conventional problem focus of many programs for youth, especially those funded by the federal government. In her pathbreaking book *Adolescents at Risk*, Joy Dryfoos (1990) documented the division of federal funding and programs among four major types of problem behavior: teenage pregnancy, substance abuse, delinquency, and school failure. She pointed out that because each problem is the domain of a different federal agency and the source of categorical funding, local prevention and treatment programs mirror the federal structure. Each draws on funding from its own federal agency and applies it to trying to prevent or treat the designated problem in a targeted set of youth, typically those considered at risk of the problem. The system is so well established that each problem also has its own researchers and research literature. In addition to demonstrating a lack of connection among these different enterprises, Dryfoos went on to show that, according to the research in each one, the presumably separate problems and solutions were actually quite closely related. This insight illustrated how shortsighted it is to consider and try to alleviate youth problems (or any human problems) one-at-a-time. Drugs, alcohol, risky sexual behavior, delinquency, school failure, and other problems are best conceived as part of a "problem behavior syndrome" (Jessor & Jessor, 1977) that often has common roots and is best treated as a whole.

Building on Strengths

There is another consideration, too, which is that often the best way to solve problems is to build on strengths. This approach has been validated by research on resilient children, that is, children who grew up under conditions that usually lead to serious problems but somehow managed to thrive. (See the treatment of this perspective in the juvenile justice chapter.) Among the drawbacks of emphasizing problems is the self-fulfilling prophecy or labeling effect. When youth are selected to participate in a program because they are at risk or enmeshed in problem behavior, selection confirms their identity as troubled. Furthermore, being thrown together with others who are also stigmatized may unintentionally reinforce undesirable behavior. (See "deviancy training" in the peers chapter.)

Universality

The emphasis on a positive orientation is closely related to the principle of universality. If all youth need support in their development, then participating in a program is no longer stigmatizing. At one extreme, some would say that youth development programs can never be targeted to a defined group and can never engage problem behavior. We reject this extreme. The fact that all youth are developing and that their development can be either enhanced or impeded by the opportunities available to them in their families, schools, and communities definitely does not mean that all youth need the same thing. One youth may need a chance to practice leadership skills, while another's most pressing need may be a safe place to spend the night. Applying the principles of youth development to the second youth means that providing a shelter for the night is necessary but not sufficient; he or she needs opportunities for growth as well.

Services, Supports, and Opportunities

The distinction among services, supports, and opportunities (Pittman et al., 2002) helps illustrate how a positive orientation and universality are consistent with the need for access to individualized treatment. Opportunities should be available to all. Opportunities—to learn, explore, play, express oneself—are, by definition, taken up voluntarily by a young person once they have been made available. This makes them both universal and individualized. The young person selects from among possibilities. Supports are also available to all. Supports include connections between a young person and others; mentoring is a good example. Services are provided for or administered to a young person. They include health care, housing, social services, compulsory schooling, and drug treatment. Most services are available, in principle, to anyone who needs them. Specific services are targeted, but the safety net of services is universal.

The tension between a positive, universal approach and a more problem-focused, targeted approach is vividly represented in practice by two of the organizations that have done the most to apply and disseminate youth development: the Search Institute and the Social Development Research Group at the University of Washington, originators of Communities That Care. Communities That Care draws on a solid and growing base of research in prevention of youth risk behavior (Catalano, Berglund, Ryan, Lonczak, & Hawkins, 1998; Catalano & Hawkins, 1996; Developmental Research and Programs, Inc., 2000). A community that uses this approach begins by determining which youth problems are most prevalent relative to other communities and then selects a validated program, or programs, to reduce those problems. In contrast, the Search Institute helps communities to identify their assets and those of their youth and then to work together to build both. As a result, it is less prescriptive and less focused on problem identification and reduction. Although financial and other constraints often mean communities must choose between the two, we regard these frameworks as potentially complementary, addressing as they do different aspects of a comprehensive, community-wide youth development initiative (Whitlock & Hamilton, 2003).

Race, Ethnicity, Class, and Gender

Youth differ along other lines, too, in addition to the degree of risk they face or the level and type of problem behaviors they engage in. Most notably, they reflect the stratification of society in the United States according to race and ethnicity, social class, and gender. In general, the cultural backgrounds of European American youth and those with other backgrounds, especially African American and Latino, will differ, not totally, but enough to require attention. Yet the experience and meaning of being African American can vary dramatically from one young person to another, even within the same family. Therefore, prescriptions for action tailored to racial categories are of little use. They are more likely to perpetuate stereotypes than to overcome them.

As an illustration, many mentoring program staff believe that matching young people with adult mentors of their own race is critical. However, the most rigorous empirical test of that assumption, in the context of an experimental evaluation of Big Brothers/Big Sisters (Rhodes, Reddy, & Grossman, 2002) found no effect for race of mentor on the behavior of young people. The most persuasive post hoc explanation for the lack of difference is that racial matching probably matters a great deal for young people who are grappling with issues of racial identity and of how they cope in a racist society, but it may matter not at all for others who either have not yet begun to grapple with such issues or are doing so with some success in other venues, such as family, school, or religious organization.

Gender is another powerful source of difference. Certainly, for some purposes and at some times, boys and girls need different opportunities and different treatment. But gender is not always primary. We have to be able to recognize and accommodate gender differences while recognizing that sometimes gender is less important than race or class or age or simply interests and aspirations.

Social class is another major category, closely associated with race and ethnicity, but not identical. Youth development in an impoverished community differs in important ways from youth development in an affluent one. The principles are the same, but the needs and strategies for meeting them may vary enormously. Sometimes, they vary in unexpected ways that test common assumptions about youth needs.

Challenging Activities and Supportive Relationships

Urie Bronfenbrenner's ecological perspective (Bronfenbrenner, 1979; Bronfenbrenner & Morris, 1998) provides a solid theoretical grounding for a range of youth development principles, in particular, the importance of engagement in challenging activities and supportive relationships, both of which endure and change over time. For Bronfenbrenner, development means growing competence. (Contrary to Dewey, who defined development as inherently positive, Bronfenbrenner sees development as including the loss of capacities, as happens in aging, and dysfunction, which may result from harmful developmental influences.) "The engines of human development," according to Bronfenbrenner, are "proximal processes" (Bronfenbrenner & Morris, 1998, p. 996). Proximal processes are activities that occur regularly over a long period of time and become progressively more complex. Learning to play piano, soccer, and chess are all examples.

Bronfenbrenner's conception of human development suggests that development is generally promoted by engagement in activities that are regular and enduring and that are challenging in the sense of increasing in complexity as people gain competence. Such activities may be performed solo with objects (e.g., photography or pottery) or symbols (e.g., writing poetry, writing a computer program) or both (e.g., painting, playing a musical instrument), but often, they also involve relationships with others. Those relationships are also most beneficial when they are regular, enduring, and reciprocal. Although relationships with adults are especially important, relationships with peers and with younger children also contribute to development. Bronfenbrenner's theory explains why playing soccer or chess, learning to dance, or planning and carrying out a community service project are more beneficial developmentally than watching television or gossiping with friends.

Bronfenbrenner conceives of the environment in which development occurs as a set of nested contexts ranging from families and peer groups (microsystems) to the culture and government (macrosystems) and proposes a series of hypotheses about how these contexts or systems interact (Bronfenbrenner, 1979, p. 22). Those who would promote youth development can use this conception to understand where a program, organization, or initiative fits among the contexts in which young people develop, and the range of influences on that process. Imagine two young people serving as interns in a hospital in a program like the one described in the chapter on work and service. What is most important for one may be the skills learned while helping patients do their exercises and the chance to learn about a potential career. What matters most for the other may be that the nurse in charge takes a personal interest in him, asks about his progress in school, his family, and his friends, and encourages him to continue his education.

The best-designed program is, by itself, neither the sole nor even the strongest influence on the attitudes and behavior of the participants. Young people are also influenced by their peers, families, neighborhoods, the media, their perceptions of their chances to "make it," and the interactions among all these influences and more. Add to this mix the variety of interests, genetic endowments (including talents and temperament), and previous experiences different people bring with them, and it is no wonder that one hospital intern becomes a physical therapist as a result of the experience, whereas the other takes an entirely different career direction but attributes his success in part to the mentoring he experienced as an intern.

Youth programs and organizations affect participants differently. Outcomes will never be uniform regardless of how good programs and organizations are. Such inescapable differences reinforce the importance of both variety and choice. One activity is not developmentally appropriate and enhancing for all.

Youth Participation

A corollary to the observation that youth have different interests and needs and therefore respond differently to the same opportunities is that they should have choices about which activities they participate in and they should have a chance to help shape those activities. This principle also follows from Bronfenbrenner's definition of proximal processes as reciprocal. Human beings develop through active engagement with their environment; by making choices and shaping that environment, they also direct their own development. They are more than passive recipients of external influences (Bronfenbrenner, 1979, p. 21).

Development is not simply something that happens to a person; *agency* refers to the developing person's active involvement in shaping the process of development, for example, by choosing challenging activities and seeking supportive relationships. This conception underlies the principle that youth are participants rather than simply recipients; they are responsible actors. This principle goes by many names, such as youth voice, participation, and empowerment. It is rooted in the rights young people have as citizens of a democracy and in what is most beneficial to their development (Convention on the Rights of the Child, 1989). In addition, when programs engage participants in serious decisions, those programs usually benefit and as a result can be more responsive, more attractive, and more effective (Zeldin, McDaniel, Topitzes, & Calvert, 2000). The rights of both adults and youth are constrained and balanced by responsibilities. Emphasizing youth engagement and responsibility does not mean leaving young people to make all the decisions all the time. Older youth in general have greater capacity and opportunity to make decisions that affect themselves and others than do young children. (See chapter on youth organizations.)

Practices for Promoting Youth Development

If the foregoing principles are valid, then putting them into practice will promote youth development. This assertion is consistent with the recommendation of the Committee on Community-Level Programs for Youth (National Research Council and Institute of Medicine, 2002, Table 4-1, pp. 90-91; see Table 1.3), which produced a list of features of settings that promote youth development based on the best available research:

Physical and Psychological Safety

Appropriate Structure

Supportive Relationships

Opportunities to Belong

Positive Social Norms

Support for Efficacy and Mattering

Opportunities for Skill Building

Integration of Family, School, and Community Efforts

According to the Committee, these features are associated with progress toward the developmental goals they identified (i.e., "assets"). Note that these features correspond to the Search Institute's 20 "external assets" and are also quite consistent with the principles of youth development stated at the beginning of this chapter. This list also echoes Maslow's (1970) hierarchy of human needs, which begins with survival needs and proceeds to self-actualization. We have not emphasized safety, but it is clearly fundamental.

The challenge to practitioners is to figure out how to create environments that bring these features to life. The last feature, "integration of family, school, and community efforts," raises an added and exceptionally complex set of issues. It recalls Bronfenbrenner's (1979) enumeration of the different systems that comprise the ecology of human development and his propositions about the value of connections among them. Trying to integrate efforts across settings involves building systems in the sense of linked and mutually reinforcing places that promote the development of all.

The term *community youth development* is often used to capture this aspect of youth development, emphasizing what we call *community-wide initiatives* (Villarruel, Perkins, Borden, & Keith, 2003). For some, this modifier seems redundant because by definition, youth development entails attempts to make communities healthier places for youth to live and grow. However, we find it helpful because it distinguishes community-wide mobilization from efforts within individual programs or organizations. Many of the illustrations in the chapters describe youth development programs in larger organizations (e.g., faith-based organizations and parks and recreation departments) and organizations that have additional purposes (e.g., juvenile justice). Although we do not include a community-wide focus as a critical component of our basic definition of youth development, the importance of the community is emphasized in the chapters on neighborhoods and community-wide initiatives.

✳ Youth development is more than helping one young person at a time; it entails the creation of a range of contexts or settings, including people and activities that promote youth development. Ideally, they constitute a system in the sense that they are inclusive, enduring, connected to each other, and connected to the larger macrosystem that surrounds them (e.g., labor market, government, mass media). This definition of a system as inclusive, internally coherent, connected to other systems, and enduring (Hamilton & Hamilton, 1999, p. 7) differentiates a system from a program. First, a system is *inclusive* by being large enough to accommodate all those who qualify. A public school system, for example, which must find classroom space and teachers for every first grader who enrolls each fall, may be contrasted with a Head Start program, which typically turns away half to two thirds of eligible applicants. Second, a system is *internally coherent.* It provides guidance to participants on how to move through it, and what a person does in one part of the system counts in another. An after-school program that is systematic is more than a menu of activities. Students can move sequentially through increasingly complex activities, taking more responsibility as they go, just as Algebra II builds on Algebra I. Third, a system is *externally connected,* or formally linked to other systems. For example, if a school requires students to perform community service, it should recognize service activities done under the auspices of a Boy Scout troop or religious youth group, provided they meet certain standards. Finally a system *endures;* it is not dependent on year-to-year allocations of "soft money."

Our hope for this book is that it will give youth development practitioners some information, ideas, sources, and models to use in trying to build youth development systems. We have organized the book principally around the settings youth inhabit, believing that this fits with the way in which practitioners work. They are usually associated with one or more of these settings. However, as we planned a volume that would be brief enough to be usable, we realized that most readers would find the chapters on the settings they know best to be less informative for them than chapters on other settings. We urge readers to consult chapters on the settings they do not know well, to learn about and thereby work more effectively with people in them who share the goals and principles of youth development.

We also made a choice not to include separate chapters on two important topics: youth participation and differences by race, ethnicity, class, and gender. Like the policy topic, we believe these issues are best understood in relation to the content of each chapter. Therefore, we asked chapter authors to discuss them. We do return to these issues again in the concluding chapter.

Table 1.2   40 Developmental Assets

Category	Asset Name and Definition
	External Assets
Support	1. Family Support—Family life provides high levels of love and support.
	2. Positive Family Communication—Young person and her or his parent(s) communicate positively, and young person is willing to seek advice and counsel from parents.
	3. Other Adult Relationships—Young person receives support from three or more nonparent adults.
	4. Caring Neighborhood—Young person experiences caring neighbors.
	5. Caring School Climate—School provides a caring, encouraging environment.
	6. Parent Involvement in Schooling—Parent(s) are actively involved in helping young person succeed in school.
Empowerment	7. Community Values Youth—Young person perceives that adults in the community value youth.
	8. Youth as Resources—Young people are given useful roles in the community.
	9. Service to Others—Young person serves as in the community one hour or more per week.
	10. Safety—Young person feels safe at home, school, and in the neighborhood.
Boundaries & Expectations	11. Family Boundaries—Family has clear rules and consequences and monitors the young person's whereabouts.
	12. School Boundaries—School provides clear rules and consequences.
	13. Neighborhood Boundaries—Neighbors take responsibility for monitoring young people's behavior.
	14. Adult Role Models—Parent(s) and other adults model positive, responsible behavior.
	15. Positive Peer Influence—Young person's best friends model responsible behavior.
	16. High Expectations—Both parent(s) and teachers encourage the young person to do well.
Constructive Use of Time	17. Creative Activities—Young person spends three or more hours per week in lessons or practice in music, theatre, or other arts.
	18. Youth Programs—Young person spends three or more hours per week in sports, clubs, or organizations at school and/or in the community.
	19. Religious Community—Young person spends one or more hours per week in activities in a religious institution.
	20. Time at Home—Young person is out with friends "with nothing special to do" two or fewer nights per week.
	Internal Assets
Commitment to Learning	21. Achievement Motivation—Young person is motivated to do well in school.
	22. School Engagement—Young person is actively engaged in learning.
	23. Homework—Young person reports doing at least one hour of homework every school day.
	24. Bonding to School—Young person cares about her or his school.
	25. Reading for Pleasure—Young person reads for pleasure three or more hours per week.
Positive Values	26. Caring—Young person places high value on helping other people.
	27. Equality and Social Justice—Young person places high value on promoting equality and reducing hunger and poverty.
	28. Integrity—Young person acts on convictions and stands up for her or his beliefs.
	29. Honesty—Young person "tells the truth even when it is not easy."
	30. Responsibility—Young person accepts and takes personal responsibility
	31. Restraint—Young person believes it is important not to be sexually active or to use alcohol or other drugs.
Social Competencies	32. Planning and Decision Making—Young person knows how to plan ahead and make choices.
	33. Interpersonal Competence—Young person has empathy, sensitivity, and friendship skills.
	34. Cultural Competence—Young person has knowledge of and comfort with people of different cultural/racial/ethnic backgrounds.
	35. Resistance Skills—Young person can resist negative peer pressure and dangerous situations.
	36. Peaceful Conflict Resolution—Young person seeks to resolve conflict nonviolently.
Positive Identity	37. Personal Power—Young person feels he or she has control over "things that happen to me."
	38. Self-Esteem—Young person reports having a high self-esteem.
	39. Sense of Purpose—Young person reports that "my life has a purpose."
	40. Positive View of Personal Future—Young person is optimistic about his or her personal future.

Source: ©1997 by Search Institute. www.search-institute.org This page reproduced, with permission, for educational, noncommercial use only.
Note: Search Institute has identified the above building blocks of healthy development that help young people grow up healthy, caring, and responsible.

Table 1.3   Features of Positive Developmental Settings

	Descriptors	*Opposite Poles*
Physical and Psychological Safety	Safe and health-promoting facilities; and practices that increase safe peer group interaction and decrease unsafe or confrontational peer interactions.	Physical and heath dangers; fear; feeling of insecurity; sexual and physical harassment; and verbal abuse.
Appropriate Structure	Limit setting; clear and consistent rules and expectations; firm-enough control; continuity and predictability; clear boundaries; and age-appropriate monitoring.	Chaotic; disorganized; laissez-faire; rigid; overcontrolled; and autocratic.
Supportive Relationships	Warmth; closeness; connectedness; good communication; caring; support; guidance; secure attachment; and responsiveness.	Cold; distant; overcontrolling; ambiguous support; untrustworthy; focused on winning; inattentive; unresponsive; and rejecting.
Opportunities to Belong	Opportunities for meaningful inclusion, regardless of one's gender, ethnicity, sexual orientation, or disabilities; social inclusion, social engagement, and integration; opportunities for sociocultural identity formation; and support for cultural and bicultural competence.	Exclusion; marginalization; and intergroup conflict.
Positive Social Norms	Rules of behavior; expectations; injunctions; ways of doing things; values and morals; and obligations for service.	Normlessness; anomie; laissez-faire practices; antisocial and amoral norms; norms that encourage violence; reckless behavior; consumerism; poor health practices; and conformity.
Support for Efficacy and Mattering	Youth based; empowerment practices that support autonomy; making a real difference in one's community; and being taken seriously. Practice that includes enabling, responsibility granting, and meaningful challenge. Practices that focus on improvement rather than on relative current performance levels.	Unchallenging; overcontrolling; disempowering; and disabling. Practices that undermine motivation and desire to learn, such as excessive focus on current relative performance level rather than improvement.
Opportunities for Skill Building	Opportunities to learn physical, intellectual, psychological, emotional, and social skills; exposure to intentional learning experiences; opportunities to learn cultural literacies, media literacy, communication skills, and good habits of mind; preparation for adult employment; and opportunities to develop social and cultural capital.	Practices that promote bad physical habits and habits of mind; and practices that undermine school and learning.
Integration of Family, School, and Community Efforts	Concordance; coordination; and synergy among family, school, and community.	Discordance; lack of communications; and conflict.

SOURCE: Adapted from National Research Council and Institute of Medicine (2002), Table 4-1, pp. 90-91. Reprinted with permission from Community Programs to Promote Youth Development. ©2002 by the National Academy of Sciences, Washington, DC.

Additional Resources on Youth Development

The American Youth Policy Forum is an excellent source of policy-related material and other information. Available at: http://www.aypf.org/index.htm.

The Center for Youth Development and Policy Research has helped shift the public debate from youth problems to youth development and makes resources available. Available at: www.cyd.aed.org.

Child Trends has a large and diverse list of publications, including research papers, research briefs, literature reviews, and a growing collection of "what works" interactive tables that identify programs proven by research to be effective in promoting child and youth development. They also have an on-line data bank that offers continuously updated trend data with the latest national estimates for all indicators, including downloadable graphics and tables. See especially, American Teens: A Special Look at "What Works" in Adolescent Development. Available at: http://www.childtrends.org.

Community Youth Development is a journal published by the Institute for Just Communities (IJC) and the Institute for Sustainable Development, Heller School of Social Policy and Management, Brandeis University, in collaboration with the National Association of Extension 4-H Agents (NAE4-HA). Available at: http://www.cydjournal.org/.

CYFERnet is a Web site containing program materials, research, and other information from land grant universities and county cooperative extension offices across the country. Available at: http://www.cyfernet.org//.

The Forum for Youth Investment (Karen Pittman) has a wealth of information. Their newsletter is always valuable. Available at: http://www.forumfor-youthinvestment.org/.

The National Training Institute for Community Youth Work provides curricula and training to strengthen youth worker practice. Available at: www.nti.aed.org.

The National Youth Development Information Center is maintained by the National Collaboration for Youth, whose members include the National 4-H Council and other major youth-serving organizations. It contains a wealth of information on programs, funding, and research. Available at: http://www.nydic.org/nydic/.

Public/Private Ventures conducts excellent research on youth programs. Available at: http://www.ppv.org.

The Search Institute (Peter Benson) promotes community youth development using its 40-assets framework. It provides support to communities and extensive research. Available at: http://www.search-institute.org/.

The Social Development Research Group, University of Washington School of Social Work, is the origin of "Communities That Care" (Catalano & Hawkins), the best source for youth programs that have been validated by research. Available at: http://depts.washington.edu/sdrg/. A commercial publisher handles some of their materials: http://www.channing-bete.com/positiveyouth/.

Notes

1. S.F. Hamilton devised and contributed this definition to a New York State policy statement (Partners for Children Adolescent Project Team, 2000). He later found a parallel three-part definition on the Web site of the National Youth Development Information Center (www.nydic.org), attributed to Edginton & deOlivera (1995, Spring), "A Model of Youth Work Orientations," *Humanics*, pp. 3-7.

2. Pittman, Irby, and Ferber (2000) distinguish the following domains: cognitive, social, physical, emotional, personal, civic, and vocational development.

References

Benson, P. L. (1997). *All kids are our kids: What communities must do to raise caring and responsible children and adolescents.* San Francisco: Jossey-Bass.

Bronfenbrenner, U. (1979). *The ecology of human development: Experiments by nature and design.* Cambridge, MA: Harvard University Press.

Bronfenbrenner, U., & Morris, P. (1998). The ecology of developmental processes. In R. M. Lerner (Ed.), *Handbook of child psychology: Vol. 1. Theoretical models of human development* (5th ed.). New York: Wiley.

Catalano, R. F., Berglund, L. M., Ryan, J. A. M., Lonczak, H. S., & Hawkins, J. D. (1998). *Positive youth development in the United States: Research findings on evaluations of positive youth development programs.* Report prepared for U.S. Department of Health and Human Services, Office of the Assistant Secretary for Planning and Evaluation, and the National Institute for Child Health and Human Development. (Available at: http://aspe.os.dhhs.gov/hsp/positive-youthdev99/)

Catalano, R. F., & Hawkins, J. D. (1996). The social development model: A theory of antisocial behavior. In J. D. Hawkins (Ed.), *Delinquency and crime: Current theories* (pp. 149-197). New York: Cambridge University Press.

Convention on the Rights of the Child. (1989). Retrieved on March 17, 2003, from http://www.unicef.org/crc/crc.htm.

Developmental Research and Programs, Inc. (2000). *Communities That Care: Prevention strategies: A research guide to what works.* Seattle, WA: Author.

Dewey, J. (1938). *Experience and education.* New York: Collier.

Dryfoos, J. (1990). *Adolescents at risk: Prevalence and prevention.* New York: Oxford University Press.

Hamilton, M. A., & Hamilton, S. F. (1999). *Building strong school-to-work systems: Illustrations of key components.* Washington, DC: U.S. Government Printing Office. (Also available at: http://www.human.cornell.edu/youthwork/)

Jessor, R., & Jessor, S. L. (1977). *Problem behavior and psychosocial development: A longitudinal study of youth.* New York: Academic Press.

Kohlberg, L., & Mayer, R. (1972). Development as the aim of education. *Harvard Educational Review, 42,* 449-496.

Maslow, A. H. (1970). *Motivation and personality.* New York: Harper & Row.

National Research Council and Institute of Medicine. (2002). *Community programs to promote youth development.* J. Eccles & J. A. Gootman (Eds.). Board on Children, Youth, and Families, Division of Behavioral and Social Sciences and Education. Washington, DC: National Academy Press.

Partners for Children Adolescent Project Team. (2000). *Promoting positive youth development in New York State: Moving from dialogue to action.* Albany, NY: Author. (Available at http://www.nyspartnersforchildren.org/teen.htm)

Pittman, K., Irby, M., & Ferber, T. (2000). *Unfinished business: Further reflections on a decade of promoting youth development.* Washington, DC: Forum for Youth Investment.

Pittman, K., Irby, M., Tolman, J., Yohalem, N., & Ferber, T. (2002). *Preventing problems, promoting development, encouraging engagement: Competing priorities or inseparable goals?* Washington, DC: Forum for Youth Investment.

Rhodes, J. E., Reddy, R., & Grossman, J. B. (2002). Volunteer mentoring relationships with minority youth: An analysis of same versus cross-race matches. *Journal of Applied Social Psychology, 32,* 2114-2133.

Scales, P. C., & Leffert, N. (1999). *Developmental assets: A synthesis of the scientific research on adolescent development.* Minneapolis, MN: Search Institute.

Villarruel, F. A., Perkins, D. F., Borden, L. M., & Keith, J. G. (Eds.). (2003). *Community youth development: Programs, polices, and practices.* Thousand Oaks, CA: Sage.

Whitlock, J. L., & Hamilton, S. F. (2003). The role of youth surveys in community youth development initiatives. *Applied Developmental Science, 7*(1) 39-51.

Zeldin, S., McDaniel, A. K., Topitzes, D., & Calvert, M. (2000). *Youth in decision-making: A study on the impacts of youth on adults and organizations.* Chevy Chase, MD: National 4-H Council.

Part I

PROCESSES AND PRACTICES IN YOUTH DEVELOPMENT CONTEXTS

2

Youth C--anizations

From Prin·   ce

Morva McDonald, an.   *nes,* *hlin*

C ommunity programs for youth exist in most neigh̲   ds. From national organizations such as the Boys and Girls Clubs of America or Girls, Inc., to local innovative and resourceful grassroots agencies, these community organizations open doors and create much-needed opportunities for young people. Many of the national groups have long histories of youth programming; in others, local inventions such as mural art projects or community service opportunities spring up as expressions of adult interests and investments in youth. The missions and goals of community-based youth programs are equally diverse: assistance with academic work, recreation, community service, moral development, and safety. Local structures vary, too. Some locally supported organizations are autonomous community creations, others are associated with public sector institutions such as libraries, and still others are affiliated with private community groups such as adult service clubs, museums, or religious organizations.

The vast and varied landscape of community-based youth programs defies any effort to compile accurate figures about the number of these organizations or participating youth.[1] Yet as a broader perspective of the personal and social assets youth need for healthy development gains credence at national, state, and local levels, policymakers, funders, practitioners, and others have begun to consider the value of community-based organizations to youth and their communities. More than a decade of research suggests that community-based youth organizations can play a vital role in youth development and education, particularly for urban youth whose families and schools are not able to meet their needs (McLaughlin, 2000; McLaughlin, Irby, & Langman, 2001; National Research Council and Institute of Medicine, 2002; Pittman, Ferber, & Irby, 2000). We also know that positive youth development requires learning across multiple domains, physical, social and emotional, as well as intellectual (National Research Council and Institute of Medicine, 2002).

As a clearer picture emerges of what youth need to aim for and attain a productive, healthy adulthood, we also understand more about the organizational structures, program features, functions, and contexts that support these youth development goals. Important features include the following:

- *Youth-centeredness.* Effective youth organizations put youth at the center, and adults who work with them know about their interests and what they bring to the organization. They know about their lives at home, at school, and in the community. Youth-centered programs make an effort to build on strengths as they respond to diverse interests, talents, and circumstances. Youth-centered programs feature youth leadership and responsibility as well as youth voice for important aspects of the organization and its activities. Activities offer multiple ways to get involved, so even the least-skilled youth can find a place to belong, and are age appropriate.

- *Clear focus.* Community organizations that engage young people are about something: the arts, sports, or leadership development as examples. Generic "club programs" hold little appeal for teens who are focusing on their own identities and concerns. They may drop in to such organizations to hang out or shoot some hoops, but they are unlikely to attend consistently.

- *Embedded curriculum.* Effective youth programs have an "embedded curriculum," or activities that deliberately teach a number of lessons across the domains of social, emotional, physical, and cognitive development. Every activity provides occasion to teach many lessons. Conflict management, cultural heritage, and nutrition, for example, all might be taught as a sports team learns athletic skills.

- *Cycles of planning, practice, and performance.* Successful youth programs provide ongoing feedback to young people about how they are progressing, and with this assessment comes recognition for growth and accomplishment.

- *Caring community.* Critical and nonnegotiable for youth is an organizational setting in which they feel physically and emotionally safe, respected, and accepted. — *Key words*

Deliberate attention to developmental needs, individuality, and promise are common to community-based organizations that succeed in the eyes of youth. Yet despite accumulating evidence about the important and possibly singular contribution youth development programs can make, such programs generally are the exception rather than the rule (Pittman et al., 2000). Youth workers and community groups find it is not so easy to design, carry out, or sustain programs that are deliberate about youth development and effective in engaging adolescents' participation. Although youth development ideas find enthusiastic support in principle, in practice they have been difficult for youth organizations to put into place. This mismatch between knowledge base and practice raises a question: If we know so much about features of positive youth development settings, why don't more community programs provide them?

This chapter takes up that question by first considering the challenges practitioners face when navigating the institutional environments in which their programs are situated. We then turn to case examples of three quite different programs that have nonetheless managed to meet these challenges and provide youth with rich, supportive, and engaging opportunities. Finally, we examine the lessons these cases teach us about how youth organizations put youth development principles into practice, especially in ways that attract and retain the involvement of older youth.

Institutional Challenges to a Youth Development Agenda

All youth organizations must navigate an institutional setting defined by organizational structures, funding arrangements, local political economy, and the other agencies and interests that work with youth, such as schools, justice, and health. The institutional landscape of youth organizations contains fundamental challenges to a youth development agenda. Ever-changing goals of funders top the list of constraints mentioned by the adults responsible for program design and development. "Flavor of the month" describes perceived shifts in the interests of private and public funders. Large organizations have become skilled at repackaging parts of their overall programming to match funders' guidelines, but small groups or groups with a single focus do so with difficulty. The clear and particular focus associated with effective youth programs can become a liability in a context in which support for a program's goals is displaced. In many communities, for example, interest in activities that focus on literacy has eroded backing for sports and arts organizations.

Programs and organizations that attend to developmental needs of youth are not inexpensive. Yet it is difficult for adults to attend to a young person's interests and needs in the context of "herd programming," in which large numbers of youth are served in a relatively impersonal environment. But for local agencies stretched to make budgets balance, simply making space available with some adult oversight may be all that is possible. Quality materials, adult attention, and learning opportunities can be costly. Programs operating on a shoestring confront practical limits on what they can do to attend to the individual interests, needs, and circumstances of youth.

Strong adult-youth relationships are important to a safe, caring environment. Yet youth organizations everywhere struggle to hire and retain qualified youth workers. Staff turnover typically is high, especially in high-poverty, high-crime urban areas. Youth often experience the short tenure of staff as betrayal by adults. Equally problematic is the challenge of finding staff with the necessary skills and background to carry out a high-quality, youth-centered, learning-focused program. In many organizations, staff lack both knowledge of youth development principles and training or background in program content.

Coordination with other youth-serving institutions has been difficult, especially for smaller, grassroots efforts. Despite attention to the benefits of collaboration and coordination from many quarters, youth organizations have had a hard time establishing productive relationships with other organizations, especially with schools. Priorities differ, rules and routines often conflict, and practical concerns such as care of space and liability issues often sink even the best collaborative intentions.

Three Cases of Youth Development in Practice

The case studies presented here originated with a 2-year study of youth development organizations in the San Francisco Bay Area.[2] In this research, we found several examples of strong youth development practice in youth organizations that successfully navigated these institutional challenges.[3] Here, we highlight three organizations and their efforts to provide opportunities that support youth learning and development. These cases of Bay

Area youth organizations include East Oakland Youth Development Center, an organization that fosters mutual respect and a caring community in the context of arts, employment, and physical development programs; HOME, a youth-run organization with an emphasis on community involvement; and Jamestown Community Center, with its school-based arts and sciences programs and neighborhood-based emphasis. Each organization has a full membership that includes teens. Each organization serves a community struggling with the manifestations of poverty, violence, and deficient social institutions.

Each case demonstrates how individual organizations put in place youth development practices that include opportunities for youth to develop relationships with other youth and adults, participate in decision making and leadership roles, become involved in the larger community, and develop skills and knowledge through their participation in challenging and interesting opportunities. We highlight how their practices represent the youth development features discussed above—youth-centeredness; clear focus; embedded curriculum; cycles of planning, practice, and performance; and caring community—and describe how program leaders have productively managed challenges in their institutional settings to enact a youth development agenda.

East Oakland Youth Development Center

For many of the youth of East Oakland, the East Oakland Youth Development Center (EOYDC) is a place of hope. The surrounding neighborhood is one of Oakland's poorest and most violent. One third of the adults in East Oakland do not have a high school diploma or equivalency; the dropout rate at the local high school is over 50%, and the average grade point average hovers around 1.28, or a D. In the midst of these conditions, EOYDC provides a safe environment for youth to explore their interests, develop their talents, and achieve their goals both as individuals and as members of a community.

History

In collaboration with community members and under the guidance of former Clorox CEO Robert B. Shetterly, the Clorox management proposed a youth center to target the particular needs of East Oakland's youth, and in 1978, EOYDC opened its doors. EOYDC has been offering youth programs in three core areas: job opportunities for youth (JOY), physical development, and the Kuumba After School Arts program. The three departments provide the foundation for all EOYDC activities, including classes in computers, drawing and painting, steel pans, West African dance, ceramics and photography, General Educational Development certificate (GED) preparation and testing, cooking, karate, basketball, track and field, and Scholastic Aptitude Testing (SAT) preparation.

Approximately 45% of EOYDC's operating budget comes from the interest generated by their endowment, freeing them to a significant extent from annual "funding sambas." In 1983, the EOYDC was established with a $1.5 million grant from the Clorox Company, followed by the company's two $1 million matching-grant challenges, which EOYDC met. Today, the endowment totals about $7 million. The executive director has noted that the endowment "has really helped us be more self-sufficient so we can focus on the work of developing programs and interacting with youth."[4]

The executive director has ensured this focus by streamlining EOYDC's programs. The organization expanded in the 1990s to include counseling services because there was "lots of money" at that time for organizations that offered mental health services to youth and their families. When the director came to EOYDC in 1994, the organization had a $2.2 million budget, of which only $700,000 was supporting their three core programs. In recognition that the counseling services EOYDC had offered were not adding to their core programs for youth, EOYDC began to refer youth out for mental health services and shrank their budget to a total of $650,000 in 1995. In the director's own words,

We were never experts in counseling, we want to do chicken and just chicken and we want to do that right. You're not going to come in here and find a smorgasbord. We started out doing job opportunities for youth, art, and physical development and we're going to do it well or we're not going to do it at all.

Implementation of Positive Youth Development

Four practices are instrumental to EOYDC's implementation of positive youth development: caring community, clear focus, embedded curriculum, and cycles of planning, practice, and performance.

Caring Community. EOYDC establishes a caring community through norms and values that encourage self-respect, respect among youth, respect between youth and adults, and respect among adults. At the beginning of African dance, for example, a staff member called for all basketballs and practice jerseys, and the youth playing a pickup game ran their final play down the court. The members of the African dance troupe slid off their shoes and stored them under the bleachers. The dancers took the floor, and the drummers beat a rhythm that accompanies the warm-up. The dancers, ranging in age from 4 to 17, listened while the dance teacher reminded them about the history of the Lindy Hop, the music of Duke Ellington, and the Harlem Renaissance. Just before beginning the practice, the teacher broke into song with "It don't mean a thing if you ain't got no swing." Joining in, the youth filled the gym with their voices. The subtle interactions among people are evidence of the importance and the ubiquitous presence of respect at EOYDC. The youth who were playing basketball, for example, understand and respect those who participate in the African dance troupe, as indicated by their quick departure from the gym floor.

Youth are supported, encouraged, and expected to demonstrate their talents, knowledge, and interests. This performance aspect of EOYDC builds the confidence and self-respect of those involved in any particular activity while also demanding the respect of others who witness the developed talents and skills of those participating. For instance, when the chefs in the culinary arts program share their creations, the fruits of their labor encourage the respect of other participants, both youth and adults.

Establishing a caring community takes more than warmth. Staff set clear rules and enforce them consistently. During one observation, an adult in the homework center walked three girls to the front desk to relay to a staff member that they were calling each other names. The other staffer said to the girls, "That is not acceptable here. We're calling your parents, and you can't come back for a whole week." These rules function as guideposts for youth and help them learn EOYDC norms and values. Consistent adherence to the rules is as important as the rules themselves. The director of the physical education department indicated that the behavior of youth becomes everyone's responsibility. He said,

> Sometimes when a kid is acting up, I put the basketball hoops up and no one plays. [The youth] start to check each other. I want them to know how to confront negative behavior. So, if they're at school and someone pulls out a beer or a cigarette, I want them to know how to confront them. They have to be willing to take people on, to be responsible for each other.

EOYDC manages to balance strict expectations regarding behavior with day-to-day practices and interactions with youth that construct norms and values of mutual respect.

Youth have the opportunity to participate in many of the activities at EOYDC starting as early as age 4, and they can continue to develop and grow with the support of the center through early adulthood, fostering a long-term commitment between youth and EOYDC. One youth began her involvement at EOYDC with the West African dance troupe at the age of 4; at the age of 12, she volunteered to be one of the receptionists at the front desk; and at 14, she had a paying job as an EOYDC receptionist. Recently, she completed two of the computer classes offered through the JOY program. This youth's long-term involvement is not unusual. The staff of EOYDC support and witness the academic, social, and emotional growth of youth over many years and, as a result, have the opportunity to adapt their expectations to fit the particular age-specific needs of youth over time. Unlike some organizations that offer only drop-in activities for youth, many of EOYDC's activities require youth to commit to regular attendance, and, as a result, they become more than participants in an activity; they become members of teams, dance troupes, and clubs. Many even keep in touch with the center after their formal participation has ended. This membership structure encourages youth to identify with particular programs and perhaps helps to sustain their interest.

Clear Focus. EOYDC offers a mix of activities that require a long-term commitment and emphasize particular interests such as dance, sports, and job preparation. The culinary arts program engages youth by developing their cooking skills and understanding of nutrition, while the computer classes attend to their particular interests in the Internet and learning different software packages. For some youth, the programs' clear focus enables them to identify with others who share the same interests, as is the case for many of the African dancers or members of the basketball team. The identification among youth with specific teams or activities may strengthen their commitment to each other and to EOYDC.

Although its programs are focused, EOYDC structures activities so that youth have various avenues for participation. For example, a youth can be a member of the West African dance troupe while at the same time drop into the homework center or arts room on any given day. This combination of structure and flexibility allows youth to explore multiple dimensions of their identities and interests through a variety of activities. The nature of participation at EOYDC is dynamic. The executive director captures the underlying philosophy that requires the center to create and sustain multiple avenues of participation: "If [youth] can't achieve success, they're going to walk away, so give them something that is of themselves, that can be celebrated, and that they can feel good about." This very simple philosophy sustains many of the practices at EOYDC and inspires the staff to understand that it is their responsibility to assist youth in finding and accessing opportunities that motivate, interest, and challenge them.

Embedded Curriculum. Combined with the clear focus of programs at EOYDC is the quality of the content and instruction. Each staff member responsible for a program—whether basketball and track, culinary arts, dance, or computers— demonstrates extensive knowledge and understanding of the content that underlies each activity. Staff's extensive knowledge allows them to adapt activities to the interests and skill levels of individual youth.

The quality of the instruction observed at EOYDC is related to the center's philosophy that youth are allowed to participate in ways that are developmentally appropriate. Individuals of different ages, abilities, and interests engage in many of the activities at EOYDC, and the instructors make intentional efforts to manage the differences among them. For example, often before the core programs start, a staff member organizes a pickup basketball game for anyone interested. The participants in these games span multiple ages and abilities. Instead of simply allowing the youth to choose teams at random, the staff member carefully selects youth for each team and then matches them up to guard one another. His ability to match up teams is an indication of his knowledge and understanding of each individual's abilities. This casual pedagogical technique is beneficial for two reasons. First, it creates fairly equal teams, thus avoiding the complete domination of one team over another. Second, it places younger with older youth, in effect allowing the older individuals to encourage the younger ones, as when an older player announced to the staff and other players, "Did you see that? Robert knows how to shut down the base line!" And he said this even though the younger player failed to prevent him from scoring. The staff's instructional strategies support and encourage positive relationships among the youth of different ages and abilities and are central to EOYDC's youth development practices.

Cycles of Planning, Practice, and Performance. Youth at EOYDC have multiple opportunities to demonstrate their knowledge and skills. Practice and performance are integral features of many activities and provide opportunities for them to receive both formative and summative assessments of their individual progress. The chefs of the culinary arts program share their creations, the basketball team practices and plays in official games, the African dance troupe presents at the winter celebration, and artists display their work in the foyer. The demands of performing do not become exclusionary, but rather act to encourage many youth to participate.

The West African dance troupe practiced 3 days a week while preparing for the winter celebration, a community event held with a school of dance at the Alice Arts Theatre in downtown Oakland. The practices and final performances included youth of all ages, regardless of experience and ability. During one of the last practices before the final performance, the instructor reviewed the details with the participants. She reminded them,

> On Saturday, we have a technical rehearsal. We call it technical because it's like a car and we have to get it to run. Rehearsal for the young kids is from ten to eleven, and then the big girls come. Sunday is the show, you will be expected to sing and dance. Those of you who aren't dancing we need as greeters, dressed up like you dress up for Easter. The greeters are only for those of you who don't know all the steps. Trust me, everyone will take part.

The instructor was committed to involving everyone, even youth who acknowledged that they didn't know the steps. Then she began dance practice as usual, and despite the pressure to solidify the final performance, she allowed anyone who wanted to participate to join in. The West African dance troupe performed in front of a community audience of approximately 400 adults and youth, all of whom celebrated their efforts, knowledge, and talents as dancers.

HOME

At HOME, youth generate, design, implement, and assess project ideas and participate in constructing the governance and operating structure of the organization. HOME provides resources and supports for youth to pursue their own goals related to personal growth and community involvement. With the support of adult coaches and consultants, youth develop their strengths and expand their interests by participating in any one of HOME's projects.

History

HOME began in September 1996, when the executive director asked the Alameda School Superintendent to pull together 20 youth and release them after fourth period to participate in a series of electives called "Effective Citizenry." This group of youth, referred to as "the founders," developed the frame for HOME. As the director explains,

> I laid down only one law—by the end of the first semester you had to have a C in every subject in order to remain in HOME. They came up with an evaluation system for their participation and grading.

This first cohort of HOME youth facilitated a youth conference attended by 150 adults and 250 youth. In the second year, HOME extended their programs into the after-school hours, beginning what they called the "Real World Labs."

With the ongoing support of adult staff, the youth of HOME have implemented a variety of projects, including the following:

- HOMEstead: the new location for HOME's projects, located on the former Alameda naval base
- Community Build: bringing together more than 500 youth and adults volunteering over $750,000 in labor and materials to renovate HOME's new building
- HOME Sweet HOME: an all-day child care center located at HOMEstead
- Bay Area School of Enterprise (BASE): the first youth-created charter high school
- Work for Alameda Youth (WAY): a youth employment agency
- Cityview Skate Park: the largest outdoor skate park in Northern California
- Expression: an Intergenerational Women's Conference
- Real World Lab: an after-school project for elective credit.

The relationship between community involvement and youth development has been a theme throughout HOME's growth. In its first 3 years, HOME grew rapidly in size and capacity. HOME's focus on community projects that are youth designed and youth implemented establishes the setting in which the features of positive youth development are enacted. HOME offers a perspective on youth development practices that captures the importance of process. Although the content and emphasis of the projects change from year to year, the commitment to involving youth in all aspects of the process and the organization remains consistent. Youth development practices at HOME are situated in a zone of tension between involving the broader community and maintaining a youth focus.

Implementation of Positive Youth Development

Caring Community and Youth-Centeredness. HOME's youth-centeredness is key to the nurturing community that has developed among youth and adults. From its inception, HOME has integrated youth perspective and voice into the organization's structure and operation in two important ways. First, the organization is structured in such a way that youth have authentic opportunities to share their perspective in individual conversations as well as through structured activities. Second, the organization and the adult coaches look to youth for advice, and listen and respond in real ways to the issues and ideas that youth generate.

These two aspects of HOME's environment were evident during a daylong retreat. The agenda of the retreat included giving youth an opportunity to conceptualize a new structure for the organization, in response to their interest in rethinking the structure specifically in consideration of the HOMEstead project as well as the adult coaches' acknowledgement that the internal structure of HOME needed to be revisited and perhaps reconceived. During the retreat, one participant indicated her view of the current structure:

> I think we've had a lot of confusion over the structure, people can't commit because they don't know where to commit. A new structure would help us minimize part of people's frustrations. Maybe we need to create ongoing activities, so we're not always stuck in this process—we need some real specific things we're creating so we can hang our hat on something.

In response to many of the youth raising similar concerns, the adult coaches redesigned the agenda to include an activity in which the participants, in groups, brainstormed about possible new structural arrangements.

This group activity surfaced many issues and generated a number of creative and thoughtful ideas for developing a new organizational structure. One group agreed that they wanted a core group of 10 youth who would help guide the organization and take leadership roles. However, one youth interjected, "We don't want to set it up so it's a privilege to be in this group. I'm worried it will create a hierarchy." Another youth responded, "But we have to have some kind of council or something—an internal structure that delegates responsibility." At the completion of this activity, one of the adult coaches reflected back to the youth some of the common themes:

> I heard that we don't want a hierarchy—we want a democratic way—and that you want to share the leadership and the power. Also the theme of communication ran through your brainstorms. I think next week we should get together to create a structure, goals, and a vision so that we have some tangible evidence of this meeting today.

HOME's incorporation of youth into its day-to-day practices and overall structure helps it become a caring community respectful of the opinions, talents, and interests youth bring to the organization.

In combination with incorporating youth voice, HOME provides multiple ways for youth to engage in the projects and builds on their interests. Because youth invent, design, and implement the projects, they can access the resources and support of HOME in ways that are meaningful and responsive to their particular interests. The evolution of the Cityview Skate Park, an idea initially generated by two young individuals, grew to involve many of the youth at HOME and encouraged individuals to participate in the project in ways that built on their unique skills and capabilities. For some, participation included mobilizing community volunteers, while for others, it included speaking with consultants regarding design issues. This is also evident in how youth have participated in the HOMEstead project. Some participated in the research group, some considered issues of funding, and others worked to build relationships with the community.

Cycles of Planning, Practice, and Performance. Cycles of planning, practice, and performance are integral to many of the HOME activities in which youth participate. This youth development practice seems to be a constant presence in the work of HOME. Because HOME is project based and follows a cycle in which youth develop a project idea, design it, implement it, and assess it, they have the opportunity to reflect on their efforts at varying stages of the process.

Youth participants' meeting with community members, including politicians, corporate executives, and foundation officers, to get support for HOMEstead is evidence of this cycle. The participants planned for that meeting in numerous ways. Some made phone calls to invite community members, some organized the conference room and decorated the walls, some made charts of their business plans for the adults to examine, and others organized the plan for the presentation and prepared to facilitate. In essence, the meeting was the performance that required all the individual and small-group preparations to come together.

HOME has added another aspect of the cycle, "reflections," that may enhance what individuals learn by participating. Following many of the presentations, the adult coaches allow time for reflection and provide a structure in which youth can consider lessons learned from their experience. After the annual youth conference, the young organizers met to reflect on the conference day. The reflection was guided by two questions: "What worked?" and "What didn't go well?" One youth was particularly distraught by the long list of items under the question "What didn't go well?" The executive director's philosophy is as follows:

> If you care about doing something well, you always have a long list of things to do better. The challenge for new kids is to understand that failure doesn't get codified as a D and then you forget about it. In this case they have to try to make sense of why it worked and didn't work.

This view of trying to understand both the successes and failures represented in a performance challenges youth to learn from their experiences.

Tension Between Youth-Centeredness and Community Involvement. The building of the Cityview Skate Park was a defining moment in the history of HOME. Up until that time, many of the projects the youth of HOME had designed and implemented were realized with the support and con- sultation of a few adults and minimal collaboration with community insti- tutions. In many respects, this was HOME's initial experience of engaging the broader community in one of the organization's projects. During the 10-day construction of the skate park, 900 community members volun- teered supplies, time, and energy. The building of the skate park demanded intense collaboration between HOME and other organizations within the community. According to the executive director,

> With the skate park it became clear that we couldn't have done it without the city council and other organizations in Alameda. It was the first time we expe- rienced true collaboration, and by collaboration I mean that we needed other people to make something happen.

The success of the skate park set the stage for HOME's launching of HOMEstead and in important ways has informed the process of how HOME incorporates adults, other organizations, and community members in the process of realizing a project idea. Their understanding that collabo- ration with the community will be essential to the success of HOMEstead has meant that during this planning period, youth have structured oppor- tunities for city officials, potential corporate supporters, and funders to participate in the initial stages of development.

The toll the skate park took on HOME's organizational capacity has increased HOME's commitment to involving the community. However, by collaborating with the broader community, HOME felt the tension between what the community considers to be feasible and what the youth themselves feel to be attainable. The feedback from many of the adults in the HOMEstead meeting emphasized their concern with the logistical and prac- tical aspects of implementing a plan as large as HOMEstead, and they were reluctant to offer their support without more tangible information regard- ing the exact course of action. For example, one funder commented, "I have a lot of concerns, and I can't say what I'll contribute until I have some of my questions answered. We need to have more of a dialogue. We may renew our grant [next year], but we need to have more in-depth informa- tion." Another funder added, "We've given a 1-year planning grant of sorts. It's hard to commit to a second year since the plans for that year are so unclear." In many regards, the feedback during this meeting suggested that HOME abandon its plan because the initial support from the adult community was tenuous at best. HOME's response, however, was to learn from the meeting, consider the concerns of the adults, perhaps recognize the limitations of collaboration at this stage, and adapt their process. This is the point at which HOME took a proactive stance to balance community involvement and youth development.

HOME struggles with the desire to involve the community, with its commitment to remain youth centered, and for the projects to remain youth directed. In the particular example of HOMEstead, the youth and the adult coaches suspended their timeline commitments with funders and potential corporate sponsors, relaxed their own target dates and goals, and created the opportunity to learn from the dialogue with community members and reconsider their own commitment to the project idea as presently conceived. This opportunity for the youth to reconceptualize the project, considering the feedback they had received, allowed the project to remain youth centered and youth driven.

HOME's ability to balance its involvement with the community and maintain a youth-centered approach is a complicated process that influences all aspects of the organization. The emphasis on process, whether focused on group dynamics or planning and implementing a project, allows HOME's participants consistent opportunities to listen and learn from the direct experiences of the youth involved. This attention and respect for youth's voice and interests lies at the heart of the learning experiences and youth development practices implemented at HOME. HOME's focus on learning and continual improvement also lies at the heart of its collaboration with community. Although the organization has had its trials and disappointments, especially with the schools, it has been more successful than many youth organizations in enlisting the support of important agencies and organizations in the community. To a significant extent, their positive experience with collaboration reflects their insistence on leading with youth and involving others in their vision, rather than merely asking for strategic or financial support.

Jamestown Community Center

Jamestown Community Center has a long history of working with youth and the community in San Francisco's Mission District, evolving from a recreation center and surviving a rough period in the early 1990s with the help of neighborhood residents to flourish in recent years with a number of exciting and innovative programs for Mission District youth. The center represents what one might think of as a truly neighborhood-based organization: one that serves youth from the Mission or Mission schools, was founded with immense support from the Mission, and is struggling with issues affecting the whole Mission District, such as gentrification and gang violence. They are educating the neighborhood as they are using the neighborhood to educate Jamestown youth. It is an example of a grassroots, community-based organization creating a supportive learning environment for youth who face challenging social and economic conditions in their neighborhood. Unlike EOYDC and HOME, Jamestown does so through many programs run in public schools.

Important learning takes place at Jamestown, both informal and formal. Young people learn skills such as acting and community organizing, while they also learn respect, conflict negotiation, teamwork, and goal setting. What sets Jamestown apart in terms of its focus on learning are the deep-rooted connections to learning resources in the community and the emphasis on making learning relevant to both the youth and the community context. The organization also recognizes its difference from school settings:

> With such poor skills, children are frustrated with school and resistant to educational programs. When given the opportunity to express themselves in an environment that is not explicitly academic, however, they are bright, articulate, and eager to participate. Jamestown's programs tap these positive attributes to spark young people's natural inclination to learn and grow. (Profile of Jamestown Community Center)

At the same time, though, Jamestown acknowledges its role in more formal kinds of learning and intentionally structures some activities to complement school.

History

Jamestown Community Center was founded in 1971 to 1972 as a Catholic Youth Organization (CYO) program, on 23rd and Fair Oaks Street, in the Mission District, taking its name from the surrounding St. James parish. It provided free activities and services for neighborhood youth of all ages and was housed in its own building. In the 1980s, the diocese encountered financial trouble and wanted to find ways to generate income, so they started a day care center at Jamestown and charged a fee for it. CYO viewed having these younger children mingling with older neighborhood youth as a problem and tried to reduce the youth's presence in the building. Neighbors saw that the youth were then "hanging out" more on Fair Oaks Street, and some of them joined together to keep Jamestown open for all neighborhood youth. They sent young people out on the streets with petitions, wrote letters to the mayor, and picketed CYO fundraisers.

In 1989, the San Francisco Community Boards Program came in to mediate among the church, Jamestown, and the neighborhood, without much success. Between 1989 and 1994, neighborhood youth had limited access to the Jamestown building, so neighbors organized volunteer activities for them—sewing, athletics, and arts, among others. In 1994, the neighbors received a grant from the Mayor's Office of Children, Youth, and Families (MOCYF) to restart Jamestown programs, and Edison Elementary School gave them space in which to run these programs. Many of the neighbors who organized these efforts are still on the Jamestown Board of Directors today and see their efforts as part of "a neighborhood raising its children" (Profile of Jamestown Community Center).

Having left Edison and after holding classes in local nonprofits for a brief time, Jamestown now has programs for elementary school children at Cesar Chavez Elementary School and for middle school students at Horace Mann Academic Middle School. Jamestown also runs a youth leadership program and hires teens, many of whom have participated in Jamestown programs, as teaching apprentices to Jamestown program staff. In addition, there are summer programs and several sports teams that play in citywide leagues. Jamestown serves about 130 young people a year through its school-based educational enrichment and tutoring programs.

Implementation of Positive Youth Development

Many factors make up Jamestown's supportive learning environments, but here we focus on the following: the embedded curriculum in all their programs, the structure of youth involvement and feedback, their creation of caring communities, and throughout, their sharp focus on what youth need through a neighborhood-based curriculum.

Embedded Curriculum. Jamestown structures its Learning Clubs and After-School Explorations to help students learn skills and activities. Much of this occurs in connection with Jamestown's regular events, such as their winter performance, and the products required for these as youth carry out the cycles of planning, practice, and performance. As part of these curricula, though, youth are learning not only the skills they need for the performances but also "softer" skills such as teamwork, respect, self-presentation, and community participation.

For example, the middle school dance program has a strong embedded political curriculum. The dance teacher incorporated many different kinds of learning into what might otherwise be a typical dance class. Even though the class was billed as a hip-hop class, she introduced other styles into the curriculum, such as stepping and tap, to expose her students to a variety of cultural and artistic forms. She also incorporated political education into her classes, something that several Jamestown classes have done. According to one of Jamestown's codirectors, this teacher worked with the students one year on the growing presence of chain stores in the Mission and the importance of supporting locally owned businesses. The next year, classes talked about what they could do to protest a youth crime bill on the spring ballot. Through these instances of cultural and political learning woven into the dance curriculum, youth benefit from this after-school setting not only in dance skills but also in their understanding of their neighborhood and issues confronting urban youth.

Another manifestation of Jamestown's embedded curriculum is its use of the neighborhood and neighborhood contexts as learning resources, and this is seen most prominently in the Youth Power program. The neighborhood-centered nature of Jamestown's work strengthens its learning environments by providing students with rich sources of learning materials as well as relevant and contextualized knowledge. As a group, the Youth Power participants choose a community problem they want to work on and devise a strategy for solving the problem. They have, among other things, talked about ways to help students and teachers respect each other more and have tried to improve the food in their school cafeteria. In Youth Power, middle school students, according to one participant, "learn about community organizing, leadership, group work and their ethnic history" in addition learning about the issues they address.

Working on these neighborhood and school-community issues is structured to be a privileged and important assignment. There is an application process to get into Youth Power. Students must write an essay, and then some are chosen to be interviewed by current Youth Power participants. Students in the program are paid a stipend for the school year and are also paid if they participate in summer workshops. This stipend acknowledges that the work the youth do is more than participation in an after-school program, and it fosters a sense of loyalty to the program.

By using knowledge about the neighborhood and working on problems affecting the neighborhood and the young people's community, Youth Power strengthens the kind of learning that takes place through Jamestown and gives these Horace Mann students an opportunity they would not otherwise have.

Youth-Centeredness. Youth are involved at all levels of Jamestown activities and planning, from choices about what to include in a winter performance to sitting on the board of directors. Although youth do not run the organization, they have a say in the kinds of learning environments they find engaging, and Jamestown is able to serve them better as a result. The organization has also adopted an individualized youth-centered approach to meeting the needs of its participants.

Youth in Charge (YIC) is a group composed of longtime Jamestown participants who are now teenagers and are charged with the responsibility of being both Jamestown's representatives in the community and their source of important feedback about programs and activities. YIC members participate in Jamestown events; they act as security at the Halloween block party and as volunteer waiters at the poetry night fundraiser. They carried out a community mapping project with the residents of the Fair Oaks neighborhood, and they participated in a MOCYF meeting on their Children's Services Plan. Some of these members have also been involved in an internal assessment of Jamestown and have been helping Jamestown meet the need of its youth more effectively.

Jamestown also implements a youth-centered approach through its attention to individual youth's needs. The structure and culture of Jamestown programs allow for different learning styles and different kinds of interests, and the organization promotes "unconditional acceptance" of youth, regardless of where they are in their development, what they have done in the past, or what their strengths are. One part of this acceptance is providing many different entry points into Jamestown, as there are in HOME and EOYDC. A youth might be interested in theater, art, community building, dance, or sports and find a place to "belong" at Jamestown. Within each of these interests, there are again many different ways to get involved. In the middle school "Claymation" class, for instance, students can work on characters, sets, lighting, camera work, or as part of general support. Older youth have options as well. They can be part of YIC, assist the Youth Power facilitators, or act as teaching apprentices in the Learning Clubs and After-School Explorations.

Jamestown's focus on youth needs seems to have had an impact on its organizational structure. Several times, the codirectors have spoken of the benefits of their small size, including greater interaction with youth and parents, more involvement in day-to-day activities, and a fluid connection between staff and codirectors. These factors point to the importance of knowing firsthand what youth in the programs are doing and what they need.

Caring Communities. Jamestown provides strong communities for youth on many levels, with its students, individual programs, and the larger community. With students, Jamestown strives to create long-term relationships. It is structured to work with students from elementary school through high school. Several of the 15 YIC participants have been with Jamestown for 5 or more years. One of the art teachers started working with Jamestown at the age of 16. One of the high school teaching assistants began Jamestown programs when she was 10 years old and at age 17 was working with the elementary programs.

Within programs, students create norms that build "minicommunities." The Youth Power group, for instance, was having trouble with students coming back late from their afternoon breaks. They proposed sanctions such as having to miss break the next day, having to talk to a codirector after being late three times, being fined for being late, and missing a whole week of breaks after three warnings. They discussed the pros and cons of each proposal, and took a vote on what to do. In this way, they were policing themselves but also learning about debate, the democratic process, and responsibility to their group.

Jamestown builds its relationship with the larger Mission community in multiple ways. Most important, it was the Mission neighborhood of Fair Oaks that helped Jamestown through its break with CYO. Jamestown's aim now is to mobilize "the support and resources of parents, neighborhood residents, and other community members to help young people realize their full potential as responsible and empowered members of society." It has recently instituted a parent group that meets on Fridays to talk about youth and how Jamestown can support them and their families. Jamestown youth have been involved in several community campaigns, including "Speak Up for Kids Day" with the San Francisco Board of Supervisors, the campaign to get a bike lane on Valencia Street, and the community mapping project of the Fair Oaks neighborhood. Jamestown also finds it important to expose its youth to what is happening in the Mission District culturally. They take trips to the Mission Cultural Center and other organizations to see what their fellow community members are doing in arts and music, and for cultural events such as the Day of the Dead.

Jamestown's organizational structure and culture clearly allow them to create positive and supportive environments for youth. They are particularly adept at using neighborhood resources, building connections with the community, and creating minicommunities in their programs. They have also recognized that the after-school setting affords them many unique opportunities to work with youth outside an academic setting, and Jamestown youth benefit from this insight. And like HOME, Jamestown sees collaboration in terms of education and reaches deep into its setting to engage commitment, support, and neighborhood resources.

Lessons for Youth Development Practice

The complexities of creating engaging and challenging opportunities presented in these three case studies suggests that a youth development approach takes shape in a variety of ways in practice. Local knowledge and expertise in the Bay Area confirm that organizations implementing positive youth development attend to pressures and demands from multiple sources and that directors of youth organizations make difficult decisions about how their organizations can best support youth. The absence of a cookie-cutter implementation process suggests that putting a youth development approach into action is itself an iterative process—a process by which those participating consistently reflect on, adapt, and improve their practices in order to support youth. There is no right way, and there is no one way.

To some, the diversity in youth development programming might suggest that there are no shared experiences across contexts and that no common threads unite the practice of a youth development approach. However, a number of lessons can be learned because of the diversity of youth organizations, not in spite of it. The lessons below identify some of the qualities that help our case study organizations create supportive environments for youth, and they are common to the successful youth development organizations we have studied.

Reconceptualizing Learning:
Connections Between Practice and Outcomes

Interpreting the relationship between youth development principles and youth development outcomes from the perspective of practice benefits from a broad conceptualization of learning that emphasizes the role of social relationships, the significance of context, and the importance of participation. A more traditional perspective on learning that emphasizes individual attributes and a direct relationship between what is taught and what is learned minimizes the complex connection among practices that focus on building supportive relationships, participation in meaningful decision-making opportunities, involvement in the broader community, and the multiple competencies youth need to develop. Programs based on traditional prevention approaches narrowly target strategies to change individual behaviors. However, the youth development organizations we studied intentionally construct environments to provide youth with multiple opportunities for substantive involvement and learning. These organizations and their programs defy simple attempts to connect a particular practice with youth's demonstration of a particular outcome.

An integral part of this reconceptualization is the recognition that there is an embedded curriculum within each of these youth organizations' programs and activities. Whether they are learning about the democratic process in Youth Power or respect for others in a basketball game at EOYDC, participants are exposed to an intentional layering of curricula. They gain valuable "hard" skills, such as job readiness or dance, while they also learn teamwork, negotiation, respect, and resilience.

Organizations implementing a youth development approach and those supporting their efforts have the challenge of paying attention to the content of their programs, the structure of learning environments, and the array of outcomes youth need to achieve for their positive development. A narrow focus on outcomes in the absence of attention to the broader context in which youth grow restricts an organization's capacity to influence the many factors that intersect to support youth's learning.

Incorporating Youth Voice

The three organizations value and emphasize the interests and desires of each of their participants, though this process looks different in each program. This youth-centeredness is often expressed through attention to *youth voice*. Youth not only have a say in their activities within these programs but are also important in guiding the organizations. They are deciding on the organizational structure of HOME, they are sitting on the board of directors of Jamestown, and they answer the phone, greet visitors, and manage youth traffic at EOYDC.

These organizations respect youth voice, and in turn, they foster respect among youth. As in the examples of the basketball players leaving the court before the African dance practice and the enforcement of rules about respectful language at EOYDC and HOME, organizations that implement programs according to youth development principles and skillfully provide supportive environments make respect a central part of what they do.

Youth voice is also central to the caring communities that these organizations create. Adults in these organizations listen to what participants have to say about what happens at the organizations and in programs as well as about what happens outside the programs in the lives of young people. This kind of sharing of concerns and responses to them deepens the trust inside the organization and fosters a stronger community as a result.

Although implementing a youth development framework does not always mean incorporating youth voice in practice, our examination of these organizations suggests that youth voice needs to be a central part of efforts to involve adolescents and to construct activities and settings they find engaging, safe, and worth their time. One foundation's youth program motto, "Nothing about us without us," applies to every aspect of a youth organization.

Keeping Youth Development Goals in View

Directors remind us that youth organizations cannot fulfill every component of a youth development approach simultaneously. Often, one or two practices take center stage for an organization, while other practices find themselves a part of the backdrop. For example, some organizations that are directed and run by youth find it difficult to balance that with the practice of involving them in broader community issues. Other organizations that clearly focus on providing youth with academic or leadership skills pay less attention to their development of physical or emotional competencies. As is evident from the case studies, high-quality youth organizations often emphasize particular youth development practices and outcomes without necessarily compromising the other competencies needed on their paths to adulthood.

Recognizing the importance of keeping broad youth development goals in view, the funding community and others interested in supporting positive youth development should look broadly across youth organizations within a neighborhood to assess opportunities for youth. Individual youth organizations cannot provide youth with opportunities to develop every competency successfully, but funders and other stakeholders can play roles in establishing neighborhood and regional perspectives to ensure that participants have access to youth development practices and outcomes in a variety of their communities' institutions and organizations.

Negotiating Institutional Environments

Staff in youth organizations daily face the need to make decisions about how to handle factors in their external and internal environments. These decisions might focus on how to respond to new federal, state, or city level policy, or they might involve internal issues of organizational staff or program size. What the organizations in this study have been able to do is take advantage of the opportunities they see in their external environments and often turn external challenges into opportunities. Although each organization negotiates these environments in unique ways, they all have done this with a focus on what is best for their youth rather than what will make the organization look good or keep them funded.

EOYDC's insistence on "doing chicken right" illustrates this focus. The director decided that counseling services were not essential to the core programs of the organization and cut them from their offerings even though there was a lot of money available for these programs. Jamestown has had to negotiate relationships with schools, and despite other organizations' difficulty with or hesitation about schools, Jamestown has been able to establish these relationships while implementing a youth development framework. HOME has resisted pressures to relax its requirement of at least a C grade point average and so expand its membership base, on the belief that students who were not achieving at least passing grades would compromise the norms established for the program.

In another type of negotiation, EOYDC has intentionally structured its programs so that its large size would not lead to a sense of impersonality and lack of belonging among its participants. The programs are organized under three departments—physical development, job opportunities for youth, and arts—with staff focused on incorporating diverse interests of youth in the programs and providing meaningful opportunities. The philosophy of the organization and the decisions it has made about how to structure and offer programs have focused on giving youth activities and opportunities that are important to them, so that despite its large size, each participant can feel at home and valued in his or her own way.

Engaging Teenagers

These organizations attend to complex implications associated with "age-appropriate" programming and structure.[5] Organizations have found that strategies successful with youth 10 to 12 years old do not work with teenagers, and they struggle to redesign their practices to reach out to older youth. Efforts to engage teenagers have focused on expanding outreach strategies. They feature youth decision making about the kinds of activities, rules, and responsibilities that should be part of the organization or particular program and act on those recommendations rather than supplanting them with adults' preferences. The organizations featured here also teach the importance of providing older youth with opportunities to build on their particular interests and talents and allowing them to contribute to their communities in some way, though a performance, service, leadership, or other ways of making valued contributions. Maintaining the participation of older youth is not a matter of getting the word out, but of providing opportunities that highlight the importance of their participation.

HOME has demonstrated this through youth's involvement in all aspects of the creation of the skate park and in their varied modes of participation at the HOMEstead meeting.

Teenagers have developmental needs different from those of younger youth, and these organizations have recognized this. In the case of EOYDC, teenage youth have opportunities to develop job-related skills and knowledge through the Job Opportunities for Youth program. In addition, EOYDC offers classes for older youth studying for their GEDs as well as SAT classes for youth applying to college. Jamestown offers teens opportunities to be teaching assistants and evaluators, in support of their need to gain work experience. Targeting particular programs to address the needs of older youth has helped maintain their participation in the organizations. An important aspect of these targeted programs is that they are not prevention programs, but programs that enable youth to take small steps toward reaching future goals. The intent and structure of each is to enhance the capacity of individuals as they look to the future.

These organizations stand out because of the success they have had in implementing youth development programs and engendering the active, committed participation of teens from some of the Bay Area's most distressed neighborhoods. They have overcome numerous institutional challenges to provide safe, nurturing, and productive programs for youth. Whether it is a conscious effort to stay small and focused or a commitment to make large programs feel small, these organizations have seen their way through the "herd programming" problem. They have also prevented the organizations from being impersonal by emphasizing respect, youth voice, and strong adult-youth relationships. They have made their way through the collaboration maze to partner with schools, in the case of Jamestown, and other organizations, in the case of HOME. They were able to do so much of this because of their negotiation of external environments, their focus on appropriate and specific outcomes, and their commitment to programming excellence and to the best interests of youth.

Notes

1. Both the Carnegie Council on Adolescent Development (1992) and the National Research Council and Institute of Medicine (2002) panel on community programs for youth attempted such a compilation, and both concluded that it could not be done given lack of documentation of many local opportunities.
2. Our research was supported by grants from the Walter and Elise Haas Fund and the San Francisco Foundation. Meredith Honig was part of the project team

that conceptualized and carried out the research on which this chapter draws. Her insights are found throughout. Jennifer O'Donoghue continued work with HOME and provided an update to that case material.

3. See McDonald, McLaughlin, and Deschenes (2002).

4. This quotation and others without text citations come from researchers' field notes.

5. Both practitioners and researchers note the difficulty of involving older youth in out-of-school community programs. See, for example, Public/Private Ventures' conclusions about low levels of teens' involvement in the extended-service schools initiative (Grossman et al., 2002).

References

Grossman, J. B., Price, M. L., Fellerath, V., Jucovy, L. Z., Kotloff, L. J., Raley R., & Walker, K. E. (2002, June). *Multiple choices after school: Findings from the extended-service schools initiative.* Philadelphia: Public/Private Ventures.

McDonald, M., McLaughlin, M., & Deschenes, S. (2002). *Mapping opportunities to learn: Youth development programming in the Bay Area. Final report to the Walter and Elise Haas Fund.* Stanford, CA: Stanford University School of Education.

McLaughlin, M. (2000). *Community counts: How youth organizations matter for youth development.* Washington, DC: Public Education Network.

McLaughlin, M., Irby, M., & Langman, J. (2001). *Urban sanctuaries: Neighborhood organizations in the lives and futures of inner-city youth* (2nd ed.). San Francisco: Jossey-Bass.

National Research Council and Institute of Medicine. (2002). *Community programs to promote youth development.* J. Eccles & J. A. Gootman (Eds.). Board on Children, Youth, and Families, Division of Behavioral and Social Sciences and Education. Washington, DC: National Academy Press.

Pittman, K., Ferber, T., & Irby, M. (2000). *Unfinished business: Further reflections on a decade of promoting youth development.* Takoma Park, MD: International Youth Foundation.

3

Organizations Serving All Ages

Geoffrey L. Ream and Peter A. Witt

Organizations that serve youth exclusively clearly have a mandate to promote youth development. Other organizations serve youth as but one part of their memberships or target groups. Examples of such organizations include government-run parks and recreation departments, public libraries, museums, Cooperative Extension, the American Red Cross, YMCAs, YWCAs, and faith-based entities. Some of these comprehensive organizations have sought to serve a wide spectrum of age groups since their inception, whereas others have expanded their missions over time to meet the needs of youth.

Implementing a youth development approach may be more complicated in these organizations because they involve administrators whose responsibilities go beyond youth issues, use facilities that have been designed for multiple audiences, and divide their funds among often competing interests. However, the opportunity is arguably greater because organizations that serve all ages are specially suited to reach into multiple contexts of youths' lives by creating networks of community-based resources. They also provide young people with ways to contribute directly to the community, sometimes working with adults, or even doing the same jobs as adults. Thus, organizations serving all ages have a unique opportunity to provide what Karen Pittman (1994) calls "S.O.S." for youth: services, opportunities, and supports. According to this perspective, although some young people need services for clear problems such as mental disorders, "If the goal is youth development . . . then the strategies have to be broader than service provision" (Pittman, 1994, p. 46). Organizations serving all ages provide supports in the form of intergenerational interaction on an equal plane and opportunities to make contributions that are of real value to their communities. These are not just service organizations, but communities in which people of multiple age groups both contribute and receive each other's contributions, such as high school age youth providing services to children and the elderly while adult staff mentor them in the process. With respect to several categories of developmental assets (constructive use of time, perceived and actual support, understood boundaries and expectations, social competence, etc.; National Research Council and Institute of Medicine, 2002, Box 3-1, pp. 74-75, see Table 1.1, p. 7, this volume), organizations serving all ages go beyond making youth ready to be constructive members of society. They integrate youth into an intergenerational community, providing them with the challenges and rewards that go along with it. Although some organizations have a distinctly youth-focused wing (such as 4-H as the youth component of Cooperative Extension), they still fit into this definition because of the rich intergenerational contact that they provide and the interdependent relationships they create between age groups.

In this chapter, we review how these comprehensive organizations have successfully implemented a youth development framework and associated practices. Cases from parks and recreation departments (PARDs) and faith-based organizations will illustrate best practices. Emphasis on these two kinds of organizations reflects the authors' expertise and interests. We believe that many of the issues we address apply as well to other organizations that serve all ages. We begin by briefly describing the youth mission of each of these two types of organizations. Next, we address some of the distinctive contributions that these organizations can make to youth development, which we categorize as *health and well-being* and *socialization and social support*. We then describe some of the challenges to sustaining organizations of this kind, namely, staffing, funding, and evaluation, and close with some final thoughts about the current and potential contributions to youth development of organizations serving all ages.

Integrating Youth Development Principles

As much as in an organization that serves primarily youth, implementation of youth development principles is an intentional, deliberate, and evolving process. Space for young people must not only be made and maintained, but its boundaries protected by caring adults committed to principles of youth development at all levels within organizations serving all ages.

The History and Youth Mission of Parks and Recreation Departments

Parks and recreation departments began with the vision of creating a space for community to form. From that followed efforts to provide youth with structure and support via recreational activities and, more recently, intentional implementation of youth development principles and making room for youth leadership. In the late 1800s, urbanization, immigration, and the changing nature of family life led to concerns about the time citizens spent outside work, especially youth. Many of the major nonprofit youth-serving organizations active today were created in response to these influences. There was a humanitarian concern for the welfare of those who found themselves with few resources, places to recreate, and/or skills to undertake recreational activities. Comments by Jane Addams in 1893 are reminiscent of those by social commentators today:

> The social organism has broken down through large districts of our great cities. Many of the people living there are very poor, the majority of them without leisure or energy for anything but the gain of subsistence. They move often from one wretched lodging to another. They live for the moment side-by-side, many of them without knowledge of each other, without fellowship, without local tradition or public spirit, without social organization of any kind. (Addams, 1893/1960, p. 4)

More than merely decrying urban pathos, Addams (1893/1960) noted the lack of connection and shared experience between people who might live right next door to each other: "The clubhouses, libraries, galleries, and semipublic conveniences for social life are also blocks away" (p. 4). Thus was born the idea of the "settlement house," as Addams called Hull House, considered to be the precursor of the modern recreation center. (Addams's work also spawned the profession and practice of social work.) The belief on which recreation centers are founded is that opportunities for recreation can make a substantive contribution to alleviating the impact of nonproductive, personally destructive, and/or antisocial actions by youth. This fact alone provided PARDs with a reason for being. However, since its inception, the movement has been seen as providing more than fun and games; activities are designed to do more than simply keep kids off the streets and occupied.

In PARDs that are successfully employing a youth development perspective, adult staff plan *with* youth, not *for* them. This requires a great deal of flexibility from adult staff to give full creative license to the youth while maintaining boundaries and keeping everyone safe. In Richmond, British Columbia, staff recognized the importance of process over product by giving youth a facilitative role in an organization that had previously delivered services and opportunities directly to youth (Witt & Crompton, 2002). Under the mentorship of adult workers, a group of high school students organized the first annual Hip-Hop Games for community youth in the spring of 2002, an event that includes an emcee competition and turntable exhibition. In the words of one of the workers,

> The purpose of planning these events is to be able to give a group of youth the experience of organizing an event of their own design for their peers. It's what we call the "Youth Involved Process" and it's the model upon which we conduct the entire youth strategy in Richmond. (City of Richmond, 2002)

PARDs are increasingly adopting either the *developmental assets model* (Search Institute, 1998) or the *protective factors/resiliency model* (Jessor, 1992). These models have helped delineate both the role of PARDs in the overall youth development framework and the components that make up quality programs. Among these elements are (a) a sense of safety, but accompanied by challenging and interesting activities; (b) a sense of belonging; (c) supportive relationships with adults; (d) involvement in decision making and opportunities for leadership; and (e) involvement in community (Gambone & Arbreton, 1997). These models emphasize the need to design programs to deliver desired attitudinal and behavioral outcomes, rather than to merely keep youth occupied. Table 3.1 portrays aspects of the "evolving mission" of parks and recreation departments and identifies some of the issues addressed.

Faith-Based Organizations' Vision for Youth

All major religions involve young people, though they may treat them differently than adults. Religious organizations are sincerely committed to youth, and many are sincerely committed to youth development, although the lack of research attention to their efforts can make it difficult for them to clearly articulate that commitment and put it into practice. There exist several examples of religious organizations celebrating youth and their contributions and socializing them with developmental assets. Sometimes, this is done by a time-honored rite-of-passage ritual; other times, it is

Table 3.1 The Shifting Paradigm of Park and Recreation Department (PARD) Youth Development Programs

Theme	From	To
Antecedent conditions	Resources stimulated by high-visibility violent incidents	Resources stimulated by desires for enhanced cultural assimilation and educational attainment
	Political skepticism toward investing in youth programs	Conventional wisdom that youth programs are good investments
Youth involvement	Programs initiated and planned by professional leaders	Programs planned and initiated by youth, with support from professionals and other adults
The evolving mission	Keep children safe, off the streets, and out of trouble through fun activities	Use programs to build individual and community assets, reduce risk behaviors, promote resiliency
	Limited to targeted groups of "at-risk youth"	Comprehensive, recognizing that youth development programs offer potential benefits to all young people
	Focus on the activity	Focus on "intentionality" and instrumentality emanating from engaging in the activities
	Short-term, one-shot programming	Commitment to ongoing programs
Collaborations and partnerships	Myopic focus on recreation activities	Adoption of a holistic perspective integrating an array of services
	PARD as an independent, compartmentalized provider of services	PARD as a component of youth development systems involved with multiple collaborations and partnerships
	PARD as a direct provider of services	PARD as a way to leverage resources: facilitator, coordinator, refiner, and residual supplier when there are no other viable delivery alternatives
Service delivery vehicles	Youth activities in multipurpose centers	Youth activities in teen centers
	Youth come to programs: Programs are building and center based	Services reach out to contact and attract uninvolved youth

(Continued)

Table 3.1 (Continued)

Theme	From	To
Staffing	Part-time staff fulfilling a "minder" role	Full-time staff fulfilling a "mentor" role
Resource support	Short-term funding from grants and special city funds	Base funding from a city's general fund
Evaluation	Focus on attendance, service quality, and satisfaction measures	Focus on outcomes (increased protective factors or developmental assets, or reductions in risk behaviors)

SOURCE: Adapted from Witt and Crompton (2002, p. 32).

done by means of a recently developed youth-oriented movement within a denomination.

In a section of the recent *Handbook of Applied Developmental Science* devoted to faith perspectives (Dowling & Dowling, 2002), Protestant (Roehlkepartain, 2002a), Jewish (Friedland & Berkson, 2002), and Muslim (Hadi & Al-Fayez, 2002) voices all articulated their faiths' commitments to positive youth development ideology. Although secular youth developmentalists are often skeptical of the motivations behind faith-based contributions to youth development (Roehlkepartain, 2002b; Trulear, 2000), empirical research has found no faith-based organizations that even remotely fit the stereotype of outwardly purporting to carry on youth development work while being secretly interested only in proselytizing (Branch, 2002).

Rituals such as Confirmation and the Bar/Bat Mitzvah draw families together in support and affirmation of a young person's beginning the journey into adulthood. An ethnographic study of the Bar Mitzvah ritual by Davis (1989) includes several stories of a young man at the center of a process that involves the entire family and community. Depending on context, the Bar Mitzvah ritual allows a young man to demonstrate his worth to the faith community (via the *haftorah* reading), to make a social debut, to maintain connection among extended family, and to reaffirm the family's Jewish identity and status with respect to a larger Jewish community. By means of these rite-of-passage rituals, the transition to adulthood is a time of great investment of religious human capital in youth and a time of significant returns of that investment to the religious community.

It is possible, however, to have the ritual without either a sincere investment in the young person or a meaningful change in that youth's status with respect to the community. In a mixed-methods study (Ream, 2001a) of 74 participants (out of 96 total) who had been through a ceremonial rite of passage such as a Bar/Bat Mitzvah, Confirmation, or "adult" baptism, only 34% described it as having been meaningful to their spiritual development. Those who said it had been meaningful cited a voluntary commitment and a real change in their status within the religious community; those who had said it was not meaningful described the event as having been obligatory and adult oriented. In contrast, of participants who had experienced a youth-oriented religious context, such as a youth trip to Israel or youth group involvement and retreats, 85% described it as having been meaningful to their spiritual development. The 85% cited positive interactions with peers, mentorship relationships with older youth, and a chance to live out the faith through volunteer activities as having been significant; the other 15% had wanted to seek their own paths spiritually or had been "turned off" by cliques.

Every Catholic diocese and nearly every moderately sized to large Protestant congregation has youth ministry staff and youth groups. Ministry staff often do not connect with secular youth development efforts or even workers from other congregations or parishes, and the research community is only beginning to pay sufficient attention to their efforts to be helpful (Roehlkepartain, 2002a). However, within larger religious denominations, there do exist what could be called youth development movements that articulate a common mission and approach and allow workers and youth to connect and grow together. Although these youth-serving offshoots have the potential to alienate young people from the rest of the congregation (one Young Life worker known to the first author feels the congregations have contracted out to him work that they should be doing themselves), it should be noted that youth are already alienated from society by secular cultural forces (Males, 1996). A review of the evidence suggests that these movements act to create a space for young people within the denominations and bring them back in.

Young Life is Evangelical Christianity's flagship youth development organization. It was born in 1940, when seminary student Jim Rayburn took it on himself to go where young people were, meet them on their own turf, and find a creative way to share the love of God with them. During 2001 to 2002, they involved 773,496 high school age youth and 175,254 middle school age youth. In addition, they had 341 ministries in 52 countries outside the United States (Young Life Service Center, 2002).

The formula is simple. Young Life believes that "kids" today need caring adult role models, constructive ways to spend time, clear information to make decisions, and unconditional acceptance. They follow the model of evangelical catechesis that G. Stanley Hall first articulated (1904), that young people's agency and freedom of choice need to be respected and nurtured and that they need to be given clear information about Christianity to develop a mature, adult faith. Meanwhile, the energy of youth is given opportunity for positive expression at adventure camps and other activities, as well as a purpose and direction in finding meaning to life through making contributions to their religious communities that only young people can (Young Life Service Center, 2002).

New Beginnings and Happening are part of the renewal movement of the Episcopal Church in the United States. (Information here is taken from the first author's own experience as a member of the steering committee for Vocare of Central New York and assistant rector for Vocare #2 of the Episcopal Diocese of Central New York.) New Beginnings is designed for youth in grades seven through nine, and Happening is for high school youth. Happening is an intensive weekend retreat planned and staffed by youth, for youth. Although the general structure of the weekend is prescribed by the Happening quality control manual, which is maintained under the auspices of the National Happening Leadership Committee, the youth decide specific features of the weekend. Youth empowerment is built into Happening's structure and functioning: The National Happening Leadership Committee contains two clergy, three adult laypeople, and six youth. Thus, youth have the controlling interest on the leadership committee.

New Beginnings and Happening are not youth-only spaces; they are truly intergenerational events, meant to create youth-adult partnerships and incorporate young people into the life of the church as full members. For all the dioceses for which information was available, any parish sending youth to New Beginnings must send adult sponsors with them. The sponsors reportedly benefit as much from the weekend as the youth do. New Beginnings and Happening both have "prayer staff," usually adults, who work behind the scenes to do things such as setting up folding chairs and processing paperwork, freeing up youth leaders to do the visible leading. Prayer staff also offer the opportunity for intergenerational cooperation between renewal groups (including Vocare, for 19 to 30-year-olds, and Cursillo, for adults) while still providing each generation its own space.

Distinctive Contributions to Health and Well-Being

Both PARDs and faith-based organizations are specially suited to provide certain developmental assets. Spiritual development, a connection with higher powers, and a personal relationship with God are known to be developmental assets (Scales & Leffert, 1999) and are the almost exclusive province of religious organizations. These assets are concentrated in the areas of identity development and psychological resiliency. Involvement in sports and recreation has psychological benefits for youth, as well. In addition, organizations that serve all ages can provide powerful opportunities for youth to acquire the knowledge, attitudes, and behaviors expected of them as members of society—the process developmental scientists refer to as *socialization* (not to be confused with "socializing" at a party). They can also provide social support, meaning both the emotional assistance afforded by being with other caring people and more material assistance.

Personal Well-Being and Health

Religion and Spirituality

James Garbarino (1999) writes of the spiritual connection that some of his "lost boys" (boys convicted of murder) found through involvement with religion:

> In the storm of his life, Dennis becomes a devout Christian, and it brings him peace and direction. Facing ten years of imprisonment, Kevin embraces Islam and finds in its teachings ways to deal with his anger and fear. Allan becomes a practicing Buddhist, and it brings him peace. (p. 154)

One of Garbarino's "lost boys," who sits on death row for killing two gang rivals, "now wears a cross around his neck and a locket; in the locket are pictures of his two sons. 'I live for them,' he says, 'and for God. All I ask now is the opportunity to live to see my boys grow to be men and for the time to make my peace with eternity'" (p. 155). Garbarino explains further,

> Spirituality and love can fill in the holes left in the story of a [young man's] life and help him develop both a strong positive sense of self and healthy limits, thus forestalling the need to compensate with grandiose posturing and deadly petulance. . . . When it is grounded in spirituality and love, religion infuses life with purpose by connecting the ups and downs of everyday life to something permanent and beyond the reach of day-to-day experiences. (p. 155)

A compelling narrative has grown around the efficacy of faith-based interventions in making lasting change in the lives of incarcerated individuals (Johnson, 2002).

These principles are applicable beyond youth who are institutionalized. Adolescents are in the process of negotiating their identities and places in society in the contexts of peers and of social forces and institutions greater than themselves (Erikson, 1968; Hall, 1904; Strommen, 1979). In this journey, contact with faith-based communities can provide meaning and purpose that adolescents need in the identity achievement process. For youth who have experienced significant stress, such as family problems that would lead to an avoidant attachment style, there is a distinct attraction to religious groups in which the doctrine provides clear, firm, and easily understood expectations, and the potential for life transformation is strong (Kirkpatrick & Shaver, 1990; Streib, 1999).

Religious involvement has several significant psychological benefits for youth. For rural high school students from low-income families (Markstrom, Marshall, & Tryon, 2000), religious involvement was correlated with higher levels of "ego strengths," including hope, will, fidelity, love, and care. Data from the "Monitoring the Future" survey revealed that religious adolescents are almost 3 times as likely as nonreligious youth to engage in community service and that they demonstrate great concern for the welfare of others (Youniss, McLellan, & Yates, 1999).

Religion and spirituality are intertwined in the psychological attachment process. A positive relationship with God can compensate for insecure attachments to parents (Kirkpatrick & Shaver, 1990). Religious involvement can also guide parents' youth development efforts. Workers for Campus Crusade for Christ's Family Life ministry (FamilyLife, 2003) in the Ukraine relate stories of how the parents in their organization noticed differences in their children's behavior. The workers' children did not have, according to the best translation available, a "complex." The workers explored this concept and found that among the families with whom they were working, it was customary for mothers to be the only effective parent and to use primarily shame and guilt to control the children so that they developed this "complex." The workers reasoned that this was not a cultural difference, but a psychological response to the ineffective parenting that had become normative in that area, because of environmental stress and lack of positive role models. The workers thus worked to foster egalitarian family styles and authoritative parenting among the families they served.

Thus, religious organizations work on several levels to create developmental assets. They augment community and parental support by supplying material and human resources that might not be otherwise available. They provide social support and control and associations with positive role models and peers. They also offer psychological benefits to youth who internalize values of universal love and care, which are at the core of many religions.

Sports for Health

Aside from the obvious contribution that opportunities for physical exercise make to the physical well-being of youth (Tuckman & Hinkle, 1988), some research exists on the positive contributions of youth sports and recreation to the psychological health of youth. They can provide an inclusive, lower-key alternative to the highly competitive sports environments of many middle and high schools, which have known associations with alcohol and other substance use (Scales & Leffert, 1999). Given the proven efficacy of exercise in helping adolescents cope with stressors (Brown & Siegel, 1988), PARDs have an important role in making low-competition and noncompetitive organized physical activity available to all youth. Best practices are suggested in, among many other places, the Michigan State University's Youth Sports Institute's Bill of Rights for young athletes (Martens & Seefeldt, 1979), which includes many youth development principles.

Independent of the level of competition involved, sports involvement is associated with academic aspirations and social status among all African American youth, and decreased social isolation and more positive teacher appraisals among African American young women. Research also suggests that recreation and sports involvement is particularly important for young women's identity development, giving those that chafe against the strictures of feminine gender socialization a chance to develop self-efficacy in other domains (Scales & Leffert, 1999).

Socialization and Social Support

A cornerstone on which public recreation services were founded was the belief that recreation can make a substantive contribution to alleviating the impact of nonproductive, personally destructive, and/or antisocial actions by youth. A caveat: There was no equivocation among early commentators about the "rightness" of providing recreation for this instrumental purpose. These sentiments were especially pervasive in the field's formative years in the first three decades of the 20th century(see Box 3.1).

Box 3.1   Supervised Amusement Cuts Juvenile Crime

Supervised playgrounds, parks, amusements, manual labor classes and boys' clubs have in 5 years reduced juvenile crime and delinquency 96% in the industrial center of Binghamton, in New York State, according to figures recently compiled by the Broome County Humane Society and Relief Association (Engle, 1919).

(Continued)

Box 3.1 (Continued)

L.H. Weir, Chief Probation Officer of Cincinnati says,

In 1906 there were 1,748 children legally before the Juvenile Court and 410 were handled unofficially making a total of 2,158 children. Of these, 1,450 were delinquents. In the Fall of that year a beginning was made in opening playgrounds in the downtown portions of the city. In the year just closed there were 993 delinquent children before the court. Each year has noted a marked decrease. While some of the decrease may be due to other causes, the work of the courts for instance, we are perfectly sure that one of the main factors has been the opportunity afforded the thousands of children in the most congested district of the city to play in a natural and spontaneous manner. (Van Ingen, 1922, p. 6)

In the late 1980s and early 1990s, during the contemporary renaissance of youth programs, the mission of most agencies was defined in terms of targeting programs to keep at-risk youth off the streets and out of trouble by engaging them in "fun and games." Most communities recognized that PARDs could be effective in this assignment. This narrow perspective often resulted in limiting expectations to opening facilities and hiring minimum-wage, part-time employees to "baby-sit" youth and the facility. This approach, trying to remove the potential for antisocial behavior by diverting youth into positive activities in a recreation center, is of limited value specifically because it is time bounded and place bounded. When youth are not in recreation centers, which is by far the largest amount of time during the day, their proclivity for antisocial behavior remains (Witt & Crompton, 2002).

As programs matured and stakeholders have acquired a more sophisticated understanding of the potential of youth programming, the mission has become more holistic. The focus on youth development encompasses both amelioration of problem behaviors and helping youth increase prosocial attitudes and behaviors. According to Furstenberg, Cook, Eccles, Elder, and Sameroff (1999),

Youth in American society must be given a fair chance (1) to acquire the cognitive skills and resources to become educated to their highest potential; (2) to accumulate psychological and social skills that foster a positive identity, including a person sense of well-being and self-efficacy; and (3) to participate in activities that foster a capacity to perform as family members, workers, and informed citizens in their communities. (pp. 9-10)

Although faith-based organizations are not founded, like early incarnations of PARDs, for the explicit purpose of regulating behavior, classical understandings of religion describe it as an agent of social control and integration (Durkheim, 1915) and a source of empowerment for the underprivileged (Weber, 1922). Modern sociology of religion describes it as a source of human capital, a set of social and cultural resources, that helps individuals cope with unpredictable, undesirable, and uncontrollable circumstances of life (such as death) under supernatural assumptions (Stark & Bainbridge, 1996). Although a purely sociological understanding of religion is inadequate for articulating the complete picture of its role in the lives of youth (Ream, 2001b), religion definitely performs the functions that this perspective prescribes. Arlene Sanchez Walsh (2000) writes of a meeting of "Barrios for Christ," Victory Outreach's ministry to gang members based in La Puente, California:

> On this particularly hot summer evening, GenX leader Manuel Alvarez invites a new convert to give his testimony to the crowd of about a hundred. . . . Juan is in his late twenties, and tattoos cover his arms. His hairstyle and clothing represent a past era of gangster, late 1970s, old guard—*veterano*. . . . He speaks about how grateful he is to Alvarez for taking the time to help him and lead him to God. (p. 74)

Juan has done more than join a new peer group and assent intellectually to a doctrine. He has replaced his former way of life with new norms and expectations. He has made a connection with a positive role model. He has broken a connection with a delinquent peer group and made a new connection with a faith-based community. He has made an important contribution to the church by undertaking a quasi-sacramental role in the ministry through his testimony. He has offered himself to the teenage gang members in front of him, no longer someone whom they would look up to as a mentor in the gang lifestyle, but as a living example of a positive alternative possible self.

Religious involvement is an important developmental asset (Benson, 1997), and religion can be an important socializing force (Benson & Saito, 2000). Sociologists and criminologists argue that religion has significant potential for keeping youth out of trouble, and religious involvement and commitment are positively associated with prosocial values and behavior (Donahue, 1995; Dor-Shav & Maslovaty, 1993; Youniss et al., 1999). Religious involvement and commitment are negatively associated with suicide attempts and suicidal ideation (Donahue, 1995); premarital sexual involvement and teenage pregnancy (Donahue, 1995; Rubin, Billingsley, & Caldwell, 1994); substance use (Bahr, Hawks, & Wang, 1993); and delinquency (Benda, 1995). In large-scale studies, the negative correlation between religion and delinquency is strongest in "moral communities" where the majority of people attend religious services, and it is weak to nonexistent in areas where relatively few people attend religious services (Stark, 1996). This is evidence that over and above the aforementioned positive effects of voluntary religious involvement on spiritual and psychological health, religion also works as a less voluntary agent of behavioral control, but the strength of this effect is proportional to the importance of religious involvement to the community as a whole.

Although religious involvement is negatively correlated with problem behaviors in youth, one might plausibly argue that the correlation is not causal because—although existing data are not understood to support this argument—only less troubled youth participate in faith-based organizations. Membership is, according to this line of reasoning, a sign of prosocial attitudes and behavior, not a cause. Although this matter cannot be examined empirically (by randomly assigning some youth to be religious), understanding how religious involvement (independent of religious commitment) leads to asset development adds substance to the contention that youth religious involvement is an important context for youth development.

Religious involvement facilitates disassociation from delinquent peers and association with a positive peer group. It provides a supportive faith community of peers and adults and gives youth an opportunity to contribute meaningfully to that community. It sets boundaries for behaviors such as substance abuse, sexuality, and aggression. It provides a source of resiliency against the detrimental effects of neighborhood disorder. Religion creates positive outcomes for youth via all these paths, and yet these explanations do not fully account for all its salutary effects (Johnson, Jang, Larson, & Li, 2001; Johnson, Jang, Li, & Larson, 2000).

Thus, religious organizations offer something to youth that other institutions cannot. There is, however, concern with faith-based organizations gaining market share in the provision of social services because of the potential that they will discriminate against certain populations of youth, such as sexual minorities (i.e., lesbian, gay, transgendered, etc.). Although anecdotal evidence suggests that faith-based youth-serving organizations discriminate against sexual-minority youth (Ryan & Futterman, 1997), secular organizations such as schools discriminate against these youth as well (Herr, 1997), and there is currently no evidence that religious organizations are any better or any worse.

Differences in the role of religion within the socialization process also exist across racial lines. On average, African American youth attend religious services more frequently than do white youth (Donahue, 1995). Although work that would investigate whether religion is more significant as a developmental asset for black youth than for white youth has yet to be done (Ream, 2003), religion is known to be a positive factor in resiliency against the unique stressors faced by black youth. In one study of African American youth, religious involvement was found to ameliorate subjective stigmatization, or internalized racism (Brega & Coleman, 1999). Religion also buffers the impact of neighborhood disorder on black youth crime, and this resiliency effect is stronger against serious crime than minor crime (Johnson et al., 2000).

Building and Maintaining the Organization

Workers in organizations that serve all ages are obliged to make sure that the organization remains in place from one year to the next for the benefit of all of the people whom it serves, and to maintain the organization's commitment to youth development principles. This involves ensuring the availability of human (staff) and economic (funding) resources and engaging in evaluation work to ensure effectiveness.

Staffing

When PARDs, faith-based organizations, and other organizations accept youth development as a major purpose, they must find, train, and maintain capable staff members. Key staffing issues include redefining staff roles and assuring that the staff are well qualified and diverse.

Staff Roles

Job descriptions for staff are often not rigidly defined in organizations serving all ages that contribute significantly to youth development. These organizations provide a variety of resources and become facilitators, rather than direct providers of some services. Reaching out to the community and maintaining connections with other organizations and with individuals in the community are central to their methods. Successful organizations are innovative in their use of resources, adapting the role of staff, the mode of service delivery, and the function of the physical facilities to the community's needs.

Parks and recreation workers who adopt a youth development community-serving approach to their jobs increasingly find themselves doing things related to neither parks nor recreation. To adapt to the needs of the population they are serving, recreation professionals have been required to adopt different modes of operation and acquire a new knowledge base and new skills (see Box 3.2).

Box 3.2   Changing Staff Roles

A former Director of the Phoenix Parks, Recreation, and Library Department observed,

> My staff say we are becoming counselors and social workers. That's fine, I believe we should be. We have always done this, but there is much more emphasis on it now than there has been in a couple of decades. My philosophy is that if a young man comes in on drugs or a young woman comes in who is pregnant, we have to help. I would not have a problem with my Department being called a Department of Community Services. Our job is to make young people whole in any way we can, and offering wholesome recreation activities is only one aspect of that. It's a way of reaching them and gives us an opportunity to help them straighten out other parts of their lives. (Witt & Crompton, 1996, p. 16)

PARDs programs frequently include after-school tutoring, community service, job training, leadership development, health education, and the development of social skills. Often, existing staff are not equipped to direct such programs, but recognize the need to view their roles as part of a system that holistically serves youth, rather than being concerned only with the recreational needs of youth.

In many cases, PARDs assume leadership to coordinate community services. Acting as facilitators, PARD personnel bring youth development agencies together to develop community-wide service plans. The Director of Portland Parks and Recreation observed:

> This is the chance for us to demonstrate the full value of who we are and what we can do. . . . Society needs help with its youth, and we have a piece of the solution. While retaining our uniqueness and autonomy, we in the field of recreation, who share the same values and goals, can accomplish more by working together than we can on our own. (Witt & Crompton, 1996, p. 19)

Adoption of the facilitator role requires the agency to serve as an enabling agent and take on the tasks of coordination, referral, and technical assistance. In Richmond, British Columbia, youth wanted a place in the community where they could have ownership and responsibility, feel welcome and safe, socialize, obtain information, and receive services. They desired more autonomy and independence in adult-like facilities. Hence, the task force called for separate dedicated spaces in which youth could hang out.

Recognizing that the single most important factor in reaching adulthood is a positive relationship with a caring adult, many PARDs are replacing part-time jobs with full-time adult leadership positions. Full-time positions enable staff to develop a stronger rapport with youth, reduce staff turnover, and provide time to establish relationships with complementary youth-serving organizations.

Staff Training and Qualification

Staff training remains a challenge to most agencies because there is frequently no provision for training in budgets. Nevertheless, PARDs strive to provide training in mentoring skills and group facilitation, community development, youth development principles, understanding the broader youth development system, financing and acquiring resources, and marketing. Training should take place both before a service is initiated and regularly, on an ongoing basis, so the knowledge base is consistently enhanced. In-service training is all the more important because, although postsecondary education is available for youth workers, the majority of youth work is performed by individuals who have no educational or professional background in a related area.

Outreach programs of PARDs pose special challenges for staff development. Mobile recreation facilities and "Roving Leader" programs (such as those in Austin and San Antonio) encounter young people on their own turf, in their own neighborhoods. In these programs even more than in facility-dependent services, leadership is more important than program content. Roving Leaders have to gain and retain the trust of youth, their parents, and the institutions that cooperate with them; be able to organize and teach recreational activities; and know the array of referral services that are available to support youth. Thus, when hiring for these Roving Leader positions, managers are inclined to be less concerned with formal academic credentials and more concerned about applicants' understanding of the neighborhood and their chemistry with resident youth (Witt & Crompton, 2002).

Religious organizations also struggle to reach youth who need but have not sought their services. Many churches develop small Bible study groups and house churches to increase accessibility. Their efforts center on connectivity between members, and thus they search for means to create additional membership and involvement.

Jonathan Kozol (1995) writes of Reverend Overall of St. Ann's Episcopal Church, in Mott Haven, a neighborhood in New York City:

The pastor rises at five a.m. She seldom seems to finish work much before ten at night. When people are sick, she takes them to the hospital. When their sons are arrested, she goes with them to court. When they are born, she baptizes them. When they die, she buries them. . . . If she had remained a lawyer, she could be at home now getting ready to go out for dinner. (p. 255)

Several functions of churches as youth-serving organizations are evident in Reverend Overall's work. First, an Episcopal diocese supports her ministry and maintains her building. To do outreach, a church can take advantage of its existing infrastructure rather than having to create a presence where one did not previously exist. Second, Reverend Overall was not educated as a youth worker, but rather as a lawyer. Like many workers in faith-based organizations, she brings special skills and legitimacy gained in secular contexts to apply to her work. Finally, the church provides a safe space in a fixed physical location that is less likely than governmentally financed PARDs to disappear as a result of politics or budget cuts.

Staff Diversity

Public/Private Ventures undertook a study on the role of religious organizations in reaching high-risk youth (Trulear, 2000). Inspired by the success of Boston's Ten Point Coalition of religious congregations that banded together to reduce youth crime, the study identified interfaith coalitions in eight cities and tracked their efforts and successes over time. Initial findings challenged expectations. The ecumenical nature of the groups was particularly impressive. The researchers found Christians working alongside Muslims in Detroit and Jews in Boston. Interdenominational squabbling did not significantly interfere with these organizations' youth development work. The organizations were open to the involvement of outsiders and to evaluation. The primary goal of the youth development efforts of these religious groups was to minister, not to proselytize.

In selecting workers who will be involved with youth, a diversified staff (race, gender, age, and education) is desirable. An ethnically diverse staff that includes individuals from a number of different service backgrounds (recreation, arts, education, social work, criminal justice, psychology) is likely to be more comprehensive and responsive in their approach to youth development. Adults are most effective who "work in partnership with young people, who see themselves as supportive friends and advocates in contrast to adults motivated to save, reform, or rescue young people from their circumstances" (Walker & White, 1998, p. 15). The caring adults may be parents or volunteers from the community, but the central responsibility is likely to reside with staff.

Funding

External funds are usually short-term, relatively unstable, and often designated for tightly defined programs. Some congregations that dropped out of the Public/Private Ventures study cited earlier (Branch, 2002) chafed against what they perceived to be the narrow agenda that came with outside money. Faith-based organizations that reject outside money can lean instead on their own sources of funding, such as donations and endowments. In contrast, for the purposes of PARDs, experts recommend that external funds be regarded as temporary resources that provide an opportunity to pilot test programs and to demonstrate to elected officials that they have positive outcomes that make them worthy of support from the city's general fund. In some cases, this has occurred, and they have become a line item in the general fund.

In Phoenix, the At-Risk Youth Division increased from 11 to 52 full-time equivalent staff (FTEs) in the past decade, and its general fund budget grew from $400,000 to more than $2 million. In addition, a surcharge of 25¢ imposed on each round of golf played at city courses goes into a dedicated fund (approximately $150,000 per year) to support paid youth internships at the recreation centers, youth golf clinics, and staff training. However, too often, effective outcomes and positive benefit-cost analyses do not result in permanent funding. Outreach programs tend to be especially vulnerable to budget cutbacks because there are no tangible assets, such as buildings, that will not be used if these programs are cut. At such times, cities give priority to programs based in physical facilities (Witt & Crompton, 2002).

For ideological reasons and to avoid the instability of government funding, faith-based youth-serving organizations generally rely on donations from individuals and congregations rather than public money, even when they can apply for it. In a recent study of a nationally representative sample of 1,236 congregations nationwide, 57% were found to have social service projects, and 36% (clergy were asked this question) said they would apply for government funds to support social service projects; but only 11% were receiving outside funds, and 3% were receiving government funds (Chaves, 1999). Some (15%) actually had policies against receiving government funds, reflecting the assertion made by a clergy respondent in the Public/Private Ventures study: "You can't fund Moses' movement with Pharaoh's money" (Trulear, 2000, p. 8). Others simply do not have the time or expertise to seek grant funding. In a nationwide study, congregations indicated greater willingness to seek government funding for social service projects if they were large (more than 900 people in attendance); Roman Catholic or liberal/moderate Protestant (rather than conservative/Evangelical Protestant); more than 80% black; and/or if they regularly invited secular visiting speakers. Congregations from the South that described themselves as theologically and politically conservative and/or regularly and frequently invited religious visiting speakers were significantly less likely to indicate willingness to apply for government funding for social service programs (Chaves, 1999).

Discussing his findings, Chaves (1999) notes an obvious disconnection between word and deed on the part of the religious conservatives: Although they are the most vociferous proponents in the public sphere of expanding Charitable Choice and increasing the role of religious organizations in providing social services, they are taking the least advantage of the money made available by legislation President Clinton signed into law in 1996. Although amendment and expansion of Charitable Choice was a major issue in the 2000 elections, it has not yet been acted on at the time of this writing, and specifically what, if anything, the George W. Bush administration will manage to do to modify or expand this legislation, as well as its potential impact, are unknown.

Evaluation

Evaluation is key to both continued funding and to guiding managers' continuous improvement efforts. Elected officials are likely to require evidence of a program's success before appropriating public tax dollars for its continuation. At the beginning of the 1990s, PARD evaluation efforts focused almost exclusively on measuring attendance, service quality, and user satisfaction. However, the forces driving the funding support from youth programs are concerned with outcomes: "What happened to Jose, Mary, Sam, and Juanita as a result of this experience?" and "What return did the community receive on its investment of resources in this program?" (Gray & Greben, 1974).

The role of evaluations in faith-based youth work is no smaller than its role in secular youth work. However, it is debatably even more important because of the dearth of research support available for faith-based youth development (Roehlkepartain, 2002b) and the settings and circumstances available to faith-based organizations, which often have entrée and trust in communities where government entities are unable or, sadly, unwilling to go (Trulear, 2000). The efficacy of faith-based initiatives often depends on the ability of a leader, or group of leaders, who is able to face the "tyranny of need" that afflicts religious organizations faced with many more ministry needs on their doorstep than they could possibly find human or financial resources to meet and articulate a comprehensive focus of ministry. More efforts like the Public/Private Ventures study cited earlier would help religious organizations be accessible for communities.

Conclusions

Erik Erikson (1968) asserted that young people are the lifeblood of any social institution. Youth invest their energy by their own choice in organizations and institutions that they perceive to be worthy. Those that are perceived to be paternalistic or patronizing toward youth, insensitive to the values of the younger generation, unreceptive to the contributions of youth, or interested only in keeping them out of trouble will not receive an investment of time and energy by youth and thus cannot expect to survive. When organizations that serve the whole community invest in youth, they are also investing in their own health and that of the community as a whole. Thus, although it is more of a challenge for organizations serving all ages to integrate youth development practices and principles into their overall missions, the rewards are greater and more comprehensive if they succeed.

Organizations that serve all ages have both the challenge and opportunity to provide organizational resources to young people and to help them develop responsibility for them. To meet this challenge, adults must make sure that youth have a place at the table in decision making regarding finite resources. Adults may occasionally have to advocate for youth if other voices within the organization attempt to deprioritize youth concerns or reenvision youth as simply appropriated human capital meant to contribute to the vision of adults. However, inasmuch as young people are working with real money, adults have the responsibility to provide the "scaffolding development" (Pittman, Irby, & Ferber, 2000) necessary for youth to handle adult-like responsibilities, understanding that any new leader will need training and mentoring to adjust to a new role. This involves being realistic about which youth will be able to handle which jobs and helping young leaders to "reality-check" their goals against their resources, without becoming overly directive or reactive to problems.

PARDs and religious organizations are two of the many components of a community's investment in youth. Through these settings, young people acquire developmental assets, while being encouraged to themselves be assets to their communities: Activity involvement can yield contact with caring adults; youth leadership creates innovation in programming and facilities and helps young people shape the future of their communities; and church youth groups enable involvement with adult role models in faith-based environments.

Community-based initiatives, such as those undertaken by PARDs and religious institutions, need to be engaging enough to hold the attention of young people and provide meaningful ways for them to avoid boredom and be involved in constructive activities. Enabling and valuing the contributions of young people are critical to keeping them involved. These agencies work best when they partner with other community resources to foster a supportive network of youth development supports and opportunities.

References

Addams, J. (1960). The subjective necessity for social settlements. In *Philanthropy and social progress* (pp. 1-26). Freeport, NY: Books for Libraries Press. (Original work published 1893).

Bahr, S. J., Hawks, R. D., & Wang, G. (1993). Family and religious influences on adolescent substance abuse. *Youth and Society, 24*(4), 443-465.

Benda, B. B. (1995). The effect of religion on adolescent delinquency revisited. *Journal of Research in Crime and Delinquency, 32*(4), 446-466.

Benson, P. L. (1997). *All kids are our kids: What communities must do to raise caring and responsible children and adolescents.* San Francisco: Jossey-Bass.

Benson, P. L., & Saito, R. N. (2000). The scientific foundations of youth development. In *Youth development: Issues, challenges and directions* (pp. 125-148). Philadelphia: Public/Private Ventures.

Branch, A. Y. (2002). *Faith and action: Implementation of the national faith-based initiative for high-risk youth.* Retrieved January 11, 2003, from: www.ppv.org.

Brega, A. G., & Coleman, L. M. (1999). Effects of religiosity and racial socialization on subjective stigmatization in African-American adolescents. *Journal of Adolescence, 22,* 223-242.

Brown, J. D., & Siegel, J. D. (1988). Exercise as a buffer of life stress: A prospective study of adolescent health. *Health Psychology, 7,* 341-353.

Chaves, M. (1999). Religious congregations and welfare reform: Who will take advantage of "Charitable Choice?" *American Sociological Review, 64*(6), 836-846.

City of Richmond, British Columbia, Canada. (2002, April 2). *Richmond to host Hip-Hop Games.* Retrieved February 10, 2003, from: http://www.city.richmond.bc.ca/webnews/city/0402_hiphop_games.htm.

Davis, J. (1989). Mazel Tov: The Bar Mitzvah as a multigenerational ritual of change and continuity. In E. Imber-Black, R. Whiting, & J. Roberts (Eds.), *Rituals in families and family therapy* (pp. 177-208). New York: Norton.

Donahue, M. J. (1995). Religion and the well-being of adolescents. *Journal of Social Issues, 51*(2), 145-160.

Dor-Shav, Z., & Maslovaty, N. (1993). Structure and salience of Israeli adolescent values within the text and context of Judaism. *Journal of Psychology and Judaism, 17*(1), 5-28.

Dowling, E. M., & Dowling, R. J. (2002). Youth development through youth ministry: A renewed emphasis of the Catholic Church. In R. M. Lerner, F. Jacobs, & D. Wertleib (Eds.), *Handbook of applied developmental science: Promoting positive child, adolescent, and family development through research, policies, and programs* (Vol. 3, pp. 475-494). Thousand Oaks, CA: Sage.

Durkheim, E. (1915). *The elementary forms of the religious life* (J. W. Swain, Trans.). London: George Allen & Unwin.

Engle, W. I. (1919). Supervised amusement cuts juvenile crime. *The American City, 21*(6), 515-517.

Erikson, E. H. (1968). *Identity, youth, and crisis.* New York: Norton.

FamilyLife. (2003). *Presentation given at Bethel Grove Bible Church on July 7, 2002, in Ithaca, NY.* Retrieved March 2, 2003, from: http://www.familylife.com.

Friedland, S. J., & Berkson, W. (2002). Jewish youth and family development programs. In R. M. Lerner, F. Jacobs, & D. Wertleib (Eds.), *Handbook of applied developmental science: Promoting positive child, adolescent, and family development through research, policies, and programs* (Vol. 3, pp. 495-514). Thousand Oaks, CA: Sage.

Furstenberg, F. F., Cook, T. D., Eccles, J., Elder, G. H., & Sameroff, A. (1999). *Managing to make it: Urban families and adolescent success.* Chicago: University of Chicago Press.

Gambone, M. A., & Arbreton, A. J. A. (1997). *Safe havens: The contributions of youth organizations to healthy adolescent development.* Philadelphia: Public/Private Ventures.

Garbarino, J. (1999). *Lost boys: Why our sons turn violent and how we can save them.* New York: Free Press.

Gray, D. E., & Greben, S. (1974, July). Future perspectives. *Parks and Recreation,* pp. 26-33, 47-56.

Hadi, F., & Al-Fayez, G. (2002). Islamic Arabic youth and youth development: An example from Kuwait. In R. M. Lerner, F. Jacobs, & D. Wertleib (Eds.), *Handbook of applied developmental science: Promoting positive child, adolescent, and family development through research, policies, and programs* (Vol. 3, pp. 455-473). Thousand Oaks, CA: Sage.

Hall, G. S. (1904). *Adolescence, its psychology, and its relations to physiology, anthropology, sociology, sex, crime, religion, and education* (Vol. 2). New York: Appleton.

Herr, K. (1997). Learning lessons from school: Homophobia, heterosexism, and the construction of failure. In M. B. Harris (Ed.), *School experiences of gay and lesbian youth* (pp. 51-64). New York: Harrington Park.

Jessor, R. (1992). Risk behavior in adolescence: A psychological framework for understanding and action. In D. E. Rogers & E. Ginzberg (Eds.), *Adolescents at risk: Medical and social perspectives* (pp. 19-33). Boulder, CO: Westview.

Johnson, B. R. (2002). Assessing the impact of religious programs and prison industry on recidivism: An exploratory study. *Texas Journal of Corrections, 28*(1), 7-11.

Johnson, B. R., Jang, S. J., Larson, D. B., & Li, S. D. (2001). Does adolescent religious commitment matter? A reexamination of the effects of religiosity on delinquency. *Journal of Research in Crime and Delinquency, 38*(1), 22-44.

Johnson, B. R., Jang, S. J., Li, S. D., & Larson, D. (2000). The "invisible institution" and Black youth crime: The church as an agency of local social control. *Journal of Youth and Adolescence, 29*(4), 479-498.

Kirkpatrick, L. A., & Shaver, P. R. (1990). Attachment theory and religion: Childhood attachments, religious beliefs, and conversion. *Journal for the Scientific Study of Religion, 29*(3), 315-334.

Kozol, J. (1995). *Amazing grace: The lives of children and the conscience of a nation.* New York: Crown.

Males, M. A. (1996). *The scapegoat generation: America's war on adolescents.* Philadelphia: Common Courage.

Markstrom, C. A., Marshall, S. K., & Tryon, R. J. (2000). Resiliency, social support, and coping in rural low-income Appalachian adolescents from two racial groups. *Journal of Adolescence, 23*(6), 693-703.

Martens, R., & Seefeldt, V. (1979). *Bill of rights for young athletes.* Retrieved February 20, 2003, from: http://ed-web3.educ.msu.edu/ysi/bill.html.

National Research Council and Institute of Medicine. (2002). *Community programs to promote youth development.* J. Eccles & J. A. Gootman (Eds.). Board on Children, Youth, and Families, Division of Behavioral and Social Sciences and Education. Washington, DC: National Academy Press.

Pittman, K. (1994, September/October). S.O.S. for youth. *Youth Today,* p. 46. Retrieved May 5, 2003, from http://www.forumforyouthinvestment.org/yt-sos-pfv.htm.

Pittman, K., Irby, M., & Ferber, T. (2000). Unfinished business: Further reflections on a decade of promoting youth development. In *Youth development: Issues, challenges, directions* (pp. 17-64). Philadelphia: Public-Private Ventures.

Ream, G. L. (2001a). *The development of intrinsic religious commitment and religious participation in young adulthood, and the religious development of gay, lesbian, and bisexual adolescents.* Unpublished Master of Arts thesis, Cornell University, Ithaca.

Ream, G. L. (2001b). Religion, spirituality, and belief systems. In J. V. Lerner, R. M. Lerner, & J. Finkelstein (Eds.), *Adolescence in America: An encyclopedia* (Vol. 2: N-Y, pp. 576-584). Santa Barbara, CA: ABC-CLIO.

Ream, G. L. (2003, August 7-10). *Religion as resiliency: Sex, sexual orientation and race differences.* Paper presented at the annual meeting of the American Psychological Association, Toronto.

Roehlkepartain, E. C. (2002a). Building strengths, deepening faith: Understanding and enhancing youth development in Protestant congregations. In R. M. Lerner, F. Jacobs, & D. Wertleib (Eds.), *Handbook of applied developmental science: Promoting positive child, adolescent, and family development through research, policies, and programs* (Vol. 3, pp. 515-534). Thousand Oaks, CA: Sage.

Roehlkepartain, E. C. (2002b). Making room at the table for everyone: Interfaith engagement in positive child and adolescent development. In R. M. Lerner, F. Jacobs, & D. Wertleib (Eds.), *Handbook of applied developmental science: Promoting positive child, adolescent, and family development through research, policies, and programs* (Vol. 3, pp. 535-563). Thousand Oaks, CA: Sage.

Rubin, R. H., Billingsley, A., & Caldwell, C. H. (1994). The black church and adolescent sexuality. *National Journal of Sociology, 8*(1-2), 131-148.

Ryan, C., & Futterman, D. (1997). *Lesbian and gay youth: Care and counseling.* Philadelphia: Hanley & Belfus.

Scales, P. C., & Leffert, N. (1999). *Developmental assets: A synthesis of the scientific research on adolescent development.* Minneapolis, MN: Search Institute.

Search Institute. (1998). *Helping youth thrive: How youth organizations can—and do—build developmental assets.* Minneapolis, MN: Author.

Stark, R. (1996). Religion as context: Hellfire and delinquency one more time. *Sociology of Religion, 57*(2), 163-173.

Stark, R., & Bainbridge, W. S. (1996). *Religion, deviance, and social control.* New York: Routledge.

Streib, H. (1999). Off-road religion? A narrative approach to fundamentalist and occult orientations of adolescents. *Journal of Adolescence, 22,* 255-267.

Strommen, M. P. (1979). *Five cries of youth.* San Francisco: Harper & Row.

Trulear, H. D. (2000). *Faith-based initiatives and high-risk youth: First report to the field.* Philadelphia: Public/Private Ventures.

Tuckman, B. W., & Hinkle, J. S. (1988). An experimental study of the physical and psychological effects of aerobic exercise on schoolchildren. In B. G. Melamed, K. A. Matthews, D. K. Routh, B. Stabler, & N. Schneiderman (Eds.), *Child health psychology.* Hillsdale, NJ: Lawrence Erlbaum.

Van Ingen, W. B. (1922, November 26). Crime statistics show most offenders are under 21 years and the figures drop whenever recreation is provided. *The New York Times, IX,* p. 6.

Walker, J., & White, L. (1998). *Caring adults support the healthy development of youth.* St. Paul: University of Minnesota, Center for 4-H Youth Development. Retrieved May 5, 2003, from: http://www.fourh.umn.edu/educators/research/Center/PDF/Center-Story3.pdf.

Walsh, A. S. (2000). Slipping into darkness: Popular culture and the creation of a Latino evangelical youth culture. In R. W. Flory & D. E. Miller (Eds.), *GenX religion* (pp. 74-91). New York: Routledge.

Weber, M. (1922). *The sociology of religion* (E. Fischoff, Trans.). Boston: Beacon.

Witt, P. A., & Crompton, J. L. (1996). *Recreation programs that work for at-risk youth: The challenge of shaping the future.* State College, PA: Venture Publishing.

Witt, P. A., & Crompton, J. L. (2002). *Best practices in youth development in public park and recreation settings.* Ashburn, VA: National Recreation and Park Association.

Young Life Service Center. (2002). *Facts at your fingertips.* Retrieved February 20, 2003, from: http://www.younglife.org/pages/faf2002.pdf.

Youniss, J., McLellan, J. A., & Yates, M. (1999). Religion, community service, and identity in American youth. *Journal of Adolescence, 22*(2), 243-253.

4

Bridging Juvenile Justice and Positive Youth Development

William H. Barton

P lacing juvenile justice and positive youth development in the same sentence is somewhat like mixing oil and water. The reader may recognize each of these concepts individually but have great difficulty imagining how they could be merged into an integrated whole. On one hand, the juvenile justice system embodies the tension between criminal justice and child welfare, seeking to address youthful misbehavior with a combination of punishment and rehabilitation. On the other hand, positive youth development advocates seek nothing less than a transformation of public consciousness and resource commitments, from a concern with preventing and treating youth problems to a comprehensive approach providing supports and opportunities enabling all children to develop optimally.

This author has attended numerous public meetings highlighted by angry and mistrustful exchanges between positive youth development advocates and traditional service providers, including juvenile justice professionals. The former argue that resources are excessively earmarked for expensive and ineffective interventions with "problem youth" while ignoring basic supports for families and children. In response, the other side expresses fears that redirecting resources toward universal supports and opportunities compounds the privileges already realized by the "best and brightest" while relegating those most "at risk" to what would remain of the juvenile justice (or mental health or child welfare) system. The two sides, both genuinely concerned with young people, seem to talk past each other. Recalling the oft-repeated line from the movie *Cool Hand Luke,* "What we have here is a failure to communicate."

This chapter offers an attempt to bridge these two worlds. For its conceptual underpinnings, the bridge rests on a great deal of theory, research, and practice wisdom converging from several disciplines to identify a set of risk and protective factors that influence the course of human development. These factors exist at multiple levels—the individual, family, school, neighborhood, and broader environment—which raise or lower the odds of positive life outcomes (Kirby & Fraser, 1997; Masten, 1994). Attention to these factors, that is, promoting resilience, strengthening protective factors, and reducing or buffering risk factors, is the key both to the promotion of positive youth development and the prevention of youth problems. But identifying conceptual underpinnings is not enough; the political environment and organizational culture of juvenile justice are among the many logistical obstacles to constructing a bridge (Schwartz, 2001). Several progressive approaches to contemporary juvenile justice and other service arenas—community prevention, a balanced approach, a comprehensive strategy with an increased emphasis on evidence-based practice, restorative justice, and systems of care/wraparound services, all to be described later in this chapter—may provide the means to overcome these obstacles.

The chapter begins with an overview of the juvenile justice system, its history, structure, programs, and policies. Juvenile justice is described as one among many distinct service systems traditionally dealing with youth problems. A synopsis of evidence indicates what does and does not work in juvenile justice and the inherent limitations of an approach based on "the medical model." Recent progressive approaches in juvenile justice are more hospitable to positive youth development principles than are previous approaches. In contrast to the traditional response to youth problems, one embracing positive youth development requires a strengths-based, ecological view that integrates services across systems. The chapter concludes with applications of juvenile justice programs that incorporate positive youth development principles and recommendations for further action to bridge these two seemingly incompatible worlds.

Overview of the Juvenile Justice System

The juvenile justice system is responsible for dealing with young people who have allegedly committed a crime or a status offense. A *status offense* is behavior, such as school truancy, running away from home, or "incorrigibility," that would not be a crime if committed by an adult. The system consists of two main parts, a judicial component (juvenile court) and a correctional component (probation, training schools, treatment programs, etc.) (Schwartz, 2001). Philosophically, the system is grounded in the belief that children are different from adults—less culpable for their behavior, more salvageable or amenable to treatment, for example—and thus should not be treated in the same manner as adults in the criminal justice system.

Although we speak of "the juvenile justice system," it is not necessarily a single, coherent entity in every locale. Some juvenile justice functions may be the responsibility of state governments, others of the counties, and still others of private agencies (Schwartz, 2001). Moreover, there is no common jurisdictional definition of *juvenile*. States vary in the lowest age of juvenile court jurisdiction; many have no statutory lower limit, while others range from 6 (North Carolina) to 10 years (e.g., Arkansas, Colorado) (Snyder & Sickmund, 1999). Although most states set the upper age limit at 17 years, in some states the upper age is 15 (e.g., Connecticut, North Carolina) or 16 (e.g., Illinois, South Carolina, Texas) (Snyder & Sickmund, 1999). Many states have now passed laws that transfer jurisdiction to the adult criminal courts for young people accused of committing certain crimes (usually extremely violent or drug-related offenses).

History of Juvenile Justice

A brief historical review highlights how shifting views of children and the tensions between punishment and rehabilitation have led to the present juvenile justice system. In the 19th century, rapid industrialization, the growth of cities, and immigration accompanied a growing and increasingly visible class of urban poor. Children of the poor, viewed as potential paupers, were subject to legal intervention for a variety of behaviors, including activities such as frequenting pool halls and associating with undesirable people. For either such unruly behaviors or for the commission of what would normally be considered crimes, they could be removed from their families and sent to institutions (houses of refuge and, later, reform schools) or "placed out" with rural Midwestern families (Bernard, 1992).

Concerned with the way young people in trouble with the law were treated, child advocates successfully created the first juvenile court in Chicago, in 1899 (Bernard, 1992). By the middle of the 20th century, all states had established juvenile courts. The guiding principle of the juvenile court was *parens patriae*, that is, the state acting in the place of parents "in the best interests of the child." Early juvenile court procedures were relatively informal. In place of the criminal court's notions of trials, verdicts, and sentencing, the juvenile court instead conducted hearings during which a judge reviewed the facts of the case, came to a decision (a finding not of criminal guilt beyond a reasonable doubt, but of delinquency based on a preponderance of the evidence), and mandated a dispositional plan ostensibly in the best interests of the child.

The early juvenile justice system relied on the discretionary judgment of presumably well-intentioned authorities. As the 20th century progressed, many viewed the unbridled discretion of the juvenile justice system with skepticism, noting inconsistent and harsh treatments afforded to some children. A series of court cases gradually introduced into the juvenile justice system many of the due process protections afforded to adults. These rights included basic due process for a youth being transferred to the adult criminal justice system (*Kent v. United States*, 1966); the right to notice of charges, legal counsel, questioning of witnesses, and protection against self-incrimination (*In re Gault*, 1967); and the necessity of establishing guilt beyond a reasonable doubt (*In re Winship*, 1970). However, the juvenile justice system did not take on all the trappings of the adult system, as other cases upheld some distinctions. Jury trials are not required in juvenile court cases (*McKeiver v. Pennsylvania*, 1971), and preventive, pretrial detention of juveniles is permitted in some circumstances (*Schall v. Martin*, 1984). Contemporary critics of the juvenile justice system (e.g., Feld, 1999) argue that, despite the increase in due process protections, the juvenile justice system still treats children, especially minority children, inconsistently and ineffectively.

Bernard (1992) has convincingly described the "cycle of juvenile justice," characterized by periods alternating tough or lenient treatment of delinquents. Because neither approach to juvenile justice appears to solve the problem of delinquency, whichever approach is currently used is blamed for the failure, and the other approach is tried until it, too, is seen as inadequate. And so the cycle continues.

At the beginning of the 21st century, we may be nearing the end of a long "get tough" period of the cycle. The last decade or so has produced "get tough" policies such as transferring increasing numbers of young offenders to the adult criminal justice system, determinate terms of incarceration, and zero tolerance, fueled by fear and an exaggerated sense of the extent of youth violence. Widely publicized events such as the horrendous school shooting at Columbine High School provided the impetus for such retributive approaches.

Stages of the Juvenile Justice System

The juvenile justice system may be best understood as a series of stages at which the fate of a child who has come to the attention of the authorities is decided by various adults (police, court intake workers, probation officers, prosecutors, judges, correctional administrators, treatment professionals, etc.). Together, these stages constitute the system. Although the options available to various decision makers may vary based on the nature of the complaint and specific state or local policies and resources, some discretion is usually possible. The decision may be to do nothing, to arrive at an informal resolution of some sort, or to proceed to the next stage of the formal juvenile justice system.

Prevention

Delinquency prevention programs, although not part of the juvenile justice system itself, may be usefully discussed as a precursor to the juvenile justice system. *Primary prevention* programs, such as local parks and recreation activities, Boy Scouts, Girl Scouts, YMCAs, YWCAs, and many school-based programs, are directed at all young people. *Secondary prevention* programs target young people "at risk" for delinquency, based on characteristics such as income, neighborhood, or known involvement in minor misbehaviors.

Court Processing

The juvenile justice system only becomes engaged when the police or juvenile court authorities intervene, either at the request of a complainant or through police detection of an offense (see Figure 4.1). The stages of court processing include intake, detention, adjudication, and disposition. At intake, a court official decides whether or not to file a petition for a formal hearing and whether or not to detain a youth prior to court hearings (preadjudication). If the decision is to detain the youth, a detention hearing is held at which a judge decides whether or not to continue the preadjudication detention. There may be several court hearings, although some of these may be collapsed at times, designed to determine the facts of the case (initial hearing), to render a judgment (adjudication hearing), and to decide what to do with the child (disposition hearing). That decision may be to release, place on probation, or commit to the custody of the state for placement in a residential or nonresidential program.

Both informal and formal resolutions at any stage typically involve assigning the youth to a program of some kind. These programs may be categorized as diversion, preadjudication, probation, placement, and aftercare. In some circumstances, to avoid proceeding further into the formal system, the youth and the youth's family may agree to voluntarily participate in

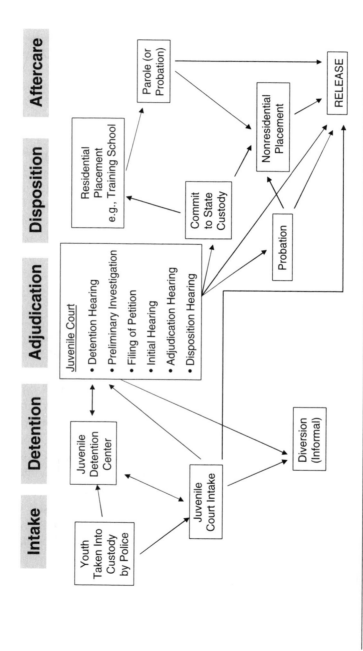

Figure 4.1   The Juvenile Justice System

SOURCE: Adapted from Indiana Youth Institute (n.d.).

some kind of diversion program, perhaps counseling, and a court official will then agree to dismiss formal charges. Preadjudication programs deal with the youth between the time of arrest and juvenile court disposition. These include confinement in a secure detention facility, or nonsecure alternatives such as home detention, perhaps augmented with electronic monitoring. The main preadjudication concerns are protection of the youth and the community prior to court processing and guaranteeing that the youth will appear in court.

Disposition

If the case proceeds to a formal hearing in juvenile court and the youth is adjudicated ("found delinquent"), a disposition follows. Dispositions range from supervised probation, perhaps supplemented with participation in specific treatment programs and/or community service activities, to placement in residential programs of varying degrees of restrictiveness. These latter may be small, relatively open, community-based programs or large, secure institutions often called *training schools*.

At the dispositional stage, a youth adjudicated delinquent may be assigned to a nonresidential or residential program. Compared with out-of-home placements, in-home programs have far greater potential for incorporating aspects of positive youth development simply because they permit the youth to remain connected to their communities and families. A considerable body of research suggests that in-home programs are at least as effective as residential placements in reducing recidivism, at far less cost (for a recent review, see Loeber & Farrington, 1998). Among the most effective nonresidential programs for children with serious emotional and behavioral problems is *multisystemic therapy* (MST) (Henggeler, Schoenwald, Borduin, Rowland, & Cunningham, 1998). With its emphasis on involving the family and addressing a range of community factors as well as the individual, MST is consistent with several principles of positive youth development.

Aftercare

Following residential placement, aftercare programs may help youth reintegrate back into the community. In an ideal world, aftercare would never, or rarely, be necessary because youth would no longer be incarcerated in institutions separated from their families and communities. In the real world, incarceration will always be with us, at least for some. Interestingly, a by-product of the nation's prison expansion in the last few decades is a growing recognition that most of those locked up will eventually return to their communities and that reentry challenges need to be addressed (e.g., Travis, Solomon, & Waul, 2001). In the juvenile justice arena, inadequate aftercare has often been cited as a main reason for the high recidivism rates of residential placements such as training schools.

It may be difficult at first to imagine a juvenile court imbued with positive youth development principles; its adversarial process seems antithetical to them. Yet if the courts were to fully embrace their original charge to act "in the best interests" of the youth, then positive youth development principles would become more salient. In any event, the court must perform its functions of fact-finding and disposition of cases. Regarding the former, youth development is probably best served by a commitment to due process. The latter function is the one most amenable to change in ways consistent with positive youth development. Currently, dispositional decisions are made by judges, based on recommendations of probation officers, from a limited menu of available programs. These decisions tend to be driven by a concern for public safety addressed by the level of behavioral control or restrictiveness mandated, and slots available in specific programs. What if these recommendations were instead developed by community teams? Public safety protection would remain a necessary component, but the individualized recommendations would probably result in fewer residential placements and stronger, more effective collaborative community support networks. Coming full circle, the juvenile court might then return to its roots of acting in the best interests of the child (and family and community).

What Works and What
Doesn't in Juvenile Corrections

Recidivism rates of juvenile correctional programs are notoriously high, with practice wisdom suggesting that anything better that 50% is good. In the 1970s, a review of research regarding the effectiveness of juvenile correctional programs (Lipton, Martinson, & Wilks, 1975) was commonly misperceived as proving that "nothing works." This pessimistic view has been challenged by several more recent reviews (Andrews et al., 1990; Howell, Krisberg, Hawkins, & Wilson, 1995; Lipsey, 1992; Lipsey & Wilson, 1998; Mendel, 2000) suggesting that some approaches, appropriately targeted, can effectively reduce recidivism and promote other positive outcomes as well.

A brief summary of recent research on juvenile justice programs reveals the following findings:

- Less than half of juveniles in secure facilities are serious and/or chronic offenders (Snyder & Sickmund, 1999).
- Transfers to the adult system are not effective in most cases (Bishop, Frazier, Lanza-Kaduce, & Winner, 1996; Snyder & Sickmund, 1999).
- Boot camps (Peters, Thomas, & Zamberlan, 1997) and other "shock incarceration" programs (Lipsey, 1992; Parent, 1989) are not effective for juveniles.
- Probation is more effective than commonly assumed: 54% of males and 73% of females who enter the juvenile justice system never return on new referrals (Snyder & Sickmund, 1999).
- Less restrictive settings are at least as effective as incarceration for most offenders, even serious offenders, and cost less (Lipsey, 1992; Loeber & Farrington, 1998).
- Effective intervention programs exist, even for serious offenders; these include interpersonal skills training, cognitive-behavioral treatment, and teaching family home programs (Lipsey & Wilson, 1998). Community and family-focused interventions, especially multisystemic therapy (Henggeler et al., 1998), have strong empirical support of effectiveness. When out-of-home placement is necessary, treatment foster care has demonstrated effectiveness, even for children with severe emotional and behavioral disorders (Chamberlain, 2002).
- Aftercare is currently a weak link in the system, although the Intensive Aftercare Program (IAP) is emerging as a promising national model (Altschuler & Armstrong, 1991; 1998; Altschuler, Armstrong, & MacKenzie, 1999). This model features close collaboration with community service providers, small caseloads, services integrated into the facilities prior to release, and a system of graduated sanctions upon release.

Juvenile Justice and the "Medical Model"

The juvenile justice system is but one of several created to address selected "youth problems." Other systems include child welfare, mental health, and special education. Each has its perspective on problem assessment and its interventions of choice. Just as physicians diagnose illness and prescribe treatment, human service professionals often see each kind of problem behavior as the manifestation of a specific deficit or dysfunction within the individual, with occasional recognition of environmental influences. Research is designed to isolate specific causes (etiological pathways) of the deficit or dysfunction. Once these are discovered, appropriate "treatments" can be developed and administered. This approach is often termed *the medical model*.

Sometimes, the particular system that becomes involved seems to be mostly an accident of where the disturbing behavior or condition was observed and/or a function of the family's resources and awareness of service options. For example, a child who acts out aggressively at home may be more likely to end up in the mental health system (possibly assigned to special education) than one who behaves similarly in school or in a public place (possibly handled in the juvenile justice system). Depending on the system that is "managing" the case, a young person whose aggressive behavior precipitated intervention may receive one or more of the following: prescribed medication, placement in a psychiatric residential program, placement in a special-needs classroom, or adjudication as delinquent followed by placement on probation or confinement in a juvenile correctional institution.

All traditional human service systems that address youth problem behaviors through this medical model approach serve to further isolate youth from conventional influences. The isolation is often physical (spatial removal from the home or classroom), and it is always at least symbolic in terms of labeling (i.e., the "problem" becomes a pivotal lens through which others think of the youth). Is it really any wonder that positive youth development, which results from positive connections among individuals and between individuals and institutions in the community, is not well served by these systems?

Applications of Progressive Approaches In the Juvenile Justice System

Researchers who have investigated the causes of youth "problem behaviors" (e.g., delinquency, substance abuse, teenage pregnancy, school dropout) over the last few decades have concluded that most of these behaviors have a common or overlapping set of causal influences (Dryfoos, 1990; Hawkins, Catalano, & Miller, 1992). Moreover, the identified causes are not only within the individual but also reflect the influence of family, school, neighborhood, and the broader community. In contrast to the study of medicine, in which most physical diseases are traceable to specific pathogens such as viruses or bacteria, investigation of problem behaviors involves causal influences that operate with less certainty and specificity. Rather than following the medical model, it is more helpful to view problem behaviors ecologically, as occurring in a web of *risk and protective factors,* in which the presence of risk factors increases the probability of problem behaviors and the presence of protective factors decreases that probability. The presence or absence of problem behaviors, then, is the result of combinations of these factors, which may not have the exact same effect on all individuals at all times.

Risk and Protective Factors

Kirby and Fraser (1997, p. 29) have summarized these risk and protective factors well. At the individual level, psychosocial and biological risk factors include biomedical problems and gender (males are at greater risk). An "easy" temperament, high self-esteem, competence in normative roles, and high intelligence serve as protective factors. _Mesolevel_ (family, school, and neighborhood) risk factors include child maltreatment, interparental conflict, parental psychopathology, and poor parenting, whereas social support, presence of caring adults, positive parent-child relationships, and effective parents provide protection. _Macrolevel_ risk factors include limited educational or employment opportunities, racial discrimination, and poverty; protective factors include the presence of opportunities for education, employment, growth, and achievement. Additional research has demonstrated the cumulative effect of these risk and protective factors on youth outcomes (Pollard, Hawkins, & Arthur, 1999).

Resilience

Interestingly, another set of researchers investigating _resilience,_ or why some people's life outcomes seem positive despite apparent disadvantages or stresses, have come to similar conclusions about the multiple levels of influences on behavior. In a landmark longitudinal study, for more than 30 years researchers followed the development of a cohort of children born on the island of Kauai, to trace their pathways from birth to various adult outcomes (Werner & Smith, 1992). These researchers identified many of the same risk factors discussed above. They were also able to identify early influences that enabled some of the high-risk children to succeed, or to "overcome the odds." These factors included several personal characteristics (e.g., a more easygoing temperament as an infant; more alertness, autonomy, and social orientation as toddlers; more interests and better academic attitudes, effort, and performance; more achievement orientation, assertiveness, and independence) but also included family factors (fewer siblings, fewer prolonged separations from a primary caretaker, a close bond with at least one caregiver) and outside influences as well (e.g., at least one close friend, participation in extracurricular activities).

Other resilience research has examined children who succeeded despite the presence of a variety of risk factors: having parents with mental illness (Anthony, 1987; Worland, Janes, Anthony, McGinnis, & Cass, 1984); experiencing child abuse (Egeland, Jacobvitz, & Sroufe, 1988); and growing up in impoverished and disorganized neighborhoods (Furstenberg, Cook,

Eccles, Elder, & Sameroff, 1999; Gordon & Song, 1994; Long & Vaillant, 1989; Luthar, 1991). Masten (1994) summarizes the resilience research, listing the following factors as promoting resilience:

> Effective parenting; connections to other competent adults; appeal to other people particularly adults; good intellectual skills; areas of talent or accomplishment valued by self and others; self-efficacy, self-worth and hopefulness; religious faith or affiliations; socioeconomic advantages; good schools and other community assets; and good fortune. (p. 14)

The reader will recognize the congruence of these factors with positive youth development.

Progressive Approaches

This ecological perspective combined with the cumulative evidence summarized above of what does and does not work have led many to question reliance on incarceration and other "get tough" measures, such as boot camps or "scared straight" deterrence approaches. As alternatives, at least five major progressive approaches have emerged in recent years that are relevant for juvenile justice and potentially amenable to positive youth development principles. Progressive approaches that permit the infusion of youth development principles are not all of the same kind, nor have they all originated from within juvenile justice. They are like paradigms, or narratives, through which juvenile justice professionals and others may view issues and problems and seek solutions in contrast to the prevailing "get tough" narratives.

Community Prevention

Community prevention addresses risk and protective factors. Communities That Care (CTC) exemplifies this approach. CTC provides communities with a framework for community mobilization, local assessment of risk and protective factors, and a collection of empirically proven or promising programs that can be tailored to meet specific communities' needs (Hawkins, Catalano, & Associates, 1992; Hawkins et al., 1992). CTC has been adopted by several communities, including several counties in Pennsylvania. A recent evaluation of the Pennsylvania trial showed CTC counties with modestly reduced delinquency rates, with the caveats that implementation was inconsistent and that longer follow-up times may provide a better test (Greenberg & Feinberg, 2002). The CTC model of prevention also serves as an integral part of the Office of Juvenile Justice and Delinquency Prevention's (OJJDP) comprehensive strategy (Howell, 1995; Wilson & Howell, 1993) discussed earlier in this chapter. CTC, with its emphasis on risk and protective factors at the micro-, meso-, and macrolevels, is highly compatible with a positive youth development perspective. Other examples of specific prevention programs with empirical support may be found in the *Blueprints for Violence Prevention* (Mihalic, Irwin, Elliott, Fagan, & Hansen, 2001).

Some feel that targeted prevention and diversion programs have limited prospects for success due to the unintended consequences of "net widening," that is, expansion of formal justice system intervention to lower-risk populations (Austin & Krisberg, 1981; Macallair & Roche, 2001). Early intervention, prevention, and diversion, then, may unwittingly make it *more* likely that young people in such programs will have further contact with the juvenile justice system. Nevertheless, communities that adopt a strategy such as CTC can avoid these negative side effects by actively applying the positive youth development perspective. Their programming then will be directed at reducing risks and enhancing protection at the community level, rather than at monitoring and changing individuals. The CTC community mobilization strategy parallels that used in many other comprehensive initiatives promoting positive youth development. Although this strategy is time-consuming and laborious, it offers an opportunity for inclusion of a full range of community participants. Thus, a community that mobilizes initially for delinquency prevention may have taken the first steps in the paradigm shift towards the positive youth development perspective.

Balanced Approach

The "balanced approach" (Maloney, Romig, & Armstrong, 1988) seeks to transcend the debate over punishment versus rehabilitation by recognizing that the juvenile justice system must pursue a balance among three goals: accountability, competency development, and public safety protection. Although it was originally developed for probation, the balanced approach can be applied to juvenile justice more generally.

Comprehensive Strategy

In the mid-1990s, the OJJDP issued a comprehensive strategy that incorporated both delinquency prevention and evidence-based juvenile justice interventions (Howell, 1995; Wilson & Howell, 1993). This strategy includes using validated risk and needs assessments, developing a continuum of evidence-based program alternatives, limiting the use of incarceration, and investing the resulting cost savings into prevention. A number of jurisdictions have followed the lead of federal funding to implement elements of this strategy.

Restorative Justice

Drawing on work initiated in Australia and New Zealand, restorative justice advocates have proposed an alternative paradigm for justice (Bazemore & Terry, 1997; Bazemore & Walgrave, 1999). In the current retributive system, the state acts on behalf of the community by punishing offenders. In contrast, a restorative justice approach seeks a mediated solution between offenders and victims to restore the community as far as possible to its condition prior to the transgression.

In a restorative approach, dispositions are more accurately viewed as mediated resolutions in which the offender, victim, and their representatives all have input into the outcome. An example may be found in Denver's Community Accountability Board, described in Case 4.1.

Case 4.1   Community Accountability Board, Denver (CO) District Attorney's Office

The Community Accountability Board (CAB) Program[1] implements restorative justice values and principles by providing a forum for neighborhood residents to meet with juvenile offenders who commit property-related crimes in six target areas encompassing 26 Denver neighborhoods. Through the CABs, community stakeholders conduct group conferences with the juvenile, his or her parents, and other interested parties to develop ways of repairing the harm caused by the offense, holding the youth accountable to the communities that have been victimized by their crimes and building on the strengths and competencies of the juvenile.

Community representatives gain a sense of justice through participation. By personalizing the victim, the CAB program gives the offender a sense of the degree of damage the offense caused. The CAB then works with the youth and his or her family to develop solutions that not only hold the youth accountable but also build his or her sense of belonging in the community. These solutions are

"It takes a village..."

formalized in a CAB agreement that is signed by the youth, parents, and the CAB members present.

The solutions recommended by the CAB go beyond traditional punitive sentences to plans that increase the youth's competency and attachment to the community. CAB volunteers share in the responsibility of supporting the juvenile's completion of the CAB agreement and often work directly with the juvenile as part of the agreement. Everyone, including the juvenile, agrees to the terms of the CAB agreement.

Teen courts represent another promising way of incorporating some positive youth development and restorative justice principles (Butts, Buck, & Coggeshall, 2002). In these programs, young, usually first-time offenders charged with nonviolent offenses may be diverted from formal court processing. The offender and his or her family agree to abide by the "sentence" imposed by a teen court; in return, the formal delinquency charge is dropped. In teen courts, young people, either volunteers or former offenders themselves, fill roles analogous to jurors, bailiff, court clerk, prosecutor, defense attorney, and sometimes even judge. Acknowledging that teen courts have potential value in encouraging volunteerism and enhancing skills in the teen volunteers, a national evaluation of teen courts in four sites also reported moderately favorable results in terms of offender recidivism (Butts et al., 2002).

System of Care/Wraparound Services

Perhaps the best examples of assessments and interventions based on the ecological framework are *system of care* and *wraparound* services. Some professionals in several service arenas began to recognize the similarities between children who had appeared in the various service systems and noticed that the same children and families often appeared in more than one system. The National Institute of Mental Health funded the Child and Adolescent Service System Program (CASSP), the first major attempt to integrate services across systems. The system of care approach (Stroul & Friedman, 1986) emerged from this initiative. Services in this approach are (a) strengths based, driven by the needs and preferences of the child and the family; (b) provided through a multiagency collaborative environment; and (c) culturally competent (Duchnowski, Kutash, & Friedman, 2002).

Whereas payments for traditional services come from system-specific funding streams, a system of care approach pools monies from these streams and makes them accessible to a case manager according to the needs identified by the collaborative plan.

Wraparound services, developed over the last 15 years, take the system of care elements even further (Burchard, Bruns, & Burchard, 2002; Goldman, 1999; VanDenBerg & Grealish, 1996). In the words of Burchard and colleagues (2002), "The philosophy that spawned wraparound is relatively simple: Identify the community services and supports that a family needs and provide them as long as they are needed" (p. 69). Wraparound places an even greater emphasis on involving children and families as partners in intervention planning, building on strengths, drawing on informal supports as well as the professional service community, and maintaining an unconditional commitment to provide support as long as needed (Goldman, 1999). Although developed initially by mental health systems, wraparound in practice has often involved the juvenile justice system as well (Franz, 1994; 2001; Northey, Primer, & Christensen, 1997). Indeed, wraparound may be one of the most promising ways to incorporate positive youth development principles into juvenile justice practice. The history, structure, and culture of juvenile justice, however, present challenges to those who would introduce wraparound or other progressive approaches into juvenile justice.

Taken together, these approaches signal a potential shift in juvenile justice toward a more ecological view of the causes and correlates of delinquency, an emphasis on competency development, and recognition that the evidence base favors community-based, strengths-focused, integrative services. It is no accident that the most effective or promising programs involve the families of the youth, maintain or reestablish connectedness to the community, provide some continuity in relationships, and help youth develop social skills. These characteristics echo the themes and principles of positive youth development. Herein lies the opportunity for building the bridge between juvenile justice and positive youth development.

Nonresidential programs are amenable to the wraparound approach. Probation departments could adopt or be a collaborative participant in a wraparound approach that tailors interventions to the unique individual and incorporates many of the principles of positive youth development. Several communities have developed wraparound programs in recent years. An example is the Dawn Project in Indianapolis, described in Case 4.2, which draws about one third of its referrals from the juvenile court.

There are also creative ways to engage probation youth in activities or settings promoting positive youth development. A study in Pennsylvania suggests

Case 4.2   The Dawn Project, Indianapolis (IN)

"Cal" spent most of his young life in the "system," including more than 30 placements and a long history with juvenile court. Although a previous independent living program had been unsuccessful, the Dawn Project[2] team realized during its strength-based discovery process that Cal was determined to live independently; the team also knew that it would be able to offer any support needed to help the transition go smoothly. Cal did move into his own apartment and, since then, has learned to use public transportation, is gainfully employed, and is building relationships with people in the community who will continue to be supportive in his life. Cal knows how to access Dawn team members in an emergency; he's been staying out of trouble and enjoying his independence.

The Dawn Project is a wraparound service program in Indianapolis responsible for developing a coordinated, family-centered, community- based system of services that builds and enhances the strengths already possessed by families and surrogate families of children with serious emotional disturbances. It involves a collaboration among three state and three county agencies: the state Division of Mental Health and Addiction (DMHA), Division of Family and Children (DFC), Department of Education, the Marion County Office of Family and Children, Superior Court (Juvenile Division), and Mental Health Association.

A managed care organization created specifically for this project assigns a service coordinator to each family, who convenes a service coordination and planning team (including the family and other involved individuals). The team develops a service plan tailored to the individual needs of each child and family. The service coordinator is responsible for authorizing payment and assessing progress toward the goals of the service plan. Services are paid from a pool of funds, available on a capitated rate basis, from three of the participating agencies. About one third of the referrals to the Dawn Project come from the juvenile court. Results from the first several years of the Dawn Project show reduced reliance on residential placements and reduced costs. The program has received federal support for continuation and expansion and serves as a model for replication in several sites in Indiana.

that probation services provided directly in schools are more effective than regular probation (Griffin, 1999). The Unity Soccer Clinic, described in Case 4.3, developed by the Santa Cruz Probation Department, clearly embodies several principles of positive youth development (safety and structure, opportunities to belong and for skill building, support for efficacy and mattering). The probation youth who serve as soccer clinic staff gain valuable, potentially marketable skills, are empowered by the control they have in the clinic, and gain a sense of usefulness by serving younger children.

Although residential programs, especially detention and training schools, are often overused (Schwartz & Barton, 1994; Snyder & Sickmund, 1999), there will always be some circumstances in which a young person must be held securely prior to court hearings or after adjudication. A classic study (Haney, Banks, & Zimbardo, 1973) suggested that the situational role demands of "prisoner" and "guard" create dehumanizing behavior, even in typical college students. Certainly, such behavior may be found in many juvenile detention centers and training schools, as well as in adult prisons. Conditions of confinement are often atrocious, and overcrowding is common (Parent et al., 1994; Snyder & Sickmund, 1999). Such conditions and behaviors clearly are not conducive to the promotion of positive youth development, but these may not be inevitable.

Effective intake screening based on rational criteria and case-monitoring systems can prevent overcrowding by limiting incarceration to those for whom it may be appropriate and by reducing unnecessarily long stays (Schwartz & Barton, 1994; Wiebush, Baird, Krisberg, & Onek, 1995). Careful staff hiring and training in youth development principles can promote more positive, respectful interactions. Programming in secure facilities should provide safety and structure while providing competency development opportunities, including meaningful interactions with the community.

An example is the partnership among a juvenile detention center, community parks and recreation department, and local arts council in Columbus, Indiana, described in Case 4.4. In this "Mural Project," home detention and shelter youth along with other young people participate in the planning and implementation of a community arts project. The goals of this project are to engage young people and other community members in the production of a collaborative work of art that enriches the community and to set a standard for creative partnering among other local agencies. A national initiative to encourage the use of the arts to prevent or reduce delinquency has been evaluated and found promising (Clawson & Coolbaugh, 2001).

In addition to finding creative ways to involve incarcerated youth in community activities beyond the walls, secure facilities can bring the community in. The requirement that detention centers and training schools

Case 4.3   Unity Soccer Clinic, Santa Cruz (CA) Probation
Department

The Unity Soccer Clinic[3] is a summer job program that had its
beginnings in the participation of probation youth in a city indoor
soccer league. Unity fielded a co-ed team of teens deemed by the
court to be "at risk of out of home placement." The profiles of these
youth included significant substance abuse, particularly heroin, and
gang entrenchment. The activity was chosen because of its popularity with the youth, the prosocial nature of the sport, and because it
helped fill otherwise unsupervised free time. In 1999, the probation
department partnered with Job Training Partnership Act (JTPA) to
pay 10 youth to put on a summer soccer clinic through the
Watsonville Parks and Recreation and Community Services
Department. The youth first participated in 2 weeks of training in
teaching techniques, specific soccer games and drills, conflict resolution skills, and first aid. Following an example set by the director of
a nearby soccer camp, the youth planned out each day of the 3-week
clinic. They divided up the responsibilities for leading each activity
from welcome to clean-up.

During a final week, they practiced connecting their newly
acquired experience with future employment possibilities. They drew
up résumés, practiced filling out job applications, and took turns in
mock interviews. They toured the Police Athletic League facilities and
learned about recreation-related high school course work. Their written evaluations reflected a very positive experience. Throughout the
2-week training, 3-week clinic and 1-week "next steps," this group of
chronic offenders had no new offenses and only two probation vio-
lations. More than $225 in restitution was paid. Four of the 10 par-
ticipants found jobs during the following school year. Five of the
original 10 clinic coaches are now off of probation entirely.

What had begun with league play as a way to increase community
safety during nonschool hours soon became one of the most complete examples of balanced and restorative justice practice in the
Juvenile Probation Department. Unity Soccer Clinic developed new
competencies and offered a way for young offenders to be accountable to their victims by paying restitution and to their community by
serving its children.

Case 4.4   Mural Project, Columbus, IN

Youth in the juvenile justice system, youth with disabilities, and young people in underserved areas of Columbus, Indiana, create large-scale works of art within the city parks system in The Mural Project.[4] The Columbus Area Arts Council, in partnership with the Columbus Parks and Recreation Department and the Bartholomew County Youth Services Center (a juvenile detention center), administers this multiyear youth development project. Youth collectively engage in brainstorming, collaboration, negotiation, planning, preparation, implementation, and evaluation—valuable life skills for all citizens. Returning participants are encouraged to take leadership and mentoring roles.

Project 1: "The Calm at the Center" (Summer, 2000). Just across Haw Creek from the Columbus Regional Hospital, Lincoln Park is visible and accessible to patients, visitors, hospital staff, and the general public. With the location in mind, young people and their adult partners painted the first mural on the east wall of the handball court facing the hospital. Two artists, 17 teenagers, and seven Youth Services counselors created a bold, colorful work that reflects ideas and images pulled from sketchbooks, group work, "top 10" lists, and intimate conversations.

Project 2: "Flight" (Summer, 2001) at Jolie Crider Memorial Skate Park. The skate park, recently built as a result of a youth-led initiative to honor the memory of a high school student, seemed the perfect location for the second mural. During 2 weeks of painting, the project involved 25 at-risk teens and 12 Youth Services employees, in addition to skaters, Parks Department and Arts Council staff, and a large number of community volunteers. Three teens from the 2000 project returned to lend a hand.

provide education is one opportunity. The same detention center in Columbus, Indiana, for example, is one of the few that provides a full day of school, 5 days a week, year round to all detention residents. The detention education program is considered a satellite program of the school corporation, allowing the corporation to include the youth in their head count (for funding purposes) (P. Clark, personal communication, May 20, 2002).

The detention center in Columbus makes a conscious effort in its programming to reflect the concepts in the CUBE model (Boys & Girls Clubs of America, 2000) of youth development (P. Clark, personal communication,

May 20, 2002). The young people participating in detention, shelter, and day treatment programs are provided with *competency development (C)* in the areas of problem solving and decision making, a *useful role (U)* to play in the program in terms of providing assistance to others, a sense of *belonging (B)* to a group, and a sense of *empowerment (E)* as they are afforded the opportunity to continue to make choices and earn extra privileges, albeit limited, while they are at the center. Not coincidentally, the director of this center previously played a major role in that community's comprehensive initiative to promote positive youth development.

Summary and Conclusions

The preceding analysis yields two recommendations for the integration of positive youth development and juvenile justice. First, those who would advocate broad-based, community strategies to promote positive youth development should not ignore the differential and inequitable distribution of risks and supports in contemporary United States communities. Their strategies must include ways to address these inequities and truly embrace all children and families. These approaches should also involve effective collaborations with professionals from the various human service systems, including juvenile justice.

Second, the juvenile justice system, though dealing with the most troubled and troubling young people in our communities, should incorporate the fundamental principles of positive youth development in its decision making and programming. The examples highlighted in this chapter are but a few ideas of how this can be done. The juvenile justice system must give more than lip service to the "competency development" portion of its threefold mission and resist the politically expedient tendency to maximize only accountability (the contemporary code term for punishment) and public safety protection (through behavioral supervision and restrictive placements). Competency development means much more than recidivism reduction. It means attending to supports and opportunities that can foster positive life outcomes. This can best be done by including youth and their families in planning, building on existing strengths of the young people, and incorporating the community, both in terms of informal supports and professional services, as appropriate for each individual youth.

Just as any specific human behavioral act can be viewed as the combination of an individual's ability to perform the act plus a motivation to do so, a combination of a valid mechanism and a political commitment are necessary for any innovation or major change to succeed. This chapter has attempted to describe some evidence-based, conceptual underpinnings for building a bridge between positive youth development and juvenile justice. Of course, that bridge also spans the other systems affecting children and families, such as education, child welfare, and mental health.

Generating the political will to build this bridge is a more daunting challenge. It will take both widespread and persistent education of all community stakeholders regarding the positive youth development perspective, the theoretical and research bases on risk/protection and resilience, the evidence regarding what does and doesn't work in juvenile justice, the promise of balanced and restorative justice, and wraparound approaches, to name several key elements.

Training and cross-training of professionals who work with children and families will be important. In addition, fiscal incentives will be required in order to change the way human services systems do business. Federal initiatives such as CASSP and the OJJDP comprehensive strategy are examples of attempts to redirect resources towards more promising models. Even greater integration across service sectors at all levels, from local communities to states and even federal agencies, will be required. Above all, what is needed is a sincere public commitment to the well-being and healthy development of all children, including those in trouble with the law.

Notes

1. The description of this program is excerpted with permission from: Motika, S., & Ritter, B. Jr. (2001). *Community accountability board.* Denver, CO: Denver District Attorney's Office. Retrieved June 3, 2002, from: http://www. denverda.org/ html_website/denver_da/community_justice_Accountability.html.

2. This program description is based on the Dawn Project's (2001) printed and on-line program materials, Indiana Behavioral Choices, Inc., Indianapolis, IN. Retrieved November 4, 2002, from: http://www.kidwrap.org/.

3. The description of this program is excerpted from information provided by T. Spencer, Assistant Division Director, Santa Cruz County Probation, Santa Cruz, CA (personal communication, May 31, 2002).

4. This program description was excerpted from information provided by K. Shrode, Columbus Area Arts Council (personal communication, May 28, 2002).

References

Altschuler, D. M., & Armstrong, T. L. (1991). *Intensive community-based aftercare prototype: Policies and procedures.* Baltimore, MD: Johns Hopkins University, Institute for Policy Studies.

Altschuler, D. M., & Armstrong, T. L. (1998). Recent developments in juvenile aftercare: Assessment, findings, and promising programs. In A. R. Roberts (Ed.), *Juvenile justice: Policies, programs, and services* (2nd ed., pp. 448-472). Chicago: Nelson-Hall.

Altschuler, D. M., Armstrong, T. L., & MacKenzie, D. L. (1999). Reintegration, supervised release, and intensive aftercare. *OJJDP Juvenile Justice Bulletin.* Washington, DC: U.S. Department of Justice, Office of Juvenile Justice and Delinquency Prevention.

Andrews, D. A., Zinger, I., Hoge, R. D., Bonta, J., Gendreau, P., & Cullen, F. T. (1990). Does correctional treatment work? A clinically-relevant and psycho-logically-informed meta-analysis. *Criminology, 28,* 369-404.

Anthony, E. J. (1987). Children at high risk for psychosis growing up successfully. In E. J. Anthony & B. J. Cohler (Eds.), *The invulnerable child* (pp. 147-184). New York: Guilford.

Austin, J., & Krisberg, B. (1981). Wider, stronger, and different nets: The dialectics of criminal justice reform. *Journal of Research in Crime and Delinquency, 18,* 165-196.

Bazemore, G., & Terry, W. C. (1997). Developing delinquent youths: A reintegra-tive model for rehabilitation and a new role for the juvenile justice system. *Child Welfare, 76,* 665-716.

Bazemore, G., & Walgrave, L. (Eds.). (1999). *Restorative juvenile justice: Repairing the harm of youth crime.* Monsey, NY: Criminal Justice Press.

Bernard, T. J. (1992). *The cycle of juvenile justice.* New York: Oxford University Press.

Bishop, D., Frazier, C., Lanza-Kaduce, L., & Winner, L. (1966). The transfer of juvenile to criminal court: Does it make a difference? *Crime and Delinquency, 42,* 171-191.

Boys & Girls Clubs of America. (2000). *Who we are.* Retrieved June 13, 2002, from: http://www.bgca.org/whoweare/.

Burchard, J. D., Bruns, E. J., & Burchard, S. N. (2002). The wraparound approach. In B. J. Burns & K. Hoagwood (Eds.), *Community treatment for youth: Evidence-based interventions for severe emotional and behavioral disorders* (pp. 69-90). New York: Oxford University Press.

Butts, J. A., Buck, J., & Coggeshall, M. B. (2002). *The impact of teen court on young offenders.* Washington, DC: Urban Institute, Justice Policy Center.

Chamberlain, P. (2002). Treatment foster care. In B. J. Burns & K. Hoagwood (Eds.), *Community treatment for youth: Evidence-based interventions for severe emotional and behavioral disorders* (pp. 117-138). New York: Oxford University Press.

Clawson, H. J., & Coolbaugh, K. (2001). The YouthARTS development project. *OJJDP Juvenile Justice Bulletin.* Washington, DC: U.S. Department of Justice, Office of Juvenile Justice and Delinquency Prevention.

Dryfoos, J. (1990). *Adolescents at risk.* New York: Oxford University Press.

Duchnowski, A. J., Kutash, K., & Friedman, R. M. (2002). Community-based inter-ventions in a system of care and outcomes framework. In B. J. Burns &

K. Hoagwood (Eds.), *Community treatment for youth: Evidence-based interventions for severe emotional and behavioral disorders* (pp. 16-37). New York: Oxford University Press.

Egeland, B., Jacobvitz, D., & Sroufe, L. A. (1988). Breaking the cycle of abuse. *Child Development, 59*, 1080-1088.

Feld, B. C. (1999). *Bad kids: Race and the transformation of the juvenile court.* New York: Oxford University Press.

Franz, J. (1994). *Wraparound and the juvenile court: Practical problems in inter-galactic communication.* Retrieved June 6, 2002, from: http://www.paperboat.com/calliope.juvcourt.html.

Franz, J. (2001). *Therapeutic jurisprudence.* Retrieved June 6, 2002, from: http://www.paperboat.com/calliope/Therapeutic.html.

Furstenberg, F. F. Jr., Cook, T. D., Eccles, J., Elder, G. H. Jr., & Sameroff, A. (1999). *Managing to make it: Urban families and adolescent success.* Chicago: University of Chicago Press.

Goldman, S. K. (1999). The conceptual framework for wraparound: Definition, values, essential elements, and requirements for practice. In B. J. Burns & S. K. Goldman (Eds.), *Systems of care: Promising practices in children's mental health, 1998 series: Vol. IV* (pp. 27-34). Washington, DC: Center for Effective Collaboration and Practice, American Institutes for Research.

Gordon, E. W., & Song, L. D. (1994). Variations in the experience of resilience. In M. C. Wang & E. W. Gordon (Eds.), *Educational resilience in inner-city America: Challenges and prospects* (pp. 27-43). Hillsdale, NJ: Lawrence Erlbaum.

Greenberg, M., & Feinberg, M. (2002). *An evaluation of PCCD's Communities that Care delinquency prevention initiative. Final report.* Harrisburg, PA: Pennsylvania Commission on Crime and Delinquency. Retrieved May 31, 2002, from: http://www.pccd.state.pa.us.

Griffin, P. W. (1999). Juvenile probation in the schools. *In Focus, 1*(1), 1-12.

Haney, C., Banks, C., & Zimbardo, P. (1973). Interpersonal dynamics in a simulated prison. *International Journal of Criminology & Penology, 1*(1), 69-97.

Hawkins, J. D., Catalano, R. F., & Associates. (1992). *Communities that care: Action for drug abuse prevention.* San Francisco: Jossey-Bass.

Hawkins, J. D., Catalano, R. F., & Miller, J. Y. (1992). Risk and protective factors for alcohol and other drug problems in adolescence and early adulthood: Implications for substance abuse prevention. *Psychological Bulletin 112*(1), 64-105.

Henggeler, S. W., Schoenwald, S. K., Borduin, C. M., Rowland, M. D., & Cunningham, P. B. (1998). *Multisystemic treatment of antisocial behavior in children and adolescents.* New York: Guilford.

Howell, J. C. (Ed.). (1995). *Guide for implementing the comprehensive strategy for serious, violent, and chronic juvenile offenders.* Washington, DC: U.S. Department of Justice, Office of Juvenile Justice and Delinquency Prevention.

Howell, J. C., Krisberg, B., Hawkins, J. D., & Wilson, J. J. (1995). *Sourcebook on serious, violent, and chronic juvenile offenders.* Thousand Oaks, CA: Sage.

Indiana Behavioral Choices, Inc. (2001). *The Dawn Project.* Indianapolis, IN. Retrieved November 4, 2002, from: http://www.kidwrap.org/.

Indiana Youth Institute. (n.d.). *The juvenile justice system in Indiana.* Indianapolis, IN: Author.

In re Gault, 387 U.S. 1, 87 S.Ct. 1428 (1967).

In re Winship, 387 U.S. 358, 90 S.Ct. 1068 (1970).

Kent v. United States, 383 U.S. 541, 86 S.Ct. 1045 (1966).

Kirby, L. D., & Fraser, M. W. (1997). Risk and resilience in childhood. In M. W. Fraser (Ed.), *Risk and resilience in childhood: An ecological perspective* (pp. 10-33). Washington, DC: NASW Press.

Lipsey, M. (1992). Juvenile delinquency treatment: A meta-analytic inquiry into the viability of effects. In T. Cook, D. Cordray, H. Hartman, L. Hedges, R. Light, T. Louis, & F. Mosteller (Eds.), *Meta-analysis for explanation: A casebook* (pp. 83-127). New York: Russell Sage.

Lipsey, M. W., & Wilson, D. B. (1998). Effective intervention for serious juvenile offenders: A synthesis of research. In R. Loeber & D. P. Farrington (Eds.), *Serious and violent juvenile offenders: Risk factors and successful interventions* (pp. 313-345). Thousand Oaks, CA: Sage.

Lipton, D., Martinson, R., & Wilks, J. (1975). *The effectiveness of correctional treatment: A survey of treatment evaluation studies.* New York: Praeger.

Loeber, R., & Farrington, D. P. (Eds.). (1998). *Serious and violent juvenile offenders: Risk factors and successful interventions.* Thousand Oaks, CA: Sage.

Long, J. V. F., & Vaillant, G. E. (1989). Escape from the underclass. In T. F. Dugan & R. Coles (Eds.), *The child in our times: Studies in the development of resiliency* (pp. 200-213). New York: Brunner/Mazel.

Luthar, S. S. (1991). Vulnerability and resilience: A study of high risk adolescents. *Child Development, 62,* 600-616.

Macallair, D., & Roche, T. (2001). *Widening the net in juvenile justice and the dangers of prevention and early intervention.* Washington, DC: Center on Juvenile and Criminal Justice. Retrieved June 6, 2002, from: http://www.cjcj.org/jpi/netwid.html.

Maloney, D., Romig, D., & Armstrong, T. (1988). Juvenile probation: The balanced approach. *Juvenile and Family Court Journal, 39*(3), 1-62.

Masten, A. S. (1994). Resilience in individual development: Successful adaptation despite risk and adversity. In M. C. Wang & E. W. Gordon (Eds.), *Educational resilience in inner-city America: Challenges and prospects* (pp. 3-25). Hillsdale, NJ: Lawrence Erlbaum.

McKeiver v. Pennsylvania, 403 U.S. 528, 91 S.Ct. 1976 (1971).

Mendel, R. A. (2000). *Less hype, more help: Reducing juvenile crime, what works—and what doesn't.* Washington, DC: American Youth Policy Forum.

Mihalic, S., Irwin, K., Elliott, D., Fagan, A., & Hansen, D. (2001). Blueprints for violence prevention. *Juvenile Justice Bulletin.* Washington, DC: U.S. Department of Justice, Office of Juvenile Justice and Delinquency Prevention.

Motika, S., & Ritter, B. Jr. (2001). Community accountability board. Denver, CO: Denver District Attorney's Office. Retrieved June 3, 2002, from: http://www.denverda.org/html_website/denver_da/community_justice_Accountability.html.

Northey W. F. Jr., Primer, V., & Christensen, L. (1997). Promoting justice in the delivery of services to juvenile delinquents: The ecosystemic natural wraparound model. *Child and Adolescent Social Work Journal, 14,* 5-22.

Parent, D. (1989). *Shock incarceration: An overview of existing programs.* Washington, DC: U.S. Department of Justice, National Institute of Justice.

Parent, D. G., Leiter, V., Kennedy, S., Levins, L., Wentworth, D., & Wilcox, S. (1994). *Conditions of confinement: Juvenile detention and corrections facilities. Research summary.* Washington, DC: U.S. Department of Justice, Office of Juvenile Justice and Delinquency Prevention.

Peters, M., Thomas, D., & Zamberlan, C. (1997). *Boot camps for juvenile offenders: Program summary.* Washington, DC: Office of Juvenile Justice and Delinquency Prevention.

Pollard, J. A., Hawkins, J. D., & Arthur, M. W. (1999). Risk and protection: Are both necessary to understand diverse behavioral outcomes in adolescence? *Social Work Research, 23*(3), 145-158.

Schall v. Martin, 467 U.S. 253, 104 S.Ct. 2403 (1984).

Schwartz, I. M., & Barton, W. H. (Eds.). (1994). *Reforming juvenile detention: No more hidden closets.* Columbus: Ohio State University Press.

Schwartz, R. G. (2001). Juvenile justice and positive youth development. In P. L. Benson & K. Pittman (Eds.), *Trends in youth development: Visions, realities and challenges* (pp. 231-268). Boston: Kluwer.

Snyder, H., & Sickmund, M. (1999). *Juvenile offenders and victims: 1999 national report.* Pittsburgh, PA: National Center for Juvenile Justice.

Stroul, B. A., & Friedman, R. M. (1986). *A system of care for seriously emotionally disturbed children and youth.* Washington, DC: CASSP Technical Assistance Center, Georgetown University Child Development Center.

Travis, J., Solomon, A. L., & Waul, M. (2001). *From prison to home: The dimensions and consequences of prisoner reentry.* Washington, DC: Urban Institute.

VanDenBerg, J. E., & Grealish, M. E. (1996). Individualized services and supports through the wraparound process: Philosophy and procedures. *Journal of Child and Family Studies, 5,* 7-21.

Werner, E. E., & Smith, R. (1992). *Overcoming the odds: High risk children from birth to adulthood.* Ithaca, NY: Cornell University Press.

Wiebush, R. G., Baird, C., Krisberg, B., & Onek, D. (1995). Risk assessment and classification for serious, violent, and chronic juvenile offenders. In J. C. Howell, B. Krisberg, J. D. Hawkins, & J. J. Wilson (Eds.), *Serious, violent, and chronic juvenile offenders: A sourcebook* (pp. 171-212). Thousand Oaks, CA: Sage.

Wilson, J. J., & Howell, J. C. (1993). *A comprehensive strategy for serious, violent, and chronic juvenile offenders: Program summary.* Washington, DC: U.S. Department of Justice, Office of Juvenile Justice and Delinquency Prevention.

Worland, J., Janes, C. L., Anthony, E. J., McGinnis, M., & Cass, L. (1984). St. Louis Risk Research Project: Comprehensive reports of experimental studies. In N. F. Watt, E. J. Anthony, L. C. Wynne, & J. Rolf (Eds.), *Children at risk for schizophrenia: A longitudinal perspective* (pp. 105-147). Cambridge: Cambridge University Press.

5

Youth Development and Health

Richard E. Kreipe, Sheryl A. Ryan,
and Susan M. Seibold-Simpson

This chapter addresses youth development from the perspective of health and health care. Because the processes and structures fostering youth development are often viewed as social phenomena, modern medicine and health care are sometimes considered peripheral or tangential to youth development. However, we shall demonstrate that both the health of and health care for youth benefit from a youth development approach. Furthermore, professionals concerned about the health of the next generation of adults increasingly apply the principles of youth development in direct health care services as well as in policy development.

The first section of this chapter will focus on changes in causes of sickness and death, in addition to changes in health care over time. Contemporary adolescent health issues at the national level will be addressed next, followed by the national agenda of leading health indicators and critical health outcomes for this age group. Youth development as a public health practice will be explored, using the example of a county health department in a metropolitan area in upstate New York. This will be followed by concrete examples of youth development activities with respect to reducing teen pregnancy and substance use. Although youth development initiatives are generally community based, health care providers would also benefit from adopting a youth development approach in encounters with individual adolescents and their families. Methods to do this will be discussed. Finally, we conclude with an example of how a youth development approach turned a deadly health crisis in a rural community into a structured framework to address health needs of the entire community, not merely its younger residents.

Medicine, Public Health, and Youth Development

From the mid-1880s to the mid-1900s, significant discoveries in biochemistry, pathology, microbiology, physiology, physics, and genetics resulted in a scientific revolution in medicine. As a result, beliefs in concepts such as diseases being caused by a poisonous atmosphere (miasma) or one's state of mind being influenced by the balance of body fluids (humors) gave way to germ theories of infectious diseases and treatments targeted at specific organs or tissues. This revolution in medicine and health care paralleled, and was in part driven by, the industrial revolution that has resulted in the highly mechanized and technological society in which we live. However, major reductions in morbidity and mortality over the last century have occurred more because of public health measures than because of encounters with individual health care providers or treatments. Improved sanitation, work environments, and immunization programs as well as safety measures, such as food inspection or the use of safety belts in motor vehicles, have done more to improve health than one-to-one medical treatment. Furthermore, because we made major strides in preventing devastating diseases in the first half of the 20th century, many of the problems now facing youth have social or environmental roots, what Haggerty and colleagues labeled the "new morbidity" (Haggerty, Roghmann, & Pless, 1992).

Thus, the majority of poor health and death for individuals 10 to 20 years of age at the beginning of the 21st century is attributable to preventable causes, such as injuries (motor vehicle accidents, homicide, or suicide) and behaviors such as substance use and abuse or sexual activity (American Academy of Pediatrics, 2001). These differ from conditions that threatened young people at the beginning of the 20th century, such as infections or untreatable medical conditions. One infectious agent stands out as a significant cause of death among young people in the beginning of the 21st century, the human immunodeficiency virus (HIV); the resultant acquired immune deficiency syndrome (AIDS) is now the third leading cause of death for individuals 25 to 30 years of age (Centers for Disease Control and Prevention, 2002). However, because there is a 10- to 15-year latency period between HIV acquisition and death due to AIDS, young adults who die from AIDS have generally acquired their HIV infection during adolescence, when they engaged in risky behaviors with an infected individual, such as injecting drugs or sexual activity. Health problems resulting from substance use, sexual activity, and risky behaviors have not responded to traditional medical approaches.

Therefore, this chapter, focused on youth development and health, warrants a comparison of traditional medical care and public health approaches (see Table 5.1). In this context, youth development approaches are best considered as a type of public health activity because they represent actions with demonstrated effectiveness in improving health outcomes for individuals but are targeted at populations. By focusing on the group level rather than the individual, public health measures benefit all young people. The World Health Organization (1948), the largest public health organization, defines health as "a state of complete physical, mental and social well-being and not merely the absence of disease or infirmity" (p. 100). This definition conceptually embraces assets associated with health within various domains, rather than merely the absence of deficits and problems associated with illness. Thus, health in this broader perspective and public health approaches to achieve this state find parallels in youth development approaches, both philosophically and in practice.

Youth Development in the Health Care System for Adolescents

The Modern Medical Care System

In *Primary Care,* Starfield (1992) cited the dilemma facing our medical care system with its emphasis on fragmentation and technology-driven specialization rather than primary care:

> Specialization oriented toward treating disease cannot maximize health because preventing illness and promoting optimal functioning requires a broader perspective than can be achieved by the disease specialists. . . . Effective medical care is not limited to the treatment of disease itself; it must consider the contexts in which the illness occurs and the patient lives. (p. 19)

The difficulties inherent in incorporating and combining the elements of highly specialized medical care with those of primary health care are directly analogous to those currently experienced by professionals working

Table 5.1   Comparison of Traditional Medicine and Public Health

Traditional Medicine	*Public Health*
Primary focus on individual	Primary focus on population
Personal service ethic, conditioned by awareness of social responsibilities	Public service ethic, tempered by concerns for the individual
Emphasis on diagnosis and treatment, care for the whole patient	Emphasis on prevention, health promotion for the whole community
Medical paradigm places predominant emphasis on medical care	Public health paradigm employs a spectrum of interventions aimed at the environment, human behavior and lifestyle, and medical care
Well-established profession with sharp public image	Multiple professional identities with diffuse public image
Uniform system for certifying specialists beyond professional medical degree	Variable certification of specialists beyond professional public health degree
Lines of specialization organized, for example, by: – organ system (cardiology) – patient group (pediatrics) – pathophysiology (oncology, infectious disease) – technical skill (radiology)	Lines of specialization organized, for example, by: – analytical method (epidemiology) – setting and population (occupational health) – substantive health problem (nutrition) – skills in assessment, policy development, and assurance
Biologic sciences central, stimulated by needs of patients; move between laboratory and bedside	Biologic sciences central, stimulated by major threats to health of populations; move between laboratory and field
Numeric sciences increasing in prominence, though still a relatively minor part of training	Numeric sciences an essential feature of analysis and training
Social sciences tend to be an elective part of medical education	Social sciences an integral part of public health education
Clinical sciences central to professional training	Clinical sciences peripheral to professional training

SOURCE: Adapted from Harvey Fineberg, MD, PhD, Dean, Harvard University School of Public Health (1990).

Table 5.2   Analogies Between Deficit Reduction vs. Youth Development
Models and Conventional Medical vs. Primary Health Care Models

	Youth Models		Health Care Models	
	Deficit Reduction	Youth Development	Conventional Medical	Primary Health Care
Focus	• Specific problem or health-compromising behavior	• Community infrastructures that support youth	• Illness • Cure	• Health • Preventive care
Content	• Programs to control risks in vulnerable or at-risk youth	• Programs that enhance protective factors in *all* children and youth	• Treatment • Episodic care • Specific problems	• Health promotion • Continuous care • Comprehensive care
Organization	• Specific agencies that provide specific prevention or intervention programs	• No one agency • Community wide encompassing all citizens to act on shared vision	• Specialists • Physicians	• General practitioners • Interdisciplinary team
Responsibility	• Professionals in involved agencies • Crisis management teams	• All individuals within a community	• Health sector only • Professional dominance • Passive reception	• Intersectional collaboration • Community participation • Self-responsibility

SOURCE: Adapted from: Benson (1997), Starfield (1992), and Vuori, (1984).

in the youth development field and attempting to reconcile the tenets of problem-oriented deficit-reduction models versus the positive youth development models that are the focus of this book (see Table 5.2).

Traditional medical care systems are designed to provide narrowly focused care that emphasizes the treatment of medical disease, rather than those that emphasize health promotion and disease prevention as in primary health care. These traditional *disease-reduction* or *deficit-reduction* models place the responsibility for care and cure on the shoulders of the medical specialists or professionals. The primary care model, with its emphasis on prevention and health promotion and its inclusion of individuals and members of the community as important in enhancing the health of all the members of a community, is consistent with the goals of public health and would embrace positive youth development efforts. Therefore, it is important for providers of health care to adolescents to apply the principles of youth development.

In *All Children Are Our Children,* Benson (1997) discusses ways in which the health care system can readily incorporate elements of youth development in both the structure and manner that care is delivered. For example, he states that the health care system has the power to be a strong presence, to advocate for community-wide health promotion strategies that address health in ways that are meaningful to communities, and to infuse asset building into routine encounters with parents and youth, as described later in this chapter.

Disease Prevention, Health Promotion, and Healthy People 2010

Adolescent health concerns in the 21st century are dominated by preventable conditions such as obesity and inadequate physical activity, tobacco and other substance use or abuse, high-risk sexual behaviors, mental health problems, and injury and violence. The blueprint for the health of our nation, *Healthy People 2010* (2000), targets 21 outcomes for adolescents and young adults, of which 9 reflect critical health outcomes and 8 represent leading health indicators related to modifiable behavior (see Tables 5.3 and 5.4). Practitioners in the adolescent health care field need to embrace the principles of youth development, both in their roles in the public health arena (e.g., Health Action, 1999) as well as during individual interactions with youth and their families (e.g., Bright Futures, 1994), both of which are discussed below.

Youth Development in Public Health Practice

Although public health approaches hold greater promise than traditional medical models for improving the health of adolescents as a group, the extant public health system in the United States may not be adequate to bring about the necessary changes. In its report, *The Future of Public Health,* the Institute of Medicine (Institute of Medicine, 1998) described public health as "what we as a society do collectively to assure the conditions for people to be healthy" (p. 19). However, the report criticized the existing public health system as being in "disarray." As a result of this report and continued concerns about the "crumbling infrastructure" of

Table 5.3   Healthy People 2010 Has Eight Leading Health Indicators for Adolescents and Young Adults

Leading Health Indicators Are **Bold**; *Those That Are Also Critical Health Outcomes Are* Underlined

Obj. #	Objective	Baseline (Year)	2010 Target
15–15	Reduce deaths caused by motor vehicle crashes.	25.4 per 100,000 (1998)	[1]
15–32	Reduce homicides.		
	– 10- to 14-year-olds	1.5 per 100,000 (1997)	[1]
	– 15- to 19-year-olds	13.6 per 100,000 (1997)	[1]
26–11	Reduce the proportion of persons engaging in binge drinking of alcoholic beverages.	8.3% (1997)	3.0%
26–10	Reduce past-month use of illicit substances.	9.4% (1997)	0.7%
25–11	Increase the proportion of adolescents who abstain from sexual intercourse or use condoms if currently sexually active.	85% (1997)	95%
27–02	Reduce tobacco use by adolescents.	43% (1997)	21%
19–03	Reduce the proportion of children and adolescents who are overweight or obese.	10% (1994)	5%
22–07	Increase the proportion of adolescents who engage in vigorous physical activity that promotes cardiorespiratory fitness 3 or more days per week for 20 or more minutes per occasion.	64% (1997)	85%

SOURCE: Adapted from "Critical and Leading Objectives for Adolescents and Young Adults" in Healthy People 2010, and National Adolescent Health Information Center.

NOTE: [1] 2010 target not provided for adolescent/young adult age group.

public health in America, new studies are ongoing to determine the best strategies to assure the health of the public in the 21st century (Institute of Medicine, 2001).

Traditionally, public health has used a predominantly deficit-based, medical model in its measurement of "health," so that it generally measures the reduction of morbidity rather than an improvement in health. Although there has been a need to shift to a more positive standpoint, performance measurement continues to focus on decreases in morbidity and not increases in developmental assets. In part, this is because the measures used to determine progress are often related to reduction in prevalence rates for certain conditions; in part, this is because we have only recently begun to measure assets in relation to health assessments.

However, as an example of an innovative community health initiative, HEALTH *ACTION* builds positive youth assets as a focus of improving health. The overall goal of HEALTH *ACTION* is to improve the health of the citizens of Monroe County (Rochester), New York, including youth, by aligning community resources toward selected priorities for action. HEALTH *ACTION* facilitates collaboration and cooperation among providers, agencies, and businesses to benefit the community by concentrating resources where they are most likely to improve health. In this initiative, a *healthy community* is defined as one in which the objective measures of health status are at optimal levels and there exists a commitment to health at all levels of the community. This commitment is required to institutionalize a sustained and continuous health improvement effort (see Figure 5.1) (Health Action, 1999).

To monitor the health status of adolescents, HEALTH *ACTION* uses an instrument that measures the 40 external and internal assets developed and refined in the Search Institute's Survey of Student Resources and Assets (Search Institute, 2000). Grounded in findings of a 1998 survey of almost 1,800 middle school students in Monroe County and 16 focus groups comprising over 200 community residents including many youth, HEALTH *ACTION* identified two youth-oriented priorities for community action beginning in 2001: (a) Reducing Tobacco Use and (b) Building Youth Competencies to Promote Healthy Lives (Health Action, 1999).

As noted in the HEALTH *ACTION* Web-based materials, the survey measures strengths and skills that allow youth to make good choices about a range of health problems. Youth with more assets are less likely to smoke, use drugs or alcohol, or to engage in risky sexual or violent behavior than those with fewer assets (Health Action, 1999; Search Institute, 2000). Therefore, this health-focused youth development intervention measures youth assets in addition to other traditional public health measures and also makes increasing youth assets a major priority. Of interest, many programs designed to

Table 5.4   Healthy People 2010 Has Nine Critical Health Objectives for
Adolescents and Young Adults

Critical Health Outcomes Are <u>Underlined</u>*; Those That Are Also Leading Health
Indicators Are* **Bold.**

Obj. #	*Objective*	*Baseline (Year)*	*2010 Target*
16–03	<u>Reduce deaths of adolescents and young adults.</u>		
	– 10- to 14-year-olds	21.8 per 100,000 (1998)	16.8/100,000
	– 15- to 19-year-olds	69.7 per 100,000 (1998)	43.2/00,000
	– 20- to 24-year-olds	93.8 per 100,000 (1998)	57.3/100,000
15–15	**<u>Reduce deaths caused by</u> <u>motor vehicle crashes.</u>**	25.4 per 100,000 (1998)	[1]
26–01	<u>Reduce deaths and injuries caused by alcohol- and drug-related motor vehicle crashes.</u>	11.7 per 100,000	[1]
18–01	<u>Reduce the suicide rate.</u>	[2]	[2]
15–32	**<u>Reduce homicides.</u>**		
	– **10- to 14-year olds**	1.5 per 100,000 (1997)	[1]
	– **15- to 19-year olds**	13.6 per 100,000 (1997)	[1]
09–07	<u>Reduce pregnancies among adolescent females.</u>	72 per 1,000 females (1995)	46 per 1,000
13–05	<u>Reduce the number of cases of HIV infection among adolescents and adults.</u>	[4]	[4]
25–01	<u>Reduce the proportion of adolescents and young adults with chlamydia trachomatis infections.</u>		
	– Females attending FP clinics	5.0% (1997)	3.0%
	– Females attending STD clinics	12.2% (1997)	3.0%
	– Males attending STD clinics	15.7% (1997)	3.0%

(Continued)

Table 5.4 (Continued)

Critical Health Outcomes Are <u>Underlined</u>; *Those That Are Also Leading Health Indicators Are* **Bold.**

Obj. #	Objective	Baseline (Year)	2010 Target
19–03	<u>Reduce the proportion of children and adolescents who are overweight or obese.</u>	10% (1994)	5%

SOURCE: Adapted from "Critical and Leading Objectives for Adolescents and Young Adults" in Healthy People 2010, and National Adolescent Health Information Center.

[1] 2010 target not provided for adolescent/young adult age group.
[2] Baseline data and 2010 target not provided for adolescent/young adult age group.
[3] Baseline and target include age groups outside of adolescent/young adult age parameters.
[4] Developmental objective—baseline and 2010 target to be provided by 2004.

enhance youth development maintain an emphasis on the reduction of risky behaviors, which tends to draw attention to "high-risk" or "at-risk" youth for special programs that are administered by professionals who tell them "how to behave properly." This limits their effectiveness. However, youth are much more likely to respond favorably when teachers, coaches, and friends help them build on their strengths and abilities. This approach has become central to the youth development activities in Monroe County, New York, as a result of the public health goals for adolescents in the community.

Examples of community-based efforts in HEALTH *ACTION* that are focused on asset building include (a) the formation of a "school support" asset called "Circle of Friends" in a local school district to build a sense of family for younger children, who then remain in the same club throughout their elementary school careers; (b) the construction of a skateboard park in a nearby rural community when youth identified having "nothing to do" as a reason for them not to feel connected to their community; (c) the renovation of an old building into a new teen center donated to a suburban village, with admission to the activities dependant on youth participating in community service projects; (d) the creation of a group of residents at a local senior center to serve as "greeters" at a nearby high school, leading one student to note, "It seemed like a joke at first, but it makes you feel a little better when someone goes out of their way to say hello to you in the morning"; (e) the inclusion of an assessment of strengths and assets by many agencies, including local United Way funded groups linked with the health department, as part of their intake process; and (f) the development of an outcome-oriented

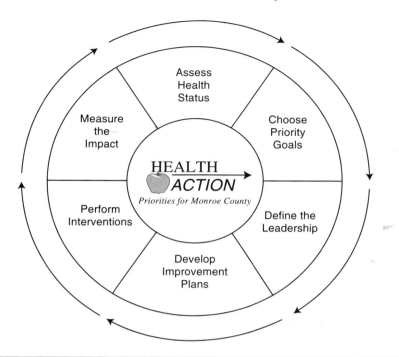

Figure 5.1   HEALTH *ACTION* Initiative

evaluation by the local Big Brothers, Big Sisters program that is built on assessing changes in the participants' assets in this mentoring program.

In these examples, leadership has been defined at the neighborhood level, and plans to improve youth assets have been developed and implemented. These efforts will continue, and other youth asset-building efforts will be added as new ideas, leaders, and needs emerge. The next step in the cycle portrayed in Figure 5.1 is to measure the impact and report the findings on "adolescent health report cards" that will be used to monitor changes in the health status of youth (Health Action, 1999) and to inform any changes needed in priority goals.

Youth Development in Relation to Teen Pregnancy and Substance Use

Although the measurement of health outcomes remains somewhat deficit focused, interventions to improve health indicators have been influenced by the youth development movement. Two areas in particular are (a) adolescent pregnancy/childbearing and (b) alcohol, tobacco, and other drug (ATOD) use.

Adolescent pregnancy rates in the United States have fallen consistently for the past decade. Although the overall rate of adolescent pregnancy has declined 22%, falling from a peak of 62.1 births per 1,000 teenagers 15 to 19 years old in 1991 to 48.5 in 2000, this rate is still high, and rates in selected subpopulations are even higher. The teen pregnancy rate in the United States remains among the highest in industrialized countries (Ventura, Mathews, & Hamilton, 2002). The research group, Child Trends, reports that the U.S. teen birthrate per 1,000 individuals by race/ethnicity group for females 15 to 19 years old in 1999 was 93 for Hispanics, 84 for blacks, and 34 for whites (Child Trends, 2002).

Some of the factors that contribute to adolescent pregnancy include poverty, early school failure, early behavior problems, and family dysfunction. A report on efforts to implement teen pregnancy prevention programs and measure their effectiveness identified several factors that can help protect against teen pregnancy, including positive relationships with parents and positive connections to a school community (U.S. General Accounting Office, 1998). Youth development programs are one way to enhance these protective factors and decrease the risky behaviors that lead to adolescent pregnancy. As Franklin & Corcoran (2000) note, youth who have higher achievement orientation, grades, aspirations, and economic opportunities are more likely to delay early sexual intercourse and childbearing. Two particular programs using a youth development approach have demonstrated a high level of rigor in evaluation as well as program success: the CAS-Carrera program and the Seattle Social Development Project.

The CAS-Carrera program includes a work-related intervention, an academic component, comprehensive family life and sexuality education, an arts and individual sports component, as well as providing mental health care and medical care (Philliber, Kaye, Herrling, & West, 2002). Philliber and colleagues (2002) recently demonstrated that, compared with controls, female program participants were half as likely to be sexually active and only one third as likely to have experienced a pregnancy. The program evaluation used a random-assignment design for 484 students and demonstrated positive findings over several years.

A second program that demonstrated success in reducing sexual risk behaviors is the Seattle Social Development Project. Lonczak and colleagues (2002) found that, compared with the control group, the youth who completed the program reported significantly fewer sexual partners and experienced a marginally reduced risk for initiating intercourse by 21 years of age. The Seattle Social Development Project sought to promote bonding to school and family by enhancing opportunities and reinforcement for a youth's active involvement in family and school, and by strengthening a youth's social competency. The study included 349 full-intervention and control participants. The study reported on the following factors: age at first sexual experience, condom use, sexual partners, sexually transmitted disease (STD) diagnosis, and pregnancy and birth. Significantly fewer females in the full-intervention group than in the control group had been pregnant and had given birth by the age of 21 years. The Seattle Social Development Project has demonstrated reductions in antisocial behavior, improved academic skills, greater commitment to school, reduced levels of alienation and better prosocial bonding with peers and adults, less misbehavior in school, and less drug use in school (National Institute on Drug Abuse, 2001).

Other programs designed to prevent adolescent pregnancy using a *community-based life options* perspective include the Teen Outreach Program, the Youth Incentive Entitlement Pilot Project, Quantum Opportunities Program, and the American Youth and Conservation Corps (Kirby, 1999; Nitz, 1999). Kirby (1999) indicates that it is thought that youth development programs may increase youth connection with adults, reduce discretionary time and subsequent opportunities for unprotected sex, and improve adolescents' beliefs and hopes for the future. Nitz (1999) noted, "Community-based life options programs appear to be a promising approach in teen pregnancy prevention, perhaps because they are ecologically oriented and focus on skill-building in areas that extend beyond pregnancy" (p. 464). The Alan Guttmacher Institute (Boonstra, 2002) also found evidence that youth development programs reduce adolescent pregnancy in France, Sweden, and to a lesser extent in Great Britain and Canada.

Prevention of ATOD has also been found to result from youth development programs. The National Institute on Drug Abuse, in cooperation with the scientists who conducted the research, described youth development interventions that have been evaluated. These include Project STAR, which includes a middle school-based component, a parent program component, and a health policy change component. The school-based component uses a social influence curriculum, and the parent component addresses family communication skills.

Social influence is one method of changing people's attitudes, values, and behavior. The National Institute of Mental Health (1995) describes *influence* as including advertisers, the media, family, friends, neighbors, as well as our own "social influenced 'inner voices' of conscience, self-concept and deep-seated stereotypes." It provides three examples of social influence research: the impact of persuasive messages, self-persuasion, and resisting pressure to change and conform. An example of a persuasive message is the "Not me, not now" media campaign to prevent adolescent pregnancy. Self-persuasion refers to coordinating attitudes with behaviors, such as providing incentives. Resisting pressure to change or conform includes teaching teenagers refusal skills as well as counteracting harmful peer influence with positive peer influence.

Lantz (2000) and colleagues reviewed youth smoking prevention and tobacco control strategies and noted that approaches based on the social influence resistance model are effective in preventing tobacco and other drug use. Interventions focus on building skills needed to recognize and resist negative influences, such as decision-making skills and assertiveness. An example that has been used widely but to date has not shown long-term effectiveness is the Drug Abuse Resistance Education (D.A.R.E.) program. D.A.R.E. has recently added a new middle school component that is currently being evaluated. Improving academic skills, creating a sustained relationship with adult advisors or mentors, and family-focused interventions are also included.

As Ethier and St. Lawrence (2002) remarked, "Strengthening social and psychological skills, rather than targeting specific risk behaviors, can protect against an array of health risks, including STDs, human immuno-deficiency virus infection, and pregnancy in adolescents and young adults" (p. 429). Ethier and St. Lawrence observed that there is a potential role for health care providers in such prevention programs. By increasing and changing the interactions between children and their health care providers from an early age, "Children could be prepared to actively seek appropriate and timely health care as adolescents, communicate effectively with their health care providers, and make healthier decisions" (p. 430).

Adolescent Medicine and the Provision of Preventive Health Care

Adolescent medicine is a subspecialty within health care that is not based on a particular technology, but instead uses an interdisciplinary team approach to adolescent health issues, addressing specific biologic, psychologic, social, and environmental factors in a manner that combines traditional medical care with public health measures. For example, one of the major elements of health counseling of adolescents is the use of "guided decision making," often used in smoking cessation interventions described below. In this process, adolescents are engaged as active participants in achieving and maintaining their own health. This closely parallels the "youth involvement" element of youth development, in which youth are fully engaged as participants, especially as they relate to issues of personal relevance to them. Youth participants in an innovative public health initiative sponsored by the New York State Department of Health, Assets Coming Together (ACT) for Youth, have developed the motto "Don't make decisions about us, without us" to capture the centrality of youth involvement in youth development programming. Similarly, active involvement of youth in their health care and wellness are central to adolescent health care.

Adolescent health care is also characterized by the application of the *readiness to change* model developed by Prochaska, DiClemente, and colleagues (Plummer et al., 2001) to motivate individuals to improve their health. Whereas traditional health care often formulates interventions in a "one-size-fits-all" approach, practitioners who use the readiness-to-change framework gauge the motivation of an adolescent to modify behaviors that would reduce risk and promote wellness. For example, a teenager who smokes but is in *precontemplation* about smoking cessation (i.e., wants to continue to smoke) would be advised to stop smoking, offered help to do so, and also given information about the benefits of smoking cessation but would not be "lectured" about the risks of lung cancer or chronic lung disease. The purpose of providing advice and information is to help move the youth along the continuum toward more healthy behaviors by having the teen consider the *possibility* of smoking cessation. Once the teen considers his or her smoking a problem, he or she has entered the *contemplation* stage and would be more amenable to weighing the pros and cons of smoking versus not smoking. The goal of intervening at this stage is for the clinician to generate an awareness of the dissonance between present behavior and long-term goals, so that the teen would want to stop smoking because smoking is not in concert with his or her goals.

When the teenager is ready to stop smoking, he or she has entered the "ready for action" stage, in which assisting him or her to make plans such as setting a quit date, developing a support system, and using nicotine replacement are appropriate. Again, the intention of the clinician being more actively involved in decision making is to help the young person move toward more healthy behaviors and ultimately stop smoking but to do so in a manner that is perceived as being under his or her control and power. Once the teen has taken action to stop smoking, there is a need for close follow-up and social support because "failure" rates are high at this stage; old habits, especially ones compounded by biological addiction, are difficult to change. Furthermore, social structures, such as associating with family or peer group members who still smoke, may make smoking cessation nearly impossible. Therefore, relapse is common.

In *Why We Do What We Do,* Deci and Flaste (1996) point out that "autonomy alignment" is one of the most important things that a teacher or clinician can do to help motivate a person to change. That is, one of the key features of adolescent development is the movement from the dependence of child-hood to the interdependence of adulthood through the emergence of a sta-ble identity and a sense of autonomy. Studies have shown that adolescents are much more likely to be motivated to change when professionals and parents acknowledge, respect, and nurture this emerging autonomy by help-ing to support and encourage it, within limits. That is, when adults provide feedback about how a youth's behaviors are in concert—or in conflict—with the youth's own autonomous goals, that individual will be more pre-pared to change and more likely to make healthy choices. This is paralleled in youth development approaches, in which community interventions are most likely to have youth "buy in" if the goals are in keeping with what the youth want to have happen and if they respect the unique contributions that youth can make to their own growth and development.

Furthermore, youth development approaches, as described elsewhere in this book, follow an ecological model in which the effects of the individual on the environment and the effects of the environment on the individual are con-sidered in a dynamic and interactive manner. The *biopsychosocial* model, described by Engel (1977) at the University of Rochester 25 years ago, takes an ecological approach to health. The biopsychosocial approach acknowl-edges uncertainty, subjectivity, and interactions at various levels, from mole-cules within cells to society at large as determinants of health. This renders health problems much more complex and contextual than the more mecha-nistic approach of traditional medicine, in which a diagnosis of a disease is made and a treatment is prescribed with an expected outcome in mind.

With a common adolescent health problem such as substance abuse, for example, the biopsychosocial approach in adolescent medicine would entail consideration of the biological properties of the substance itself (effects, side effects, addiction potential) as well as the predisposition a young per-son might have to addiction (based on family history of substance abuse or depression and his or her personal experience with various substances). One would also take into consideration the developmental stage of the indi-vidual, realizing that a younger person who has a "positive" experience when using a substance might be more likely than an older adolescent to again seek that experience. The psychological context of self-esteem and the presence of an underlying mental health condition, such as depression, anxiety, or learning disability, may all make the use and abuse of substances more likely. In addition, there are numerous "protective" factors that mitigate the likelihood of use or the progression from use to abuse of substances. Finally, the social realm of school environment, neighborhood, parental monitoring, peer group membership, religious affiliation, and future orientation all can influence substance use, and the use/abuse of substances can lead to changes in these spheres of influence. This begs the question, however, of the need for a more preventive approach to such problems.

Prevention, a central public health function, exists in three levels: (a) primary prevention, focused on preventing the acquisition of disease or illness; (b) secondary prevention, in which an individual is identified early in the course of an illness and remedial treatments are provided; and (c) tertiary prevention, in which an individual who has a health problem receives rehabilitation to prevent worsening of the condition or to return toward normal and preventing recurrence. There are many practical applications of preventive efforts within a youth development framework.

For example, youth development activities that enhance a 15-year-old female's connectedness with her school and that empower her to resist peer pressure to become sexually active by remaining abstinent represent primary prevention of high-risk sexual behaviors. If such a girl were later to become sexually active, secondary preventive efforts would then include helping her to return to being abstinent as well as screening for sexually transmitted infections (STI) or pregnancy and providing services that would help her to prevent acquiring a STI or becoming pregnant unintentionally if she were to remain sexually active. If these primary and secondary prevention efforts failed and she did acquire a STI, tertiary preventive efforts would include prescribing antibiotics and instructing on their proper use to minimize the likelihood of complications such as infertility. If primary and secondary efforts failed and she became pregnant, tertiary prevention would be focused on prevention of a repeat pregnancy and ensuring that she completed her education as planned.

Although hierarchical, these prevention levels are not mutually exclusive. Thus, primary and secondary measures are still applicable when tertiary prevention efforts are used, with the assumption that it is "never too late." Obviously, as one moves from primary to tertiary prevention, the focus is much more on the individual. However, the principles of youth development for populations can still be applied to individuals. In fact, a caring adult helping an adolescent through such difficult situations can be a catalyst to empowering an adolescent to engage in youth development activities in which they might not otherwise engage.

Youth Development and
Health Care of the Individual

Bright Futures, a national pediatric health promotion and disease prevention initiative based on published guidelines for health supervision, is an example of what can be accomplished in the health care setting between a health care provider and individual patient (Green, 1994). Health maintenance visits include asking the adolescent about friends, family, recreation, school, and behaviors. Health education in these visits addresses not only topic areas such as high-risk behaviors and health habits (e.g., smoking avoidance, benefits of physical activity) but also includes counseling about the positive effects of being involved in community service activities, school achievement, and developing skills that reflect personal responsibility and social competence, such as restraint of immediate gratification and respect for diversity.

The Bright Futures guidelines also include comprehensive information for incorporating parents in the health visit and pinpoint specific areas for questions. Following these guidelines, clinicians ask parents about their son's or daughter's functioning, as well as their own parenting and ability to promote positive aspects of their offspring's development. Clinicians are guided to ask parents about specific activities in which they engage as a family; their parenting styles and practices; expectations, rules, and supervision that they have for their child's behavior; their child's school performance and plans for the future; and their support for healthy behaviors and personal safety.

Thus, the focus in Bright Futures is the promotion of health and optimal well-being and the prevention of behaviors that would lead to medical problems and poorer developmental outcomes. Embedded in a developmental framework that is the cornerstone of any clinician's approach to children and youth, these clinical interactions represent developmental asset building at the individual adolescent and family level. One-on-one enhancement of positive development can occur whenever a clinical provider is interacting with an adolescent alone or with his or her family. There are many opportunities for clinicians to infuse this approach in their clinical interactions. For example, during a brief preparticipation sports physical, one can inquire about the role of sports as a positive use of time and how that is balanced with other creative and school activities. One can further inquire about the coach as a mentor and adult role model, as well as other nonparent adults whom the teen can identify as being important in his or her life. Similarly, many youth seek medical services through school-based health centers, and these encounters represent rich opportunities for the clinician to promote health by inquiring about and encouraging specific developmental asset areas. There is evidence that providing preventive services using a structured format such as Bright Futures increases the likelihood that such services will be received during clinical encounters, but there is not yet evidence that the receipt of these services changes long-term health outcomes (Hedberg, Klein, & Andresen, 1998).

Turning Deadly Health Crises into Youth Development Opportunities

In response to the need to transform and strengthen the existing public health infrastructure in America so that states, local communities, and their private and their public health agencies can collaborate more effectively, the W.K. Kellogg Foundation and the Robert Wood Johnson Foundation jointly funded an innovative health-oriented program called Turning Point (W.K. Kellogg Foundation and the Robert Wood Johnson Foundation, 1998). Initially, 14 state level partnerships and 41 communities received 2- to 3-year grants in 1998 to address issues specific to their needs. Baxter (2001) reviewed the program and suggested an exploration of implications for national public health policy. One of the communities that received a Turning Point grant was a small, rural community in upstate New York, Chautauqua County. This community had become the focus of national and international media attention in 1997 because an older nonresident adolescent male had had sexual intercourse with approximately 50 local teenage females over a period of 18 months and directly infected 13 of them with HIV. The epidemiologic report of the case by the Centers for Disease Control and Prevention (1999) concluded,

> Unrecognized social and sexual networks of youth at high risk for HIV and other STDs exist even in rural areas where HIV prevalence is relatively low, and these networks can facilitate the rapid spread of HIV infection. It is important for public health programs to provide effective HIV prevention services to youth in rural areas. (p. 416)

Although the national media coverage of this tragedy tended to demonize the young man for his behavior, the community chose to recognize the situation as a "wake-up call" indicating that youth in the community were vulnerable to health risk behavior. The accomplishments resulting from Chautauqua County participating in Turning Point partnership activities included (a) the establishment of new community-based organizational structure, Kids First Alliance, (b) a change in organizational policies to increase youth voice, and (c) the engagement of youth and other residents in planning and decision making, with programs such as Kidsultants, Peer

Educators, Youth Summits, and Kids First Mini-Grants (http://www.naccho.org/files/documents/findings-text.pdf). Kidsultants are formally prepared to participate in planning councils and community forums, have been included in legislative meetings, and are active members in the local tobacco prevention coalition (Lewin Group, 2002).

The Kids First Alliance (KFA) is an all-inclusive decision-making body with diverse community representation, composed of various community organizations, businesses, and faith communities in addition to public health and county government officials and the Youth Bureau. It receives technical support from an Investors Support Group, a group of public and private funders that meets monthly to discuss common interests and investments. An outcome of these meetings has been an understanding of how money flows through the child and family services system and the development of shared community planning and investment databases. These outcomes will allow for the creation of a flexible funding pool in pursuit of common goals, objectives, and outcome measures to be shared across community agencies and funders, resulting in the institutionalization of KFA in the structure and function of the community.

The KFA is committed to mapping and tracking county youth assets to evaluate its effectiveness. In the process of implementing Turning Point initiatives, the Chautauqua County Health Department, which was the focal point of the epidemiologic investigation of the local HIV epidemic, had a major role in helping to coordinate 65 different coalitions, committees, and task forces; their goal was to focus on prevention and the root causes of health problems by shifting from a deficit-centered to an asset-based model and by shifting decision-making power from government, agencies, and investors to local communities (Rhein, Lafronza, Bhandari, Hawes, & Hofrichter, 2001). The venue within the KFA that enables youth and adults to prioritize neighborhood level needs and exercise their executive power is a network of neighborhood entities, Communities Connecting with Kids (CCKs).

The creation of CCKs ensures that "youth empowerment" activities are designed to work *with* youth rather than *for* youth, in a sustainable process leading to local change by providing,

[A] grassroots mechanism for actively involving kids in collecting information on community needs and assets, setting health priorities, applying for and allocating community-based funding, developing partnerships and strategies to address priorities, and developing plans to strengthen community resources. (Robert Berke, M.D., personal communication, 2003)

Local communities are provided with encouragement, technical assistance, training in asset mapping and leadership, and financial support and legitimacy.

A study of high-risk sexual activity and unintended pregnancies in the area provides a good example of how CCKs function. Kidsultants who are employed by KFA are actively engaged in ongoing community health assessment by both obtaining and providing information. In the process of community meetings of KFA, a large disparity between knowledge about risks and actual risk behaviors among youth in the area was identified. Traditional health assessment surveys were administered in schools to determine why knowledgeable youth put themselves at risk for pregnancy, sexually transmitted infections, and substance abuse. In addition, cultural anthropologists interviewed youth in nontraditional settings such as safe houses, jails, and businesses frequented by youth to explore their social networks—something that would never be considered in usual public health assessment practice. The disturbing findings from these assessments enabled community representatives, including youth empowered in their role as Kidsultants, to prioritize problems and to allocate resources to creative solutions to problems.

For example, the Town of Chautauqua Teen Pregnancy Council, which is a CCK, held youth summits (at which adults are invited to listen, but not to speak) and community forums (at which both adults and youth speak and listen) in 2001 to inform the development of effective programming to prevent teen pregnancy. In addition, smaller groups met to discuss issues relevant to their local communities. Collective action projects that resulted from these KFA activities included (a) "Can We Talk?" a parent-child communication project in which parents are helped to talk to their fourth- to sixth graders, using ideas generated by the youth themselves, (b) peer education programs to reduce risk behaviors that include at-risk youth and not only honor students, (c) mentoring programs for youth, (d) the creation of a fund to support civic involvement of youth, and (e) renovation of a closed movie theater into a dance club for teens. In addition, the teen pregnancy council provided $2000 in Kids First planning minigrants to six other CCKs in neighborhoods with high rates of unwanted teen pregnancies and offered the neighborhoods asset development training.

The experience of the Turning Point initiative in general and the Kids First Alliance in particular has resulted in seven valuable "lessons learned": (a) community engagement evolves over time, (b) partnerships need to recruit an array of formal members to establish a base for engaging other parts of the community, (c) partnerships must reach beyond formal members to engage diverse sectors of the community in planning and decision making, (d) successful community mobilization requires explicit commitments to broad civic involvement, (e) explicit policy and resource investments are required to sustain or institutionalize community participation, (f) community education and technical assistance programs enable citizens to participate in public health activities, and (g) neighborhood work groups are instrumental in generating and sustaining support for public health improvements (Lewin Group, 2002).

Although the impetus for this youth development initiative (Kids First Alliance, Kidsultants, Communities Connecting with Kids, etc.) was a potentially deadly public health crisis related to adolescent behavior, the community-wide collaboration that resulted promises to improve the health of adolescents throughout the community. The lessons learned in the process should be used to inform strategies to effectively address public health problems of youth in the future.

Summary

Positive youth development, health, and health care are intimately linked to each other. Providers of adolescent health care should be involved in youth development at the individual and family levels. In addition, health care providers, especially adolescent medicine specialists, need to be "at the table" when community- and school-based youth development strategies are being developed. They are in a unique position to encourage youth involvement because effective clinical interventions are, at their core, supportive of positive youth development. Future research and action need to focus on effective strategies that bring professionals involved with youth development and adolescent health into closer approximation and partnerships.

References

American Academy of Pediatrics. Committee on Psychosocial Aspects of Child and Family Health. (2001). The new morbidity revisited: A renewed commitment to the psychosocial aspects of pediatric care. *Pediatrics, 108*(5), 1227-1230.

Baxter, R. J. (2001). *What Turning Point tells us: Implications for national policy.* Lewin Group, Falls Church, VA. Retrieved January 8, 2003, from: http://qtrducms03.interpath.net:8080/content_files/spotlight_docs/TPoint.pdf.

Benson, P. (1997). *All children are our children.* San Francisco: Jossey-Bass.

Boonstra, H. (2002). Teen pregnancy and lessons learned. *Alan Guttmacher Institute: Issues in brief.* Retrieved January 8, 2003, from: http://www.guttmacher.org/pubs/ib_1–02.html#top.

Centers for Disease Control and Prevention. (1999). Cluster of HIV-positive young women–New York, 1997-1998. *MMWR, 48*(20), 413-416.

Centers for Disease Control and Prevention, National Center for HIV, STD and TB Prevention. (2002). *Divisions of HIV/AIDS Prevention.* Atlanta, GA. Retrieved on January 8, 2003, from: http://www.cdc.gov/hiv/pubs/facts/compyout.htm.

Child Trends. (2002). Teen pregnancy. *Child Trends data bank*. Retrieved on January 8, 2003, from: http://www.childtrendsdatabank.org/socemo/childbearing/14TeenPregnancy.htm.

Deci, E. L., & Flaste, R. (1996). *Why we do what we do: Understanding self-motivation*. New York: Penguin.

Engel, G. L. (1977). The need for a new medical model: A challenge for biomedicine. *Science, 196*(4286), 129-136.

Ethier K., & St. Lawrence, J. S. (2002). The role of early, multilevel youth development programs in preventing health risk behavior in adolescents and young adults. *Archives in Pediatric and Adolescent Medicine, 156*(5), 429-430.

Franklin, C., & Corcoran, J. (2000). Preventing adolescent pregnancy: A review of programs and practices. *Social Work, 45*(1), 40-52.

Green, M. (Ed). (1994). *Bright futures: Guidelines for health supervision of infants, children and adolescents*. National Center for Education in Maternal and Child Health. Arlington, VA. Retrieved on January 8, 2003, from: http://www.brightfutures.org.

Haggerty, R. J., Roghmann, K. J., & Pless, I. B. (1992). Child health and the community. In *Health and illness: The new morbidity* (2nd ed.). New York: John Wiley.

Health Action: Priorities for Monroe County. (1999). Retrieved on January 8, 2003, from: http://www.healthaction.org/.

Hedberg, V. A., Klein, J. D., & Andresen, E. (1998). Health counseling in adolescent preventive visits: Effectiveness, current practices, and quality measurement. *Journal of Adolescent Health, 23*(6), 344-353.

Institute of Medicine, Board on Health Promotion and Disease Prevention, Committee on Assuring the Health of the Public in the 21st Century. (2003). *The future of public health in the 21st century*. Washington, DC: National Academy Press.

Institute of Medicine, Division of Health Care Services, Committee for the Study of the Future of Public Health. (1998). *The future of public health*. Washington, DC: National Academy Press.

Kirby, D. (1999). Reflections on two decades of research on teen sexual behavior. *Journal of School Health, 69*(3), 89-94.

Lantz, P. M., Jacobson, P. D., Warner, K. E., Wasserman, J., Pollack, H. A., Berson, J., & Ahlstrom, A. (2000). Investing in youth tobacco control: A review of smoking prevention and control strategies. *Tobacco Control, 9*, 47-63.

Lewin Group. (2002). *Community participation can improve America's public health systems*. Battle Creek: W. K. Kellogg Foundation.

Lonczak, H. S., Abbott, R. D., Hawkins, J. D., Kosterman, R., & Catalano, R. F. (2002). Effects of the Seattle Social Development Project on sexual behavior, pregnancy, birth, and sexually transmitted disease outcomes by age 21 years. *Archives in Pediatric and Adolescent Medicine, 156*, 438-447.

National Institute of Mental Health. (1995). *Basic behavioral research for mental health: A national investment. A report of the National Advisory Mental Health Council*. Retrieved on January 24, 2003, from: http://www.nimh.gov/publicat/baschap5.cfm.

National Institute on Drug Abuse. (2001). *Some research-based drug abuse prevention programs.* Retrieved on January 8, 2003, from: http://165.112.78.61/prevention/PROGRM.html.

Nitz, K. (1999). Adolescent pregnancy prevention: A review of interventions and programs. *Clinical Psychological Review, 19*(4), 457-471.

Philliber, S., Kaye, J. W., Herrling, S., & West, E. (2002). Preventing pregnancy and improving health care access among teenagers: An evaluation of the Children's Aid Society-Carrera Program. *Perspectives on Sexual and Reproductive Health, 34*(5), 244.

Plummer, B. A., Velicer, W. F., Redding, C. A., Prochaska, J. O., Rossi, J. S., Pallonen, U. E., & Meier, K. S. (2001). Stage of change, decisional balance, and temptations for smoking: Measurement and validation in a large, school-based population of adolescents. *Addictive Behaviors, 26*(4), 551-571.

Rhein, M., Lafronza, V., Bhandari, E., Hawes, J., & Hofrichter R. (2001). *Advancing community public health systems in the 21st century: Emerging strategies and innovations from the Turning Point experience.* Washington, DC: National Association of County and City Health Officials. Retrieved on January 8, 2003, from: http://www.naccho.org/files/documents/tp1.pdf.

Search Institute. (2000). *The power of assets.* Retrieved on January 8, 2003, from: http://www.search-institute.org/research/assets/assetpower.html.

Starfield, B. (1992). *Primary care: Concept, evaluation, and policy.* New York: Oxford University Press.

U.S. Department of Health and Human Services, Office of Disease Prevention and Health Promotion. (2000). *Healthy People 2010.* Retrieved on January 8, 2003, from: http://www.healthypeople.gov/default.htm.

U.S. General Accounting Office, Report to the Chairman, Committee on Labor and Human Resources, U.S. Senate. (1998). *Teen pregnancy: State and federal efforts to implement prevention programs and measure their effectiveness* (HEHS-99-4). Washington, DC: General Accounting Office.

Ventura, S. J., Mathews, T. J., & Hamilton, B. E. (2002). Teenage births in the United States: State trends, 1991-2000, an update. *National Vital Statistics Reports, 50*(9). Retrieved on January 8, 2003, from: http://www.cdc.gov/nchs/data/nvsr/nvsr50/nvsr50_09.pdf.

Vuori, H. (1984). Primary health care in Europe: Problems and solutions. *Community Medicine, 6,* 221-231.

W. K. Kellogg Foundation and the Robert Wood Johnson Foundation. (1998). *Turning Point: Collaborating for a new century in public health.* Washington, DC: National Association of County and City Health Officials. Retrieved on January 8, 2003, from: http://www.naccho.org/project30.cfm.

World Health Organization. (1948). Preamble to the Constitution of the World Health Organization as adopted by the International Health Conference, New York, 19-22 June, 1946; signed on 22 July 1946 by the representatives of 61 states and entered into force on 7 April 1948. *Official Records of the World Health Organization, 2,* p. 100. Retrieved on January 8, 2003, from: http://www.who.int/about/definition/en/.

6

Can High Schools Foster Youth Development?

Jerome M. Ziegler

O utside the home, schools are where the majority of adolescent youth spend most of their time. So, in thinking about youth development, it is logical to ask how schools affect what happens to young people as they grow and mature. What do schools contribute to youth development, and how does what happens in school connect to what occurs outside the school? The aim of this chapter is to explain some of the basic elements in how schools work and how their purposes, structures, and educational programs foster or impede optimum youth development, in order to give youth development professionals and others some background and guidance toward working effectively with schools for the benefit of youth. The emphasis is on high schools.

Young people in the United States are required to attend school (or be homeschooled) in most states until they are 16 years old. Thirteen states require them to stay in school until they are 17 or 18 years old. It has been commonly believed in our country at least since the first third of the 19th century that all children should attend school through the elementary grades; and as America changed from an agricultural to an industrial economy, and children were no longer needed on the farm, compulsory school attendance was extended into the middle years of adolescence (Cremin, 1980). School was the place where basic intellectual skills were taught—reading, writing, and arithmetic—for children to attain a minimum level of competence sufficient to negotiate the adult world. School was also a place (in addition to the home and church) where it was expected that children and youth would acquire character and the habits of responsibility. In short, schools became an instrument of socialization, perhaps the major instrument. We shall see that schools today retain that sense of purpose but that far more is expected now than in earlier decades.

Schools have traditionally been thought to provide a kind of universal experience for children and youth of different ethnic, religious, and social class backgrounds. Schools are what they have in common, and so the "common school" has taken on a certain mythic quality in the forging of our democratic republic, in "Americanizing" generations of immigrant children, and in preparing them for responsible adulthood. John Dewey's (1916) idea that democracy is inseparable from an educated citizenry has been a fundamental tenet of American social and political thought for more than eight decades and has animated the 20th-century discussion of educational goals and programs.

The scope of the general school enterprise in the United States, in particular the high school, is immense. In 1999 to 2000, there were 13,914 public high schools, containing 9th through 12th grades, enrolling 13,369,000 students. Those numbers will increase. In total, public school enrollment in kindergarten through grade eight rose from 29.9 million in fall 1990 to an estimated 33.6 million in fall 2001. The growing numbers of young pupils that have been filling the elementary schools in the last two decades will cause noticeable increases at the secondary school level during the next 10 years (U.S. Department of Education, 2001; see Tables 82, 95, and 98). This has been fueled in part by the steady increase in immigration since the early 1980s and the birthrate of certain immigrant populations.

These numbers alone demonstrate that what happens in schools is of enormous significance to our society. All other public institutions designed for youth combined do not approach this magnitude. The future of young people is intimately connected to the functioning of high school and the specific question of youth development, which is the subject of this chapter. The chapter is organized around five questions: What do youth experience in good schools? Why don't all schools resemble the best? How are schools structured to enhance youth development? How do adults' attitudes about youth and their willingness to share power affect schools? What is the place of schools in community-wide partnerships?

What Youth Experience in Good Schools

Since the 1983 report on the state of American public education, "A Nation At Risk," by the National Commission on Excellence of Education, there has been a profusion of writing about educational reform, including fresh ideas about curriculum improvement coupled with suggestions for structural change in the way schools are organized, instruction is delivered, and teachers are trained. We can suppose that many tens of thousands of school administrators and teachers understand most of the elements that are needed to provide better outcomes for their students. Many of these ideas are summed up in "the three highs [which] have been encouraged by the Edna McConnell Clark Foundation in New York. . . . High expectations, high content, high support," which comprise the agenda of a new principal in an urban high school, as cited by Rexford Brown (1993, p. 122) in his study of classroom literacy. These three "highs" lead to a fourth, "high achievement," which is the objective of enhanced teaching and learning and is clearly the hope and expectation for the changes in school operations and classroom practice brought about by school reform.

There is no longer any mystery, as I write in the third year of the new century, about what it takes to create an excellent school characterized by these four highs, for there are hundreds of models. The elements include, but are not limited to, the following:

- A school large enough to provide a wide-ranging curriculum but small enough to enable individual students to become well-known to the staff
- Long enough periods and small enough classes to allow teachers and students to explore topics in-depth
- Instruction that incorporates the opportunities and resources offered by the outside community, including work and service learning
- Teachers who are well prepared in their subject matter, with time to prepare creative lesson plans and for continual professional development
- An approach to students by all staff that treats young persons as capable of framing their own education and sharing in school and classroom governance
- Administrators, including central district superintendents and building principals, with strong vision and determination to acquire and make use of the foregoing elements

Since the early 1980s, educators such as Theodore Sizer, Deborah Meier, James Comer, Linda Darling-Hammond, John Goodlad, and Rexford Brown (and many others) have worked with schools to put these elements into place. The Coalition of Essential Schools and the illustrations offered in Sizer's book *Horace's School* (1992) provide us with principles for excellent practice and spell out how administrator and teacher attitudes toward student learning can and must be changed. Deborah Meier (1996), describing what she was able to accomplish as the principal of Central Park East School in the 1990s, emphasizes the necessity, first, of providing time for teachers to discuss among themselves their objectives, their programs, and their methods; second, of involving students in creating learning objectives and curricula to meet those objectives; and third, of "personalizing" high school education along the lines of typical practice in kindergarten and the early elementary grades—in short, really focusing on the individual student and using democratic norms and power sharing in the classroom and throughout the school.

Wasley, Hempel, and Clark (1997), investigating five high schools in the Coalition of Essential Schools, found that the "Nine Common Principles" of the Coalition had been used to develop a strategy of overall school reform. Results included strong teacher-student interaction, the "personalization" of the classroom, the integration of subject matter, small classes and Socratic seminars, and the use of student portfolios and student team research projects, together with the strong involvement of parents and other community resources, all resulting in higher student achievement.

These examples of schools that operate on the elements outlined above tell us that educational reform can work and that teachers can perform and students learn at much higher levels than in the standard American high school. In addition to improving academic achievement, such schools are models for the promotion of youth development. They are places where the competence and character of young people are fostered. But when considering the majority of high schools across the country, the question naturally arises: Why aren't all high schools of similar quality? To answer that question, we have to look briefly at the obstacles to educational reform.

Why All High Schools Don't Resemble the Best

What are the barriers to schools promoting youth development? The answers to this question fall into one or more of the following categories: accountability, order, inadequate resources, and student needs.

Accountability

In a democratic republic, accountability is a political and administrative norm. Up to a point, it is a good thing. It allows citizens to be assured that their tax monies are being used for the purposes for which they are intended. Accountability results in voluminous record keeping and reporting required by government agencies. The level of detail required is staggering. Public school principals spend a significant part of almost every day responding to requests for information and writing reports. Advances in technology (e-mail and fax machines) make swiftness of reply an additional burden. Clerks and administrative personnel in the central district administration buck the pressure they get from state and federal agencies down to the building principal. The current policy of using standardized tests as the sole measure of a school's performance and holding administrators accountable for increasing test scores represents a new level of accountability that carries even more serious consequences.

Demands for accountability tend to overwhelm other priorities, unintentionally but inexorably placing the administration at the center of the educational enterprise where student learning and development should be. In addition to the record keeping and reporting required for accountability, principals spend major portions of their time with the following tasks: budgeting, labor relations, relations with central district administration, student discipline, school safety, community relations, and managing teachers, librarians, coaches, and other staff. It is easy to see that high school principals are badly overburdened, with far less time than they would wish to attend to substantive teaching-learning issues and the process of youth development as a major element in the school's functioning.

Order

Principals are, in a sense, accountable first for maintaining order because it is widely considered to be essential to academic learning. Anyone observing the movement of high school students from class to class in a medium- or large-sized building immediately understands that school administration has to be concerned about order. Control is an important element in the safety and security of a school. Both are fundamental to a decent learning environment. Students do not learn effectively when they are scared or worried (Garbarino & deLara, 2002). Therefore, it is entirely reasonable to have quiet and decorum in the classroom and elsewhere in the building. However, maintaining order is not identical to controlling students. When the quest for order pits adults against youth, the result is rigid practices that impede learning and development and give many students the idea that the adults are "against" them.

Among the many high schools I visited in the past decade in five large cities on the East Coast, there was not one in which the students were invited to talk with their teachers about the issue of control and order.

Students are merely recipients of rules, and often enough of adults shouting at them in class to be quiet or in corridors to move quickly from one class to another. The question of how to maintain order could be seen as one requiring intensive discussion and negotiation leading toward the creation of a civil society in a high school, with rules and routines that students have a share in defining and maintaining. Sharing power in this manner might be seen as a way to foster youth development. It would convey school administrators' and teachers' trust in students and encourage them to be trustworthy.

The quest for order also leads to routinized processing of students and rigid organization of the curriculum, exemplified in the "egg crate" scheduling of classes and activities. Classes are 42 to 50 minutes long, with five or six class periods per day. Such schedules allow for little variation and little or no free time in the school (Sizer, 1984). The routine is the control; it is characterized by constant adult supervision and a set curriculum.

Although time is linear, learning may not be; in fact, it is more likely to be circular or jagged, interrupted in the adolescent personality by a-thousand-and-one other forces. Individual development and academic learning, therefore, run counter to the traditional linear organizing framework of the curriculum. Administrators and teachers, then, must take account of the nonlinear learning process and of different learning styles in their students (Gardner, 1991) while at the same time bearing in mind the necessities of organizing the school to be efficient and effective. This is one of the burdens of management in a school setting.

Developmentally, high school students are ready to become more independent, but they are in fact not permitted much independence in school. Other than choosing to take one foreign language or one science course instead of another, or band instead of chorus, they are typically not given much chance to choose their curricula. Flexibility for individual curriculum is distinctly rare (Clinchy, 1997), so opportunities for taking responsibility for one's own curriculum are also rare. The kind of independent thinking and personal responsibility that can lead to interesting personal growth for students are sadly all too often absent from schools.

Teachers, too, are constrained by routinized processing and a rigid curriculum. Teaching five class a day, five days a week, and often at two grade levels does not give much time for individual attention except by an extraordinary teacher. That person must be adept enough to organize the class in such a way that individual students can be acknowledged, that different learning styles are accepted, that individual student interest is encouraged, and that "learning for understanding," in Linda Darling-Hammond's apt phrase (1997), is the result achieved.

Inadequate Resources

When measured against the multiple needs of a modern high school, available resources are always inadequate. The principal constantly addresses shortfalls in resources by negotiating with central district administration over the school's budget, shifting monies within the budget, writing grant proposals to government agencies and philanthropic foundations, trying to raise funds from local community and business sources, and just getting by without necessities. It is a never-ending struggle to fit the official budget received from the district office to the needs of the school and to find supplementary funds that can plug the holes, or in better times provide enrichment to the curriculum and after-school activities. The quest for funds to meet the school's needs is another demand that keeps the principal from creative work with the instructional staff on curriculum improvement and youth development.

Student Needs

For too many adolescents, the conditions of their homes and neighborhood environments are, it is not too strong to say, horrible. Schools must deal with the malign effects of conditions far beyond their control: poor mental and physical health, emotional instability, bad nutrition, drug and alcohol abuse, teen pregnancy, the problems of parental unemployment, family instability and dysfunction, neglect and brutality, bad housing, and neighborhoods.[1] These conditions contribute to *unreadiness to learn* and impede students' educational progress. Some of these conditions affect students at every socioeconomic level, not just those from low- and very-low-income families. Teachers and administrators have to cope with them every day of the school year, and, as many writers have pointed out (Dryfoos, 1994; Schorr, 1988; Sizer, 1984), these conditions result in disruptive behavior and consequent discipline problems and inability or unwillingness to learn.

How Schools Are Structured to Enhance Development

Restructuring is the general term that describes the different ways to change the organization of the school, all aiming to markedly improve the teaching-learning process. We can think of restructuring as a process of confronting the four formidable obstacles just listed—accountability, order, inadequate resources, and student needs—and putting in place the elements of good schools identified above: well-prepared teachers, strong administrative leaders, right-sized schools, flexible schedules, links between classroom and the world outside, and trust in students.

One form of restructuring, *site-based management,* changes accountability by giving the building principal and teachers far more authority to decide how their budgets are spent and to introduce innovations. The following forms of restructuring usually include some degree of site-based management but emphasize smaller classes and small "learning communities," team teaching, and flexible schedules.

Alternative Schools

Small schools established as alternatives to standard high schools often use block scheduling so that teachers and students have more time to explore topics in depth (although this is not confined to alternative schools). They are also more likely to use team teaching, in which different subjects such as math and social studies or science and writing are integrated. Students, too, may work in teams, as in a science and history class I visited in Central Park East High School, in New York City, where the first-year students offered 15-minute reports on their research topics. Students may also spend time working in agencies and groups outside the school that provide learning opportunities quite different from regular classwork.

Alternative schools can take risks with new approaches to school organization and curricula that standard high schools are loath to try. As a rule, alternative schools attract instructional staff who want to do new things, which makes it easier for administrators to mark out new directions. Alternative schools can break at least some of the constraints that bind standard high schools, thereby becoming institutional models for replication if their students perform well. Local and state educational agencies must be convinced, so students from alternative schools must do at least as well as those in the standard schools, and probably better.

Performance on Standardized Tests

This is a difficult educational issue that must be addressed when attempting to measure the results of various means of restructuring. The positive influence of a stronger educational program and of deeper learning in any given student may not become apparent until some years later as that young person develops in life; in other words, the benefits may not show up in tests taken in the later grades of high school, but rather as young people become successful adults in whatever sphere they choose. Improved test scores in school are only one measure by which restructuring and alternative schools should be assessed, although they are sure to be highly sought after and accorded great value by the larger society as indices of success. Test scores may not, however, be the best instruments for assessing youth development. Alternative and other restructured schools may well be succeeding in creating competence and character in their students even if their test scores do not climb off the charts.

Whole-School Restructuring

Different approaches to school organization and instruction are not only occuring in alternative schools. Restructuring is occurring in many of the 16,000 school districts, although usually only in some or a very few of a district's schools. For example, the programs described in the Wasley et al. (1997) report on the five schools they visited in different sections of the country, part of the Coalition of Essential Schools, all employed team teaching, created small classes, used the seminar method of teaching, and developed assessment of students through portfolios and student exhibitions. These five high schools also created partnerships with universities and businesses, brought families into closer relation with the schools, including the provision of child care facilities for their students who had babies and toddlers, and provided clinics and social services along the lines of the ideas presented by Joy Dryfoos in her book *The Full Service School* (1994).

Interviews recorded by the authors with students in these schools show plainly that the combination of new ways of organizing the curriculum and new methods of teaching were improving the educational programs. Students were thinking about school and themselves in new ways. In short, they had become engaged. The authors concluded that although much remained to be done to ensure the full development and permanence of the reforms, these schools were on the path to success (Wasley et al., 1997). Thomas Toch (1991) describes schools in all sections of the country that have introduced one or more of the reforms associated with restructuring and provides many interesting examples of schools breaking the mold (see also Steinberg & Allen, 2002).

Schools-Within-a-School and Houses

Much of the writing on educational reform has addressed the problems associated with the large urban or central high school. One answer to the condition of a few thousand students packed into one building has been the movement toward schools-within-a-school. It has caught on in many districts as a method of breaking down, say, 4,000 students into four schools of 1,000 each, or eight schools of 500 students. This approach is based on the belief that teachers and students will relate to one another better in smaller units and that the anonymity experienced by many students in the large schools will be overcome.

Many administrators and teachers believe that even groups of 1,000 or 500 students are too big and should be divided again into smaller units or "houses," as they are sometimes termed. Houses or schools-within-a-school are usually organized around curricular themes, with the students able to choose among them according to their interests. They work with the same group of teachers over a period of years, which allows both students and teachers to come to know and understand each other. Subjects can be integrated into a new whole, with connections and relationships established among ideas and events, something that is simply not possible in the standard curriculum (see Cases 6.1 and 6.2).

Case 6.1   Small Learning Communities in Philadelphia

Under Superintendent David Hornbeck, all comprehensive high schools in Philadelphia were reorganized into small learning communities (SLCs). These smaller schools-within-a-school are often organized around a theme or career area with a team of teachers who stay with the same students for 3 or 4 years. The SLC structure makes it possible to design a curriculum that is more relevant to individuals, more open to real-life applications, and more continuous over time. At many high schools, such as Bartram, Kensington, and Olney, ninth graders explore career areas in a career Awareness Community and choose an SLC for grades 10, 11, and 12 in career areas that interest them. Some SLCs operate with support from outside organizations, such as Communities in Schools and Philadelphia's High School Academies, the latter having created career academies, the earliest forms of SLCs in Philadelphia. Other SLCs are homegrown.

SOURCE: Adapted from Hamilton & Hamilton (1999, pp. 47-48).

Case 6.2   Career Academies

The San Juan Unified School District (in the Sacramento, California, metropolitan region) has 22 career academies in its nine high schools. Encina High School has "wall-to-wall academies," meaning that every student is in one of its four career academies. The school board has allocated money to pay for field trips and to employ "youth employment technicians," or job developers who find related work-based learning opportunities for all seniors in career academies. Merle Padilla, San Juan's retired former school-to-career director, talked about how participation in a career academy affects teachers and students:

> The teachers really like it. It's such a support for them. They have other teachers to depend on and they'll do anything for each other. We try to help them figure out ways they can get together, but nothing quite does it like the common prep [preparation period]. Most of the teachers and students now eat lunch together in the academy rooms, so they truly do become a school-within-a-school. Students know the teachers are there and they know they can get in touch with them during lunch. It's great for the students to know that those teachers care a lot about them.

SOURCE: Adapted from Hamilton & Hamilton (1999, p. 55).

Academies

Sometimes, the schools-within-a-school are called "academies," as in the 18 high schools in Philadelphia organized by subject matter themes, each with a top limit of 400 students. Themes range widely, and students choose according to their interests and typically spend 4 years at it. A 6-month follow-up study of the 2001 class showed a 92% "productively engaged" rate after graduation: college, trade school, the military, or employment (Philadelphia Academies, 2002). A central idea in the academy or school-within-a-school organization is that it permits and encourages different approaches to teaching and learning according to the interests of the faculty and the students. It allows for variation, and it supports risk taking and experimentation. In short, the factory model of processing students in a large school and moving them according to a rigid schedule from one subject to another is discarded and replaced by a far more dynamic and interactive way of providing education to masses of students (see Box 6.2).

City in School

The "City in School" program, used in several Boston schools and elsewhere, is another example of school organization and curriculum development that makes use in new ways of the community in which the school resides. The city becomes the focus of different parts or aspects of the school curriculum and draws both teachers and students into a new kind of study that presumably is of more direct interest to them because they live in urban or suburban locations and can easily recognize the connections. In this way, they come to see the greater relevance of their studies.

Cooperative Education

Alternating classroom instruction with work experience in an organization or outside group is another approach to the organization of the instructional program. A first- or second-year high school student spends 3 days in the school's classes and 2 days outside; by the senior year, he or she will be spending 1 or 2 days in class and 3 or 4 days outside. This is also the typical pattern for a full vocational school, such as the six vocational high schools in Chicago, except that the work supervisors are closely tied to the academic staff. Vocational high schools in general throughout the country employ classroom instructors from the trades. Therefore, the school curriculum is developed by persons who have been practitioners and is designed to give students sufficient skill to go to outside work sites and make reasonable contributions in their job situations (see Box 6.3).

Common Themes in Restructuring

What these new structures of school organization have in common is an understanding by administrators and teachers that the average student must be given *different kinds of learning opportunities* than have been customarily available to them in the past and are current practice in the standard high school (see Case 6.3). Students must be *engaged* in order to learn well. They must be given responsibility in the classroom for their own learning and responsibility for contributing to the governance of the unit or school of which they are a part. Engagement and responsibility bring about the development of competence and character. Schools that are organized in these new and different ways produce heightened individual growth and maturity because students are taken more seriously, more is required of them, and their daily living experience in the schools is one of accomplishment and recognition.

Case 6.3   The Met

The Metropolitan Regional Career and Technical Center, known as "The Met," occupies multiple buildings in Providence, Rhode Island, each housing no more than 100 students. The school turns inside out the usual relationship between work-based internships and school classes. The fundamental unit of instruction is the LTI, Learning Through Internships. Every student is matched with a workplace mentor to pursue a specific set of learning objectives related to the school's goals, which encompass communication, empirical reasoning, quantitative reasoning, social reasoning, and personal qualities. Learning at work is complemented by individualized and small-group study in school, especially in math and science but also including other academic subjects. Teachers visit work sites and communicate with mentors frequently. Parents receive weekly reports on their children's work performance. Each student has a "learning plan team" including the mentor, teacher, and parent(s), who meet four times a year with the student to assess progress and plan next steps. Work placements are maintained or changed depending on this group's deliberations. Each trimester concludes with a student exhibition presenting the results of a long-term project relating work experience to academic learning.

SOURCE: Adapted from Hamilton & Hamilton (1999, p. 31).

The Coalition of Essential Schools and the Effective Schools movement emphasize the involvement of students in these new ways of learning, which can essentially be described as *partnership*. Students are not merely receptacles into which information is poured by the instructor standing at the front of the class. They are involved in projects, in research on topics of their own choosing, in peer groups, in tutoring younger children in earlier grades, in meetings with school administrators on serious subjects of school governance, in serving a variety of outside agencies, or in cooperative work programs. To repeat, students in these schools are taken seriously, and that is why they can achieve at higher levels and develop the qualities the adult world regards as positive.

The aim of restructuring, then, is to change the teaching-learning environment from what it was into something new, to make it more dynamic and interactive, and to involve students in their own education in new ways so that their learning will be enhanced. Students want to learn, and they want to be challenged—all the recent literature points to this (see citations above). Once they become truly interested in what the school offers, deeper learning, growth, and maturity follow: in youth development terms, *competence* and *character*.

Beyond Restructuring: Changing Attitudes and Sharing Power

In addition to the kinds of structural changes just described, transforming schools into settings that consistently promote the development of all students entails (a) changes in the way adults in schools think about youth and (b) sharing of power over what happens in school. These two changes depend, in turn, on the vision of the school leader. The examples of school reform described earlier indicate how school personnel have changed from treating young students as cogs in a wheel to treating them as persons with talents and abilities, who to a large extent can take responsibility for their own learning when instructors act as mentors and coaches as well as teachers in the traditional sense. Changes in the attitudes of the adults will draw a like response from the students.

Power Sharing

The single most significant element in transforming schools is power sharing by administrators with teachers and students, and by teachers with their students. With power sharing comes respect for the ideas of others and a willingness to give to others responsibility for school operations. Power sharing depends on trust; trust develops among individuals and across status levels when attitudes change and experience bears out that others can do the work. This is a kind of circular process, but it has to start somewhere. And although energy for transformation can arise at many points—with parents, teachers, district superintendents and school boards, community leaders, and state legislators—it usually starts with the building principal, whose leadership is the crucial element in the process of transformation, as recent research literature affirms (Clinchy, 1997; Toch, 1991). For it is the building principal who is held accountable by the central administration, by the parents, and by the community at large for the performance of the school.

Vision

Transformation in a high school must begin with a vision of what the school can be, and the school principal is the one who establishes the vision. Others may play a role, but it is the building principal who sets forth the vision of how to achieve academic excellence, care for the individual student, and connect the school to the community. It is the principal who must speak about the willingness to experiment and take some risks with respect to changing curricula and incorporating new practices such as those described above. It is the principal who must challenge the staff to create a caring environment and who must set an example by sharing power with students in decision making of consequence, not just asking for advice or comment on the usual student government problems (although some of these can be important). The principal must be a powerful role model in leadership for risk taking and reform for all staff, teachers, coaches, librarians, guidance counselors, social workers, and indeed all support staff; for secretaries, custodians, and cafeteria workers also have an important influence on students.

In the early 1990s, the new principal of Tilden High School in New York City had a huge banner in purple and white, the school colors, hung across the entrance hall with the words "Tilden Pride." I heard him talk to a group of freshmen about what that slogan meant in terms of regular attendance, academic integrity, doing homework, and staying away from drugs and alcohol. Those two words took on meaning for the students; they established a different way of thinking about schooling and about themselves. In Philadelphia, I listened to a principal in a vocational agricultural high school explain to the teaching staff what he meant by staff attention to every individual student, with emphasis on students who came with aggravated behavioral problems. He knew that the vocational agriculture curriculum was a means of developing skills in teenagers who came from disadvantaged backgrounds, which they could use to make futures for themselves, and he knew that if the teachers connected with their students, the students would think about their own learning in a different way, and succeed.

Transforming a school means transforming each individual classroom as well as the overall school environment. In addition to learning from observation and from professional development programs, teachers can learn new practice by contacts with agencies outside the school that work with high school youth, many of which provide interesting and successful models of youth development (Zeldin, McDaniel, Topitzes, & Calvert, 2000). The central insights offered by Zeldin et al. and other writers about youth decision making in community organizations and structures and applied to the school setting is that adults have to *advocate* on behalf of young people (trust), *listen* to them (hear them), and *let them in* (power sharing). When adults do these things, young people can take up their new roles in affirmative and useful ways, develop habits of responsibility for self-learning, and make progress in their march toward acquiring competence and character. Are these insights applicable to schools? Certainly. Every item in the list of "conditions" that Zeldin and his colleagues (2000, pp. 45-47) posit for successful youth development in organizations can be applied to schools in the transformation process:

"Condition one, the Board of Directors is committed to youth governance and entrepreneurial decision-making" [school board].

"Two, adult leaders strongly advocate for including young people in decision-making roles" [high school principal and teachers].

"Three, youth provide pressure and support for increasing youth participation in governance" [leaders of student organizations].

"Four, adults need a variety of experiences with youth" [teachers, guidance counselors, and coaches in their classes].

"Five, organizations provide support for youth to advance through a variety of decision-making opportunities" [as students advance from grade to grade, they assume increasing decision-making responsibility in class, in student organizations, in school governance, and in fieldwork].

"Six, organizations involve older youth in governance positions early on in the organizational change process" [students are invited by teachers at the beginning of a school year to talk about their interests and make suggestions about the dimensions of the content to be covered in the class and methods of presentation for that year—suggestions of books, videos, group projects, and the like].

Putting these conditions into practice requires building administrators and all instructional personnel to accept and internalize the two basic elements of transformation: taking students seriously and sharing power.

In the end, the process of transformation, I believe, involves thinking about power in a different way and using it in a different way. Those who want to effect true change in high school education programs should understand that their power must be tempered by concepts of partnership and inclusion, first, throughout the school and second, by the community. School board members, central district administrators, and building principals need to realize that progress in educational reform will occur only if the "ground troops," the teachers and the students, are truly included in decision making (Sarason, 1990; Sizer, 1992). Not only do teachers have a formal right to be included, usually through the union contract, but they are also the ones who have to make the actual process of reform *work*. In their classrooms, the year's curricular objectives, the daily lesson plans, and classroom management and student learning and development occur. The students have a right to be included because they are on the receiving end and they offer critical perspectives about school programs. Students' ideas may not be correct, and they may not know all the factors, and they may be impractical. But students must be heard and involved if transformation is to succeed. These two elements of transformation, then, must be at the heart of schools' acceptance of youth development as a central objective of their missions.

The Place of Schools in Community-Wide Partnerships and Initiatives

Cooperative education and vocational schools are illustrations of efforts to put public high schools in place as significant actors in communities. These efforts change the way the public regards the high school as an institution "out there," disconnected, and serving mainly as a means of controlling all that adolescent energy for at least 5 or 6 hours a day, 5 days a week, 30 weeks a year. Despite the success of vocational high schools in making job sites available to their students, true partnerships between the standard high school and other institutions or groups in the community are not easy to create. Schools exist in their own realm; they have separate taxing authority; their staffs think of themselves as members of a special profession, subject to the profession's norms and expectations but not really beholden to anyone else; and the incentives and rewards for involvement in community-wide partnerships or initiatives related to youth development, such as neighborhood youth groups or settlement house programs, are not readily apparent to most administrators and instructors. When school personnel become involved with officials in other systems, such as juvenile justice or social services, this is seen as a distraction from the primary purpose of providing instruction in class.

The "full-service school" described by Joy Dryfoos (1994) may be an excellent idea, but it is difficult to put into practice because it requires more than casual relationships among service organizations and school administration, and, of course, it takes additional funding. Nevertheless, as examples described in other chapters in this volume show, there are models of school-to-work programs and the involvement of schools in community-wide partnerships that present students with opportunities for growth and development beyond what is ordinarily available in the standard high school curriculum.

The Beacons initiative (described in detail in Chapter 12 in this volume) illustrates how schools are responding to a rapidly growing need for after-school care. It makes use of a significant community resource, the school building, at a time when it is otherwise unoccupied. However, it is worth noting that hosting programs for all ages during nonschool hours, as the Beacons do, does not have a direct impact on what happens in the school building during the day. It is possible for the school building to serve as a hub of community activity when classes are not in session but for classes to be uninteresting and ineffective during the day. Opening the school building to the community is not the same thing as school restructuring.

Anyone outside the school system who wishes to engage schools in youth development must be aware of the barriers to school reform, as well as the many successful models. They must be patient to work with a large and slow-moving bureaucracy. Most important, they must understand that simply having a proposal that would be good for youth is not sufficient incentive to secure collaboration. Dealing with inadequate resources as they always do, educators resist pleas to "do more with less." A far more promising approach is to demonstrate how collaboration can help the school achieve its multiple goals. For example, the Learning Web, an informal apprenticeship program, has enjoyed a close working relationship with the Ithaca Public Schools, especially with guidance counselors, for more than 25 years, because it has demonstrated its capacity to find valuable learning opportunities for students who are not thriving in school.

Conclusions

What would a high school look like where youth development was *the central object* of the educational program? It would be a place where, first and foremost, the entire school staff—instructors, counselors, librarians, coaches, custodians, and administrators—were imbued with the idea that students should be taken as serious partners in their own learning. It would be a place where trust and democratic norms were the basis for the school's operations and power was shared willingly. It would be a place where adults responsible for the school shared a vision of what young people can become, and were willing to change, to experiment, to take risks as the process of transformation proceeds, and not to be discouraged if success proved to be illusive. It would be a place where the teachers were given a high degree of autonomy so that their own creativity and energy could be liberated from the many constraints and old ways of doing their work. And it would be a place where students were in the center of the circle.

In such a school, students would be held to high expectations, and they would perform at higher levels because they would be involved in their own education in new ways: They would be *engaged*. And as they achieved success in school, they would come to believe and imagine their futures as varied and exciting paths into adulthood. To achieve such a school, the community must be educated about what it means and what it takes to bring it about. Time and resources are necessary—time for the elements of change and experimentation to work and resources to give substance to the transformation process. This is a task of leadership by the school board and central administration and by parents and teachers and legislators who believe it can be done.

The purpose of schools is to give young children and youth the means toward self-fulfillment: intellectual and social skills and, in the United States, a sufficient understanding of democracy and responsible citizenship so that not only individuals but also communities and the whole society will thrive. John Dewey, in *Democracy and Education* (1916), wrote, "A democratic community [is] more interested than other communities have cause to be in deliberate and systematic education. The devotion of democracy to education is a familiar fact" (p. 87). Progress in creating high schools that foster youth development rests on democratic values, on administrators sharing authority and power with their teacher colleagues and with students, and on the idea of community in which students and their families have as much to contribute as school personnel. If youth development as a central organizing concept for the public school finds broader recognition and acceptance, it will go a long way toward fulfilling the hope for true educational reform and the belief that public education should educate the whole child, in which youth development is vital; and that, in turn, will make our democracy vibrant and long-lasting.

Note

1. The Federal Interagency Forum on Child and Family Statistics is the central compendium of data on the living conditions and status of children and youth. It appears yearly.

References

Brown, R. G. (1993). *Schools of thought*. San Francisco: Jossey-Bass.
Clinchy, E. (1997). *Transforming public education*. New York: Teachers College Press.

Comer, J. P. (1997). *Waiting for a miracle.* New York: Dutton.

Cremin, L. A. (1980). *American education: The national experience 1783-1876.* New York: Harper & Row.

Darling-Hammond, L. (1997). *The right to learn.* San Francisco: Jossey-Bass.

Dewey, J. (1916). *Democracy and education.* New York: Macmillan.

Dryfoos, J. (1994). *The full service school.* San Francisco: Jossey-Bass.

Garbarino, J., & deLara, E. (2002). *And words can hurt forever.* New York: Free Press.

Gardner, H. (1991). *The unschooled mind.* New York: Basic Books.

Goodlad, J. I. (1994). *Educational renewal.* San Francisco: Jossey-Bass.

Hamilton, S. F., & Hamilton, M. A. (1999). *Building strong school-to-work systems: Illustrations of key components.* Washington, DC: U.S. Government Printing Office. (Available at http://www.human.cornell.edu/youthwork/)

Meier, D. (1994). *The power of their ideas.* Boston: Beacon.

Philadelphia Academies, Inc. (2002). *Offering public school students a supportive academic environment: Exposure to a spectrum of career options & marketable occupational skills* [Brochure]. Philadelphia: Author.

Sarason, S. B. (1990). *The predictable failure of educational reform.* San Francisco: Jossey-Bass.

Schorr, L. B. (1988). *Within our reach.* New York: Anchor Press/Doubleday.

Sizer, T. R. (1984). *Horace's compromise.* Boston: Houghton Mifflin.

Sizer, T. R. (1992). *Horace's school.* Boston: Houghton Mifflin.

Steinberg, A., & Allen, L. (2002). *From large to small: Strategies for personalizing the high school.* Boston: Jobs for the Future. (See also http://www.jff.org)

Toch, T. (1991). *In the name of excellence.* New York: Oxford University Press.

U.S. Department of Education. (2001). *Digest of educational statistics.* Washington, DC: National Center for Educational Statistics.

Wasley, P. A., Hempel, R. L., & Clark, R. W. (1997). *Kids and school reform.* San Francisco: Jossey-Bass.

Zeldin, R. S., McDaniel, A. K., Topitzes, D., & Calvert, M. (2000). *Youth in decision-making.* Madison: University of Wisconsin–Madison.

7

Designing Work and Service for Learning

*Mary Agnes Hamilton
and Stephen F. Hamilton*

Work and service-learning both give youth the chance to explore new worlds; to learn new things about themselves and others; to act with more independence; to increase their responsibilities, skills, and understanding of how the world works; and to do things for others. In contrast to the typically passive role of student, a role in which they are treated primarily as recipients of knowledge, work and service place youth in roles that are adult-like and that make them less dependant and more accountable. Many benefits may flow from such experiences. Young people make discoveries about themselves, about others, and about the world they live in that can help them form values, set goals, and develop identities. To be most beneficial, both kinds of experiences must be selected and shaped according to the principles of youth development. In other words, their design must be intentional.

Work and service are treated together in this chapter because they offer many of the same developmental opportunities. Indeed, we believe viewing the two as parallel opportunities broadens the range of community settings in which youth can acquire and exercise both work-related and civic competence. This perspective is not widely shared and is therefore not reflected in the ways these two kinds of activities are organized or in research on the topic. Most youth employment is not sponsored by schools or youth-serving organizations at all. It occurs "naturally" as young people find opportunities to earn money. Service-learning, in contrast, is a sponsored activity almost by definition. Whereas youth may engage in community service individually and in an ad hoc manner, combining service with learning almost always entails sponsorship. Many youth-serving organizations sponsor it; the largest numbers of youth participate through school-sponsored programs.

Work and service are common among youth. Including informal jobs such as baby-sitting and lawn mowing, 69% of youth work for pay at some time when they are age 15. During the year when they are age 18, 91% work (U.S. Department of Labor, 2003, p. 3). In 1999, 52% of students in grades 6 through 12 participated in community service (Wirt et al., 2001, Table 16–1). Indeed, rising rates of community service are one of the bright spots in the usually dreary statistics on youth (Putnam, 2000).

This chapter examines work and service as contexts for youth development. Although the two are not typically considered together, we argue that they offer some of the same opportunities for gaining technical, personal, social, and academic competence. Research on both generally confirms their beneficial effects. In both domains, quality is critical. We begin by describing in some detail the experience of a high school student volunteer in a hospital, based on interviews we conducted with her and her mentor. This case usefully illustrates many of the overlapping characteristics of work and service; she might have been paid to do the same thing. Our interview and the case description emphasize what she learned from the experience.[1]

A Hospital Volunteer

Pam volunteered in an inner-city hospital for 10 hours a week during her senior year of high school as part of her service requirement for graduation. At the end of an interview about what she had learned during her volunteer internship, she was asked, "What do you think will be most helpful in your next steps in life?" Pam responded,

> Well I think *becoming more assertive*. I think that's going to help me a lot in college with getting what I want done and not being afraid to ask questions in classes. Also I mean, of course, *being a team player*. I mean, *all of the things I mentioned* [during the interview], I think, are, I mean, they're all so important, and so necessary and vital. I know *how to communicate* well with others is very important. I can use each thing in different situations. There was not one thing I learned that wasn't necessary. They are all so important.

Mapping a Career Path

Pam describes how Lucy, the nurse manager who is her supervisor and mentor, opens doors and engages her in reflecting on her experiences around the hospital:

> [Lucy] asked me to make a goal list or a goal sheet and I told her on it what I would like to accomplish during my stay there. And she really helped me out with that. Like each week, she would let me work in the post-op area, or she would call up the minor surgery room and have me observe there, or she would let me go to the OR and observe there, and like let me follow a social worker or a PA, which is a physician's assistant. So I had the opportunity to work with a lot of different types of people.

"To see the big picture": Lucy explained how she arranged for Pam to observe a patient's stay from registration to discharge:

> Every time [the staff] looks at a situation, they always have to look at the bigger picture, so that they can make good decisions that can influence how they do their work too. I told her that it's important to know the contribution of other people. "What are the things that the registrar has to do?" Right now the insurance information is extremely important. A patient cannot go into surgery unless it is preauthorized. So at least [Pam] sees the big picture, so that [she] will not be self-centered.

Reflective questioning about college plans: When Pam told Lucy that she planned on working for a year before going to college, Lucy asked her a series of questions to encourage her to think more deeply about the reasons behind her decision and what she hoped to accomplish in the long run:

> I said, "Why?" and she said, "Well I'm not sure what degree I'm going to take." And I said, "What are you going to do while waiting to figure out what to take in the future?" She said, "Well, I'll work." I said, "So if you work then you start to earn money. You're going to find somebody, you're going to get married, you're going to start having children. You know the best time to go to college is when you're single. As soon as you get out of school just for a year, it's hard to go back again." So she said that, "Well I think you're right." So I said, "What did your parents say? Did they agree with you staying out of college? Well I think there are lots of scholarships you could check if there is anything that you are qualified. Even if you haven't decided what course to take, you can always take a general AA degree just to get your feet in college. But if it's a financial issue, that's a different story because you can apply for student loans and stuff like that." Because I know that she's a bright kid. So I said, "Did you explore that already?"

Learning How to Be a Team Player

In the process of carrying out her volunteer work, Pam learned not only about the health care field but also about teamwork within the medical profession:

> I learned how to be like a team player and help out in different situations. It really like tuned in my thinking skills I guess to think on my feet because situations I was put in weren't like my normal or typical everyday situation.

"Being a part":

> Originally my main goal was to help people and to talk with them, but also to experience new things. At first I would help like clean up the post-op area and even though I wasn't too keen on doing that I did it anyway. When they had a shortage at the desk, I did clerical work and I would answer the phones. If they had computer problems I would try to help them there. And I worked in ER. I kind of spread myself around if they needed help anywhere. I wouldn't force myself to go up to the OR that day or minor surgery, I would stay put and help them out there. Basically I learned I don't always get to do what I want or what my goal was and I basically helped them out when they needed it and I know they helped me out when I needed help, if I didn't understand a certain thing. I remember an emergency, we all got together and we all ran with different ways of getting certain things for the patient. So you know just being a part of it. I learned that unless everyone works together, it's not going to get done. At times that was more important because we were there in an area where the patient is the number one important, their highest priority. And so I realized that if there is no one else there who's going to do it, then the patient's going to ultimately be suffering and it will take longer for them to be cared for. So [I] just pieced it together and just helped out where I could.

Pam recalled the staff Christmas party. "It was just amazing," Pam said. "I really felt like part of the family, and it's really, I think, all thanks to Lucy, who introduced me to the staff and I think she told the staff to treat me as one of them with respect."

Learning to Work With People

Lucy involved Pam in designing and conducting a survey of patient satisfaction with their stay in the hospital. They discussed the reasons for conducting the survey and the rationale behind the questions, and role-played mock interviews. Lucy expressed great satisfaction with Pam's input when formulating questions to get helpful information from the patients that the nurses could use. During the course of her internship, Lucy's practice of pointing out to Pam the value of her contributions increased Pam's sense of efficacy and mattering as well as her professional identity. Lucy commented about Pam's work on the survey:

> She gave us a good suggestion—keeping the patients updated while they're waiting for the OR or medication. She also suggested that nurses have to consistently ask the patient if they need anything so [patients] don't feel like they are left out even if they're not. So she gave us a really good, well-thought-out suggestion that we incorporated in our script. And I shared that with the nurses; they were impressed that she came up with all those.

"Becoming More Assertive"

Pam had commented that she thought the internship was helping her become "more assertive":

> As I mentioned before, I am usually shy. But I noticed my parents used to comment, "You're taking more initiative and you're saying and doing certain things and certain tasks." And in class I've noticed myself becoming less fearful of doing different jobs where I might have a weakness. And I would pride myself on working harder at that particular area but knowing that I'm doing it with I guess more ease and taking initiative to perfect it. I'm usually very shy and here I wasn't afraid to ask questions. It really became like more of a family to me. At first I felt intimidated somewhat but the people there were really open to me and so I had no problem asking them, like you know the surgeon says, "I'm going to do like a [specific procedure]," and I had no idea what that meant, he would explain it to me and stuff like that.
>
> Basically you know in school, since I know these kids for years now, I'm not afraid. But you know coming into a new situation, a new area where there aren't other kids was kind of intimidating. But, thankfully, the people there were very open and open-minded and really helped me to make me feel comfortable. And so once I felt comfortable I had no problem asking questions, saying, "What does this mean?" and "What is this?" I would watch surgery, minor surgeries, and you know each doctor does have their own way of doing things. I remember I observed surgery with one doctor and she basically went through the whole surgery not talking to me. She was there to do a job, which is fine. But then I remember there was another doctor who I came to love. Every time he would explain things to me on my own and he would talk while he was doing surgery and I would ask him questions, "Well what happens if this occurred?" and "Will there be scarring involved?" or just whatever came to the top of my head. So I felt really comfortable in doing that.

What Is Learned From Work and Service?

Working with educators and employers to develop a youth apprenticeship demonstration project, we developed a framework for stating and assessing apprentices' learning that included technical, personal, and social competence (Cornell Youth and Work Program, 2002). *Technical competence* refers to job skills that enable a person to complete specific work tasks successfully. *Personal* and *social competence* refer to qualities that enable a person to function effectively in the social environment of the workplace, to perform the role of worker. Effective functioning in the work world requires a combination of basic academic competence, technical competence sufficient to perform work tasks that add value, and the personal and social competence needed to participate within a complex social organization and to relate to customers, suppliers, and others. (Murnane & Levy, 1996, characterized what we called personal and social competence as "soft skills.") The personal and social competencies identified by employers in our demonstration project were uniform across very different work environments: manufacturing, health care, and office administration (Hamilton & Hamilton, 1997). These same competencies are also critical to success at school, in civic activity, and in families, a convergence that is part of our motivation for addressing paid work alongside service-learning. Employers might once have considered schools effective if their graduates were minimally literate and maximally compliant, but contemporary work requires all the personal qualities traditionally associated with a liberal education. (See National Center for Education and the Economy, 1990; Secretary's Commission on Achieving Necessary Skills, 1991.)

Much of what Pam talked about learning as a hospital volunteer are personal and social competencies: Mapping a career path and becoming more assertive are personal competencies; learning to be a team player and to work with people are social competencies. Learning how to design and conduct a survey or the proper procedure for moving a patient into a wheelchair are technical competencies. Some youth in similar situations describe learning academic competencies in a workplace that they might also have learned in school, such as facts about physiology or how to write paragraphs with topic sentences to make their reports clearer.

Youth Work Experience

Unlike Pam's volunteer internship, most of the jobs young people perform for pay are low skill by definition. High school students, by definition, cannot fill jobs that require a high school diploma. Sixty-two percent of jobs held by 16- to 17-year-olds are in retail trade. Eating and drinking places account for the largest share of these jobs. The service sector, including health, education, households, recreation, and entertainment, employ about a quarter. The remaining workers are distributed among agriculture, mining, construction, and manufacturing, and an undefined "other" category (U.S. Department of Labor, 2000, Chart 4.7, p. 37). Males and females are almost equally likely to be in retail trade (60% and 63%, respectively), but females are more likely to be in services than males (29% compared with 19%), while males are more likely to be in agriculture, mining, construction, manufacturing, and other (21% compared with 7%). White youth work more than nonwhites, but this difference is attributable to family income more than either desire to work or racial discrimination. Nonwhites tend to live in neighborhoods with fewer job opportunities and to lack transportation to suburban malls, where retail jobs are concentrated (Ruhm, 1997, pp. 752-753).

Studies of the impact of work experience on youth have not used the framework of technical, personal, social, and academic competence. However, it is possible to apply this framework to some of their findings.

Opportunities for gaining technical competence and for applying academic knowledge are limited in most youth jobs. However, they can contribute to personal and social competence. Tannock (2001, p. 45) describes the "local expertise" needed by grocery store and fast-food workers, who must know how to deal with individual managers and customers, which rules to follow and which to bend, and how to make do when machines and standard processes break down. Katherine Newman wrote about the skills youth and young adults demonstrated in fast-food restaurants in Harlem:

> Workers who know the secrets of the trade—how to cut corners with the official procedures mandated by the company on food preparation, how to "trick" the cash register into giving the right amount of change when a mistake has been made, how to keep the orders straight when there are twenty people backed up in the drive-through line, how to teach new employees the real methods of food production (as opposed to the official script), and what to do when a customer throws a screaming fit and disrupts the whole restaurant—keep the complicated ballet of a fast-food operation moving smoothly. When "experts" disappear from the shift, nothing works the way it should. When they quit, the whole crew is thrown into a state of near chaos. (Newman, 1999, p. 147)

The value of such skills in well-paid jobs can be considerable. They are also skills that would be welcome in a political campaign office or a community-based organization.

The nature of youth jobs helps to explain Greenberger and Steinberg's (1986) mostly negative findings about their effects, including greater use of alcohol, tobacco, and illegal drugs and more engagement in negative behavior such as stealing and lying. Youth who work more than 20 hours per week also have lower school grades. Several other longitudinal studies using appropriate statistical controls have confirmed many of the negative outcomes Greenberger and Steinberg found to be associated with long hours of work by high school students (National Research Council/Institute of Medicine, 1998, pp. 131-134), but have found moderate work hours to be generally beneficial.

The Impact of Youth Work on Later Earnings

Recent research tends to support a more favorable view and to shed light on how different kinds of work experience affect different youth. Ruhm (1997) found no evidence of serious negative economic consequences of school year employment in an analysis of data from the 1979 National Longitudinal Survey of Youth. Employment during 12th grade but not before was associated with higher earnings and more prestigious jobs. Ruhm statistically controlled for a large number of variables to counter the explanation that post–high school differences in employment reflected differences that were already visible in high school, such as work ethic or responsibility.

Ruhm (1997, p. 767, Table 10) estimated that seniors who worked 10 hours per week earned 14% more than nonworkers 6 to 9 years after graduation, reflecting both more hours worked and higher hourly pay. Young women who worked moderate hours had a larger increase in post–high school earnings than young men; working 10 hours per week boosted women's subsequent earnings by 23% and men's by only 13%. But working 20 hours per week did not increase their subsequent earnings as much as it increased young men's. These earnings advantages occurred despite a slightly lower level of educational attainment among working than nonworking youth. This effect was much more pronounced for women than for men. Ruhm pointed out that the negative effects are quite small and apply to a small proportion of working youth. The positive associations suggest that youth who work while in high school gain competencies that help them in subsequent jobs. Somewhat lower educational attainment suggests that extensive working may compromise academic competence.

Patterns and Quality of Youth Work

Mortimer, who has conducted the most extensive longitudinal study of youth employment and synthesized the literature as well, shares the view that youth employment is mostly beneficial. By examining not only number of hours worked per week but also different patterns of employment and by asking youth questions about the nature of their work experience, Mortimer (2003) came to the conclusion that the critical question to ask is not about whether youth work, but about the nature and quality of their work. She distinguished four different patterns of work experience based on both intensity and duration. Working 20 or more hours per week is defined as "high intensity" and less than 20 hours as "low intensity." Duration refers to whether the youth works regularly or intermittently (pp. 70-75). In general, working at high intensity is most likely to be harmful, whether of high or low duration. Low-intensity and low-duration employment is benign, showing few effects either positive or negative. The most favorable pattern is low intensity, high duration, that is, regular employment at less than 20 hours per week. Mortimer found, for example, that workers in this "steady" category were 3 times more likely to earn a bachelor's degree than those in the high-intensity/high-duration category (p. 190). Intriguingly, youth who showed low educational promise upon entry into high school but maintained this "steady" pattern of employment were far more likely to receive a bachelor's degree than others of low educational promise (23% compared with less than 3%; p. 203). Under most circumstances, in other words, work does not compromise academic competence and may even boost it.

Like Ruhm (1997), Mortimer (2003, pp. 157-159) also found provocative differences between males and females. Although all youth who were employed showed gains in self-efficacy from 9th to 10th grades, boys' self-efficacy improved when they said they could advance in their jobs, were not closely supervised, and did not see conflicts between school and work. Girls' self-efficacy improved when they said they were well paid and could help others. These and the previous interactive effect of the nature of work and gender on personal competence are further illustrations of the validity of the ecological perspective.

> During high school, the quality of work experience appears to matter far more than hours of work for the psychosocial outcomes under scrutiny. That is, youth who have more successful experiences in the workplace become more competent, in terms of both a general, global sense of efficacy and efficacy in the economic domain. There is also evidence that high-quality work experiences involving learning opportunities help adolescents acquire occupational values. Opportunities for learning and advancement on the job, the perception that one is being paid well, and limited stressors at work all appear to have significant psychosocial benefits. (Mortimer, 2003, p. 181)

Stern and his colleagues (Stern, Finkelstein, Urquiola, & Cagampang, 1997) added to this generally positive portrayal that the negative effects of working are reduced and the positive effects accentuated when work experience is connected with schooling, once more affirming its potential value as a learning opportunity.

A logical way to create work experiences that promote youth development is through subsidized employment programs for low-income youth. YouthBuild, described in the chapter on neighborhoods, is exemplary. However, federal employment policy has shifted toward short-term programs, most emphasizing job placement and aimed at adults (Bailey & Morest, 1998; Zuckerman, 2001). However, the Workforce Investment Act calls for youth councils to guide local programs and to coordinate with other efforts, encouraging collaboration among various organizations and agencies. Although funding for subsidized programs has been drastically reduced, they can be an important part of a larger initiative to make work a positive experience for youth, especially in low-income communities.

The Impact of Service-Learning

Pam's unpaid hospital internship typifies a kind of service-learning in which youth as individuals fill roles in established organizations. When they are regular, such activities appear to offer many of the same developmental opportunities as paid work, along with the benefits of performing service. In fact, because volunteers can choose sites that match their interests and because their supervisors realize they may not return if the work is too unpleasant, they may be asked to do more interesting tasks than paid workers. Another type of service-learning involves groups of youth who identify community needs and then collectively take the initiative to meet them, such as the R.I.V.E.R. Team, an environmental action group (Case 7.1).

Case 7.1   R.I.V.E.R. Team Reclaims Bronx River

In New York City, the R.I.V.E.R. Team (Reaching & Including Youth Voices for Environmental Rights) is reclaiming the lower reaches of the Bronx River. When it enters their community, it is a pleasant and scenic stream, but after flowing past the Botanical Garden and Zoo, both the banks and the water degenerate drastically. An abandoned cement plant, auto repair shops, factories, and sewage pollute the water. A neglected park deters rather than invites human activity. A community organization, Youth Ministries for Peace & Justice, has helped organize 13- to 21-year-old youth to clean up the river and its environs. Working with adult groups, the youth have participated in setting and pursuing an ambitious agenda that includes lobbying representatives at the city, state, and federal levels for funds to clean up the river and actively engaging in public awareness and clean-up activities. With the aid of the National Guard, they removed 27 abandoned automobiles from the river and captured national media attention. They have won some of their battles and lost others, but they continue to improve their neighborhood and to demonstrate the power of people working together.

SOURCE: What Kids Can Do (2001).

A service-learning activity of the magnitude and complexity of R.I.V.E.R. Team offers multiple opportunities for gaining technical, personal, social, and academic competence. In the absence of careful research on this project, we cannot say with certainty whether any or all participants grasped or benefited from these opportunities. But the possibilities are easy to see. Beginning with a 2-year study of their neighborhood and the river, the youth needed academic skills related to natural science but also communication. Designing and conducting surveys of residents entailed another kind of research, plus communication skill (social competence). Effective appeals to government require detailed knowledge of which levels and branches of government are responsible, who has funds, and how to approach both elected representatives and agency officials. Because the entire enterprise is couched in terms of environmental justice, these working-class youth of color also had the chance to learn about ethical and political principles and of how to act on them (social and technical competence, also character). Growing Up in Cities (Chawla, 2002) is another excellent example of young people studying their communities and then taking action to improve them. This international project has successfully engaged youth in some of the world's poorest cities in participatory action research (Driskell, 2002).

Without denigrating paid employment, which, as we have seen, can build competence, it seems plausible that the depth and richness of this kind of service experience could have a profound effect on youth and that such experiences might be especially powerful for disadvantaged youth who begin to see themselves as competent advocates, leaders, researchers, and activists. A youth who has gained the competence to participate effectively and take leadership roles in a project like the R.I.V.E.R. Team can realistically aspire to getting a job and also to becoming a manager or starting a business. With this potential in mind, Gomez (1996) advocated for service-learning as an urban education reform strategy. "Social cause service" (Metz, McLellan, & Youniss, 2003, pp. 195-198) such as the R.I.V.E.R. Team as opposed to "standard service" (e.g., tutoring) has the potential to affect civic development as measured by a concern for social issues, future intentions about unconventional civic activities, and future intended service.

Although research on youth employment yields some negative results among its mostly positive findings, service-learning appears to be an unalloyed good. Indeed, the National Research Council and Institute of Medicine report on youth development (2002) frequently cited service-learning as an exemplary youth development activity. According to the research synthesized by Stukas, Clary, and Snyder (1999), service learning has been shown to have positive effects on youth in the following domains:

1. *Self-enhancement* is indicated by gains in self-confidence, self-esteem, and efficacy. Some studies show a positive impact of service-learning but not always a uniform one. Experiences that entail greater responsibility, choice, and independence appear to be most beneficial.

2. *Understanding self and the world* includes self-reported personal growth; skills such as moral reasoning, problem solving, and empathic understanding; understanding diverse groups of people; and mastering related course content. Generally, understanding is enhanced by the opportunity for guided reflection on the experience.

3. *Value expression* means that participants view their voluntary action as enacting their values, but such action can also strengthen participants' intentions to continue to volunteer and more generally their sense of social responsibility. This effect is most likely to occur in programs that allow students to make decisions, take responsibility, and engage in challenging tasks.

4. *Career development* is seldom a primary purpose of service-learning, but for some participants, volunteer activity functions as career exploration.

5. *Social expectations* refer to the place of service in the norms and values of those around them. Youth are more likely to volunteer when their schools, peers, and parents value service.

6. *Protection* may be an unexpected outcome of service, but it has been found to reduce stress, alienation, isolation, and discipline problems. This accounts for some findings indicating that "at-risk" youth benefit most from service-learning.

In our terms, these are personal competencies, except for Numbers 3 and 5, which are social competencies. Note the presence of career development among the findings, which affirms our claim that work and service overlap substantially. The authors concluded by emphasizing that positive results reported are associated with service-learning programs that support participants' autonomy, match goals with appropriate activities, attend to relationships among participants, and provide opportunities for reflection.

These findings are supported by additional studies summarized by Eyler, Giles, and Gray (1999) in an annotated bibliography on the effects of service-learning, which classified the positive effects on students in terms of personal development (sense of efficacy, identity, spiritual growth, moral development); interpersonal development (ability to work well with others, take leadership, communicate); improved cultural and racial understanding; social responsibility and citizenship; and commitment to service, as well as academic learning. These categories are comparable to ours. (Billig, 2000, provides another useful research review summarizing predominantly positive effects of service-learning.) As with work experience, research affirms the importance of high-quality service-learning; positive effects are associated most strongly with programs that meet high standards (e.g., Melchior & Bailis, 2002).

Designing Work and Service to Promote Youth Development

When properly designed, work and service enable all youth to thrive in the sense of gaining technical, personal, social, and academic competence. The principles of youth development set out in the introductory chapter provide a useful template.

Challenging Activities

Working provides an opportunity to exercise skills one brings to the job and to acquire new ones, in other words, to engage in challenging activities. Although job skills are often conceived as related to future careers, or at least to preparation for adulthood, it is important to remember that job skills are important to youth in the present, too. Dewey (1938) warned against a fixation with preparation for the future, pointing out that the best preparation for the future is "extracting at each present time the full meaning of each present experience" (p. 49).

Learning how to operate a cash register or to arrange products attractively makes a young worker more productive. It also boosts his or her sense of efficacy. However, because youth jobs are seldom directly related to careers, the specific technical competence youth learn is less important in the long run than more generic personal and social competence. As defined by employers in our youth apprenticeship demonstration project, personal competence includes taking initiative when appropriate, asking questions and seeking help in a timely fashion, performing with confidence but asking for help when needed, seeking counsel about career options and pathways, and pursuing rigorous academic courses to qualify for further education. Social competence includes adherence to workplace rules and professional norms, the ability to communicate, to work effectively with diverse groups of people, and to be trustworthy and honest. It also includes being able to work in teams and to navigate organizational systems. Working challenges youth to acquire and use all these competencies. Note that these are competencies that can continue to be challenging throughout a person's life. Communication, trustworthiness, and teamwork can always be improved.

Interviews with workplace mentors of high school interns and apprentices (Hamilton & Hamilton, 2002) confirm that they identify these competencies as goals for their teaching. Mentors of paid interns in the Automotive Youth Educational Systems (AYES) challenge youth to master complex problems (Case 7.2).

Case 7.2   Solving Auto Repair Problems

As automobiles have become more complex, auto repair technicians have had to master new skills, both technical and social. Automotive Youth Educational Systems (AYES) is a program sponsored by automobile manufacturers to enhance the preparation of technicians by improving secondary vocational education and offering internships. We interviewed several adult mentors working with high school interns in the program. The first described his intern's mastery of the technical manuals needed to guide repairs to electronic antilock brake and traction control systems.

> I thought he was pretty good in that part. He helped me a lot. He actually could read some of these [manuals]. I'd read something and go to do it

and he said, "I think you're reading that wrong." We'd reread it and [I'd say]: "Oh, I think you're right." So he actually helped me at times. (Cornell Youth and Work Program, 2002, *Problem Solve*)

In addition to being technically competent, auto repair technicians need to know how to communicate with customers to understand what must be repaired, the topic of a second mentor's description.

I've talked to him about what you need to ask [customers] if you're not sure. Sometimes the customer may not have any more information for you that will help you. They'll just come and say it's squeaking. Sometimes you may go for a ride. And [the customer] says, "Well it just made that [noise] yesterday but now it's here in the shop and it won't do it." That happens every time. I tell him he may ask, "Does it happen the first time in the morning? Does it happen over bumps? Does it happen at a certain speed? That kind of stuff." I've told him that if the customer can't seem to answer all your questions, maybe we need to talk to them together. "You'll learn as time goes on what to ask some of these people and sometimes I guess with age you're able to interpret some of these people. You see their attitude. Some people may have a real nice attitude and you can joke with them and some people are straightforward." (Cornell Youth and Work Program, 2002, *Perform Job Tasks*)

SOURCE: Cornell Youth and Work Program (2002).

These excerpts, along with Pam's hospital internship and the R.I.V.E.R. Team case, demonstrate that work and service-learning can incorporate challenging activities that foster technical, personal, social, and academic competence. Volunteers in high-quality programs are held to the same standards of performance as paid employees and learn some specific technical competencies as well.

Supportive Relationships With Peers and Adults

In paid and unpaid workplaces, youth perform challenging activities in the company of peers and adults. Work and service tend to develop a momentum that leads all participants to want to contribute to their success. Working together toward a common goal, whether it is selling more hamburgers, cleaning up a polluted river, manufacturing photographic film, or caring for seniors, tends to make young people feel connected with each other and with adults. Paid and voluntary workplaces give youth roles and responsibilities that are more adult-like than those they perform at home, in school, or in purely social peer groups. They are supported in performing these roles and meeting these responsibilities by peers but also by adults. Pam's feeling accepted at the Christmas party resulted from her work with colleagues toward shared goals in the hospital. The auto repair technician who valued his intern's skill at interpreting manuals treated him as a partner, not just a helper.

Work and service give youth the message that they are valued, even needed. People depend on them. Colleagues welcome them and express their appreciation. They take them into their social interactions, implicitly treating them as friends and colleagues, not just "kids." And in turn, the youth internalize values of the workplace, such as dedication to patients' welfare and to the smooth functioning of the unit.

Mentoring

We have argued elsewhere (Hamilton & Hamilton, in press) that workplaces (paid and unpaid) are ideal contexts for mentoring relationships. In brief, "social mentoring," exemplified by Big Brothers/Big Sisters, though demonstrably effective for elementary school and some middle school children, is less attractive to high school youth. In a study of a mentoring program for middle school students, we found that when mentors were primarily concerned with building social relationships, matches were much less likely to last than when mentors engaged in challenging activities together that built competence and character, such as repairing a bicycle and planning an extended ride (Hamilton & Hamilton, 1992). This does not mean that a mentoring relationship that begins early cannot last into the late teens, but that it becomes harder to initiate new mentoring relationships with older youth. However, most high school students are attracted to work, and workplaces offer many lessons to be learned, technical, personal, and social. We have found in our research and demonstration projects that many adults, meanwhile, are more than ready to teach and advise youth apprentices or interns, including adults who would not volunteer to be mentors in their free time. Workplaces are, in Freedman's (1993) apt phrase, "mentor-rich environments." That is, they are places where adults and youth can come to know each other without the burden of having been matched as mentor/protégé. In such an environment, mentoring is more natural.

It is often more helpful to think of "mentoring" than mentors (Hamilton & Hamilton, in press). Mentoring, broadly defined, is something that many different adults can do to a greater or lesser extent. Although having a single or main mentor who is almost like another parent can be extremely valuable, especially for youth whose own parents do not perform the role well, it is also valuable to have multiple adults who build their competence and character by teaching, advising, and serving as role models in more limited ways and for shorter periods of time. Mentoring also involves building a youth's social capital by linking him or her to other individuals and to groups and organizations. When youth are anxious to learn from experienced adults how to perform work tasks (technical competence) and how to carry out the role of worker (personal and social competence), they become open to mentoring that extends beyond the workplace to address matters of values, education, and career planning. Getting to know personally adults who are neither parents nor formal teachers is clearly an advantage for youth who are in the stage of thinking about themselves as the adults they will become. Work and service-learning create opportunities for such relationships and do so on the side, in the course of the work, which may be the best way, as illustrated in the testimony of another hospital intern (Case 7.3).

Case 7.3   An Internship in Caring

Esdras Mangual, a radiology intern at St. Christopher's Hospital in Philadelphia, explained that to enter the program, "I had to keep my grades and attendance up to par. Prior to participating in this program my attendance and grades weren't what they should be. I now had to be more responsible, reliable, and accountable. It was something new for me, you know, it really changed my life. It's not just you come here and you work. It's more than that. They treat you like their own, like family. My mother just passed away and the day my mentor found out, she came to my home, sat down, and talked to me. Also the coordinator of the program, Barbara Liccio, came over and talked to me, and it really helped me a lot. She also obtained counseling services for me. I see that they're here to support you."

Mangual plans to enter college and major in physical therapy. "After I finish and get my master's, I will give back to the community. I'd like to come back to St. Chris, probably become a mentor to young students. Before the program I was involved in gang activity. And when I joined the program, my whole life changed. I started seeing the point of my education."

SOURCE: Adapted from Hamilton and Hamilton, 1999, p. 47).

In our research on how workplace mentors teach (Hamilton & Hamilton, 2002), we have found that some teaching behaviors are universal: demonstrating, explaining how, explaining why, and monitoring performance and giving feedback. What we called "challenging teaching behaviors" are less common but potentially more powerful: reflective questioning and problem solving. Lucy, the mentor for the hospital intern described above, illustrated the use of reflective questioning about Pam's career plans. The patient survey Pam did with Lucy's guidance illustrates problem solving, as does the auto repair technician's account of working with his intern to understand the manual. We demonstrated that it is possible to increase mentors' use of these teaching behaviors with training. Such training could also be provided to mentors in subsidized youth employment programs, in service-learning programs, and to supervisors in youth jobs.

Creating High-Quality Work and Service Opportunities

Thinking about how work and service match the principles of youth development helps to identify common criteria for high quality in the two types of experiences:

1. Youth engage in productive activity individually and in groups. The work they do matters.

2. Activities are planned, with explicit learning objectives, and monitored to assure that those objectives are met and that appropriate adaptations occur. Experiences are matched with youths' individual needs, interests, and capacities. Expectations for performance and norms for behavior are reasonable and understandable; they are taught explicitly and reinforced by constructive feedback from both peers and adults.

3. Youth participate in making plans and goals for their learning and activities, as well as rules and decisions, to the degree appropriate to their developmental levels and to the situations.

4. Activities call for the exercise and acquisition of new technical, personal, and social competencies, some of which are transferable to other settings. Academic knowledge and skills are applied and reinforced. Activities are challenging enough to stretch youth but accompanied by enough support to be achievable. Youth engage in solving problems with open solutions. Projects are an ideal form of problem solving.

5. Youth have regular opportunities to reflect on their experience. They come to understand what they are doing in relation to principles and values behind their activities and behaviors. They also are challenged to understand how

their work and service fit into larger systems: work organization, corporation, government, economic institutions, and the natural ecology.

6. Adults form mentoring relationships with youth, not only about work but also about issues beyond the workplace.

7. Youth are safe, physically and psychologically. They are protected from avoidable hazards, undue stress, and exploitation.

These criteria delineate an ideal situation for work and service-learning. In an imperfect world, there is no reason to expect that only situations that meet these criteria will foster youth development. But they do provide a standard against which current opportunities may be judged and improvement efforts launched. They also imply that people who care about youth should think as seriously about how to maximize the contributions of paid work to youth development as they ordinarily do about those of service-learning. Employers who need youth employees now also need to consider how work experience promotes the career development of their future workers.

Building Systems

Work and service are best conceived as constituting a central part of a community-wide system promoting youth development. In the introductory chapter, we defined a system as being inclusive, coherent, connected, and enduring. Applying those criteria to work and service is another reason to think of them in relation to each other, rather than as separate domains.

In an ideal system, work and service-learning opportunities would be allocated with some attention to divergent needs. Youth whose families need the extra income they can generate should have access to paying jobs that are also educational. Youth who need the experience more than the money might be encouraged to seek unpaid internships. However, service should be expected of and made available to all, regardless of their personal and family situations.

Youth-run enterprises may come closest to combining the best elements of work and service-learning. Unlike most jobs in large firms or many volunteer positions in which youth perform mostly routine tasks, youth-run enterprises, such as the Alamo 4-H club sheep-raising project, provide opportunities for youth to participate in making all the important decisions (see Case 7.4). This gives them not only work experience but also management experience. For youth who may live in communities where few people have jobs, be it a desolate urban area or a remote Indian reservation, this can be a transforming experience, enabling them to see a much different future for themselves and to develop some of the competencies they will need to make that future real.

Case 7.4   Youth Entrepreneurship

More than 100 students are enrolled in the Alamo Navajo Indian Reservation 4-H club in New Mexico. Marvin Martin, the agriculture and horticulture teacher, explained that the club's favorite project is raising sheep. This year, 40 students raised $4,000 toward the purchase and feeding of the animals by organizing a basketball tournament with concession stands. "This way we ensure that all youth can buy at least one animal, and it is not such a hardship on the family. Some of these youth will get four, five, or six lambs." A Navajo club leader, Dave Piño, teaches the students about raising and showing the sheep. During the summer months, students raise their animals at home in pens they build, taking responsibility for feeding, watering, grooming, and exercising their animals. Part of this routine involves running the animals through the arroyos (sand-filled dry streambeds) to reduce their fat. They keep records of the animal's development, which are turned in at the end of the year to compete for medals and awards. Pens at the school are available for shearing and washing the animals before showing and selling in the fall. The goals of the program are to help youth start saving money for college and to teach them enough about raising sheep that they could start their own business after graduation. In another youth entrepreneurship project, the horticulture class grows and markets tomatoes.

SOURCE: Adapted from Hamilton and Hamilton (1999, p. 17).

A system of work-based learning would include a coherent sequence beginning with visits to workplaces (field trips and job shadowing), progressing to work-like experience (including service-learning and youth-run enterprises), and culminating in actual employment (including youth jobs, subsidized employment training, cooperative education and paid internships, and apprenticeships) (Hamilton & Hamilton, 1997). These experiences would be closely related to school learning. They would accumulate so that by high school graduation, most youth would have a wealth of work and work-like experience to draw on as they make decisions about education and employment.

Putting such a system in place requires an extraordinary commitment on the part of employers to help educate and develop their future workers and to work together with educators, parents, and others in the community. Such commitment is rare, but enough examples can be found to demonstrate that it is possible (Hamilton & Hamilton, 1999).

Note

1. Krista Beiswenger contributed to the development of this case study. Quotations are taken from interview transcripts and have been lightly edited. The interview was conducted as part of our Mentoring Youth at Work study. Pam and Lucy are pseudonyms.

References

Bailey, T., & Morest, V. S. (1998). Preparing youth for employment. In S. Halperin (Ed.), *The forgotten half revisited: American youth and young families, 1988–2008* (chap. 7, pp. 115–136). Washington, DC: American Youth Policy Forum.

Billig, S. H. (2000). Research on K-12 school-based service learning: The evidence builds. *Phi Delta Kappan, 81,* 658–664.

Chawla, L. (Ed.). (2002). *Growing up in an urbanising world.* London: UNESCO & Earthscan.

Cornell Youth and Work Program. (2002). *Guide to teaching and learning.* Retrieved March 25, 2003, from: http://www.human.cornell.edu/youthwork/mentoring/teaching_learning.html. *Problem solve.* Retrieved March 25, 2003, from: http://www.human.cornell.edu/youthwork/mentoring/how_challenging_solve.html. *Perform job tasks.* Retrieved March 25, 2003, from:http://www.human.cornell.edu/youthwork/mentoring/what_technical_perform.html.

Dewey, J. (1938). *Experience and education.* New York: Collier.

Driskell, D. (2002). *Creating better cities with children and youth: A manual for participation.* London: UNESCO and Earthscan.

Eyler, J., Giles, D. E., & Gray, C. J. (1999). *At a glance: What we know about the effects of service-learning on students, faculty, institutions, and communities, 1993–1999.* Unpublished manuscript, Vanderbilt University, Nashville, TN.

Freedman, M. (1993). *The kindness of strangers: Reflections on the mentoring movement.* San Francisco: Jossey-Bass.

Gomez, B. (1996). Service-learning and school-to-work strategies for revitalizing urban education and communities. *Education and Urban Society, 28*(2), 160–165.

Greenberger, E., & Steinberg, L. D. (1986). *When teenagers work: The psychological and social costs of adolescent employment.* New York: Basic Books.

Hamilton, M. A., & Hamilton, S. F. (1997). *Learning well at work: Choices for quality.* Washington, DC: U.S. Government Printing Office. (Also available at http://www.human.cornell.edu/youthwork/)

Hamilton, M. A., & Hamilton, S. F. (2002). Why mentoring in the workplace works. In J. Rhodes (Ed.), *New directions for youth development: A critical view of youth mentoring.* San Francisco: Jossey-Bass.

Hamilton, S. F., & Hamilton, M. A. (1992). Mentoring programs: Promise and paradox. *Phi Delta Kappan, 73,* 546–550.

Hamilton, S. F., & Hamilton, M. A. (1999). *Building strong school-to-work systems: Illustrations of key components.* Washington, DC: U.S. Government Printing Office. (Also available at http://www.human.cornell.edu/youthwork/)

Hamilton, S. F., & Hamilton, M. A. (in press). Contexts for mentoring: Adolescent-adult relationships in workplaces and communities. In R. M. Lerner & L. Steinberg (Eds.), *Handbook of adolescent psychology.* New York: Wiley.

Melchior, A., & Bailis, L. N. (2002). Impact of service-learning on civic attitudes and behaviors of middle and high school youth: Findings from three national evaluations. In A. Furco & S. H. Billig (Eds.), *Service-learning: The essence of the pedagogy.* Greenwich, CT: Information Age Publishing.

Metz, E., McLellan, J., & Youniss, J. (2003). Types of voluntary service and adolescents' civic development. *Journal of Adolescent Research, 18,* 188–202.

Mortimer, J. T. (2003). *Working and growing up in America.* Cambridge, MA: Harvard University Press.

Murnane, R. J., & Levy, F. (1996). *Teaching the new basic skills.* New York: Free Press.

National Center on Education and the Economy. (1990). *America's choice: High skills or low wages! The report of the Commission on the Skills of the American Workforce.* Rochester, NY: Author.

National Research Council and Institute of Medicine. (1998). *Protecting youth at work: Health, safety, and development of working children and adolescents in the United States.* Washington, DC: National Academy Press.

National Research Council and Institute of Medicine. (2002). *Community programs to promote youth development.* J. Eccles & J. A. Gootman (Eds.). Board on Children, Youth, and Families, Division of Behavioral and Social Sciences and Education. Washington, DC: National Academy Press.

Newman, K. S. (1999). *No shame in my game: The working poor in the inner city.* New York: Vintage Books and Russell Sage.

Putnam, R. D. (2000). *Bowling alone: The collapse and revival of American community.* New York: Simon & Schuster.

Ruhm, C. J. (1997). Is high school employment consumption or investment? *Journal of Labor Economics, 15,* 735–777.

Secretary's Commission on Achieving Necessary Skills. (1991). *What work requires of schools: A SCANS report for America 2000.* Washington, DC: U.S. Department of Labor.

Stern, D., Finkelstein, N., Urquiola, M., & Cagampang, H. (1997). What differences does it make if school and work are connected? *Economics of Education Review, 16,* 213–229.

Stukas, A. A. Jr., Clary, E. G., & Snyder, M. (1999). Service learning: Who benefits and why. *Social Policy Report, 13*(4). (Society for Research in Child Development).

Tannock, S. (2001). *Youth at work: The unionized fast-food and grocery workplace.* Philadelphia: Temple University Press.

U.S. Department of Labor, Bureau of Labor Statistics. (2000). *Report on the youth labor force.* Washington, DC: Author. (Also available at http://www.bls.gov/opub/rlyf/rlyfhome.htm)

U.S. Department of Labor, Bureau of Labor Statistics. (2003, January 31). *Employment experience of youths during the school year and summer* (News release USLD 03–40). Washington, DC: Author. (Also available at http://www.bls.gov/nls/)

What Kids Can Do. (2001). *Reclaiming the Bronx River in a New York City neighborhood.* Retrieved January 29, 2003, from: http://www.whatkidscando.org/studentwork/BronxRiver.html.

Wirt, J., Choy, S., Gerald, D., Provasnik, S., Rooney, P., Watanabe, S., Tobin, R., & Glander, M. (2001). *The condition of education, 2001.* Washington, DC: U.S. Department of Education, National Center for Education Statistics. (Also available at http://nces.ed.gov/pubsearch/pubsinfo.asp?pubid=2001072)

Zuckerman, A. (2001). The more things change, the more they stay the same: The evolution and devolution of youth employment programs. In P. Benson & K. Pittman (Eds.), *Trends in youth development: Visions, realities and challenges* (chap. 9, pp. 269–289). Boston: Kluwer.

8

Using and Building Family Strengths to Promote Youth Development

Catherine P. Bradshaw and James Garbarino

Parents have traditionally been the ones blamed when things go badly for youth. However, in matters of human development, when the question is "Does X cause Y?" (e.g., "Does poor parenting cause delinquency?"), the best scientific answer is "It depends." Parents do not raise children in isolation, for as children move into and through adolescence, their world expands, and other influences also shape their development; many of those influences are addressed in other chapters of this volume, including schools, popular culture and the media, and especially peers.

In this chapter, we review several studies indicating that what parents do with and to their children *does* matter. These effects are usually neither simple nor direct because the child development equation includes a constantly shifting and evolving interplay of the child's biology and the parents' action (for a review, see Collins, Maccoby, Steinberg, Hetherington, & Bornstein, 2000; Steinberg, 2001). Consequently, the success of parents in rearing healthy and prosocial children often depends largely on the difficulties posed by the children and the degree to which the social environment is toxic and hostile to both children and their parents (Collins et al., 2000;

Garbarino, 1995). We also discuss a few ways that youth development professionals can help parents combat these risks.

Families change as well as adolescents, and we discuss some of the challenges presented by various family structures and provide some suggestions for how parents can adapt their parenting behaviors to accommodate these developmental changes. Youth development professionals should both harness and enhance the strengths of families when creating and implementing youth development strategies. Because this is often difficult to do, we provide some suggestions for how youth development professionals can look for age-appropriate ways to involve parents, encourage joint participation in youth-parent activities, support parents, and foster networks among families for the promotion of positive youth development.

Families in the Ecology of Human Development

As individuals develop, they play more active roles in an ever-widening world. Newborns shape the feeding behavior of their mothers but are confined largely to cribs, laps, arms, and carriers and have limited means of communicating their needs. Adolescents develop stronger attachments to and relationships with peers, who become particularly influential regarding issues such as fashion, music, and where and how adolescents spend their time. Although parents have some control over their children's peer group, especially in early childhood, as they age youth have more freedom to choose with whom they want to associate. Adolescents, like adults, tend to seek out others who share their same beliefs, attitudes, and pastimes. These associations, in turn, reinforce their own behaviors, be they prosocial or antisocial (for a review, see Thornberry & Krohn, 1997). What appears to be peer influence is at least partly a result of youth with similar attitudes, preferences, and behaviors choosing to associate with each other.

Although many adults think peers become the guiding force in adolescents' lives (e.g., Harris, 1998), parents actually still have the greatest influence over major decisions and character development (Allen & Land, 1999). More specifically, youth who have secure relationships with their parents explore their environments, including peer relationships, with the knowledge that they have their trusted parents to rely on when needed. Furthermore, peers tend to have the greatest influence on youth with weak family support. A recent study indicated that parental attachment moderated the influence of deviant peers on problem behaviors of youth. Youth who reported having strong attachments to parents in adolescence were less likely to be influenced by deviant friends, regardless of the level of parental monitoring. Conversely, youth with low parental attachments were more influenced by their friends' deviant behaviors (Vitaro, Brendgen, & Tremblay, 2000). These findings suggest that the effect of parenting behaviors on youth development depends on the strength of the emotional relationship between parents and youth (Steinberg, 2001).

Context Matters

The most important characteristic of the ecological perspective is that it encourages us to look both inside the individual child or parent and beyond to the environment when attempting to influence behavior and development (Bronfenbrenner, 1972). When promoting positive youth development, youth development professionals must consider families, friends, neighborhood, and schools, as well as more distant forces that constitute the social geography and cultural climate (e.g., laws, institutions, the media, religious beliefs, and cultural values). Youth service workers and practitioners cannot effectively promote a child's development without knowing something about the rest of the world in which that child lives, and even then it may be very difficult. For example, much has been said about the decisive role of the early years of a child's life on later development. National media campaigns urge parents to invest in the first 3 years as a strategy to promote thriving in later years. Although there is certainly truth to this, human development is a lifelong process. More specifically, the first few years "matter" considerably, but many of the effects of adverse childhood experiences can be overcome through later nurturance (Bruer, 1999). The endurance of these effects also depends on how extremely depriving or traumatic the early experience was and what developmental opportunities the child subsequently encounters.

Biology and Environment Interact

For children born biologically at risk, such as with temperamental or genetic risk factors, the effects of adverse childhood experiences can be modulated by the environment. For example, Bohman (1996) and colleagues followed a large group of adopted children who had at least one biological parent with a criminal record. Although these children, whom the investigators classified as being born with a biological predisposition to antisocial behavior, were more likely to have a criminal record than children without such a heritage, the odds of repeating their biological parents' patterns varied significantly by the type of family that adopted them (Bohman, 1996). Of the children biologically at risk for developing criminal behavior who were adopted by high-risk families, 40% ended up with criminal records, compared with only 12% of children adopted into well-functioning families. Nonetheless, the percentage of biologically at-risk children who developed criminal behavior after being placed in the well-functioning families was well above the average for other nonadopted children raised in well-functioning families (i.e., 12% compared with 3%) (Bohman, 1996). This study illustrates how the effects of biological risk factors can be buffered or attenuated by a supportive family environment (Collins et al., 2000).

Parenting Practices

As noted above, factors outside the family can have a major effect on children and their parents. Although many of those factors are favorable and support the positive influence parents hope to have, others work against parents, acting as impediments rather than assets for youth development. One study identified four main challenges many parents face today as they seek to promote positive youth development in their adolescents (Zill & Nord, 1994). At their worst, these conditions create "social toxicity":

1. Adult authority is weaker and more fragmented.

2. Young people are spending more time with peers than adults.

3. Teenagers have more freedom in their own lives than previous generations of young people. They have greater freedom of choice regarding friends, school commitments, sexual activity, and career paths.

4. The mass media exposes adolescents to a broader range of experiences that influence young people in deleterious ways.

How can parents overcome these challenges and the threat they carry of social toxicity?

Monitoring and Disclosure

Parenting styles and behaviors depend to a certain degree on the social context in which they occur. Enhancing parental monitoring strategies by tracking and attending to the child's activities and whereabouts is one way parents can adapt to challenging environments (Dishion & McMahon, 1998). Parental monitoring can protect children from many of the temptations and dangers associated with being a young person today. More specifically, research indicates that well-monitored youth are at decreased risk for several delinquent and problem behaviors, such as smoking, using drugs and alcohol, engaging in risky sexual behavior, and socializing with deviant peers (Dishion & McMahon, 1998).

Related research suggests that it may be *disclosure* by youth to the parents, rather than parental monitoring, that has the greatest impact on their problem behaviors (Kerr & Stattin, 2000). Furthermore, youth who are more securely attached to their parents are also most likely to disclose (Allen & Land, 1999). A study of Cornell undergraduates underscores the importance of parental monitoring and disclosure, for it illustrates that a substantial number of successful youth have secret lives that their parents are not aware of (Garbarino & Bedard, 2001). Of the 275 first-year undergraduates who participated in the study, 18% reported that they had stolen from their parents, with 65% of these students reporting that their parents never found out. Fourteen percent reported that they had been arrested or detained, with 27% saying that their parents never found out. Twenty-three percent admitted to driving under the influence, of which 94% said their parents never found out. Eleven percent reported having used hard drugs, such as cocaine or Ecstasy, and 92% said their parents never knew about it. Most concerning is the 25% who reported contemplating suicide, of which 87% said their parents never knew. If this group of highly functioning students can have such dangerous secret lives, then what can we expect of less fortunate youth?

Authoritative Parenting

Several decades of research on effective parenting indicate rather consistently that an authoritative parenting style is most effective for promoting positive youth development across a number of domains (e.g., academic performance and prosocial behavior) (Baumrind, 1966; Steinberg, 2001). These authoritative parenting behaviors are characterized by firmness, warmth, and psychological autonomy granting and are more effective at promoting positive youth development than authoritarian parenting behaviors that include high control or firmness in the absence of warmth (Steinberg, 2001).

There appear to be some racial differences in the association between parenting styles and youth development; authoritarian parenting may be associated with fewer negative outcomes for African American and Asian

American youth than it appears to be for European American youth. For example, whereas previous research indicated that authoritative parenting was associated with academic achievement, more recent research has indicated that authoritative parenting is not associated with academic performance among African American and Asian American youth (Steinberg, Dornbusch, & Brown, 1992). It looks as if the peer group might exert greater influence over academic performance than the parents in these latter cultures. More specifically, it is possible that Asian American peers put a great deal of pressure on one another to excel academically. Conversely, in some African American communities, peers may undermine the influence of the parents by teasing or snubbing high academic performers (Steinberg et al., 1992).

Furthermore, there also seem to be indirect effects of authoritative parenting that operate through peers, such that a youth may benefit simply from having friends whose parents are authoritative. Similarly, it is likely that many of the positive attitudes and behaviors of authoritative parents rub off on their children, for many of the qualities of an authoritative parent are also desirable in a good friend, such as being consistent and reliable (i.e., firm), supportive (i.e., warm), and being accepting and tolerant of individual or cultural differences (i.e., autonomy granting) (Steinberg, 2001). Moreover, a whole community of authoritative parents also appears to have a cumulative effect, whereby the community has mutually agreed on norms of acceptable behavior for youth and enforces and expects those behaviors in all youth (Fletcher, Darling, Steinberg, & Dornbusch, 1995).

Adapting Parenting Behaviors to Combat Social Toxicity

In more extreme environmental circumstances, parents concerned about the physical well-being of their children may alter their parenting behavior to compensate for the toxicity of their children's social environments (Furstenberg, Cook, Eccles, Elder, & Sameroff, 1999; Garbarino, 1995). More specifically, there is some research indicating that in comparison with European American parents, African American parents are less permissive and use harsher discipline (Shumow, Vandell, & Posner, 1998). These strategies are believed to protect African American children from socially toxic environments and prepare them for life in a society that is unfortunately often discriminatory (Bell-Scott & McKenry, 1986).

Similarly, a few studies suggest that parents living in urban areas may attempt to compensate for the unpredictability of their environments by setting greater restrictions on their children's behavior and using a slightly domineering or authoritarian parenting style, which sometimes includes the threat of physical punishment (Deater-Deckard, Dodge, Bates, & Pettit, 1996; Furstenberg et al., 1999). Interviews with mothers raising children in the public housing projects of inner-city Chicago indicate that these mothers are more restrictive with their children and adolescents because they are concerned about their children's safety. These mothers report that this is the only way they feel they can protect their children from the widespread gang activity and gunfire that is characteristic of their neighborhoods (Dubrow & Garbarino, 1989).

It is clear that these parents have good intentions and are struggling to ensure the physical well-being of their children, but at what cost? There is no empirical evidence indicating that authoritarian parenting and harsh parenting strategies (including the threat of physical punishment) are necessarily more effective in these contexts. To the contrary, previous research has shown that overly restrictive and controlling parenting practices are associated with *increased* behavior problems among African American youth. However, more restrictive parenting practices appear to be somewhat effective in terms of reducing delinquency for younger African American children *when coupled with high levels of maternal warmth* (Dunifon & Kowaleski-Jones, 2002). Although these effects do not appear to hold for European American children, they are reminiscent of the larger body of research findings indicating that the emotional context of any parenting behavior is extremely important (Steinberg, 2001). Additional research on the effectiveness of different parenting strategies in high-risk environments is certainly needed.

Challenges Resulting From Developmental Changes in the Youth and Family

Although some researchers, and many parents, no doubt, have viewed adolescence as a time of storm and stress for the family, it appears that some of these derogatory characterizations were based on high-risk youth, the majority of whom had preexisting family problems. Surveys of well-functioning youth, however, indicate that approximately 75% of adolescents perceive their relationships with their parents to be positive (Steinberg, 2001). Conversely, it may be that *parents* experience greater distress over the bickering and squabbling common to many households with adolescents, for they perceive these interactions differently and often take them more personally than do the adolescents. Steinberg (2001) provides the example of a parent and adolescent arguing over how a youth is not keeping his room clean. Whereas the parent views this as a disagreement over *values* (e.g., not valuing personal property or disrespecting the parents), the adolescent views the disagreement simply as a difference of *opinion,* for he believes that it is one's personal choice how one prefers to keep one's room. This example illustrates the importance of supporting parents as they adapt their parenting behavior in response to their children's development, because many parents struggle between granting children's much-wanted autonomy and demonstrating authoritative parenting behaviors.

In addition to challenges associated with the youth's development, many parents and youth face additional challenges resulting from changes in family structure (i.e., single parent, blended families, and cohabiting couples). As a consequence, these families must decide how open they will be to others in the community and to the influence of youth development professionals. We briefly present some of these challenges and discuss their implications for youth development professionals.

Divorced and Single-Parent Families

Longitudinal studies indicate that children from divorced families are at a small but significantly greater risk than intact families for developing internalizing and externalizing symptoms and demonstrating lower academic achievement (Amato, 2000). Even more disconcerting is that divorce is often associated with "sleeper effects," meaning that the effects may take up to 10 or more years after marital dissolution to emerge (Wallerstein & Kelly, 1989). Furthermore, the cycle appears to continue, for studies show that children of divorced parents are more likely to divorce than children from intact families (McGue & Lykken, 1992). Given the high rates of divorce, it is not surprising that nearly 50% of all youth will live in single-parent homes at some point before their 18th birthdays, even if only temporarily (Amato, 2000).

Nearly a quarter of youth under the age of 18 live with a single parent during any given year, including 18% of European American children and 50% of African American children (U.S. Census Bureau, 2001). Youth who grow up in single-parent or cohabiting families are at greater risk for behavior problems and low academic achievement. However, time spent in single-parent households is not significantly associated with delinquency or math performance for African American youth (Dunifon & Kowaleski-Jones, 2002).

Studies have shown that single-parent families differ from two-parent families in the amount of time the youth spends with the parent, the amount of control and demands imposed by the parent, and the level of warmth expressed by the parent (Astone & McLanahan, 1991). There has been, however, some ambiguity over whether it matters if the "other" adult living in the home is related by marriage (i.e., a stepparent) or not (as in the case of cohabitation). A recent study indicated that for African American youth, time spent in a household with married (including both biological and step-) parents was associated with a decreased likelihood of delinquency, compared with living in a household with a parent who is cohabiting (Dunifon & Kowaleski-Jones, 2002). Although a cohabiting partner can potentially monitor the youth's behavior and foster positive development, that adult has not made a formal commitment to the parent (or the family) and thus may introduce more instability than stability. Unfortunately, it appears that the mere presence of a cohabiting adult in the home does not suffice.

It is difficult to disentangle the influence of family structure from that of socioeconomic status (Dunifon & Kowaleski-Jones, 2002), for 39% of single-parent families are poor, compared with only 7% of married-couple families (U.S. Census Bureau, 2001). Racial differences are also not fully understood.

In thinking about why single parenthood in African American families is associated with fewer detrimental outcomes than in European American families, it is helpful to consider how family might be conceptualized in African American culture. One possibility is that "family" is more broadly defined for many African Americans (Hill, 1972). For example, people outside the nuclear family with whom there are strong ties, such as distant cousins, or even neighbors or close family friends who are not biologically related, are often considered family. Similarly, a biological relative may function in a different role than is typical of his or her biological relationship, such as a grandmother who becomes a primary caregiver. Furthermore, approximately one third of African American families live in extended family homes, which is particularly advantageous in single-parent families. In many of these households, being a single parent does not have to mean single parenting (Stack & Burton, 1993).

These statistics call attention to the importance of extended family and family-like ties in promoting positive youth development. Youth development practitioners should be cognizant of these relationships and include other family members and people who are considered family in youth development programming. They are a natural resource on which to capitalize; however, this is difficult to do when a family establishes an impermeable boundary between itself and the community.

Open and Closed Family Systems

Family researchers and therapists have long known that families are on some level "open systems," meaning they are influenced by the larger social context (Minuchin, 1974). Families must create boundaries and decide how permeable these boundaries will be to the flow of information, energy, and people in and out of the family system (Garbarino, 1995). Families who become too closed off to society run the risk of depleting their own resources. Quite often, closed families set impermeable boundaries to protect a family secret, such as in the case of abuse. Family therapists have told us that when they are referred to families suspected of abuse, these families often do not have telephone service. Although there are likely economic factors that contribute to not having phone service, abusive families often attempt to insulate themselves from the community to hide their dysfunction. Canceling telephone service may be one way of limiting the flow of information and blocking people from entering their family system. These and other deliberate attempts to withdraw from society can also occur when families are concerned about perceived or real dangers in the community.

A closed family system limits children's opportunities for positive development, for there are many characteristics of the youth's environment that are outside the direct control of parents, such as a caring school climate, neighborhood boundaries, and positive peer influences (Scales & Leffert, 1999, p. 2). Parents implicitly rely on others in the community to help them raise thriving youth. Open families are therefore better able to use the support of individuals outside the family.

Open family systems are most beneficial when their environments reinforce and extend their positive influence. For example, it is easier to promote "reading for pleasure at least 3 hours per week" in a community that demonstrates its commitment to literacy via the public library. Getting youth to "spend 3 or more hours per week in lessons or practice in music, theater, or other arts" is more likely in a community that supports music and art in school and perhaps even has a community school of music and the arts. Similarly, a 1995 Gallup poll conducted for *Parenting* magazine revealed that 90% of parents said they had talked to their children about God (Brown, 2000). That is a good start, but it is most likely to translate into the asset of "young person spends 1 or more hours per week in activities in a religious institution" in a community that is rich with religious institutions and other supports for spiritual practice. These are only a few of the institutional supports that children need to develop in a positive way.

How Can Youth Development Professionals Strengthen Families?

Except in extreme cases in which youth are removed from their families and placed in institutions, youth development professionals are supplementing what families do, not replacing them. Youth development professionals can help strengthen families by focusing their efforts on the following six attributes of strong families (Stinnett, Chesser, & DeFrain, 1979, pp. 25-29). Note the consistency between these six strengths and the Search Institute's developmental assets that are within the control of the parents (see Table 1.2, this volume):

1. *Appreciation:* Members of strong families regard each other warmly and positively and give support to each other as individuals.

2. *Spending time together:* Members of strong families spend a lot of time together, often just hanging around the house or doing more structured activities such as eating together, working together, attending movies or local performances, and participating in community, school, and athletic events.

3. *Good communication patterns:* Members of strong families are honest, open, and receptive to feedback from one another. Open lines of communication help to promote stability and allow youth to become active members in making family decisions.

4. *Commitment:* Strong families place the family high on their list of priorities. They choose to participate in activities that are family rather than individual focused.

5. *Ability to deal with crises in a positive manner:* Strong families are able to manage and respond to conflict effectively by banding together in *mutual* support. They rally together to meet challenges, such as illness, employment transitions, financial problems, loss, and social toxicity.

6. *Religious orientation:* These families have a sense of purpose and a strong set of beliefs, which are usually religious or spiritual in nature. These beliefs help the family feel that it is working toward something outside itself, for humans are spiritual as well as social beings.

Unfortunately, most families fall short of displaying all these strengths. Considering what we know about how families influence youth development and the challenges they face, there are several ways youth development professionals can benefit youth while also strengthening their families. We spend the remainder of the chapter providing a few suggestions and some examples of how youth development professionals can enhance family strengths where they exist and stimulate them where they are lacking (Alvarado & Kumpfer, 2000).

Educate Parents (Builds Strengths 3, 4, and 5)

Although parent education seems most relevant when children are young, the parents of adolescents often recognize that their established patterns no longer work. Consequently, most parents are open to new information and new approaches. Parent education groups are an effective way to disseminate information on effective parenting behaviors, the importance of setting clear limits, being consistent, and avoiding coercive interactions. When youth development professionals are respected and have a close enough relationship with parents, they can work with the parents individually, educating them about the importance of using positive discipline, thereby fostering self-control and promoting nonviolent problem-solving skills. Furthermore, youth development professionals can help authoritative parents network with one another and set norms for appropriate behaviors that will be reinforced in the home, at school, and in the community (Ianni, 1989). In view of the research indicating racial differences in the effectiveness of parenting styles, however, it is important that anyone working with parents be sensitive to cultural and contextual differences and be cautious about recommending one "best" style of parenting for all.

Youth development professionals can also help educate parents and other adults in the community about the effects of social toxicity and help them appropriately adapt their parenting strategies to battle socially toxic forces in their environments. Similarly, they can help families decide how to respond to challenges, such as violent media and peers who are negative influences, and how tolerant of and welcoming they will be to other members of the community and people from diverse cultures.

Look for Age-Appropriate Ways to Involve Parents (Builds Strengths 1, 2, 3, and 4)

Parent involvement in schools and other settings declines with age. It is clear that the nature of that involvement must change to match the youth's development. However, it is equally clear that parents still care, still matter, and still have a right and responsibility to be involved as their children grow older. Schools seem to be a natural avenue for families to participate in youth development (see Case 8.1). Research indicates that parental involvement has a positive effect on academic performance (Keith et al., 1998). Furthermore,

Case 8.1   Parental Involvement in Secondary Schools

Although it may be easier to envision parental participation in elementary or preschool programs, schools on military bases sponsored by the Department of Defense Education Activity (DoDEA) have successfully involved parents throughout the education process. Not only is parental involvement expected, but service members are required to attend parent-teacher conference day and are relieved of their work responsibilities to volunteer at the school each month. This illustrates a commitment to parental involvement in the education process that is well beyond what is common in most business-education partnerships (Smrekar, Guthrie, Owens, & Sims, 2001). What is even more promising is that DoDEA schools have reduced the disparity in test scores of youth from different ethnic backgrounds. For example, the average difference between Caucasian and minority youth eighth-grade writing National Assessment of Educational Progress (NAEP) scores is around 15 points, with this disparity being even less for students attending DoDEA schools overseas. These numbers are impressive when compared with the national average, a 27-point disparity (Smrekar et al., 2001). Furthermore, 68% of DoDEA students took the Scholastic Aptitude Test (SAT) in 2002, compared with just 48% of high school students nationally (U.S. Department of Defense, 2002). It is difficult to attribute these effects to a single cause; however, parental involvement is likely a significant factor.

SOURCE: Smrekar et al. (2001); U.S. Department of Defense (2002); www.peabody.vanderbilt.edu/pdf/ DoDFinal921.pdf.

parents can influence their children's academic performance simply by talking with them about school activities and their own aspirations for their children's education (e.g., to attend college) (Keith et al., 1998).

Encourage Joint Youth-Parent Activities (Builds Strengths 1, 2, 3, 4, 5, and 6)

Rather than assuming that separation of parents from adolescents is always best, youth development professionals can emphasize the importance of families spending time together. This can be challenging, because rising parental and societal expectations infringe on parents' "free time"; however, adolescents still need time to be around their families to talk, eat meals together, and watch movies. Parents easily declare that they are committed to their families, but choosing family over other attractive alternatives is hard work.

Volunteering is a promising activity for youth and parents to participate in together, for it simultaneously benefits the youth, the family, and the community. Participating in a river or roadside cleanup, for example, can be particularly rewarding for environmentally conscious families, or, for those who possess culinary skills, preparing meals at a local homeless shelter. Providing youth and their families opportunities to volunteer also contributes to the development of assets, such as being valued by the family and community, being perceived as a resource, and providing service to others (Scales & Leffert, 1999). Furthermore, the younger people are when they first volunteer, the more likely they are to volunteer in adulthood. Sponsoring youth/parent volunteer activities is an easy way that youth-serving organizations can foster positive youth *and* family development.

There is increasing recognition throughout our society that not enough attention is paid to the development of character and values and that more and more youth are looking to peers and mass media to determine their values. Although parents teach and model positive values and virtues, they cannot do the job alone. They need the support and assistance of other adults in the community, for parenting is very much a cultural enterprise, grounded in values, beliefs, and assumptions about right and wrong and about how children develop (Ianni, 1989). Encouraging participation in religious activities and organizations is one way to engage and support parents in promoting character development, for how well we function in the world depends as much on the quality of the social environment as it does on the quality of our spiritual lives.

Similarly, youth development professionals can remind parents of the importance of being positive role models for their own children. By giving youth active roles in their own families, parents can promote the development of positive values and foster their children's ability to serve as moral leaders to their peers. Families can encourage youth participation by holding weekly family management meetings, during which the family discusses any issues or problems that occurred over the previous week and makes plans for the upcoming week (Dinkmeyer, Dinkmeyer, & Sperry, 1987). The adolescents also have the opportunity during these meetings to discuss concerns and raise questions regarding family values and ideals for behavior (see Case 8.2).

Case 8.2   Camps and Programs Building Youth/Parent Partnerships

The Player/Parent Session at the Roanoke College Soccer Camp invites youth to attend a weeklong day camp with a parent, and usually the dad enrolls. Players build soccer skills and parents also get to know their children as teammates, see their children interact with other youth, and work with them for a common goal, no pun intended. Parents also learn a little humility, for often the youth are better players and in better shape than their parents.

At Camps Seafarer and Sea Gull in Arapahoe, North Carolina, families develop new skills through land- and sea-based activities (Camp Sea Gull and Camp Seafarer, n.d.). Youth/parent outward-bound programs remove families from the everyday stress and hustle of their home environments to engage in personally and physically challenging programs. Unfortunately, too many of these types of family programs are accessible only to families with considerable resources, in terms of both money and time.

Provide the Support Parents Need to Do Their Job (Builds Strengths 2 and 5)

Research indicates that youth who begin self-care (so-called latchkey children) by the age of 8 or 9 years are twice as likely as adult-supervised youth to have experimented with alcohol, drugs, or sex by age 15 (Richardson et al., 1989). In addition, most juvenile crimes are committed between the hours of 3 p.m. and 6 p.m., roughly between the time youth get out of school and the time their parents arrive home from work (Snyder & Sickmund, 1999). Supervision is limited during the time most youth are transitioning between school and home, illustrating a weak link between schools and families. These youth not only need to be monitored but also need a safe place to be during this time. Child care programs, including after-school programs, are an ideal way to link parents with other youth-serving organizations.

After-school programs are, unfortunately, not available to all youth. Youth development professionals can create programs and networks that help parents monitor from a distance what adolescents are watching, what games they are playing, what music they are listening to, who they are hanging out with, where they are going, and how they are treating each other. In addition, they can help parents identify and select among different after-school options.

On a societal level, youth service workers, practitioners, and policymakers can work toward ensuring that after-school programs are accessible, affordable, and of high quality. Furthermore, they can work to stabilize child care resources and support the professional development of care providers. Similarly, it is important to champion public policies that enhance family stability, such as encouraging businesses to set policies that allow parents to care for their children and adolescents without jeopardizing their jobs, or policies that reward geographic stability during their employees' child-rearing years. Like traditional education, after-school programming should be recognized as part of a community's youth development system (see Case 8.3).

Promote Networking Among Parents (Builds Strength 5)

There is more to youth development than working directly with parents and children. Connecting families with each other and with other social systems is essential (Ianni, 1989). Practitioners can help and encourage parents to join forces with other parents and teachers to set norms and enforce expectations of acceptable behavior, such as the types of television programs, videogames, and Web pages children will have access to at each other's homes or at school. For example, one of the greatest obstacles to preventing bullying is the widely held view that "Boys will be boys," and similarly that boys are supposed to "fight things out." Research by Olweus (1993) and others indicates that teachers and parents know about, and often witness, children who are bullied regularly, but do relatively little to intervene. Turning a blind eye not only impedes intervention but also sends the message to the bully that the behavior is acceptable and to the victim that the assault was justified. Worse yet, the victims learn through these experiences that they cannot rely on adults to help or protect them (Garbarino & deLara, 2002). Similarly, sociologists have shown that neighbors' willingness to intervene on behalf of the common good is associated with reduced community violence (Sampson, Raudenbush, & Earls, 1997). This type of group effort requires that we let go of the "American value" of individualism, a value that promotes closed family systems (see Case 8.4).

Conclusions

Peers and socially toxic forces in the environment can at times impede parents' efforts to promote thriving in their children. Although some

---

Case 8.3   Intensive Family-Focused Services

HOMEBUILDERS intends to avert the placement of youth in residential treatment programs by providing intensive in-home intervention to families in crisis (Institute for Family Development, n.d.). The program allows youth to remain in the community, while promoting problem-solving skills that prevent future crises. Families are referred to the program because one or more of their children are at risk of being placed in foster, group, or institutional care, or when a youth is returning from out-of-home care. The therapists carry small caseloads and are available to the families 24 hours a day, 7 days a week. In addition to counseling services, therapists educate the family on effective problem-solving skills and help parents manage their own stress reactions to situations. The therapists also connect the family with other supportive agencies, such as educational services and after-school activities (Institute for Family Development, n.d.). Implemented in several communities nationwide, evaluations indicate that HOMEBUILDERS successfully averts youth placement in residential or detention facilities and promotes family stability (Alvarado & Kumpfer, 1998).

Family Solutions is a multifamily group intervention alternative to traditional probation or incarceration for first-time juvenile offenders. The family, including the youth, parents, and siblings, attend 10 weekly group sessions with approximately eight other families. The program promotes positive changes in family environments by enhancing communication, coping skills, family strengths, and resources, and altering conflictive cycles of interaction between parents and youth. Implemented in several communities, evaluations indicate that Family Solutions effectively reduces recidivism rates among first-offender participants (Quinn, VanDyke, & Kurth, 2002).

---

parents may feel that they have lost control during their children's adolescence, they continue to be the most influential force in their children's lives (Steinberg, 2001). Parents still are—or should be—children's stable base or "attachment figures in reserve" (Cooper, Shaver, & Collins, 1998, p. 1380).

Parents do, however, need to adapt their parenting behaviors to accommodate adolescent and family development changes. Youth development professionals can be instrumental in helping parents maintain a positive

---

Case 8.4   Youth Charters

One way youth development professionals can help families network with one another and set norms of acceptable behavior is by encouraging them to craft a youth charter. A youth charter is a code of acceptable and ideal behaviors that youth, parents, and others in the community will strive to uphold (Ianni, 1989). More specifically, the charter records a consensus about core standards and expectations regarding common decency, respect, honesty, fairness, and personal responsibility. Youth charters typically are developed through small- and large-group meetings, which include youth, parents, teachers, youth development professionals, police, local media, employers, religious leaders, and others from the community.

The charter addresses issues the community is concerned about. It can be either specific, focusing on issues such as reducing drunk driving or unprotected sex, or more general, such as promoting academic achieving or character development. The charter is intended to supplement the character development and values promoted in the home and extend them into the community. Working on a charter connects parents with other parents and youth-serving organizations (Damon, 1997). Youth development professionals can be instrumental in helping communities develop and abide by youth charters.

---

influence on their adolescent children by promoting family strengths and stability, for youth from strong, stable families face society with the skills to combat risk (Alvarado & Kumpfer, 2000; Coleman, 1989). Furthermore, youth development professionals can educate parents on effective parenting behaviors and help them understand that increased parental monitoring and authoritative parenting behaviors may be their best defense against social toxicity.

Although it can be challenging, it is particularly important to support and strengthen the families of biologically and temperamentally vulnerable youth. This may require intensive intervention services. However, youth development professionals can help families identify and connect with intensive services and can support parents and youth during the transitions into and out of these services. Youth development programs can also serve as follow-up or aftercare for youth and their parents in the form of parent education and support groups.

Given that parents have a substantial influence on at least a quarter of the Search Institute's 40 developmental assets (see Chapter 1), it is essential that parents be involved in promoting youth development. We have provided only a few examples of the many ways that youth development professionals can involve parents in the promotion of positive youth development. Most of all, we encourage youth development professionals to look beyond their own programs and resources to consider how they can work with the family, the community, and other institutions to raise healthy, thriving youth.

Additional Resources

It may be helpful to supplement parenting-education experiences with information and resources available on the Internet. It is important, however, to direct parents toward resources that are research based and culturally sensitive. Although there is no room here to summarize the numerous resources available, the following sites are a good place to start.

The *Center for Media Education* (CME) provides public education on quality electronic media for children, families, and communities. The center also conducts research and has been a leader in the promotion of children's educational television programming and safeguards on the Internet. Available at: http://www.cme.org or (202) 331-7833.

The *Fatherhood Project* is a national initiative that promotes books, films, training programs, and seminars on enhancing fathers' involvement in their children's lives. Sponsored by the Families and Work Institute. Available at: http://www.fatherhoodproject.org.

The *Independent Educational Consulting Association* (IECA) is an organization of professionals who help parents select schools and programs that meet the special needs of their adolescent children. Provides information about educational opportunities (e.g., summer enrichment programs and colleges) and programs for students with learning disabilities or emotional problems (e.g., wilderness programs or residential treatment centers). Available at: http://www.educationalconsulting.org/.

Educational Consulting Services (ECS) specializes in working with troubled adolescents. Available at: http://www.educationalconsultingservices.com.

The *National Parent Information Network* (NPIN) provides information and resources on education, parenting, child care, and child development. The NPIN Web site provides numerous suggested readings and some full-text articles. Sponsored by the U.S. Department of Education. Available at: http://www.npin.org/about.html.

Parents Without Partners is a volunteer organization that sponsors support meetings and educational activities for single parents. Available at: http://www.parentswithoutpartners.org.

Talking With Your Kids About Tough Issues is a national initiative that encourages parents to talk with their children about violence, sex, HIV/AIDS, and substance abuse. Sponsored by Children Now and the Kaiser Family Foundation. The Web page includes a list of suggested readings for parents and links to other sites. Available at: http://www.talkingwithkids.org or (800) CHILD-44.

References

Allen, J. P., & Land, D. (1999). Attachment in adolescence. In J. Cassidy & P. R. Shaver (Eds.), *Handbook of attachment: Theory, research, and clinical applications* (pp. 319-335). New York: Guilford.

Alvarado, R., & Kumpfer, K. (2000). Strengthening America's families. *Juvenile Justice, 7*(3), 8-18.

Amato, P. R. (2000). The consequences of divorce for adults and children. *Journal of Marriage and the Family, 62,* 1269-1287.

Astone, N. M., & McLanahan, S. S. (1991). Family structure, parental practices, and high school completion. *American Sociological Review, 56,* 309-320.

Baumrind, D. (1966). Effects of authoritative control on child behavior. *Child Development, 37*(4), 887-907.

Bell-Scott, P., & McKenry, P. C. (1986). Black adolescents and their families. In G. K. Leigh & G. W. Peterson (Eds.), *Adolescents in families* (pp. 410-432). Cincinnati, OH: South-Western.

Bohman, M. (1996). Predisposition to criminality: Swedish adoption studies in retrospect. In G. R. Bock & J. A. Goode (Eds.), *Genetics of criminal and antisocial behavior, Ciba Foundation Symposium 194* (pp. 99-114). Chichester, England: Wiley.

Bronfenbrenner, U. (1972). *Influences on human development.* Hinsdale, IL: Dryden.

Brown, H. (2000, December/January). The search for spirituality. *Parenting,* pp. 114-119.

Bruer, J. (1999). *The myth of the first three years: A new understanding of early brain development and lifelong learning.* New York: Free Press.

Camp Sea Gull and Camp Seafarer. (n.d.). *Camp Sea Gull and Camp Seafarer Family Opportunities.* Retrieved January 24, 2003, from: http://www.seagull-seafarer.org/pages/programs/extseason/fcamp.html.

Coleman, J. S. (1989). The family, the community, and the future of education. In W. J. Weston (Ed.), *Education and the American family: A research synthesis* (pp. 169-185). New York: New York University Press.

Collins, W. A., Maccoby, E. E., Steinberg, L., Hetherington, E. M., & Bornstein, M. H. (2000). Contemporary research on parenting: The case for nature and nurture. *American Psychologist, 55*(2), 218-232.

Cooper, M. L., Shaver, P. R., & Collins, N. L. (1998). Attachment styles, emotion regulation, and adjustment in adolescence. *Journal of Personality and Social Psychology, 74*(5), 1380-1397.

Damon, W. (1997). *The youth charter.* New York: Free Press.

Deater-Deckard, K., Dodge, K. A., Bates, J. E., & Pettit, G. S. (1996). Physical discipline among African American and European American mothers: Links to children's externalizing behaviors. *Developmental Psychology, 32*(6), 1065-1072.

Dinkmeyer, D. C., Dinkmeyer, D. C., & Sperry, L. (1987). *Adlerian counseling and psychotherapy* (2nd ed.). Columbus, OH: Merrill.

Dishion, T. J., & McMahon, R. J. (1998). Parental monitoring and the prevention of child and adolescent problem behavior: A conceptual and empirical formulation. *Clinical Child and Family Psychology Review, 1*(1), 61-75.

Dubrow, N. F., & Garbarino, J. (1989). Living in the war zone: Mothers and young children in public housing development. *Journal of Child Welfare, 68,* 3-20.

Dunifon, R., & Kowaleski-Jones, L. (2002). Who's in the house? Race differences in cohabitation, single parenthood, and child development. *Child Development, 73*(4), 1249-1264.

Fletcher, A. C., Darling, N. E., Steinberg, L., & Dornbusch, S. (1995). The company they keep: Relation of adolescents' adjustment and behavior to their friends' perceptions of authoritative parenting in the social network. *Developmental Psychology, 31*(2), 300-310.

Furstenberg, F., Cook, T., Eccles, J., Elder, G., & Sameroff, A. (1999). *Managing to make it.* Chicago: University of Chicago Press.

Garbarino, J. (1995). *Raising children in a socially toxic environment.* San Francisco: Jossey-Bass.

Garbarino, J., & Bedard, C. (2001). *Parents under siege.* New York: Free Press.

Garbarino, J., & deLara, E. (2002). *And words can hurt forever.* New York: Free Press.

Harris, J. R. (1998). *The nurture assumption: Why children turn out the way they do.* New York: Simon & Schuster.

Hill, R. B. (1972). *The strengths of black families.* New York: Emerson Hall.

Ianni, F. A. (1989). The search for structure and the caring community, *The search for structure: A report on American youth today* (pp. 260-283). New York: Free Press.

Institute for Family Development. (n.d.). *HOMEBUILDERS.* Retrieved March 4, 2003, from: http://www.institutefamily.org/prog_homebuilders.asp.

Keith, T. Z., Keith, P. B., Quirk, K. J., Sperduto, J., Santillo, S., & Killings S. (1998). Longitudinal effects of parent involvement on high school grades: Similarities and differences across gender and ethnic groups. *Journal of School Psychology, 36,* 335-363.

Kerr, M., & Stattin, H. (2000). What parents know, how they know it, and several forms of adolescent adjustment: Further support for a reinterpretation of monitoring. *Developmental Psychology 36*(3), 366-380.

McGue, M., & Lykken, D. T. (1992). Genetic influence on risk of divorce. *Psychological Science, 3*(6), 368-373.

Minuchin, S. (1974). *Families and family therapy.* Cambridge, MA: Harvard University Press.

Olweus, D. (1993). Bullies on the playground: The role of victimization. In C. H. Hart (Ed.), *Children on playgrounds: Research perspectives and applications* (Vol. SUNY series, Children's play in society). Albany: State University of New York Press.

Quinn, W. H., VanDyke, D. J., & Kurth, S. T. (2002). A brief multiple family group model for juvenile first offenders. In C. R. Figley (Ed.), *Brief treatments for the traumatized: A project of the Green Cross Foundation* (Vol. 39, pp. 226-251). Westport, CT: Greenwood.

Richardson, J., Dwyer, K., McGuigan, K., Hansen, W., Dent, C., Johnson, C., Sussman, S., Brannon, B., & Flay, B. (1989). Substance abuse among eighth-grade students who take care of themselves after school. *Pediatrics, 84,* 556-566.

Sampson, R. J., Raudenbush, S. W., & Earls, F. (1997). Neighborhoods and violent crime: A multilevel study of collective efficacy. *Science, 277*(5328), 918-924.

Scales, P., & Leffert, N. (1999). *Developmental assets: A synthesis of the scientific research on adolescent development.* Minneapolis, MN: Search Institute.

Shumow, L., Vandell, D. L., & Posner, J. K. (1998). Harsh, firm, and permissive parenting in low-income families: Relations to children's academic achievement and behavioral adjustment. *Journal of Family Issues, 19,* 483-507.

Smrekar, C., Guthrie, J. W., Owens, D. E., & Sims, P. G. (2001). *March toward excellence: School success and minority student achievement in Department of Defense Schools.* Nashville, TN: Vanderbilt University.

Snyder, H. N., & Sickmund, M. (1999). *Juvenile offenders and victims: 1999 national report.* Washington, DC: Office of Juvenile Justice and Delinquency Prevention.

Stack, C. B., & Burton, L. M. (1993). Kinscripts. *Journal of Comparative Family Studies, 24*(2), 157-170.

Steinberg, L. (2001). We know some things: Parent-adolescent relationships in retrospect and prospect. *Journal of Research on Adolescence, 11*(1), 1-19.

Steinberg, L., Dornbusch, S. M., & Brown, B. (1992). Ethnic differences in adolescent achievement: An ecological perspective. *American Psychologist, 47,* 723-729.

Stinnett, N., Chesser, B., & DeFrain, J. (1979). *Building family strengths: Blueprints for action.* Lincoln: University of Nebraska Press.

Thornberry, T. P., & Krohn, M. D. (1997). Peers, drug use, and delinquency. In D. M. Stoff, J. Breiling, & J. D. Maser (Eds.), *Handbook of antisocial behavior* (pp. 218-233). New York: Wiley.

U.S. Census Bureau. (2001). *Marital status and living arrangements: March 1998.* Retrieved January 31, 2003, from: http://www.census.gov/prod/99pubs/p20-514u.pdf.

U.S. Department of Defense. (2002, September 6). DoDEA students' SAT participation climbs to new high in 2002. *American Forces information services: News articles.* Retrieved January 27, 2003, from DefenseLINK: http://www.defenselink.mil/news/Sep2002/n09062002_200209062.html.

Vitaro, F., Brendgen, M., & Tremblay, R. E. (2000). Influence of deviant friends on delinquency: Searching for moderator variables. *Journal of Abnormal Child Psychology, 28*(4), 313-325.

Wallerstein, J. S., & Kelly, J. B. (1989). *Surviving the breakup: How children and parents cope with divorce.* New York: Basic Books.

Zill, N., & Nord, C. W. (1994). *Running in place: How American families are faring in a changing economy and an individualistic society.* Washington, DC: Child Trends.

9

Enlisting Peers in Developmental Interventions

Principles and Practices

Michael J. Karcher, B. Bradford Brown,
and Douglas W. Elliott

One of the hallmarks of the adolescent stage of life in the United States is a sharp increase in the amount of time that young people spend with peers (Csikszentmihalyi & Larson, 1984). Much of this time is spent in settings unsupervised by adults, and it can involve unhealthy or risky behavior. However, there is considerable evidence of the positive, growth-promoting qualities of peer interaction on adolescent development (Berndt, 1998; Youniss & Smollar, 1985). This has prompted many practitioners to design interventions that enlist adolescents in the reciprocal process of facilitating each other's development. A growing literature on this topic suggests that adults who organize peer interventions can harness young people's potential to help one another by structuring interactions through formal programs; to be effective, however, they must also prevent peer interactions from causing harm.

This chapter focuses on two questions: First, how can peers enhance one another's healthy development during adolescence? Second, how can community agency staff, school counselors, and other adults enlist the positive, growth-enhancing qualities of youth's peer interactions to create positive, peer-based interventions? We begin by reframing the traditional view of peer influences on development and then articulate principles for the design of effective, peer-based interventions. Next, we offer illustrations of several types of programs, highlighting exemplary ones.

Peer Influences on Adolescent Development

Typically, peer influence during adolescence is understood in terms of peer pressure and as a negative force to be strenuously avoided. In fact, the central objective of many intervention programs is to provide young people with "peer pressure resistance" skills, such as in Botvin's (1989) Life Skills Training; the Project Northland curricula (Williams, Perry, Farbakhsh, & Veblen-Mortenson, 1999); and Spivak and Shure's (1974) Interpersonal Problem-Solving Program. Yet this approach provides a one-sided view of peer pressure that leads to an underconceptualized understanding of the complex ways in which peers influence each other's development during adolescence.

Four Modes of Peer Influence

There are four major modes of peer influence (Brown & Theobald, 1998). The power of tacit *group norms* is one form of peer pressure. Adolescents are influenced not only by peers with whom they have formal (e.g., classmate, teammate) and informal relationships (e.g., friend, romantic partner) but also by peers and peer groups with whom they would like to have relationships. Adolescents unintentionally influence one another via efforts to emulate their peers' behaviors in order to achieve desired relationships and to fit in with general social norms (e.g., "But, Mom, *nobody* wears those kind of shoes anymore"). A second mode of influence, which happens more often within the context of ongoing relationships with friends and acquaintances, is *peer pressure*—a direct, intentional effort to shape an adolescent's attitudes or behavior. The two other modes can occur within the context of actual or desired relationships. Peers influence one another by *modeling* or displaying a behavior that either is to be copied or scrupulously avoided. Finally, peers influence one another by *structuring opportunities* or creating situations in which certain behaviors can occur.

For most adolescents, several of these modes may operate simultaneously, and these modes of influence can contradict each other (Brown, 1999). For example, an adolescent may find herself at a party at which close friends encourage her not to drink at the same time that peers she desires to befriend are bonding through the experience of drinking alcohol together. Prosocial and antisocial influences also may emerge within a single peer relationship, as when a close friend encourages trust and empathy within the relationship but at the same time goads the young person to participate in health-compromising, deviant, or unconventional activities.

This same complex set of dynamic influences is apparent in formal groups and structured activities. For example, general group norms will be established among a group of peers in a team, club, or activity, but these norms may either be incompatible or compete with behaviors modeled by group leaders. In adult-structured interventions that involve groups of peers, such as group counseling or in-class guidance curricula, the expectations of adults may conflict with pressures that participants sense from close associates within the group. Dishion, McCord, and Poulin (1999) cautioned that group interventions with teenagers can fail when they bring together a set of deviant peers who succeed in reinforcing each other's inclinations toward deviant activity. Effective interventions must be designed in a way that is mindful of all four modes of influence and with an awareness of direct as well as indirect peer influences.

Reciprocal Influences of Social Support and Interpersonal Skills

Two important ways in which peers foster healthy development are by providing social support to each other and by enhancing one another's interpersonal skills. Teenagers routinely turn to each other for advice, emotional support, and material assistance. An important aspect of autonomy during adolescence is learning to rely on peers as well as parents and other adults for these resources (Cooper, Grotevant, & Condon, 1983; Youniss & Smollar, 1985). Of course, to take advantage of these resources, adolescents must possess effective interpersonal skills. Otherwise, their relationships may be too short-lived, too ridden with conflict and mistrust, or too superficial to provide meaningful support and assistance.

Many adolescents need some help in mastering the interpersonal skills necessary to sustain meaningful peer relationships (Parker & Asher, 1987; Selman, Watts, & Schultz, 1997). These skills can be inculcated or encouraged by adults but also may be fostered by peers. Lerner (1982) suggests that one way in which youth become producers of their own development is by helping each other learn how to take feedback from others and react to conflict in positive ways. One primary developmental task for adolescents is a shift from a childhood self-centeredness toward an understanding of their embeddedness within larger communities (Yates & Youniss, 1996). This social embeddedness facilitates the development of social connectedness and caring, self-confidence, and character, as well as a number of social competencies (Catalano, Berglund, Ryan, Lonczak, & Hawkins, 2002; Karcher & Lindwall, in press). The shift from self-centeredness to social embeddedness is facilitated by peer involvement in the middle and high school years.

Constructive peer influence is contingent on the establishment and maintenance of relationships with prosocial peers as well as mastery of effective interpersonal skills, a reciprocal process. To build positive relationships, adolescents need to use appropriate interpersonal skills. Then, they can draw on the resources within these relationships to master additional prosocial behaviors and achieve important developmental milestones. Peer-based interventions can be aimed at either building social relationships or enhancing interpersonal skills, or both; social support and interpersonal skills are reciprocal.

One of the most important roles that adults can play is helping to structure opportunities and contexts so that the peer interactions are developmental and constructive (Larson, Wilson, Brown, Furstenberg, & Verma, 2002). Yet many youth development programs do not explicitly highlight the possibilities for youth, both youth at promise and those at risk, to creatively work as active agents in fostering the development of their peers and other youths. Evolving definitions of positive youth development programs should be expanded to fully encompass the use of peers in interventions. The definition must move away from the position that programs, information, and skills are to be provided by adults to youth and toward the idea that interventions also can be provided by youth to youth (Camino, 2000). Rather than unilaterally imparting program content or activities to youth, effective youth development programs need to be structured to provide opportunities for youth to participate in reciprocal, cooperative, developmental peer interactions. This may require principles and goals that differ from the traditional approach taken in primary and secondary preventive interventions.

Principles for Developing Peer Interventions

Principles for developing effective peer interventions should reflect both the social changes and expanded environments in which adolescents operate, as well as their unique developmental changes. Youth interventions should be voluntary and structured in ways that promote prosocial engagement with peers. Intervention activities and goals should include perspective taking and identity development. Finally, peer interventions should promote effective interactions among youth from diverse cultural/racial backgrounds and both genders. Each of these principles is elaborated below.

Offer Structured Voluntary Activities

Peer interventions should be structured and voluntary. Larson (2000) suggests that "boredom, alienation, and disconnection" are signs of deficiencies in positive development (p. 170), and he makes this point to reveal the conditions under which positive development occurs. Larson suggests that youth development occurs through activities in which youth are intrinsically motivated, given structure and guidelines by which to engage their environment, and presented with challenges and opportunities for sustained concentration and commitment within a widened peer group. Unless activities are both voluntary and structured (with constraints, rules, and goals), youth tend not to remain attentive, motivated, and persistent (Fantuzzo, Riggio, Connelly, & Dimeff, 1989; Larson, 2000).

The challenge of using voluntary activities with youth who may not initially want to participate is readily apparent; however, it may be just as challenging to effectively implement mandatory youth development activities with intervention-resistant youth (Gibbs, Potter, Barriga, & Liau, 1996). Forcing such youth into involuntary interventions can have deleterious effects (Catterall, 1987; Dishion et al., 1999); involuntary service activities often do not result in the same benefits for youth as do voluntary service activities (Stukas, Clary, & Snyder, 1999). Yet often youth can be motivated either by providing some nominal incentive or giving them the opportunity to choose among a variety of activities. When youth are provided opportunities to exercise their volition, this alone can be motivating, regardless of the options that are available. Simply asking a youth to help often can be sufficient motivation.

Two cross-age peer-tutoring programs, the Time Dollar Cross-Age Peer Tutoring program and the Coca-Cola Valued Youth Program (Case 9.1), offer unique solutions to the challenge of encouraging participation among a broad range of students through the use of extrinsic benefits as incentives for participating in these programs.

> **Case 9.1   Incentives in Peer-Tutoring Programs**
>
> ---
>
> *Time Dollar Cross-Age Peer Tutoring program.* Tutors participating in this program receive one Time Dollar for every hour of tutoring. Peer tutoring in reading and math is available to students for 1 hour after school, 5 days a week, for 28 weeks. After earning 100 Time Dollars and getting their parents to earn 8 Time Dollars by volunteering after school and attending local school council meetings and community-policing meetings, students earn a refurbished computer preloaded with productivity software, a mouse, mouse pad, software manual, and T-shirt. More than 200 students attended the after-school tutoring sessions in one program's first year.
>
> *Coca-Cola Valued Youth Program.* Older at-risk students are paid minimum wage to tutor younger students at least 4 hours per week in the Coca-Cola Valued Youth program, in which typically four grades separate them. Tutors also attend weekly meetings with their teacher coordinators to develop their own literacy and tutoring skills.
>
> ---
>
> SOURCE: Cardenas, Montecel, Supik, & Harris (1992); Washington-Steward (2000).

Although material incentives such as computers and money can be useful tools to encourage youth to join programs, care needs to be exercised in how incentives are employed. Such incentives may be useful in overcoming initial resistance to program participation, but they should not overshadow the main goals of the program. Through its basic structure, the program should offer some intrinsic benefits to youth. In the Time Dollar program, the experience of academic success and esteem of their younger tutees likely increase the tutors' motivation, allowing the goal of earning the computer to recede into the background.

Promote Perspective Taking and Identity Development

Successful social skills require growth in perspective taking and identity (Cooper et al., 1983; Selman, 1980), and for this reason, both have been the focus of many youth interventions (Enright, Colby, & McMullin, 1977; Selman et al., 1997). Miscommunication and misunderstanding among peers may result in adverse consequences such as violence and social isolation. To prevent such consequences, peer mediation activities can teach youth to be empathic, to restate one another's needs or beliefs, and to learn to coordinate perspectives when resolving conflict (Lane-Garon, 1998).

Promoting perspective taking in peer interventions also provides opportunities to directly address and sometimes prevent cross-cultural and cross-gender misunderstanding. For example, when youth begin to base part of their developing identities on their ethnic group memberships, they may initially base these identities on group stereotypes (Erikson, 1968; Matute-Bianchi, 1986). Peer interventions provide unique opportunities to help youth understand between-group and within-group differences and avoid foreclosing on a negative or stereotypical ethnic identity.

The Time Dollar and Coca-Cola Valued Youth programs (see Case 9.1) illustrate the importance of structuring activities that promote perspective taking and identity development. Both programs are designed to involve as tutors those students who might not ordinarily volunteer for such a role (Cardenas, Montecel, Supik, & Harris, 1992). It appears that many of these tutors are attracted to the program by the initial incentive but then become "hooked" by viewing themselves as competent at facilitating their tutees' learning. Within the Time Dollar program, several tutors suggested that seeing other students struggle to learn the material and being able to see themselves as competent in reading and math (sometimes for the first time) helped them take new perspectives on themselves and to feel better about themselves as students (Washington-Steward, 2000).

Promote Intergroup Relations

One of the biggest challenges youth will face in the future is living in communities in which multiple beliefs, opinions, and norms result from increasing ethnic and religious diversity (Larson et al., 2002). Parents who have not experienced this diversity themselves may not be able to fully pre-pare their children to develop the skills necessary to function effectively in such communities. Schools may be the main context in which youth will learn about other ethnic, class, or religious groups. Although schools may teach about diversity and tolerance, such lessons are not likely to become integrated into a youth's repertoire of interpersonal skills unless the youth has a chance to act on and practice using this information in authentic, purposeful peer interactions.

In addition to addressing between-group cultural misunderstandings and stereotypes, youth development programs should structure opportunities for youth to reevaluate within-group stereotypes. Schools and other orga-nizations can structure opportunities for peers within particular ethnic groups to reflect on how their interactions may complicate or enhance their own social or academic development. When peers within a cultural group deliberately or unintentionally encourage their peers to conform to negative group stereotypes, academic as well as social development may be thwarted. One specific problem of within-culture stereotyping, found both in communities and in schools, is referred to as the "burden of acting white," or "racelessness" (Fordham, 1988). This is a within-group phenomenon in which peers influence one another to conform to group stereotypes. Sometimes, these behavioral expectations support an anti-intellectual identity and thereby constrain both within-group and between-group relationships. Such phenomena can be addressed through structured peer dialogues.

Reinforce Prosocial Behaviors and Conventional Norms

Both the Coca-Cola Valued Youth and Time Dollar programs structure activities that encourage youth to demonstrate prosocial behaviors and conventional norms (Fashola & Slavin, 1998). Prosocial behaviors reflect attention by youth to the needs of others and to the expectations of society. Conventional norms are those of societal institutions such as the school, family, and justice system (Jessor & Jessor, 1977). Tutors are trained in how to teach and are supported in their teaching efforts. Thus, tutors are taught a socially valued skill and reinforced for its application.

It is critical that peer interventions be carefully structured to promote prosocial behaviors and skill development and do not inadvertently lead to the reinforcement of antisocial behaviors. There is a growing consensus that peer-based interventions in which high-risk, antisocial, or delinquent youth are aggregated can actually facilitate or aggravate the development of problem behaviors when the peers in these interventions subvert conventional social norms (Catterall, 1987; Dishion et al., 1999). This unintended effect is known as *deviancy training,* which occurs when communication and interaction patterns among delinquent youth undermine conventional norms and reinforce antisocial behavior (Patterson, Dishion, & Yoerger, 2000). Various types of overt and covert peer behaviors can undermine otherwise successful interventions (e.g., Dishion, et al., 1999; Patterson et al., 2000). Even well-designed programs, such as the EQUIP program for juvenile offenders (Gibbs, Potter, & Goldstein, 1995), must be very carefully implemented so as not to inadvertently create a breeding ground for delinquency and antisocial behavior.

One step that can be taken to inhibit deviancy training in peer interventions is to include a balanced number of high- and low-risk youth in peer or group interventions. But including youth who differ in their risk status will help only if the interactions in that dyad or group are actively structured by adults to support conventional norms and to reinforce prosocial behaviors. It may be necessary to work directly with influential peers or with whole groups of youth themselves to get their commitment to avoid making antisocial or authority-undermining jokes, statements, and behaviors. When youth feel that refraining from undermining the program's goals will truly be helpful to others, such as to younger students in the group, and when refraining does not detract from their own status among their peers, even aggressive, delinquent, and underachieving youth may be inclined to be helpful. Beyond the peers themselves, it may be helpful (a) to work with parents and school administrators to better understand contextual or cultural variations in what constitutes antisocial behavior or (b) to create a committee of adults and/or peers to establish guidelines for the program and to make decisions about what is appropriate behavior (Portner, 2001). It also may be helpful to include or consult with psychologists or other professionals to identify problem behaviors specific to a culture, age, or particular peer group and to make suggestions for tailoring program activities to promote specific developmental goals (Lerner, De Stefanis, & Ladd, 1998).

Meet the Needs of Girls as Well as Boys

What may be an effective intervention for boys may not be as effective for girls. For example, a recent study of mentoring found that program effects depended on the development of a significant bond between mentors and mentees. Social discussions and recreational activities were more helpful than academically focused interactions in the development of this significant interpersonal relationship (DuBois, Neville, Parra, & Pugh-Lilly, 2002), yet overall, the effect of these interactions on the mentor's eventual significance to the mentee was greater for boys than for girls. Boys also tend to benefit more than girls from serving as tutors to younger children (Yogev & Ronen, 1982); yet girls are more likely to volunteer to participate as tutors or volunteers in service-learning projects and peer interventions (Stukas et al., 1999). One study of 374 children in 15 peer tutoring programs found that same-sex pairs were good for male tutors, male tutees, and female tutees but not for female tutors (Topping & Whiteley, 1993); female-male pairs were good for the female tutors but not for their male tutees. Peer support interventions appear to be especially helpful to teenage mothers (Rhodes, Ebert, & Fischer, 1992). Girls may need peer interventions that allow them to practice particular communication skills, such as refusal skills for managing sexual advances (Foshee et al., 1996; Way, 1995). Better understanding the dynamics involved in these differential outcomes presents important challenges for future researchers and program coordinators. When developing peer interventions, it is critical to consider how the intervention approach and goals will be received differently by boys and girls.

Types of Peer Intervention Programs

Some peer interventions, like peer mentoring or peer mediation, are stand-alone programs; others occur within larger intervention programs. In their review of 25 empirically supported, positive youth development programs, Catalano et al. (2002) describe no programs that were solely peer-helping-peer interventions, but five of the programs they describe have significant peer-helping-peer intervention components that present unique opportunities for developing prosocial interpersonal relationships among peers (Catalano et al., 2002; Dryfoos, 1990). These components include peer counseling, peer mediation, peer mentoring, peer tutoring, and peer teaching. In this section, we review each of these peer intervention components and briefly highlight peer components within larger interventions in schools.

Peer Counseling Without Direct Adult Guidance

Peer counseling is based on the idea that youth may best be understood by other youth and that peers often can be the most empathic with one another's experiences and provide the best suggestions to help other youth with their problems (Haszouri & Smith, 1991). Peer counseling has not received as much research attention as other peer interventions, and this may reflect the fact that allowing adolescents to counsel their peers may be unwise if they are not carefully supervised. Peer counselors without sufficient training, supervision, and personal maturity may do more harm than good.

Peer counseling has been recommended as particularly useful for youth of color (Gibbs, 1989; LaFromboise & Bigfoot, 1988). However, there is evidence that cross-race peer counseling requires additional training. One purpose of training should be to help peer counselors understand cultural differences in the use of direct versus indirect speech (Delpit, 1988) and of self-disclosure. For example, in a study of undergraduates engaged in peer counseling (Berg & Wright-Buckley, 1988), African American students felt more positively about their experiences and about their white peer counselors when the peer counselors were more self-disclosing.

Pair Counseling With Direct Adult Guidance

Pair counseling, like peer counseling, is based on the philosophy that reciprocal interactions between youth provide unique catalysts for developmental growth (Selman et al., 1997). Unlike peer counseling, in duo- and pair counseling, neither youth is given "authority" over the other, and an adult counselor guides the intervention. Neither youth is seen solely as the counselor or the counselee. Both come to the interaction with their own problems and their own strengths, and usually they are similar in age and developmental maturity. The counselor's goal is to help them learn to interact more maturely and to better understand the importance of friendships (Selman & Schultz, 1990). Pair counseling has been shown to reduce externalizing behaviors and increase both perspective-taking and negotiation skills (Karcher & Lewis, 2002). The assumption is that if youth can be helped to develop a mature and satisfying relationship in the pair, then these skills can be generalized to other relationships (Karcher, 2002; Lieberman & Smith, 1991; Nakkula & Selman, 1991).

Pair counseling has been practiced primarily with older elementary school children and with middle school youth because it is oriented around play, and older youth usually prefer more verbal interventions. Pair counseling with older youth has been conducted primarily in residential treatment contexts, where their social skills deficits are typically more severe (Karcher & Lewis, 2002; Moody, 1997; Selman et al., 1997). Adult counselors also could use pair counseling to help adolescents in couples better understand how their individual behaviors affect their partners and their ongoing relationships and thereby increase the likelihood of satisfaction and success in their current and future relationships.

Peers as Mediators, Tutors, and Mentors

In peer mediation, peer tutoring, and peer mentoring, a clearly delineated, hierarchical relationship exists between the two peers. In the case of peer mentoring, often the youth differ in age; yet in peer mediation and peer tutoring, it is not uncommon for youth in the same grade to work with each other.

Peer Mediation

Peer mediation programs have grown steadily in popularity and number over the past 15 years and can be found in many school districts and in elementary, middle, and high schools (Johnson & Johnson, 1996). Peer mediation is designed to provide two or more youth experiencing interpersonal conflicts some assistance from a trained peer before adult intervention becomes necessary. It can both reduce the demand for intervention by adults in the school and help students learn problem-solving skills. Peer mediators are trained to help the two youth in conflict to more effectively talk about their problems and generate mutually satisfactory resolutions to their problems. The mediators help the youth articulate their own unique perspectives and restate each other's points of view (Lane-Garon, 1998). One problem with peer mediation programs is that peers rarely request these services on their own. Therefore, principals, teachers, or other disciplinarians, who often are pressured to reach swift resolutions, must take time to promote this intermediate intervention option.

Youth receiving mediation from peers may benefit, first, from being able to resolve their immediate problems by reaching an agreed-upon solution, preventing enduring hostilities, and lessening future conflicts. For this reason, peer mediation programs have been incorporated into many larger violence prevention interventions in schools (Aber, Jones, Brown, Chaudry, & Samples, 1998). Second, youth have the opportunity to practice interpersonal skills they can later transfer to other contexts and relationships, and mediators often become more integrally involved in the school.

Peer Tutoring

Peer tutors help other students develop skills or learn information about a particular subject. Peer tutoring is less hierarchical in nature than peer mediation, and therefore youth may be more likely to request peer tutoring than peer mediation. Peer tutoring typically lasts longer than mediation, sometimes the course of an academic year.

Both the tutor and the tutee benefit socially and academically from peer tutoring (Greenwood, Delquadri, & Hall, 1989; Topping & Whiteley, 1993). Cross-age and peer tutoring provided by children in elementary school may not be as effective as tutoring from adolescent peer tutors (Jenkins, Jewell, Leicester, Jenkins, & Troutner, 1991), possibly because older youth better teach problem solving and explain difficult concepts.

Tutors need sufficient training both in how to present information and in how to communicate effectively with their tutees. Seventh graders who served as tutors to each other have demonstrated significantly greater learning when the tutors were trained to ask comprehension and thought-provoking questions and to explain the material effectively (King, Staffeiri, & Adelgais, 1998). In addition, the tutees trained to ask questions of their peer tutors learned more. Peer tutors have reported stronger bonding to school; increased self-esteem, empathy, and altruism; and improved academic skills after serving as tutors (Srebnik & Elias, 1993; Switzer, Simmons, Dew, Regalski, & Wang, 1995; Trapani & Gettinger, 1989; Yogev & Ronen, 1982).

Some of the benefits of peer-tutoring programs result from the recruitment of tutors from populations of students who traditionally do not participate in tutoring programs. The Time Dollar program (described in Case 9.1) operates in low-income school districts, and the Coca-Cola Valued Youth program targets at-risk students. Evaluations of the Coca-Cola Valued Youth program suggest that after participating, the tutors were more committed to school and felt better about school, as demonstrated by improved grades, reduced absenteeism, and lower dropout rates than a control group of similar students who did not participate in the program (Cardenas et al., 1992). Although the evaluation of the Time Dollar program did not specifically investigate its effect on tutors, anecdotal information suggests similar benefits for tutors from participating in its program, especially for tutors who came from special education classes, who had attention deficits, or who had past behavior problems in the school (Washington-Steward, 2000).

Peer and Cross-Age Mentoring

Because few youth view others of their same age as their mentors, cross-age mentoring is more common than same-age peer mentoring (Hamilton & Darling, 1989). Often, high school students mentor younger students, such as when a senior mentors a freshman or a high school student mentors a middle or elementary student (Dennison, 2000; Karcher, Davis, & Powell, 2002). However, same-age peer mentoring also has been conducted. Most often, this has been regular education with special education students, high-achieving with lower-achieving students, or delinquent with previously delinquent youths (Sheehan, DiCara, LeBailly, & Christoffel, 1999). As with other peer interventions, it appears that involvement as a peer mentor has the capacity to develop character and strengthen connectedness to school (Karcher & Lindwall, in press; Sheehan et al., 1999; Srebnik & Elias, 1993) as well as to discourage youth involvement in risk-taking behavior outside of school (McNamara, 2000). The main factors of effective mentoring appear to be not the age of the mentor, but the degree of support, training, supervision, and guidance mentors are provided for their work. For both adults and youth mentors, mentors who receive ongoing training and supervision have a bigger impact than those who do not (DuBois, Holloway, Valentine, & Cooper, 2002).

School-Based Peer Intervention Programs

Schools are a primary context in which one can enlist youth to work with peers in youth development activities and programs. Although most of the youth development programs described by Roth, Brooks-Gunn, Murray, & Foster (1998) are community based, it appears that most of the youth development programs that truly utilize peers as agents of change occur within the school. Peer interventions that provide leadership, facilitator, mediator, tutor, and mentor roles can be found in several contexts within the school. Some peer interventions occur among pairs of youth, while other peer interventions occur within larger group or classroom contexts. Others take place outside the classroom, either during or after school.

Developing positive peer relations is critical to newcomers in every school. A significant need among youth transitioning into new schools and communities is the opportunity to meet, interact with, and develop social bonds with peers, particularly for youth with disabilities, low self-esteem, or poor social skills (Cornille, Bayer, & Smyth, 1983). The STEP (School Transitional Environment Project) program (Felner et al., 1993) attempts to reorganize peer relationships and facilitate a sense of connectedness to peers transitioning to a new school. This is done by organizing the school environment and schedule to create a small community within the school in which peers become more familiar with one another and minimize negative interactions with upperclassmen.

Numerous youth intervention and school guidance curricula involve peer interaction activities designed to reduce problem behaviors (e.g., substance use or violence) or promote specific types of skills (e.g., refusal skills, negotiation skills training). These have been summarized elsewhere (Catalano et al., 2002; Roth et al., 1998). The Teen Outreach Program (Allen, Kuperminc, Philliber, & Herre, 1994) uses a cross-age teaching experience to affect positive growth in middle and high school students. The BrainPower Program (Hudley & Friday, 1996) and the Anger Coping Program (Lochman, Dunn, & Klimesdougan, 1993) enlist youth to help their peers explore and correct their misattributions and thereby help youth become more empathic, sophisticated in their social perspective taking, and effective in negotiating. In fact, many youth programs that involve peer components target critical problems in peer relations and social skills, such as the attribution biases of aggressive youth, poor negotiation skills, limited empathy and perspective taking, intergroup hostilities, difficulty interpreting nonverbal communication cues, and inadequate self-management and problem-solving skills (e.g., Embry, Flannery, Vazsonyi, Powell, & Atha, 1996).

Many large-scale intervention programs attempt to capitalize on the power and influence of peer interactions. Although the core purpose of these programs may not be to develop positive peer relations, the programs create structured opportunities for youths to have a positive impact on their peers en route to achieving other developmental goals. Two examples of such programs are the Adolescent Transitions Project and Project Northland (Case 9.2).

Case 9.2   Peer Interventions in Schools

The Adolescent Transitions Program. A comprehensive prevention program aimed at middle-school-aged teens, the Adolescent Transitions Project works with parents, schools, and young teens to prevent problem behaviors by developing individual skills and changing the school environment. Although largely curriculum based, the program contains a peer component in which adolescents meet weekly in groups of six to eight participants for 12 sessions. An adult counselor meets with these groups of adolescents to give the teens a chance to learn, discuss, and practice social skills. In addition to the adult counselor, the groups also involve a peer counselor, usually a high school student who has successfully completed the Adolescents Transitions Program. The peer counselor acts as a role model for the younger teens and as a bridge between the younger teens and the adult counselor. Sometimes, the peer counselor attempts to connect with youth disliked by the rest of group and helps involve them in the group.

Project Northland. A comprehensive intervention program that aims to delay the onset of and reduce the use of alcohol by adolescents, Project Northland works with schools, communities, and the media to influence community norms associated with the demand, supply, and availability of alcohol among adolescents. Project Northland is implemented in phases, addressing the demand for alcohol in Phase 1 and the supply of alcohol in Phase 2. In both phases, adolescents are recruited to assist in affecting community norms. In Phase 1, middle school teens are helped to plan, organize, and promote alcohol-free social events for their peers. These teens are given a 1-day leadership training session that teaches them the skills they need to develop the social activities. In Phase 2, high school teens are recruited to work with part-time adult coordinators to form youth action teams. In addition to having the same mandate

(Continued)

Case 9.2   (Continued)

as the middle school youth leaders to plan alcohol-free alternative social activities, the youth action teams also participate in other activities that affect the community norms concerning alcohol use by adolescents, for example, by producing community-specific videos about adolescent alcohol use and its negative consequences.

SOURCE: Dishion, Kauanagh, Schneiger, Nelson, & Kaufman (2002); Williams et al. (1999).

Levels of Involvement

The impact that the youth components of these programs have on their participants appears to depend on the adolescent's level of involvement. Although the comprehensive Adolescent Transitions Program (ATP) has resulted in several positive outcomes for youth, involvement in the ATP peer group component had a detrimental effect on some youth (Andrews, Soberman, & Dishion, 1995; Dishion et al., 1999). Instead of reinforcing positive social skills, the peer group meetings provided a venue for deviancy training, in which members reinforced each other's negative behaviors. However, teens who went beyond simply attending the meetings and developed close relationships with their peer counselors exhibited fewer problem behaviors at the conclusion of the program than teens with more distant relationships with their peer counselors (Andrews et al., 1995; Dishion et al., 2001).

Similarly, the effects of Project Northland appear to depend on the youth's level of involvement in the program. Overall, the program appeared to reduce the tendency of participating youth to use alcohol compared with control group youth not receiving the intervention, but the level of involvement that adolescents had in the program had an additional effect (Komro & Perry, 1996). For example, after participating, the youth leaders and the youth action teams (who planned the activities) exhibited a lower tendency to use alcohol than teens who had only attended the activities.

Structured and Voluntary Participation

Both the ATP and Project Northland (see Case 9.2) illustrate that the peer components of these programs are more successful when participation is structured and voluntary. The youth leaders in Project Northland, although recruited by adults, volunteer their time and effort. Youth who volunteer are given a clear and concise goal: to reduce the use of alcohol by teens by affecting community norms associated with drinking. In addition to receiving training in planning social activities, youth leaders rely on support and suggestions from school staff. The skills, support, and clear mandate that the youth are given to guide their efforts allow the teens to better focus their time and energy into social activities that are incompatible with alcohol use.

Opportunities to Learn and Use Prosocial Behaviors

The impact of promoting prosocial behaviors is clearly illustrated in Project Northland and ATP. Adolescents who either become youth leaders or members of the youth action teams are provided the opportunity and support they need to have a positive impact on their peers. Youth involved in the peer component of Project Northland go beyond the classroom curriculum to teach the dangers of adolescent alcohol use. The youth leaders do not simply learn about the dangers associated with adolescent alcohol use but also gain skills that enable them to address the problem in positive ways, such as by planning and promoting alcohol-free social activities for their peers. The youth action team members can even have an impact on the community beyond that of their peers, such as by addressing policies concerning the sale of alcohol at community events, bringing speakers to educate students on the negative effects of adolescent alcohol use, and creating community-specific videos about adolescent alcohol use. Thus, the prosocial skills that the youth leaders learn through participating in Project Northland can have a positive effect on their peers, their community, and their own developing identities.

Conclusions

The evolving definition for youth development programs should be expanded to include peers as catalysts rather than solely as targets of growth. In this review of peer interventions, we have highlighted the numerous opportunities available to include youth who serve as leaders, guides, and facilitators to influence the development of their peers and younger youth through mentoring, tutoring, mediating, and teaching. Adults can facilitate developmental intervention programs that help peers to support one another, model and encourage one another's social skills development, and facilitate interpersonal understanding across age, gender, cultural and peer groups. Adults can guide peers within larger programs and activities to have a positive influence on one another's development. However, program coordinators must consider not only tacit, direct, and indirect peer influences but also the likelihood that negative peer influences may undermine the promotion of conventional, prosocial behaviors in their programs. Nevertheless, the advantages of enlisting peers as resources in youth development programs are great and often go untapped, and they suggest that peer interventions should be included whenever possible.

References

Aber, J. L., Jones, S. M., Brown, J. L., Chaudry, N., & Samples, F. (1998). Resolving conflict creatively: Evaluating the developmental effects of a school-based violence prevention program in neighborhood and classroom context. *Development and Psychopathology, 10,* 187-213.

Allen, J. P., Kuperminc, G., Philliber, S., & Herre, K. (1994). Programmatic prevention of adolescent problem behaviors: The role of autonomy, relatedness, and volunteer service in the Teen Outreach Program. *American Journal of Community Psychology, 22*(5), 617-638.

Andrews, D. W., Soberman, L. H., & Dishion, T. J. (1995). The adolescent transitions program for high-risk teens and their parents: Toward a school-based intervention. *Education & Treatment of Children, 18*(4), 478-498.

Berg, J. H., & Wright-Buckley, C. (1988). Effects of racial similarity and interview intimacy in peer counseling dialogue. *Journal of Counseling Psychology, 35*(4), 377-384.

Berndt, T. J. (1998). Exploring the effects of friendship quality on social development. In W. M. Bukowski & A. F. Newcomb (Eds.), *The company they keep* (pp. 346-365). New York: Cambridge University Press.

Botvin, G. J. (1989). *Life skills training teacher's manual.* New York: Smithfield.

Brown, B. B. (1999). Measuring the peer environment of American adolescents. In S. L. Friedman & T. D. Wachs (Eds.), *Measuring environment across the life span: Emerging methods and concepts* (pp. 59-90). Washington, DC: American Psychological Association.

Brown, B. B., & Theobald, W. (1998). Learning contexts beyond the classroom: Extracurricular activities, community organizations, and peer groups. In K. Borman & B. Schneider (Eds.), *The adolescent years: Social influences and educational challenges* (pp. 109-141). Chicago: National Society for the Study of Education.

Camino, L. A. (2000). Putting youth-adolescent partnerships to work for community change: Lessons from volunteers across the country. *CYD Journal: Community Youth Development,* 127-131.

Cardenas, J. A., Montecel, M. R., Supik, J. D., & Harris, R. J. (1992). The Coca-Cola Valued Youth Program: Dropout prevention strategies for at-risk students. *Texas Researcher, 3,* 111-130.

Catalano, R. F., Berglund, M. L., Ryan, J. A. M., Lonczak, H. S., & Hawkins, J. D. (2002, June 24). Positive youth development in the United States: Research findings on evaluations of positive youth development programs. *Prevention & Treatment, 5,* Article 15. Retrieved October 9, 2002, from: http://journals.apa.org/prevention/volume2005/pre0050015a.html.

Catterall, J. S. (1987). An intensive group counseling dropout prevention intervention: Some cautions on isolating at-risk adolescents within high schools. *American Educational Research Journal, 24*(4), 521-540.

Cooper, C. R., Grotevant, H. D., & Condon, S. M. (1983). Individuality and connectedness in the family as a context for adolescent identity formation and role-taking skill. *New Directions for Child Development, 22,* 43-59.

Cornille, T. A., Bayer, A. E., & Smyth, C. K. (1983). Schools and newcomers: A national survey of innovative programs. *Personnel & Guidance Journal, 62*(4), 229-236.

Csikszentmihalyi, M., & Larson, R. (1984). *Being adolescent.* New York: Basic Books.

Delpit, L. (1988). The silenced dialogue: Power and pedagogy in educating other people's children. *Harvard Educational Review, 58*(3), 280-298.

Dennison, S. (2000). A win-win peer mentoring and tutoring program: A collaborative model. *The Journal of Primary Prevention, 20*(3), 161-174.

Dishion, T. J., Kavanagh, K., Schneiger, A., Nelson, S., & Kaufman, N. K. (2002). Preventing early adolescent substance use: A family-centered strategy for the public middle school. *Prevention Science, 3*(3), 191-201.

Dishion, T. J., McCord, J., & Poulin, F. (1999). When interventions harm: Peer groups and problem behavior. *American Psychologist, 54,* 755-764.

Dryfoos, J. G. (1990). *Adolescents at risk: Prevalence and prevention.* New York: Oxford University Press.

DuBois, D. L., Holloway, B. E., Valentine, J. C., & Cooper, H. (2002). Effectiveness of mentoring programs for youth: A meta-analytic review. *American Journal of Community Psychology, 30,* 157-197.

DuBois, D. L., Neville, H. A., Parra, G. R., & Pugh-Lilly, A. O. (2002, Spring). Testing a new model of mentoring. *New Directions for Youth Development, 93,* 21-57.

Embry, D. D., Flannery, D. J., Vazsonyi, A. T., Powell, K. E., & Atha, H. (1996). PeaceBuilders: A theoretically driven, school based model for early violence prevention. *American Journal of Preventive Medicine, 12*(5), 91-100.

Enright, R. D., Colby, S., & McMullin, I. (1977). A social-cognitive developmental intervention with sixth and first graders. *The Counseling Psychologist, 6*(4), 10-12.

Erikson, E. H. (1968). *Identity: Youth and crisis.* New York: Norton.

Fantuzzo, J. W., Riggio, R. E., Connelly, S., & Dimeff, L. A. (1989). Effects of reciprocal peer tutoring on academic achievement and psychological adjustment: A component analysis. *Journal of Educational Psychology, 81*(2), 173-177.

Fashola, O. S., & Slavin, R. E. (1998). Effective dropout prevention and college attendance programs for students placed at risk. *Journal of Education for Students Placed at Risk, 3*(2), 159-183.

Felner, R. D., Brand, S., Adan, A. M., Mulhall, P. F., Flowers, N., Sartain, B., & DuBois, D. L. (1993). Restructuring the ecology of the school as an approach to prevention during school transitions: Longitudinal follow-ups and extensions of the School Transitional Environment Project (STEP). *Prevention in Human Services, 10,* 103-136.

Fordham, S. (1988). Racelessness as a factor in Black students' school success: Pragmatic strategy or pyrrhic victory? *Harvard Educational Review, 58*(1), 54-82.

Foshee, V. A., Linder, G. F., Bauman, K. E., Langwick, S. A., Arriaga, X. B., Heath, J. L., McMahon, P. M., & Bangdiwala, S. (1996). The safe dates project: Theoretical basis, evaluation design, and selected baseline findings. *American Journal of Preventive Medicine, 12*(5), 39-47.

Gibbs, J. C., Potter, G. B., Barriga, A. Q., & Liau, A. K. (1996). Developing the helping skills and prosocial motivation of aggressive adolescents in peer group programs. *Aggression & Violent Behavior, 1*(3), 283-305.

Gibbs, J. C., Potter, G. B., & Goldstein, A. P. (1995). *The EQUIP program: Teaching youth to think and act responsibly through a peer-helping approach.* Champaign, IL: Research Press.

Gibbs, J. T. (1989). Biracial adolescents. In J. T. Gibbs & L. N. Huang (Eds.), *Children of color: Psychological interventions with minority youth* (pp. 322-350). San Francisco: Jossey-Bass.

Greenwood, C. R., Delquadri, J. C., & Hall, R. V. (1989). Longitudinal effects of classwide peer tutoring. *Journal of Educational Psychology, 81*(3), 371-383.

Hamilton, S. F., & Darling, N. (1989). Mentors in adolescents' lives. In K. Hurrelmann & U. Engel (Eds.), *The social world of adolescents: International perspectives. Prevention and intervention in childhood and adolescence* (Vol. 5, pp. 121-139). Berlin: Walter de Gruyter.

Haszouri, S., & Smith, M. (1991). *Peer listening in the middle school: Training activities for students.* Minneapolis, MN: Educational Media Corporation.

Hudley, C., & Friday, J. (1996). Attributional bias and reactive aggression. *American Journal of Preventive Medicine, 12*(5), 75-81.

Jenkins, J. R., Jewell, M., Leicester, N., Jenkins, L., & Troutner, N. M. (1991). Development of a school building model for educating students with handicaps and at-risk students in general education classrooms. *Journal of Learning Disabilities, 24*(5), 311-320.

Jessor, R., & Jessor, S. L. (1977). *Problem behavior and psychological development: A longitudinal study of youth.* New York: Academic Press.

Johnson, D. W., & Johnson, R. T. (1996). Conflict resolution and peer mediation programs in elementary and secondary schools. *Review of Educational Research, 66*(4), 459-506.

Karcher, M. J. (2002). The principles and practice of pair counseling: A dyadic play therapy for aggressive, withdrawn, and socially immature youth. *International Journal of Play Therapy, 11*(2), 121-147.

Karcher, M. J., Davis, C., & Powell, B. (2002). Developmental mentoring in the schools: Testing connectedness as a mediating variable in the promotion of academic achievement. *The School Community Journal, 12*(2), 36-52.

Karcher, M. J., & Lewis, S. S. (2002). Pair counseling: The effects of a dyadic developmental play therapy on interpersonal understanding and externalizing behaviors. *International Journal of Play Therapy, 11*(1), 19-41.

Karcher, M. J., & Lindwall, J. (in press). Social interest, connectedness, and challenging experiences. What makes high school mentors persist? *Journal of Individual Psychology.*

Komro, K. A., & Perry, C. L. (1996). Peer-planned activities for preventing alcohol use among young adolescents. *Journal of School Health, 66*(9), 328-334.

King, A., Staffeiri, A., & Adelgais, A. (1998). Mutual peer tutoring: Effects of structuring tutorial interaction to scaffold peer learning. *Journal of Educational Psychology, 90*(1), 134-152.

LaFromboise, T. D., & Bigfoot, D. S. (1988). Cultural and cognitive considerations in the prevention of American Indian adolescent suicide (Special issue: Mental health research and service issues for minority youth). *Journal of Adolescence, 11*(2), 139-153.

Lane-Garon, P. (1998). Developmental considerations: Encouraging perspective taking in student mediators. *Mediation Quarterly, 16*(2), 201-217.

Larson, R. W. (2000). Toward a psychology of positive youth development. *American Psychologist, 55*(1), 170-183.

Larson, R. W., Wilson, S., Brown, B. B., Furstenberg, F. F., & Verma, S. (2002). Changes in adolescents' interpersonal experiences: Are they being prepared for adult relationships in the twenty-first century? *Journal of Research on Adolescence, 12*(1), 31-68.

Lerner, R. M. (1982). Children and adolescents as producers of their own development. *Developmental Review, 2*(4), 342-370.

Lerner, R. M., De Stefanis, I., & Ladd, G. T. (1998). Promoting positive youth development: Collaborative opportunities. *Children's Services: Social Policy, Research, and Practice, 1*(2), 83-109.

Lieberman, S. N., & Smith, L. B. (1991). Duo therapy: A bridge to the world of peers for the ego-impaired child. *Journal of Child & Adolescent Group Therapy, 1*(4), 243-252.

Lochman, J. E., Dunn, S. E., & Klimesdougan, B. (1993). An intervention and consultation model from a social cognitive perspective: A description of the anger coping program. *School Psychology Review, 22*(3), 458-471.

Matute-Bianchi, M. E. (1986). Ethnic identities and patterns of school success and failure among Mexican-descent and Japanese-American students in a Californian high school. *American Journal of Education, 95,* 233-255.

McNamara, K. (2000). Outcomes associated with service involvement among disengaged youth. *Journal of Drug Education, 30*(2), 229-245.

Moody, E. E. (1997). Pair counseling: An intervention for disturbed children when nothing else works. *Elementary School Guidance and Counseling, 31,* 171-179.

Nakkula, M. J., & Selman, R. L. (1991). How people "treat" each other: Pair therapy as a context for the development of interpersonal ethics. In W. Kurtines & J. Gewirtz (Eds.), *Handbook of moral development and behavior* (pp. 179-211). Hillsdale, NJ: Lawrence Erlbaum.

Parker, J. G., & Asher, S. R. (1987). Peer relations and later personal adjustment: Are low-accepted children at risk? *Psychological Bulletin, 102*(3), 357-389.

Patterson, G. R., Dishion, T. J., & Yoerger, K. (2000). Adolescent growth in new forms of problem behavior: Macro- and micro-peer dynamics. *Prevention Sciences, 1,* 3-13.

Portner, H. (2001). *Training mentors is not enough: Everything else schools and districts need to do.* Thousand Oaks, CA: Corwin.

Rhodes, J. E., Ebert, L., & Fischer, K. (1992). Natural mentors: An overlooked resource in the social networks of young, African American mothers. *American Journal of Community Psychology, 20*(4), 445-461.

Roth, J., Brooks-Gunn, J., Murray, L., & Foster, W. (1998). Promoting healthy adolescents: Synthesis of youth development program evaluations. *Journal of Research on Adolescence, 8*(4), 423-459.

Selman, R. L. (1980). *The growth of interpersonal understanding: Developmental and clinical analyses.* New York: Academic Press.

Selman, R. L., & Schultz, L. H. (1990). *Making a friend in youth: Developmental theory and pair therapy.* Chicago: University of Chicago Press.

Selman, R. L., Watts, C. L., & Schultz, L. H. (Eds.). (1997). *Fostering friendship: Pair therapy for treatment and prevention.* Hawthorne, New York: Aldine de Gruyter.

Sheehan, K., DiCara, J. A., LeBailly, S., & Christoffel, K. K. (1999). Adapting the gang model: Peer mentoring for violence prevention. *Pediatrics, 104*(1), 50-54.

Spivak, G., & Shure, M. B. (1974). *Social adjustment of young children: A cognitive approach to solving real life problems.* San Francisco: Jossey-Bass.

Srebnik, D. S., & Elias, M. J. (1993). An ecological, interpersonal skills approach to drop-out prevention. *American Journal of Orthopsychiatry, 63*(4), 526-535.

Stukas, A. Jr., Clary, E. G., & Snyder, M. (1999). Service learning: Who benefits and why. *Social Policy Report, 13*(4), 1-20.

Switzer, G. E., Simmons, R. G., Dew, M. A., Regalski, J. M., & Wang, C. H. (1995). The effect of a school-based helper program on adolescent self-image, attitudes, and behavior. *Journal of Early Adolescence, 15,* 429-455.

Topping, K., & Whiteley, M. (1993). Sex differences in the effectiveness of peer tutoring. *School Psychology International, 14,* 57-67.

Trapani, C., & Gettinger, M. (1989). Effects of social skills training and cross-age tutoring on academic achievement and social behaviors of boys with learning disabilities. *Journal of Research and Development in Education, 22*(4), 1-9.

Washington-Steward, E. (2000, August). *10,000 Tutors Partnership Program evaluation.* Retrieved February 28, 2003, from: http://www.timedollartutoring.org/.

Way, N. (1995). "Can't you see the courage, the strength that I have?": Listening to urban adolescent girls speak about their relationships. *Psychology of Women Quarterly, 19*(1), 107-128.

Williams, C. L., Perry, C. L., Farbakhsh, K., & Veblen-Mortenson, S. (1999). Project Northland: Comprehensive alcohol use prevention for young adolescents, their parents, schools, peers and communities. *Journal of Studies on Alcohol, 13,* 112-124.

Yates, M., & Youniss, J. (1996). A developmental perspective on community service in adolescence. *Social Development, 5,* 85-111.

Yogev, A., & Ronen, R. (1982). Cross-age tutoring: Effects on tutors' attributions. *Journal of Educational Research, 75,* 261-268.

Youniss, J., & Smollar, J. (1985). *Adolescent relations with mothers, fathers, and friends.* Chicago: University of Chicago Press.

10

How Neighborhoods
Matter for Youth Development

Ray Swisher and Janis Whitlock

Neighborhoods matter to youth development. From intelligence test scores as early as age 3, to positive engagement in educational and extracurricular activities in adolescence, and ultimately, to socioeconomic and psychosocial well-being in adulthood, the quality of the neighborhood in which one lives makes a difference.

To use this fact to shape policies and programs, we must know precisely what it is about a neighborhood that matters to youth development. Is it simply the affluence of neighbors that promotes positive outcomes for youth? Or is it other resources associated with advantaged neighborhoods, such as informal social control, greater safety, community involvement, intergenerational relationships, quality schools, and local institutions?

An important conceptual issue is how to define neighborhoods. At a minimum, neighborhoods have a geographic component, typically demarcated by identifiable physical boundaries such as major streets, railroad tracks, rivers, or other landmarks. Most important from a youth development perspective, however, are the social and perceptual components of neighborhoods. At their core, neighborhoods are constituted by social interactions between residents. As we will discuss later, these relationships among youth, their friends and peers, parents, teachers, and other adults in the community are important resources on which youth development efforts attempt to build. Though exact descriptions may vary, even between next-door neighbors, neighborhood definitions also typically involve a sense of shared history and identity for residents. In this chapter, we use an ecological perspective to organize our review of the current neighborhood research literature, highlight exemplary programs, and suggest implications for policy and program development.

How Neighborhoods Matter

We begin by reviewing one exemplary program, YouthBuild, which embodies many of the components of successful neighborhood-based youth development initiatives. Examining those components reveals some of the ways in which neighborhoods can foster youth development.

Started in 1978 as a partnership between youth and adults in East Harlem, New York, YouthBuild today is a comprehensive neighborhood-based program combining rehabilitation of low-income housing with youth education, job training, and leadership development. Although improving the stock of low-income housing for the homeless is a primary physical product, the mission and goals of the program also emphasize assisting youth to transform themselves and their communities. As stated on the YouthBuild (2003) Web site, the program aims to help youth "build skills and increase awareness of issues confronting the community and act decisively to improve it." Thus, in addition to gaining practical skills such as carpentry, youth actively work on their GEDs or high school diplomas, receive a wide variety of supportive services such as life skills and career counseling, participate in leadership development and community service projects, and may be eligible for educational scholarships.

Perhaps most unique is the program's emphasis on youth governance. YouthBuild participants are not simply recipients of services, but become fully engaged and active leaders in their communities (see Case 10.1). The success of the East Harlem program subsequently led to the development of the national YouthBuild organization, economic sponsorship by the Department of Housing and Urban Development, and myriad foundation and other private sources of funding. Today, there are more than 200 local YouthBuild programs around the country (YouthBuild, 2003).

Case 10.1 From Harlem to Capitol Hill

The story of one successful student, Trevor Daniels, illustrates the challenges of growing up in a disadvantaged neighborhood, as well as the reasons that programs like YouthBuild are effective. "I grew up in Harlem, in an environment where dreams turned into nightmares and many people made school out to be the wrong route to follow. Many adults as well as kids were into the streets, money, and other negative activities" (Daniels, 2003, p. 1). Yet Trevor managed to do well in school and stay on track, until two devastating tragedies occurred. "There was a knock on the door. . . . He informed us that one of my sister's boyfriends, whom I considered my older brother, had just been murdered in the elevator of the building across from ours" (Daniels, 2003, p. 1). Just a year later,

> I was on my way home. As I walked through the door, I was immediately stopped by my mother and three sisters. I forced my way through them to my mother's room; there were police officers standing outside the doorway. When I approached the room, I saw my father lying on the floor with one eye open and a quilt covering half of his body. I was fourteen years old and within a year I lost the only two male role models I had in my life. After the death of my father it seemed my dreams began to turn into nightmares. (Daniels, 2003, p. 1)

Though Trevor managed to finish school, after repeating his senior year and transferring to another school, his ambitions became stalled. That is when he became involved with YouthBuild and a rigorous leadership development program called "Mental Toughness." Subsequent activities have included "rebuilding affordable housing and cleaning up local parks" and quite unique opportunities, including a trip to Washington, D.C., to meet and speak to members of Congress about youth development. Trevor describes his success, as well as his ambition to give back to the community.

> At the end of the year, I graduated at the top of my class and [was] one of seven students selected to return to the organization as staff. As a peer counselor (Team Leader), I am dedicated to supporting the students and assisting them in successfully completing the program. Not only has YouthBuild taught me to become more of a leader but has showed me the importance of education. (Daniels, 2003, p. 2)

We highlight YouthBuild at the outset because it combines in one program many of the elements that we believe contribute to successful neighborhood-based youth development programs. YouthBuild improves the physical infrastructure of neighborhoods through housing rehabilitation, which may help to alleviate violence and the many other negative consequences of a neighborhood's physical deterioration. YouthBuild further contributes to the local economy by developing relationships and job opportunities with local businesses and by building storefronts in their housing rehabilitation projects to make places for local business. Moreover, it is founded on youth-adult partnerships and actively seeks to create positive relationships among youth, neighborhood adults, and institutions in the wider community (e.g., schools and businesses). Through participation, youth gain invaluable human capital—job training, education, and leadership skills—which improves their ability to pursue higher education and to take advantage of future economic opportunities. In the next section, we discuss each of these points in greater detail, drawing on recent social science research about how neighborhoods influence youth development.

The New Urban Poverty

Much of contemporary neighborhood research draws on the work of William Julius Wilson (1987, 1997) and his theory of the "new urban poverty." Wilson argues that the experience of poverty is more detrimental to youth today than it was in the past, due to changes in the economic, demographic, and social structures of the neighborhoods in which poor families often live. In the past, inner-city families represented a wider socioeconomic range. Youth from poorer families thus benefited from having middle-class families in the neighborhood who served as role models, informally monitored youth activities, and had the economic and political resources to demand quality schools and other services.

Today, by contrast, poverty is more highly concentrated and accompanied by joblessness, which Wilson argues is more detrimental than poverty alone because it undermines the attachment of neighborhood residents to the labor force. This concentration of poverty and unemployment leads to the isolation of youth from mainstream routes to success, such as higher education and stable employment, and makes alternative (often criminal) routes to self-sufficiency more appealing (Wilson, 1987, 1997). The cause of this social transformation of the inner city, Wilson contends, is a broad socioeconomic shift from manufacturing to services and information-based employment, which has radically reshaped the geography of economic opportunity. Due to the more footloose nature of industries today, low-skilled jobs have increasingly moved away from central city locations to suburbs, exurbs, and rural areas and regionally, from the older industrial cities of the Midwest and Northeast to rapidly growing areas in the South and West and overseas. Thus, the poor are caught in a "spatial mismatch," that is, a geographic disparity between the locations of low-skilled jobs and the residences of poor, low-skilled workers who might otherwise be employed (Cowie, 1999; Kasarda, 1990). As those able to follow moving opportunities do so, many of them middle-class families, the poor are increasingly left behind and isolated in the inner city (Wilson, 1987).

Inspired by Wilson's theory, researchers have begun to demonstrate that neighborhoods matter for a wide range of outcomes across the life course. Their influence begins at birth, with neighborhoods found to have significant effects on birth weight and infant mortality, and on variables typically thought to represent stable individual characteristics, such as IQ and temperament. In childhood and adolescence, neighborhoods have been found to shape negative outcomes such as aggression, delinquency, and substance use as well as positive outcomes such as high school completion, grades, community involvement, and psychological well-being. Neighborhoods have also been found to influence adult outcomes, including child abuse, single parenthood, educational attainment, crime and substance use, employment and earnings, and general well-being (Brooks-Gunn, Duncan, & Aber, 1997; Gephart, 1997; Leventhal & Brooks-Gunn, 2000).

A simplified model of how we believe neighborhoods influence youth development is presented in Figure 10.1. At the far left of the diagram are the socioeconomic and demographic characteristics of neighborhoods, which set the rough boundaries of opportunities and risks within the neighborhood. The middle two boxes contain more specific aspects of neighborhood social relationships and quality that have a more immediate and meaningful impact on the lives of local youth. At the far right are positive developmental outcomes that the youth development movement seeks to promote. The arrows suggest the general direction of causality, with neighborhood socioeconomic and demographic structure influencing the nature of neighborhood relationships and neighborhood quality, which in turn shape youth outcomes. We wish to stress that this is a simplification of a much more dynamic reality, in which the direction of causation flows in both directions and multiple factors interact with each other to shape youth development.

Neighborhood Demographics

A key insight of Wilson (1997) is that many of the negative outcomes associated with concentrated poverty, such as violence, dropping out of

Neighborhood Demographics	Neighborhood Social Capital	Neighborhood Quality	
• Income • Human Captial • Race/Ethnicity • Household & Age Structure • Population Stability	• Intergenerational Closure • Bonding Ties • Informal Controls • Bridging Ties • Institutions	• Safety • Positive Expectations • Collective Efficacy	Positive Youth Outcomes

Figure 10.1   How Neighborhoods Influence Youth Development

high school, and teen pregnancy, are ultimately attributable to a neighborhood's economic and demographic structure. In this section, we review neighborhood research that points to specific characteristics of this structure that are important to youth development.

Income

Consistent with the prominence of concentrated poverty in Wilson's theory, many studies have found that the percentage of families below poverty level in a neighborhood is associated with juvenile delinquency, high school dropout, teen pregnancy, and other outcomes (Gephart, 1997). Neighborhood income reflects local employment opportunities and is linked by Wilson (1997) to nearly all other aspects of neighborhood social capital and quality. Due to its influence on tax revenues, income may particularly influence the quality and funding of schools and other public services.

Human Capital

Other studies emphasize the benefits of high-socioeconomic-status neighbors (e.g., college educated, professionals) for promoting educational and other positive outcomes (Brooks-Gunn et al., 1997; Duncan, 1994). From this perspective, it is not so much the presence of poor families, but rather the absence of a critical mass of neighborhood human capital—residents with more education, skills, and training—that undermines youth development (Swisher, 1999). Though human capital is usually conceived of as a resource embodied in the skills, values, and habits of individuals (Becker, 1964), the presence of such individuals in a neighborhood represents potential resources that may be drawn on to achieve neighborhood goals as well.

Race and Ethnicity

Frequently associated with income is a neighborhood's racial composition. Massey and Denton (1993) contend, for example, that the concentrated poverty we observe today is the combined result of continuing racial segregation in housing and growing economic inequality between racial groups. Though fair-housing legislation has made racial discrimination illegal and blatantly discriminatory practices less common, a historic legacy of restrictive federal housing policies and the continuation of more subtle forms of discrimination leave many neighborhoods strongly segregated by race (Yinger, 1995).

Such segregation, particularly when combined with economic inequality, is detrimental to youth development and society as a whole (Yinger, 1995). Combating segregation is difficult and is made more so by the fact that increasing diversity within a neighborhood may be perceived as a sign of instability and works against the formation of relationships across racial and ethnic lines (Sampson & Groves, 1989). Reducing segregation thus requires efforts to stabilize integrated neighborhoods and increase the housing options of all races (Yinger, 1995).

Household and Age Structure

The household and age structure of a neighborhood may have important consequences for youth development, as well. A large representation of single parents within a neighborhood, for example, has been found to be negatively associated with educational attainment and positively with community disorder (Gephart, 1997). Similarly, research in Cleveland, Ohio, has shown that a neighborhood's "child care burden"—as measured by child-to-adult and male-to-female ratios and the absence of elderly residents—is associated with elevated rates of child maltreatment, drug trafficking, violent crime, juvenile delinquency, teen childbearing, and low-weight births (Coulton, Korbin, Su, & Chow, 1995). It is argued that these effects are due to a simple lack of adults within the neighborhood to socialize and monitor youth activity. Though not yet studied empirically, a similar lack of adult monitoring may contribute to a growing sense of youth alienation in more affluent, geographically isolated, suburban neighborhoods in which both parents typically work outside the home.

Population Stability

Homeownership and population stability are additional factors influencing the frequency and quality of social interactions within a neighborhood. Frequent moves disrupt social relationships and make people less likely to invest in new relationships. Home ownership, or a long residence within the same neighborhood, in contrast, gives residents incentives to make investments of self, time, and money in the neighborhood (Sampson, 1988).

Neighborhood Social Capital

Kids Don't Know diff.

An ecological perspective suggests that it is not simply the presence of affluent neighbors that matters. Rather, it is the more proximal and enduring social relationships between neighbors that make a difference in the lives of youth (Bronfenbrenner, 1979). Community Impact! is a neighborhood-based program exemplifying the importance of building social relationships. Started in 1990 in six Washington, D.C. neighborhoods, Community Impact! strives to increase the pursuit of higher education by local youth. It does so through concerted efforts to increase the "social capital" of the neighborhood (Community Impact! 2003a).

James Coleman (1988) defines social capital as a resource embedded in the social relationships between actors that may be drawn on to achieve a variety of ends, from things as simple as borrowing tools to more ambitious projects such as socializing children, going to college, or mobilizing support for social change. He describes three main types of resources that social relationships may provide: (a) trust that obligations to others will be reciprocated in the future, (b) access to information, and (c) the effective sanctioning of norms.

Intergenerational Closure   ** good. learn from elders*

Enduring relationships among parents, teachers, other adults, and youth are particularly critical for youth development because they are conducive to trust building, information sharing, and monitoring. Coleman (1988) calls attention to the value of "intergenerational closure," with *intergenerational* referring to relationships between generations, and *closure* denoting a high degree of interconnectedness in the networks of adults and youth. Closure emerges not from a single relationship between an adult and youth, but rather from the multiple relationships among parents, their children, their children's friends, their friends' parents, and other adults in the neighborhood.

Community Impact! explicitly seeks to develop social capital by building intergenerational relationships (Case 10.2). It uses a three-pronged program of training, action, and investment. Training is led by small teams of youth ("Youth Mobilizers") and adults, who teach leadership development courses in local high schools to groups of 10 to 20 neighborhood youth. Leadership training includes skills such as public speaking, community organizing, group facilitation, and conflict resolution. The action component is then carried out by partnerships of youth, adults, and community organizations in community service-learning projects. The investment component is facilitated by leveraging funds to create a neighborhood bank account, which is later used to fund college scholarships for local youth leaders and small grants to other community projects. Partnerships are also developed with neighborhood corporations to create job opportunities and train youth in school-to-work programs (Community Impact! 2003a). The secret to the program lies in creating connections among local youth, local leaders, and neighborhood adults in schools, businesses, and other community organizations. Since its inception, Community Impact! has awarded over 290 postsecondary scholarships; organized participation of more than 10,000 Washington, D.C. residents on more than 1,000 projects; and trained hundreds of youth leaders. These successes led to the formation in 1989 of a national organization, Community Impact! USA, to support affiliated programs in Austin, Baltimore, and Nashville (Community Impact! 2003a).

Case 10.2 Making an Impact!

Community Impact! contacted the owner of a local café for an annual "U Street Clean-UP" project. Though he expressed an interest in the project, he also mentioned his perception of a lack of skilled workers in the neighborhood. Community Impact! staff involved in a local "Joblink" training program put him in touch with several local high school students, one of whom was eventually given a full-time job. The owner's successful experience with local youth led him to become a vocal leader and supporter of Community Impact! He also connected the program to the local neighborhood association. Through the simple act of asking someone to get involved, Community Impact! strengthened intergenerational ties (between the owner and local youth), the human capital of local youth, economic opportunity, and the relationship between the program and other neighborhood organizations.

SOURCE: Community Impact! (2003b).

Research suggests that we must be careful to recognize the many varieties of social relationships and their potential for facilitating both positive and negative outcomes (Portes, 1998). Below, we discuss two types of neighborhood social relationships, bonding ties and bridging ties, and the importance of distinguishing the norms, expectations, and information embedded within them.

Bonding Ties

Bonding ties or relationships are characterized by frequent and sometimes intense interactions. They tend to be among persons of similar social backgrounds, though this is by no means a requirement. In a sense, bonding relationships are an extension of the family and thrive on trust and everyday interdependence. Within poor neighborhoods, bonding relationships have been found to provide much-needed support for coping with the everyday demands and stressors of poverty (Edin & Lein, 1997; Stack, 1974). Whether it is borrowing groceries or a few dollars at the end of the month, emergency baby-sitting, or getting a ride to work, neighbors can provide invaluable support.

A potential drawback of bonding relationships is that they may be constructed in opposition to some other group. Solidarity with one group of individuals is sometimes strengthened by the creation of social boundaries that exclude other groups, a factor that may work against the inclusive goals of youth development. Research also suggests that the familial or in-group orientation of intense bonding relationships may inhibit the development and freedom of individual members to pursue opportunities outside the local area (Portes, 1998; Stack, 1974).

Informal Controls

As relationships enable some activities, both good and bad, they discourage others. The research of Sampson and colleagues (1997, 1999) illustrates the benefits of informal social controls within neighborhoods. Neighborhoods in which adults are willing to watch out for each other's children and intervene when necessary are found to have lower levels of delinquency, crime, and violence than do other neighborhoods. When informal social controls are coupled with shared norms and expectations for child rearing, a growing sense of collective efficacy among neighbors may begin to emerge (Sampson et al., 1997, 1999). Thus, bonding ties may provide a basis for informal social controls that make neighborhoods better places for all.

Bridging Ties

Although bonding relationships may provide everyday support and facilitate the monitoring of neighborhood youth, they are less effective for gaining access to information about resources and opportunities beyond neighborhood boundaries (e.g., job opportunities). Because bonding relationships typically form between people of similar characteristics, they tend to provide redundant information. This is particularly true in poor neighborhoods in which fewer adults have experience with higher education, professional occupations, and institutions linked to the broader community. In contrast, bridging ties or relationships, which involve a more heterogeneous set of persons, tend to be less frequent and more instrumental in nature. These relationships might be with people met at college, a previous job, a community organizational meeting, or simply through mutual acquaintances. They are what we more commonly call "contacts" built up over time through "networking." Though one would almost never call on a business contact to borrow a lawnmower or watch the kids, such ties may prove quite useful for linking neighborhood youth to job opportunities in other parts of the city or rallying organizational and political support (Guest, 2000; Portes, 1998; Warren, Thompson, & Saegert, 2001).

An important by-product of bridging relationships is that they make possible a coordination of information across the various developmental settings of families, schools, neighborhoods, and the wider community. As Bronfenbrenner (1979) notes, such connections are most developmentally productive "when the settings occur in cultural or sub-cultural contexts that are different from each other in terms of ethnicity, social class, religion, age group, or other background factors" (p. 213). Under such circumstances, bridging relationships may help to offset the potentially exclusionary nature of more localized bonding relationships.

Neighborhood Institutions

The Neighborhood Academy (Case 10.3) illustrates how a local voluntary association can enhance social capital by increasing youth and adult participation. Such associations are the bedrock of civil society (Putnam, 2000), building trust and laying the groundwork for wider political participation. Of particular importance for present purposes is research showing that active participation of youth and parents in school, neighborhood, and other civic associations has a powerful and positive effect on youth development (Elder & Conger, 2000; Furstenberg, Cook, Eccles, Elder, & Sameroff, 1999). Several community and neighborhood institutions,

---

Case 10.3 The Neighborhood Academy

The Neighborhood Academy was launched in 1997 in a downtown San Diego neighborhood. Engaging young people as active participants in their neighborhoods and communities is a core goal of the Neighborhood Academy philosophy. This is accomplished through group facilitation skills training, balanced youth-adult partnerships, and assisting participants in assuming leadership in their neighborhoods. Currently, youth graduates are active in neighborhood associations, parent-teacher organizations, church and tutoring programs, and other community organizations. They have conducted youth leadership trainings, cocreated and provided training in youth engagement curricula, and have participated in partnerships with other local and national organizations.

SOURCE: Neighborhood Academy (2003).

---

including schools, faith-based organizations, and youth-serving organizations, are treated in detail in other chapters of this volume. Creating connections among schools, voluntary associations, religious institutions, and other neighborhood organizations should thus be an important component of neighborhood youth development initiatives.

Neighborhood Quality

Strengthening each of the forms of social capital we have described is a worthy end in itself and a goal for neighborhood-based youth development efforts. A healthy stock of social capital contributes to several dimensions of neighborhood quality that are critical to successful youth development, including a sense of safety, order and control, and positive expectations for the future.

Safety

A perceived lack of safety and uncertainty about one's chances of survival are major barriers to youth development in disadvantaged neighborhoods. Asked the classic question of what he wanted to do when he grows up, a young boy in Kotlowitz's (1987) *There Are No Children Here* responded, "If I grow up, I'd like to be a bus driver" (p. x). Another explained, "I worry about dying, dying at a young age, while you're little. . . . It aint no joke when you die" (p. 264). Constant attention to issues of daily survival distracts youth from learning opportunities and undermines long-term planning and investments. As a youth in MacLeod's (1987) *Ain't No Makin' It* explains, "All through the teenage years around here, you hafta learn to survive before you learn to do anything else" (p. 36). Another remarks, "Nobody learns anything from school around here. All it is, is how to survive" (p. 36). Young (1999) forcefully argues, based on his study of the life histories of poor African American men in Chicago, that the constant threat of violence in poor neighborhoods undermines "the essential prerequisite for conceiving of future life chances: a consistently secure belief that they could survive into adulthood" (p. 210).

Research on the effects of exposure to violence and other ambient hazards reveals serious consequences for youth well-being, including anxiety, depression, aggression, and other self-destructive behavior; post-traumatic stress disorders; a diminished sense of personal efficacy and control; high school dropout; and teen pregnancy (Aneshensel & Sucoff, 1996; Geis & Ross, 1998; Hagan & Foster, 2001; Osofsky, 1995). Furthermore, research shows that exposure to violence in adolescence results in long-term negative consequences for earning and well-being in adulthood (MacMillan, 2001).

One potential means of disrupting the cycle between neighborhood poverty, disorder, and violence is suggested by Wilson and Kelling's (1982) "broken windows" theory. They argue that broken windows and other visual signs of disorder within a neighborhood, such as abandoned housing, graffiti, litter, and youth hanging out on street corners, are cues to others that people do not care about what happens in the neighborhood. This encourages and attracts criminal behavior. The reasoning is that if neighbors allow such minor infractions to go unchecked, they are even less likely to intervene in the case of more serious incidents such as crime and violence. Increased fears of community violence, in turn, lead to the social withdrawal of neighbors and a further weakening of informal social controls. A vicious cycle of neighborhood disorder and violence thus ensues. One way in which some neighborhoods around the country are combating this cycle is through innovative collaborations between graffiti artists and local youth and adults to produce murals reflecting the history and aspirations of their neighborhoods (see Case 10.4). As youth create murals, they also develop enduring relationships within the community and build human capital and self-efficacy.

Case 10.4 The Mural and Cultural Arts Program

The Mural and Cultural Arts Program of Long Beach, California, launched in 1985 by the Departments of Parks, Recreation, and Marine and Community Development, sets program goals to increase cultural understanding, literacy, social and artistic expression, and job skills, while reducing graffiti through neighborhood improvement projects. Teams of neighborhood youth are paired with artist mentors to design murals for schools, parks, and their neighborhoods and to publish journals of each young person's experiences. Developing designs for neighborhood murals requires that youth communicate with neighborhood residents about the themes to be depicted in the mural, most often reflecting the particular cultural heritage of participating neighborhoods.

SOURCE: Mural and Cultural Arts Program (2003).

Positive Expectations

Assuming that a basic level of personal safety is secured, youth may then begin to think about their prospects for educational and economic success in early adulthood. Researchers are increasingly recognizing the importance of youth's expectations and perceptions of the economic opportunity structure in shaping decision making during adolescence and the transition to adulthood (Gould, 1999; Young, 1999). As youth move into adulthood, they make decisions about various transitions—staying in school, going to college, getting married—based in part on perceptions of each one's relative payoff and their own likelihood of success.

Wilson (1997) argues that youth living in poor neighborhoods today develop their expectations for the future based largely on the bleak educational and occupational experiences of the many unemployed and underemployed local adults. These effects on the outlook of youth make the presence of unemployment in neighborhoods devastating. Moreover, with few examples of full-time employment to draw on, youth also begin to doubt the efficacy of mainstream routes to employment, such as staying in school and pursuing job training or higher education.

The perceptions of youth in MacLeod's (1987) study illustrate these points. Asked about future employment prospects, one youth responded,

"Shitty jobs. Picking up trash, cleaning the streets. [People around here] won't get no good jobs" (p. 68). As to the wisdom of staying in school, one youth remarked,

> None of my friends take that route. . . . [Those that do] they're dopes. . . . They think that if they go through high school and college [that] they're gonna get a job that's gonna pay. . . . My diploma ain't doing me no good. . . . Look how many college graduates ain't got jobs. . . . So school ain't paying off for no one. (pp. 103-104)

Promoting more optimistic expectations is an important component of many neighborhood-based youth development programs. A guiding principle of Community Impact! for example, is to promote a "can do" attitude among youth, through positive experiences of making a difference within their communities (Community Impact!, 2003a). Yet those involved in Community Impact! know that simply saying that one expects to succeed is not enough. Such optimism will be genuine and effective only if it is built on realistic economic opportunities and reinforced by bonding and bridging ties with other local adults and youth. In other words, social capital is means of getting from here to there.

Collective Efficacy

As Wilson notes, Bandura's (1982) concept of "self-efficacy" refers not only to individuals' confidence in their ability to accomplish goals but also their belief that the social environment will be responsive to and reward such efforts. The perceived lack of responsiveness of the local opportunity structure lowers the expectations of poor youth. When such negative attitudes are held by many youth in the area, the neighborhood's sense of collective efficacy is diminished (Wilson, 1997). Sampson and colleagues also speak about the emergence of collective efficacy—the perceived ability of residents to realize collective goals—that is generated by the shared norms, trust, and informal social controls within healthy neighborhoods (Sampson et al., 1999).

Interactions Between Neighborhood and Family Resources

An ecological approach recognizes that the relationships among youth, families, and the wider contexts in which they are embedded are inherently interactive, with developmental outcomes a joint function of the characteristics of each (Bronfenbrenner, 1979). We will not fully understand the experience of a family without taking into account the social context of the neighborhood in which it is embedded. Nor will we understand the influence of a neighborhood on families without considering the diversity of families within it, each of which experiences and responds to the neighborhood in a different way.

Concentrated Disadvantage

One way of thinking about the interaction between neighborhoods and families is in terms of their resources, broadly construed to include economic, human, and various forms of social capital. Figure 10.2 is a simplified representation of the interaction between family and neighborhood resources. The top-left quadrant, "Concentrated Disadvantage," is the most disadvantaged situation, in which both the family and the neighborhood are lacking in economic resources. Wilson's (1997) description of concentrated poverty is a case in point, with poor youth living in neighborhoods surrounded by other poor families. One might also think of this as an accentuation of disadvantage stemming from the lack of resources at both the family and neighborhood levels. These communities are most in need of help but may lack many of the economic, human, and social capital on which youth development programs typically build.

Concentrated Advantage

The opposite extreme is found in the bottom-right quadrant of Figure 10.2, which we have called "Concentrated Advantage," a situation of high resources for both families and neighborhoods. Though fewer studies focus on such advantaged contexts, research does suggest that high-socioeconomic-status neighborhoods and schools may maximize the potential of youth coming from high-socioeconomic-status families (Sucoff & Upchurch, 1998). Although youth development initiatives are not likely to target advantaged neighborhoods, this finding provides support for the notion that neighborhoods matter to all youth, regardless of family socioeconomic background.

Social Buffers

Other studies suggest that the resources of good neighborhoods are most beneficial to youth from families that lack resources (see Figure 10.2, upper-right quadrant). Wilson (1997), for example, argues that

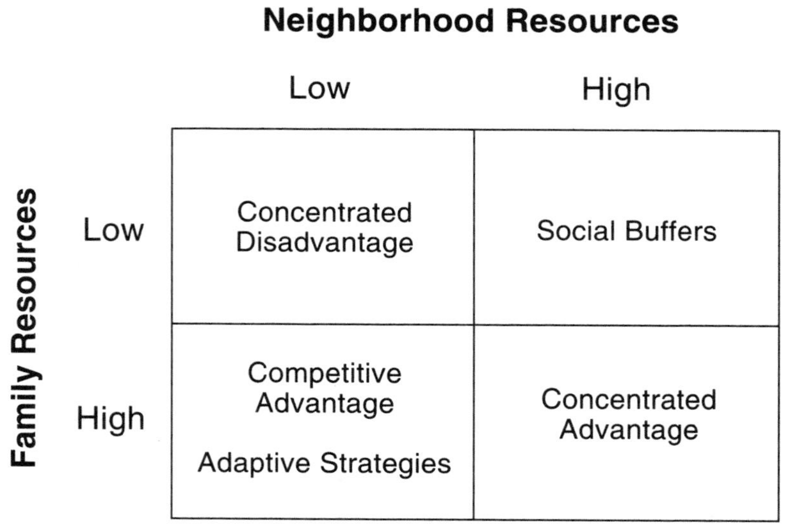

Neighborhood Resources

		Low	High
Family Resources	Low	Concentrated Disadvantage	Social Buffers
	High	Competitive Advantage Adaptive Strategies	Concentrated Advantage

Figure 10.2   Interactions Between Neighborhood and Family Resources

middle-class neighbors serve as "social buffers" for youth from poor families, acting as role models of mainstream routes to success, providing bridging ties, and monitoring and sanctioning undesired behavior (i.e., informal controls). From a youth development perspective, this implies that efforts to increase economic and social capital may be of particular benefit to disadvantaged youth. The successful experience of Trevor with YouthBuild (Case 10.1) illustrates this point. Though disadvantaged by his lack of education and the recent loss of his father, he was able to beat the odds with the reliable social support offered by YouthBuild.

One challenge to keep in mind, however, is that poor youth may be disadvantaged in competitions for scarce resources with, and by negative social comparisons to, less disadvantaged youth (Mayer & Jencks, 1989). Such a problem is suggested in a study by Brooks-Gunn, Duncan, Klebanov, and Sealand (1993), which found that the benefits of living in affluent neighborhoods were realized only by more affluent and nonblack youth.

Competitive Advantage

By the same token, youth from advantaged families (i.e., advantaged economically or by greater parental human capital) living in predominantly resource-poor neighborhoods (see Figure 10.2, bottom-left quadrant) may find themselves at a competitive advantage relative to their disadvantaged peers. This is a relatively rare occurrence, however, due to the greater ability of such families to choose more prosperous neighborhoods for their children.

Adaptive Strategies

More frequently observed, in the bottom-left quadrant of Figure 10.2, are the many coping strategies employed by resourceful parents in disadvantaged contexts. For example, in highly violent neighborhoods, many families organize their daily lives so as to avoid the most dangerous places, times of day, and people. Parents may also become highly vigilant of their children, setting strict curfews and using extended kin networks to chaperone activities. A more psychological coping mechanism is the creation of an identity in opposition to the neighborhood (Furstenberg et al., 1999; Jarrett, 1997). Anderson (1999) observed such a practice among single-parent mothers living in poor neighborhoods who actively strove to maintain their reputations as "decent" families, unlike the "street" families living nearby.

The physical and psychological distancing of families within dangerous neighborhoods represents a challenge to youth development initiatives. Yet at the same time, such strategies suggest a deep concern for the welfare of youth and adaptive capabilities on which youth development programs might build. Optimism is also suggested by the more socially engaged strategies of other families in the same circumstances, who get involved in school and neighborhood associations and seek to maximize and build on existing assets (Jarrett, 1997).

Conclusions

In this chapter, we have sought to show that neighborhoods matter to youth development. We have discussed relevant socioeconomic and demographic characteristics of neighborhoods (e.g., income), types of neighborhood social capital (i.e., bonding and bridging ties), and aspects of neighborhood quality more broadly (e.g., collective efficacy) that have consequences for youth development. As may have been obvious, few programs address only a single component of our analysis. This reflects their planners' recognition of the <u>importance of a synergy</u> among the many components of youth and neighborhood development, such as economic development, housing and physical infrastructure, social capital, human capital, and positive expectations. Although it is unlikely that any one program will be able to address all these issues simultaneously, we wish to close with suggestions for ways participants in programs can think about combining multiple objectives whenever possible.

Link Economic and Social Capital Development

A neighborhood's socioeconomic structure is a critical determinant of the quality of neighborhood life, from the availability of jobs, the intensity and nature of social capital, and the quality of schools and other community institutions to the ultimate life chances of local youth. Neighborhood-based programs must therefore actively seek to improve economic opportunities. Efforts designed to build social capital, for example, without consideration of the larger opportunity structure may offer false promises.

Yet at the same time, a neighborhood's social capital infrastructure is a precondition for successful economic development. YouthBuild and Community Impact! recognize this fact by making the enhancement of a neighborhood's economic vitality and social capital integral components. They have shown that the relationship between economic and social capital is reciprocal, so that building social capital can be an effective component of successful economic development.

Build Varieties of Neighborhood Social Capital

Youth development programs must build relationships between youth and adults of varying backgrounds, thus broadening the horizons of youth to include opportunities beyond a neighborhood's boundaries. This is where the development of both bonding and bridging relationships is critical. Warren et al. (2001) describe four types of bridging relationships to be promoted: (a) bridges between various forms of social capital within a neighborhood, (b) bridges between one poor neighborhood and another, (c) bridges between poor and affluent neighborhoods, and (d) bridges between the local and national communities. They argue that it is necessary to "build social capital locally yet connect it regionally and nationally" (p. 12). Our review further suggests developing bridges across generations (i.e., between youth and adults); local institutions (i.e., among neighborhoods, schools, and businesses); and socioeconomic and cultural differences. We also believe it is critical that relationships between youth and adults be true partnerships. We must work with youth, not simply for them.

Promote Human Capital and Collective Efficacy

Of utmost importance is that youth feel hopeful and optimistic about their futures. Yet we are not advocating a blind optimism, ignorant of the many barriers to achievement in disadvantaged neighborhoods. Optimism must be based on real educational and economic opportunities. It must also be based on the development of tangible leadership, job skills, and other forms of human capital. Youth must have access to the means to be successful, experiences of success, and models of success in their neighborhoods. This point is confirmed in the exemplary youth development programs we have discussed, all of which make some combination of leadership and career development, vocational training, mentorship, educational scholarships, and the promotion of self- and collective efficacy key program components. This combination of realistic expectations and knowledge about how to get from here to there enables youth to develop into productive, caring, and engaged adults.

References

Anderson, E. (1999). *Code of the street: Decency, violence, and the moral life of the inner-city.* New York: Norton.

Aneshensel, C. S., & Sucoff, C. (1996). The neighborhood context of adolescent mental health. *Journal of Health and Social Behavior, 37*(6), 293-310.

Bandura, A. (1982). *Self-efficacy mechanism in human agency. American Psychologist, 37,* 122-147.

Becker, G. S. (1964). *Human capital: A theoretical analysis with special reference to education.* Chicago: University of Chicago Press.

Bronfenbrenner, U. (1979). *The ecology of human development: Experiments by nature and design.* Cambridge, MA: Harvard University Press.

Brooks-Gunn, J., Duncan, G. J., & Aber, J. L. (1997). *Neighborhood poverty: Vol. 1. Context and consequences for children; Vol. 2. Policy implications in studying neighborhoods.* New York: Russell Sage.

Brooks-Gunn, J., Duncan, G. J., Klebanov, P. K., & Sealand, N. (1993). Do neighborhoods influence child and adolescent development? *American Journal of Sociology, 99*(2), 353-395.

Coleman, J. S. (1988). Social capital in the creation of human capital. *American Journal of Sociology, 94*(Suppl.), 95-120.

Community Impact! (2003a). *About CI! History and mission.* Retrieved February 26, 2003, from: http://www.community-impact.net/aboutci.html.

Community Impact! (2003b). *Getting business owners involved in their neighborhoods.* Retrieved February 26, 2003, from: http://www.community-impact.net/organizing/Ownerstory.pdf.

Coulton, C. J., Korbin, J. E., Su, M., & Chow, J. (1995). Community level factors and child maltreatment rates. *Child Development, 66,* 1262-1276.

Cowie, J. R. (1999). *Capital moves: RCA's seventy-year quest for cheap labor.* Ithaca, NY: Cornell University Press.

Daniels, T. (2003). *Personal essay.* Provided by YouthBuild.

Duncan, G. J. (1994). Families and neighbors as sources of disadvantage in the schooling decisions of white and black adolescents. *American Journal of Education, 103*(6), 20-53.

Edin, K., & Lein, L. (1997). *Making ends meet: How single mothers survive welfare and low-wage work.* New York: Russell Sage.

Elder, G. H. Jr., & Conger, R. (2000). *Children of the land: Adversity and success in rural America.* Chicago: University of Chicago Press.

Furstenberg, F. F. Jr., Cook, T. D., Eccles, J., Elder, G. E. Jr., & Sameroff, A. (1999). *Managing to make it: Urban families and adolescent success.* Chicago: University of Chicago Press.

Geis, K. J., & Ross, C. E. (1998). A new look at urban alienation: The effect of neighborhood disorder on perceived powerlessness. *Social Psychology Quarterly, 61*(3), 232-246.

Gephart, M. A. (1997). Neighborhoods and communities as contexts for development. In J. Brooks-Gunn, G. J. Duncan, & J. L. Aber (Eds.), *Neighborhood poverty: Vol. 1. Context and consequences for children* (chap. 1). New York: Russell Sage.

Gould, M. (1999). Race and theory: Culture, poverty, and adaptation to discrimination in Wilson and Ogbu. *Sociological Theory, 17*(2), 171-200.

Guest, A. M. (2000). The mediate community: The nature of local and extralocal ties within the metropolis. *Urban Affairs Review, 35*(5), 603-627.

Hagan, J., & Foster, H. (2001). Youth violence and the end of adolescence. *American Sociological Review, 66*(6), 874-899.

Jarrett, R. L. (1997). African American family and parenting strategies in impoverished neighborhoods. *Qualitative Sociology, 20*(2), 275-287.

Kasarda, J. (1990). Urban industrial transition and the underclass. *Annals of the American Academy of Political and Social Science, 501,* 26-47.

Kotlowitz, A. (1991). *There are no children here: A story of two boys growing up in the other America.* New York: Doubleday.

Leventhal, T., & Brooks-Gunn, J. (2000). The neighborhoods they live in: The effects of neighborhood residence on child and adolescent outcomes. *Psychological Bulletin, 126*(2), 309-337.

MacLeod, J. (1987). *Ain't no makin' it: Aspirations and attainment in a low-income neighborhood.* New York: Westview.

MacMillan, R. (2001). Violence and the life course: The consequences of victimization for personal and social development. *Annual Review of Sociology, 27,* 1-22.

Massey, D. S., & Denton, N. A. (1993). *American apartheid: Segregation and the making of the underclass.* Cambridge, MA: Harvard University Press.

Mayer, S. E., & Jencks, C. (1989). Growing up in poor neighborhoods: How much does it matter? *Science, 243,* 1441-1446.

Mural and Cultural Arts Program. (2003). *Mural & Cultural Arts Program.* Retrieved February 26, 2003, from: http://www.ci.long-beach.ca.us/commmunity/murals/.Muralmap.html.

Neighborhood Academy. (2003). *What is the neighborhood academy?* Retrieved February 26, 2003, from: http://www.ica-usa.org/programs/na/na_home.html.

Osofsky, J. D. (1995). The effects of exposure to violence on young children. *American Psychologist, 50*(9), 782-788.

Portes, A. (1998). Social capital: Its origins and applications in modern sociology. *Annual Review of Sociology, 24,* 1-24.

Putnam, R. D. (2000). *Bowling alone.* New York: Simon & Schuster.

Saegert, S. J., Thompson, J. P., & Warren, M. R. (Eds.). (2001). *Social capital and poor communities.* New York: Russell Sage.

Sampson, R. J. (1988). Local friendship ties and community attachment in mass society: A multilevel systemic model. *American Sociological Review, 53,* 766-779.

Sampson, R. J., & Groves, W. B. (1989). Community structure and crime: Testing social-disorganization theory. *American Journal of Sociology, 94,* 774-802.

Sampson, R. J., Morenoff, J. D., & Earls, F. (1999). Beyond social capital: Spatial dynamics of collective efficacy for children. *American Sociological Review, 64,* 633-660.

Sampson, R. J., Raudenbush, S. W., & Earls, F. (1997). Neighborhoods and violent crime: A multilevel study of collective efficacy. *Science, 277,* 918-924.

Stack, C. (1974). *All our kin: Strategies for survival in a black community.* New York: Harper & Row.

Sucoff, C. A., & Upchurch, D. M. (1998). Neighborhood context and the risk of childbearing among metropolitan-area black adolescents. *American Sociological Review, 63*(4), 571-585.

Swisher, R. R. (1999). *Neighborhood effects on adolescent college expectations.* Doctoral dissertation, University of North Carolina at Chapel Hill.

Warren, M. R., Thompson, J. P., & Saegert, S. (2001). The role of social capital in combating poverty. In S. J. Saegert, J. P. Thompson, & M. R. Warren (Eds.), *Social capital and poor communities.* New York: Russell Sage.

Wilson, J. Q., & Kelling, G. (1982). Broken windows. *Atlantic Monthly, 3,* 9-28.

Wilson, W. J. (1987). *The truly disadvantaged: The inner city, the underclass, and public policy.* Chicago: University of Chicago Press.

Wilson, W. J. (1997). *When work disappears: The world of the new urban poor.* New York: Knopf.

Yinger, J. (1995). *Closed doors, opportunities lost: The continuing costs of housing discrimination.* New York: Russell Sage.

Young, A. (1999). The (non) accumulation of capital: Explicating the relationship of structure and agency in the lives of poor black men. *Sociological Theory, 17*(2), 201-227.

YouthBuild. (2003). *History and facts.* Retrieved February 26, 2003, from: http://www.youthbuild.org/about_history.html.

11

Popular Media Culture and the Promise of Critical Media Literacy

Jane D. Brown, Rebecca Schaffer,
Lucila Vargas, and LaHoma S. Romocki

Youth today are growing up in a world saturated with the mass media (television, movies, magazines, music, the Internet). They are surrounded by a popular culture distributed through the mass media that sees young people as a market ripe for exploitation rather than as a generation that is eager to learn and act in meaningful ways.

For many young people, the mass media provide a window on a larger world beyond their families, schools, and communities. As youth grapple with questions of identity and undertake other crucial developmental tasks of maturation (e.g., developing cross-gender relationships, gaining independence from parents, and thinking about occupational and civic roles), they may see the media as accessible and safe means to explore possible ways of being.

The mass media also both reflect and influence the community norms and expectations that provide an important context for adolescent development, such as parent-child relationships, sexual orientations, racial and ethnic politics, and class relations. These norms also influence the ways in which adults, including parents and policymakers, view and act toward adolescents.

239

In the United States and other Western capitalist societies, popular culture—the set of practices and artifacts that are available to most people in a society, including leisure activities, clothing, music, and stories—is conflated with the mass media, making it difficult to distinguish between the two. In this chapter, we focus on what we call *popular media culture:* the easily accessible cultural forms available through the mass media.

Public interest in the role the media play in the lives of today's youth has escalated in recent years, owing in large part to questions concerning possible links between media portrayals of unhealthy behaviors (e.g., violence, unprotected sex, drug use) and the prevalence of such behaviors among young people. Although the growing body of quantitative research designed to assess patterns of media use among young people provides some of the information that policymakers and educators require to address such issues, it is too often based on outdated theories and/or provides general findings that are difficult to translate into policies and programs for specific cultural groups, especially for minority youth.

In this chapter, we look briefly at the findings of traditional research on patterns of media use by youth and their impact on health and well-being, which has tended to focus on the direct power of the media. We then posit the *media practice model* as an alternative, because it assumes that young people are more active than passive in their use of the media. Finally, we propose and provide examples of critical media literacy education as a strategy for enhancing and expanding the potential of youth as engaged and critical media consumers, producers, and activists who will be able to more effectively deal with popular media culture in the future.

Patterns of Media Use

Recent studies have found that young people in the United States spend more of their awake time watching television and videotapes and playing video games than doing any other activity including being in school (Robinson, 1999). The most recent study of a nationally representative sample of children and adolescents in the United States found that 2- to 18-year-olds are spending an average of 5 to 6 hours a day with some form of media (Roberts, Foehr, Rideout, & Brodie, 1999).

The information revolution has resulted in a proliferation of media channels and greater access to all forms of media than any generation of children has ever experienced before. It may also be the first time in history that most of a child's exposure to the world outside his or her family has occurred without parental supervision or interpretation. It used to be that the television set was in the "family room" and television viewing was considered a family activity. By the beginning of this century, in contrast, most households had more than one television set, and two thirds of 8- to 18-year-olds had television sets in their own bedrooms (Roberts, 2000). Most young Americans have personal control over other kinds of media as well, including radios and cassette and CD players, magazines, videotape players, video game players, and computers that provide access to more games and the Internet. Thus, today's youth frequently consume media alone and in the privacy of their own rooms, so there is less opportunity for adult intervention or conversation about what they see, hear, and read.

Although relatively little U.S. research has focused on racial and ethnic differences in media use, we do know that access to and time spent with different forms of media are disproportionately distributed in the adolescent population. African American adolescents, on average, spend the most time watching television (about 5 five hours per day), followed by Latino adolescents (about 4 hours per day). Of the racial/ethnic groups, white adolescents spend the least amount of time watching television, but still spend about 3 hours a day in front of "the tube." Boys typically spend more time watching television than girls (Roberts, 2000). Youth whose parents have less education and who live in less affluent neighborhoods tend to spend more time with media than youth with better-educated parents and those who live in communities with higher average household incomes (Roberts et al., 1999).

Children who have access to a lot of media in their bedrooms also spend more time with the media. In a national study of young people's media patterns, having a computer, video game player, and/or cable television hooked up in the child's bedroom was the strongest predictor of more time spent watching the television screen. Media use is higher also among children who live in homes where the television is on most of the time even when no one in particular is watching (about 42% of children) and among children who spend more than half their television time watching alone (about one fifth of early adolescents and one third of older adolescents) (Roberts et al., 1999).

In general, as youth get older, music becomes a more important part of their daily media diets (time spent with different media and genres) than television, and genre preferences are closely tied to gender, ethnicity, and social class. Girls, for example, spend more time than boys listening to music and watching music videos; MTV is the preferred television network for girls aged 11 to 19. Some girls also spend time playing video games, but they are far less likely than boys to do so (Mediascope, 2000).

In short, popular media culture is an important context in which young people are spending a great deal of time, often alone, without parental supervision or comment. Gender, race/ethnicity, age, and socioeconomic status all affect the frequency of attention to the media and the selection of content.

Concerns About the Health and Well-Being of Youth

Since the early days of mass-mediated forms of communication, parents, educators, and researchers have been concerned about the possible effects of popular media culture on children. Much of the attention has focused on the effects of the increasingly frequent and graphic portrayals of violence on television and in the movies, and more recently, on increasingly explicit depictions of sexual behavior. The mass media also have been found to contribute to negative stereotyping of young people and ethnic minorities.

Violence on Television

Large numbers of studies have established that exposure to media violence is related to increased fear, desensitization, and aggressiveness among young viewers. More than 1,000 studies using various scientific methods with a range of populations over three decades converge on the conclusion that viewing violence on television increases the probability that viewers will be fearful, desensitized to real-world violence, and violent themselves (Friedrich-Cofer & Huston, 1986). Some analyses have suggested that 5% to 15% of violent behavior in the United States could be attributed to viewing violence on television (Comstock & Strasberger, 1990).

Despite the certainty with which most researchers would say there are direct, negative effects of media violence and despite numerous public and legislative efforts to reduce the amount of violence portrayed in popular media, U.S. television and movies remain saturated with depictions of aggression and violence. A recent comprehensive content analysis of U.S. television non-news programming over 3 years found that more than half of all programs included violent content. Very few of the programs portrayed nonviolent solutions to conflict or the long-term negative consequences of violence, such as physical and psychological suffering (Smith et al., 1998). Thus, it would be difficult for young viewers to learn alternative, nonviolent forms of conflict resolution from current popular media, and more likely that they will learn that violence is an appropriate and relatively consequence-free way of solving conflicts.

Sex in Popular Media Culture

The frequency of sexual portrayals across media that are used by adolescents (e.g., television, radio, movies, magazines, Internet) and the relative reticence of other sources of information about sexuality (e.g., teachers, parents) suggest that the media also are important sex educators (Brown, Steele, & Walsh-Childers, 2002). Teens say they would prefer to get sexual information from their parents, but more than half of adolescents report that they have learned about sexual issues from television and movies, and more than half of teen girls say they have learned about sex from magazines (Kaiser Family Foundation, 1998).

Although all media tend to display sexual content regularly, different media and genres often provide contradictory information about "normal" or "healthy" sexual attitudes and behaviors, different depictions of the "ideal" girl and boy, and different expectations for girls' development into women and boys' development into men. In general, television and movies tend to privilege unprotected heterosexual intercourse between unmarried partners over other types of sexual encounters and fail to address the consequences of unprotected sex (i.e., pregnancy, sexually transmitted diseases) (Huston, Wartella, & Donnerstein, 1998). One study found that 40% of the sexual behaviors observed in prime-time comedies fit the legal definition of sexual harassment, often to the accompaniment of a laugh track (Skill, Robinson, & Kinsella, 1994). The Internet offers both an alarming amount of pornographic material and numerous sites operated by health and education practitioners and teens to provide information or raise questions about sexual health that adolescents can access in an anonymous, safe forum (see, for example, www.goaskalice.columbia.edu) (Stern, 2002).

Although less prevalent than studies about the effects of media violence, an emerging body of research suggests that youth learn about sexuality from the media. Girls tend to incorporate the prevailing mass media messages (e.g., that girls should be thin, fair skinned, and well dressed; that popularity is critical; that girls' bodies reflect who they really are). Adoption of these norms may contribute to decreased self-esteem, poor body images, poor nutrition, early sexual activity, and an exaggerated desire to be accepted by their peers. Furthermore, such assimilation may eclipse healthier desires (e.g., to excel at school, to take a stand on issues that are important to them, to resist popular images of femininity and masculinity) (Brown et al., 2002; Durham, 1999; Gilligan, 1982; Mazarella & Pecora, 1999; Pipher, 1994).

Stereotyping Minority Youth

The media also tend to portray youth, especially minority youth, as dangerous and uncivilized. In the United States, minority youth, especially young black men and, increasingly, young Latino men, are disproportionately associated with criminal and violent acts (e.g., drive-by shootings, armed robberies, assaults, drug use) by both the news media and the non-news media. Donna Gaines (1991), Henry Giroux (1998), and Mike Males (1999) are among a growing number of researchers who have found that portrayals of youth crime across the media create the inaccurate impression that youth, particularly minority youth, are responsible for a greater proportion of all crime than their adult counterparts, that the rate at which youth commit crimes is growing, and that we must take swift, extreme measures to control these young people. The media have exacerbated adult fears about young people, criminalized minority youth, and racialized youth violence by misrepresenting crime rates, focusing on and sensationalizing incidents of youth violence, and failing to provide alternative portrayals of youth as humanitarian, caring, and productive members of society. For example, analyses of Latino youth subcultures conclude that the media have been instrumental in shaping public opinion and in legitimizing a heavy-handed policing approach toward Latino young men (Cross, 1993).

In popular media depictions, minority youth often are positioned in antagonistic relationships to institutions such as schools and law enforcement (Seiter, 1995). Hollywood portrays public schools as not only dysfunctional but also as an imminent threat to the dominant society. Students represent a criminalized underclass that must be watched and contained through the use of high-tech monitoring systems and military-style authority (Giroux, 2000).

Narrow and stereotypical images of blacks, most notably the contemporary stereotype of young blacks as athletes, are prevalent in television advertising and other forms of popular media, as well. Most commercials featuring African Americans include a reference to rap music and/or sports (Rose, 1995). Although African American athletes such as Michael Jordan or Jackie Joyner-Kersee can serve as positive role models for black youth, focus on such stars can be problematic because it distorts the minuscule statistical realities of an African American youth's prospects of "making it big" in sports (Bristor, Lee, & Hunt, 1995).

The social construction of rap and rap-related violence is fundamentally linked to a belief that black youth and black culture are dangerous and that rap music represents an internal threat to American culture. Although popular white youth music, especially heavy metal rock music, has not been immune to criticism, the nature of the attacks on expressions from black and white youth have been different and serve as useful examples of the ways in which racial discourses inform social control efforts in the United States (Rose, 1995).

Thus, the popular media culture in the United States may contribute to the creation of a violent and sexualized youth culture and the perception of youth as dangerous and deviant by providing a narrow set of portrayals that focus on the negative rather than the positive aspects of the young. Traditional mass communication research may have assisted in these misperceptions by working from a frame of direct and powerful media effects rather than a more interactive perspective that sees the media consumer as an active participant in the process of using and applying media content.

Uses of Popular Media by Adolescents: The Media Practice Model

Throughout this chapter, we use the term *media use* to refer to two related but different sets of activities. One set of media use activities includes the numerous ways in which people use media messages, media practices (e.g., movie going), and media technologies as both social and psychological resources. For example, people use media as communicative resources for interpersonal relations (e.g., news as a conversation starter, reading the newspaper to avoid conversation) (Lull, 1990). People also use media as psychological resources to construct, for instance, a gendered identity (e.g., watching sports rather than soap operas) and to develop and assert a sense of self (e.g., watching Britney Spears to see what clothes to wear and what makeup to buy).

The second kind of media use has to do with responses to media messages, including interpretive strategies and other reactions such as acceptance and incorporation, negotiation of the messages' problematic aspects, or resistance to the messages. Some boys, for example, may reject popular notions of the need to have "six-pack abs" because they can distinguish that marketers have fostered the norm by including masculinity appeals in their advertising.

One way to describe uses of popular media by adolescents and to integrate the various meanings of media use is diagrammed in the media practice model, developed by Steele and Brown (1995). This model (see Figure 11.1) suggests that an adolescent's current and emerging sense of self (or identity)

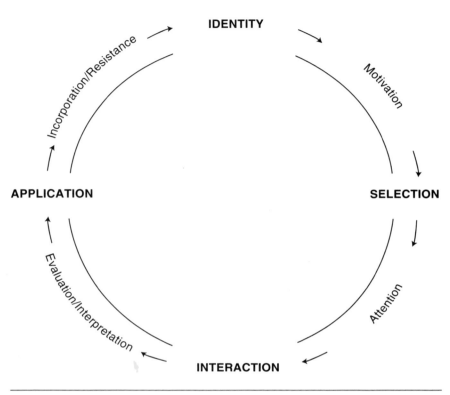

Figure 11.1   Adolescents' Media Practice Model
Reprinted by permission of Jeanne R. Steele, University of St. Thomas

is a compelling component as decisions are made about which media are selected, how they are interpreted, and how they are applied in different situations. This model works from the assumption that teens are active users of the media and bring with them a set of experiences and motivations that will affect what media they choose as well as how that content will be incorporated in their lives.

Lived Experience

Lived experience is a complex construct that sees the process of development as a constant bridging, accomplished through activity and communication, between the known and the new in specific contexts (Valsiner, 1991). Whether listening to music alone in their bedroom or dancing at a party, adolescents carry their particular life histories and knowledge of their peer cultures with them (Corsaro, 1992). With this knowledge, they build on and transform the shared sociocultural knowledge available through the media.

Media messages serve as cultural resources that youth use to reinforce or modify their sense of self and their affiliations with others within contexts shaped by gender, patterns of family life, race, ethnicity, class, sexual orientation, and other social distinctions. Stereotypical gender-based differences have been observed across countries such that some have said that girls and boys live in different media worlds.

The particular way in which a family structures its private life also sets parameters for its children's media use. In some homes, television is the primary form of entertainment. In others, the family engages in leisure and civic activities primarily outside the home. Children who are engaged in their schools and doing well academically tend to spend less time with the media. Although the influence of social class on patterns of media use has been neglected in U.S. media research, European studies have found substantial differences in time spent with media and content choices among youth in different socioeconomic circumstances. European studies also have found significant differences among countries in media use patterns by youth, suggesting that media use is related to even broader cultural norms (Roe, 2000).

Identity

The media practice model posits that each teen comes to the media with an identity or developing sense of himself or herself given by their lived experience that affects motivations for using the media as well as which medium is selected at any moment. These motivations, in turn, affect what content the teen pays attention to and to what extent the teen interacts with that content and incorporates it into what he or she already knows or does.

The model's circularity also reflects the assumption that human behavior is bidirectional and reciprocal. What an adolescent brings to the media is influenced by the media he or she uses and, in turn, will affect how he or she attends to the media in the future. In this way, we suggest also that the media's influence will almost never be as massive or direct as is often assumed. Media interaction will be conditional on who the teen is, when he or she uses the media, and the context in which the media are used. As adolescents try on different ways of being in the world, the media provide a kind of "toolkit" of beliefs, expectations, scripts, and models of behavior.

Key Moments in the Media Practice Model

The media practice model calls attention to three "moments" in the use of media. Adolescents do not come as blank slates to their use of media. Instead, they select media based on who they already are and who they want to be (Steele, 1999). They also interact with and interpret media in their own ways, and they may either incorporate or resist media messages.

Selection

As we discussed in detail earlier, teens' media diets differ dramatically by age, gender, ethnicity, and access to media. Recent ethnographic studies suggest that media selection is also affected by family and peer dynamics (Ang, 2001; Hall, 1986; Morley, 1986). For example, in some households, older siblings or adults may have more control over what is viewed, and so even though some teens may report frequent use of sexualized media content, they may not have chosen that content and thus may not "tune in" to the same extent as do teens who sought out that content. Teens in peer groups in which music plays an important role may select a specific kind of music to be more clearly identified as part of that group.

Interaction and Interpretation

Following the active process of selection, the second major step in media practice involves interaction and interpretation: Once content is selected, how is it understood? What aspects of the content are attended to and engaged with? A few studies of teens' interpretations of frequent sexual content in the media and a large body of work on the concept of selective perception tell us that all members of an audience will not see or interpret the same message in the same way (Livingstone, 1989; Zillmann & Bryant, 1985).

Brown and Schulze (1990) found a striking example of differing interpretations in their intergenerational study of one of Madonna's early music videos, "Papa Don't Preach." When first released, columnist Ellen Goodman called it "a commercial for teenage pregnancy" (1986, p. A-23), while antiabortion groups saw it as a stand against abortion. College students who saw the video differed in their interpretations of the video, too. Although most white females thought the video was about a teen girl deciding to keep her unborn child ("baby"), black males were more likely to think the girl (Madonna) in the video was singing about wanting to keep her boyfriend ("baby"). Because the young men were identifying primarily with the dilemma of the boyfriend in the video, they were less likely than the female viewers were to see or hear the cues that suggested pregnancy.

Incorporation and Resistance

As teens attend to and interpret media content, they also evaluate and sometimes incorporate what they are seeing into their own developing sense of self. Qualitative studies of how girls use the Internet (Stern, 2002; Wray & Steele, 2002) have shown that youth can be astute media critics and producers. These studies illustrate what is meant by "resistance" in the media practice model; the girls opposed the dominant ideas of attractiveness and the female's role in the dominant model of heterosexual relationships.

For example, one young female Web author posted a game she called "Make Kate Fat." Spoofing the waifish figure of supermodel Kate Moss, the game allowed site visitors to select various foods Kate Moss might choose for lunch. As they clicked on fattening food items, the model's photographic image was enhanced to make it look as if she were gaining weight. This game was a clever way for the Web author to express her dissatisfaction with the often unrealistic and unhealthy beauty standards promoted by mainstream media.

The media practice model thus provides a way of thinking about the various steps in the process of media use by youth, which include selection of, interaction with, and incorporation of popular media culture. As the model suggests, the process is somewhat different for each youth and depends on who they are and what they need in the moment, as well as who they have been, what they know and believe, and the social cultural context in which they live. Some youth will be more astute media consumers than others, some more able to negotiate, critique, and resist the dominant media messages that tend to disempower them through negative stereotypes and portrayals.

Critical Media Literacy

Over the past couple of decades, parents, educators, and media scholars and activists have been promoting *media literacy,* or *media education* or *critical media literacy,* as a useful way to empower more youth with the capacity to be critical media consumers and advocates. Two broad perspectives, the liberation and the inoculation, have guided the development of this idea.

The ultimate goal of the *liberation* perspective on media literacy is to transform society by enabling students to question the underlying assumptions of the media and to create more democratic media institutions. This perspective sees the media as key social institutions that reproduce social inequalities such as sexism, racism, and economic disparity. One of the aims is to minimize the current control of media by huge corporations, such as Disney and Time-Warner, and to create a regulatory climate in which community and public media can flourish (Lewis & Jhally, 1998). Students who participate in curricula and workshops based on this perspective come to understand how corporations and private interests have taken over the majority of "public spheres" that are vital to democratic dialogue, decision making, and community building. They learn how to reclaim these spaces by producing countercultural messages that address public issues such as poverty, the privatization of public spaces, and the lack of visible alternatives to neoliberal politics.

The *inoculation* perspective on media literacy recognizes that there are considerable problems with the U.S. commercial media system but tends to focus more on change at the level of the individual media consumer rather than on larger social structures. Although the liberation perspective sees students as citizens and envisages the democratization of the media, the inoculation perspective conceptualizes students primarily as media consumers and aims to help them make more informed choices about what media to use and how to interpret what they see, hear, and read. Inoculation perspective advocates seek to protect young people from "unhealthy" media messages by teaching them how to regulate their own media consumption and "deconstruct" media texts by identifying intended and unintended meanings.

We believe that young people today need to know more and be encouraged to be critical and active at both the societal and individual levels of media use. Because the liberation perspective includes both institutional analysis and individual critique, we focus more on that perspective here.

The Philosophical Basis: Paulo Freire

The root of the liberation perspective on media literacy is *Freirean pedagogy*. Because Freire's pedagogy is widely referred to as *critical pedagogy*, approaches to media literacy relying on the liberation perspective are also known as *critical media literacy*. Paulo Freire was an educator, who, while working on adult literacy for peasants in Brazil, developed his ideas about the "pedagogy of the oppressed," which is both a method and a philosophy of education. Freire (1973) believed that human beings are incomplete, or *becoming,* and that their "ontological vocation" is to become fully human, capable of reflecting on their immediate reality in order to transform it. Under oppressive circumstances, however, people (both oppressed and oppressors) become less, rather than more, human.

Freire (1999, p. 149) argued that conventional "banking" education produces a "culture of silence" that sustains oppression because it conceptualizes knowledge as "deposits" transferred from teacher to student. In contrast, liberatory education, which relies on reflective dialogue and problem posing, empowers students to question and name historical situations that have become naturalized over time (such as unequal gender relations based on assumptions taken for granted about men and women).

Following Freirean pedagogy, critical media literacy education prompts students to analyze the media and the role the media play in their lives and in society. Critical media literacy training provides an opportunity for students to address problems about the media content they read, listen to, or view; about the media technologies they use; about the media systems in which they participate; and about the ways people participate, or do not, in those systems. Critical media literacy also involves knowledge about global media economics and about the socializing power of today's giant media conglomerates. It also includes the development of media production skills that empower students to create media texts that speak with a liberated voice.

Media literacy programs that adhere closely to Freire's thought assume that media have become crucial institutions for the socialization of children and for the maintenance of democracy. Some of these programs aim to transform the current media system and thus encourage students to reflect on concrete ways in which mainstream media content manipulates them and to take specific actions that may reduce the manipulation (see Cases 11.1 and 11.2).

The skills and competencies that constitute critical media literacy enable students to be not only savvy users of mainstream media but also aware of the purposes of the commercial logic of these media. Most crucially, media literacy competencies are more than an end in themselves; they are also a means to an end: the practice of democratic citizenship. Critical media literacy empowers youth to relate to media texts and technologies in ways that enable them to participate more effectively in social change efforts and therefore to participate more creatively in the civic life of their communities.

Case 11.1   A Critical Media Literacy Project with Arab American
Girls

Media literacy educators Jennifer Bing-Canar and Mary Zerkel (1998) collaborated with the Arab American Community Center in Chicago to implement a successful yearlong critical media literacy program for Arab American girls. The program addressed a number of problems identified by the community center, including widespread misinformation about Chicago's Arab American community; negative stereotypes about Arab American girls; racism; and girls' invisibility within their own communities. The program was designed to accomplish two goals: (a) to develop the young women's critical thinking skills and critical consciousness through both theoretical discussions and actual practice (video production) and (b) to provide a safe and comfortable space for young women in the Arab American community to explore sensitive issues together.

The two educators and 8 to 10 participating girls accomplished the first goal by beginning to question and analyze mechanisms and structures in the mass media and by investigating representation and identity—especially that of Arabs, Arab Americans, and women—as they are constructed in the media. In addition, through the production of a video about themselves, *Benaat Chicago (Daughters of Chicago): Growing up Arab and Female in Chicago,* the young women began actively creating an alternative image of themselves and their community and initiating dialogue among other community members about a wide range of related issues.

During the weekly workshops, the educators and girls analyzed media content, discussed relevant personal and social issues, and produced a documentary video. The media analysis involved dissecting media presentations of Arab issues in the news, focusing primarily on the points of view that are included or excluded by the media. The girls considered questions such as "Whom does each speaker hold responsible for the incident?" "What is the unspoken point of view of each speaker?" "Whose point of view is missing?" "Which points of view shown here do you see on television or in newspapers?" The girls also connected their marginalization in the media with that of other cultures, women, children, and the elderly. The girls filled out a "Home TV Critic" form that asked them to identify stereotypes in their favorite shows and to decide whether each show was relevant to their lives.

The weekly sessions also included a structured time for reflection through journal writing or story telling. The girls read segments of their journals aloud to focus discussions and provide a basis of personal experience on which to build group activities. The girls also explored relevant social issues through role-playing, which enabled them to think about differing perspectives on sensitive cultural issues (e.g., gender relations within Arab communities).

Technical instruction on video production was as hands-on as possible. The educators provided handouts on every technical concept covered and ample time for each young woman to put the concept into practice. For instance, most discussions were videotaped by the girls, which allowed them to become proficient behind the camera and more comfortable in front of it. Periodically, the educators took the group on a location shoot, where they filmed scenes for the video. Although time constraints precluded involving all the girls in the editing process, the educators did hire two of the participants as production interns to shepherd the process. While editing the video, the interns discussed various issues with the rest of the group and with other community members to ensure that the final product captured the group's intended messages. Halfway through the adult producers' final edit, they previewed the video in progress with a small group from the community to gain feedback and last-minute direction. The resulting video has been a source of pride for the participating girls, their families, and the community center and a catalyst for important dialogues across Chicago.

Critical media literacy is quite different from social-change-oriented efforts that advocate simply "giving" media to the people (e.g., installing a radio station in a rural area, putting cameras in the hands of inner-city teens). Many of these projects privilege production skills and either pay insufficient attention to or completely lack the most important component of critical media literacy, which is to acquire critical thinking skills to effectively resist the mainstream media. Moreover, these projects often concentrate on change at the individual level and microlevels, failing to link local conditions to global processes. Critical media literacy aims to enable students to understand the

Case 11.2   Culture Jamming as a Set of Critical Media Literacy
                 Strategies

Culture jamming is a set of practices used to instigate community discussion about the politics of public space by parodying advertisements and hijacking billboards to drastically alter their messages (Klein, 1999). Culture jammers, also known as "adbusters" and "badvertisers," argue that the "concentration of media ownership has successfully devalued the right to free speech by severing it from the right to be heard" (Klein, 1999, p. 280). "Streets are public spaces, adbusters argue, and since most residents can't afford to counter corporate messages by purchasing their own ads, they should have the right to talk back to images they never asked to see" (Klein, 1999, p. 280). The "Joe Chemo," "Cancer Kid," "Please Do Not Feed the Models," and "Shit Happens. New Exxon" campaigns are perhaps the most widely known culture jams in this country. (These images are available online at: www.adbusters.org.)

In her book, *No Logo: Taking Aim at the Brand Bullies,* Naomi Klein (1999) reports that "for a growing number of young activists, adbusting has presented itself as the perfect tool with which to register disapproval of the multinational corporations that have so aggressively stalked them as shoppers, and so unceremoniously dumped them as workers" (p. 284). These activists are developing a network of "media collectives" that combine adbusting with zine publishing, pirate radio, activist video, Internet development, and community activism.

For example, Asian American girls have developed Internet sites that address negative (usually hypersexualized) images of Asian women and girls produced by corporations, advertising agencies, and other media producers. One such site, "Eroticize This," contains a picture of an Asian American teen in "grunge" attire throwing a fist that grows larger as it appears to approach the computer user. These sites usually contain links to other activist Internet sites and contact information for other activist resources.

Although these Internet sites and related endeavors appear to be part of grassroots campaigns initiated and maintained by teens, other "media collectives" have been established by government agencies, nonprofit organizations, and schools to engage young people in culture jamming and other liberation-oriented media education activities (e.g., The *Girls Re-Cast TV* and the American Legacy Foundation's anti–tobacco industry *Truth* campaign; see: www.thetruth.com).

role of media in both local and global processes and the way these two types of processes are interconnected. For example, critical media literacy training could increase understanding of the link between the racializing portrayal of immigrants in the media and the dependence of a number of U.S. industries (e.g., food processing) on immigrant labor.

Critical media literacy training also encourages students to inquire about the role of the media in identity construction processes. It encourages them to inquire especially about the ways in which the media constitute youth's identities in terms of gender, race, and class and about the ways in which the media contribute to how they come to see themselves. In terms of the media practice model, critical media literacy training introduces critical reflection into the three moments of media use: selection, interpretation, and application. And, as these examples of critical media literacy training demonstrate, it often adds a fourth moment: alternative media production.

Examples of Promising Critical Media Literacy Projects

Although few media literacy projects have undertaken rigorous evaluation efforts to demonstrate their effects on participants, there is a growing body of case study evidence suggesting that critical media literacy training can have a positive impact on the lives of young people. This section highlights a few programs that appear to be making a difference.

Community College Media Literacy Curriculum

In California, media activist and scholar Tara Yosso (2002) combined Freire's method with critical race theory to implement a media literacy curriculum with 35 Latino/Hispanic young adults (both native and immigrant) who were attending a community college. The curriculum was designed to analyze the racialized version of socioacademic success constructed by Hollywood films. Together, Yosso and the students discussed and critiqued cinematic representation of Latino adolescents in school settings. Yosso found that the curriculum was a powerful tool for consciousness raising among these marginalized youth and had great potential in the social justice efforts of grassroots organizations serving immigrant and minority youth.

Girls Re-Cast TV

Two national nonprofit organizations, Girls Incorporated and the Center for Media Literacy, are collaborating to sponsor Girls Re-Cast TV, a four-part media literacy program designed to promote gender equity. The program seeks to make girls aged 11 to 14 more aware of how they are portrayed on television and how such portrayals can affect how they think about themselves and others. It also focuses on issues such as gender role stereotyping, sex and power, body image, and gender violence. A discussion guide is available online at: www.girlsinc.org.

New Mexico Media Literacy Project

Another multifaceted program, the New Mexico Media Literacy Project (NMMLP; available at: www.nmmlp.org) promotes inoculation-oriented media education on issues such as substance abuse and eating disorders, and liberation-oriented media education on issues such as consumerism, corporate media monopolies, and censorship. According to its literature, NMMLP (1999) "shows teachers, students, parents, business people, professionals and other citizens how media literacy can create freedom, and how it can relieve the cynicism, apathy and stress that modern media create." Moreover, "Media literate technology develops skills to successfully approach media issues such as violence, technological education, parenting, news, democracy, compulsivity, stereotyping, reading skills, self esteem, productivity, motivation, and addictions." To reach these diverse goals, NMMLP has developed CD-ROM–based media literacy curricula, conducted approximately 500 presentations at schools nationwide, and held annual media literacy conferences at which speakers such as Neil Postman, Susan Douglas, and Howard Zinn promoted multifaceted media education programs (NMMLP, 2000).

Promoting Media Literacy in the United States

Examples indicate that liberation-oriented media literacy holds much promise. Currently, however, in the United States, media literacy training is spotty, developed and sponsored by a few organizations that have recognized its potential for helping young people gain more control over their lives and the culture. Although in a number of other countries, such as England and Australia, media education has become an integral part of the public education curricula, it is unlikely that this will happen soon in the United States, primarily because state and local school systems have such autonomy in determining curriculum. Therefore, U.S. media literacy advocates, while continuing to work toward having media education as part of school curricula, are promoting media literacy activities in other youth-serving venues, such as after-school programs and clubs for youth.

Institutionalizing media literacy education will require persuading the public that it can be an effective response to diverse, widespread concerns, such as school violence and health risk behaviors among children. It will also require conducting research on the various ways young people use media, the effects of liberation-oriented programs, and best practices in implementing these programs.

Proponents of the liberation perspective have described a number of topics of concern, or "hooks," that could be used to garner public support for implementing media literacy education more widely. The topics include diversity, critical thinking skills, the "digital divide," citizenship, and censorship. Because several of the exemplary media literacy projects we've already discussed focus on media literacy and diversity, we will briefly discuss the other four topics that can be addressed with media literacy education.

Media Literacy for Critical Thinking Skills

Media literacy advocates argue that media literacy should be considered a core competency in schools because it requires students to learn and use critical thinking skills to deconstruct and produce media messages and to analyze the contexts in which the media operate. If critical media literacy were to be taught in schools and youth groups, new types of teacher training that provide information about the various technologies and the principles and practices of media education would be necessary. Teachers and youth workers also would have to be trained in pedagogies that move away from disseminating information ("banking" education) toward coaching students and enhancing their creative and problem-solving capacities (Considine, 1997).

Such training opportunities will have great appeal to many teachers and youth workers but may intimidate others who are not comfortable with the technology and/or their new roles as facilitators in student-centered classrooms and workshops. Media literacy advocates will need to work with teachers to ease their fears, address their concerns, and learn from their experiences. Fortunately, training is available at a number of sites across the country (see Table 11.1 U.S. for a list of media literacy programs and training opportunities).

Table 11.1 U.S. Media Literacy Resources

Organization Name	Type of Organization			Target Audience			Materials Available					For more information, contact
	A	IN	SA	Y	P	E	S/PM	P/B /R	AV	C	W/C	
Action Coalition for Media Education	X					X	X				X	www.acmecoalition.org
Alliance for a Media Literate America (AMLA)		X				X				X	X	www.nmec.org
American Academy of Pediatrics		X			X		X			X		www.aap.org
American Academy of Child and Adolescent Psychiatry		X			X		X			X		www.aacap.org
American Medical Association		X			X		X			X		www.ama-assn.org
American Psychological Association		X					X			X		www.apa.org
Cable in the Classroom			X		X							800-743-5355
Center for Media Education	X	X			X	X	X	X			X	www.cme.org

Organization Name	Type of Organization			Target Audience				Materials Available				For more information, contact
	A	IN	SA	Y	P	E	S/PM	P/B/R	AV	C	W/C	
Center for Media Literary	X	X			X	X	X	X	X	X	X	www.medialit.org
Center for Media Studies		X					X				X	www.mediastudies.rutgers.edu
Discovery Communications, Inc.		X		X		X				X	X	www.assignmentmedialit.com
Just Think Foundation		X		X	X	X		X	X	X	X	www.justthink.org
Kaiser Family Foundation		X			X		X	X				www.kff.org
Kidsnet		X	X	X	X	X			X	X	X	www.kidsnet.org

Abbreviations:
A – Advocacy
IN – Information
SA – Service agency
Y – Youth
P – Parents

E – Educators
S/PM – Media scholars/Policymakers
P/B/R – Pamphlets/ Books/ Reports
AV – Audiovisuals
C – Curricula
W/C – Workshops/Conferences

(Continued)

259

Table 11.1 U. S. Media Literacy Resources (Continued)

Organization Name	Type of Organization			Target Audience				Materials Available				For more information, contact
	A	IN	SA	Y	P	E	S/PM	P/B /R	AV	C	W/C	
Mass Media Bureau		X										www.fcc.gov
Media Channel	X						X	X				www.mediachannel.org
Media Education Foundation	X					X	X	X	X			www.mediaed.org/index.html
Media Literacy Clearinghouse						X				X		www.med.sc.edu; 81 Medialit
Media Literacy Project		X				X				X		www.reneehobbs.org
Media Literacy Review	X	X		X	X	X	X	X	X	X		www.interact.uoregon.edu/MediaLit
National Institute on Media and the Family	X				X							www.mediaandthefamily.org
National PTA	X				X	X						www.danet.wicip.org/ntc

Organization Name	Type of Organization			Target Audience				Materials Available				For more information, contact
	A	IN	SA	Y	P	E	S/PM	P/B/R	AV	C	W/C	
National Telemedia Council, Inc.		X					X					www.national telemedia council.org
New Mexico Media Literacy Project	X		X	X	X	X	X			X	X	www.nmmlp.org
Project Look Sharp		X				X				X	X	www.ithaca.edu/ looksharp
Yale University Family Television Research and Consultation Center		X			X							www.yale.edu/psychology/ singerlab.html; 203-432-4565

Abbreviations:
A – Advocacy
IN – Information
SA – Service agency
Y – Youth
P – Parents

E – Educators
S/PM – Media scholars/Policymakers
P/B/R – Pamphlets/ Books/ Reports
AV – Audiovisuals
C – Curricula
W/C – Workshops/Conferences

Media Literacy and the Digital Divide

Access to media technology, particularly computers and the Internet, has become a major political issue in recent years. President Clinton promised to put computers and Internet connections in every classroom in the country and to close the widely publicized income-related "technology gap" or "digital divide." Schools are trying to figure out the best way to use these new resources. Many are finding that existing curricula and teaching strategies fail to take advantage of what these resources offer and that their efforts to use the technology end up taking the place of other subject matter. This may prove an ideal time to institute media literacy across multiple subjects as a strategy for integrating technology use with other subject matter, enhancing both in the process.

Moreover, the steadily increasing demand for school reform and restructuring may provide a related opportunity to articulate media literacy as an integral component of school curricula. A number of states are finding this strategy useful. North Carolina, for instance, has incorporated media literacy into its communication skills (English) and information skills curricula. Massachusetts has incorporated media literacy in all curriculum frameworks recently developed by the state education department (Hobbs, 2000).

In cooperation with the Discovery Channel, the State of Maryland has developed a comprehensive media education curriculum and training for teachers of grades K-12. Such partnerships with media companies concern some media literacy advocates, however, who say that it jeopardizes the potential for media criticism (Heins & Cho, 2002).

Media Literacy for Citizenship

Linking media education to citizenship and civic education can help tap into growing concerns about the changing nature of citizenship and democracy in contemporary society and the alleged failure of schools to foster a sense of civic duty in students.

Media literacy advocate Renee Hobbs (1998) argues that media literacy can help strengthen American democracy in three ways: (a) by enhancing students' access to information, analysis, and communication skills and interest in monitoring what is happening in the world; (b) by fostering educational environments in which students can practice the skills needed to participate in a democratic society, including leadership skills, free and responsible expression, conflict resolution, and consensus-building; and (c) by inspiring young people to seek out diverse sources of information representing a wide variety of groups and interests.

Hobbs (1998) explains that as media ownership is increasingly centralized, students (and adults) may require encouragement to seek out alternative sources of information. Hobbs and others believe that this articulation of the connection between media literacy and democracy will help mobilize key stakeholders, including government agencies, national nonprofits, school administrators, teachers, parents, and youth, in the interest of creating a more democratic media system and society.

Media Literacy and Censorship

Recent mergers between large media corporations such as AOL.com and Time-Warner Corp. have prompted debate over the effects of media monopolies on the public sphere. Hobbs, the NMMLP, the culture jammers, and others have argued that these monopolies limit the topics, voices, and opinions that appear in the media and thus participate in a kind of censorship of alternative ideas and voices. They argue that youth must be taught how to seek out other sources of information and be encouraged to demand more from those who control the "public" airwaves. Some argue that this issue is particularly pressing given the increasing extent to which commercial interests are targeting schools as new markets (through the installation of billboards, logos on athletic scoreboards, television in the classroom, etc.).

Conclusions

The mass media are an important context in which youth live and learn. Many young people in the United States today have almost unlimited access to a wide variety of media and spend a great deal of unsupervised time attending to them. Unfortunately, the content of much of the media does not provide a positive, empowering, healthy view of the world. Traditional communication research has found that youth are affected by what they read, see, and hear in the media and that the media contribute to increased levels of aggression and violence, unhealthy attitudes about sexuality, and negative stereotyping of minority youth.

Recent communication theory conceptualizes viewers/readers/listeners as active participants in media practices. The media practice model posits three moments in which they make choices: as they select which media and content to attend to; as they pay attention to and interpret some parts of the content and not other parts; and as they apply, incorporate, or resist applying to their own lives what they have seen, read, or listened to.

In this context, one of the most useful ways of countering the potentially negative effects of media exposure is to help young people learn more about media systems, to empower them to become media activists and producers, and to encourage them to make wiser choices at each step in their use of media.

The growing movement of media literacy education holds great promise, especially because it can simultaneously address a number of related issues, such as the need for critical thinking skills, the digital divide, and citizenship. Recent examples of successful media literacy projects with young people show that youth like thinking and talking about the media and they love producing their own. Our vision is that in the future, the media world would be a more diverse and civically engaged place in which young people could find and produce positive images of themselves. Raising a generation of media-literate citizens may help realize that vision.

References

Ang, I. (2001). On the politics of empirical audience research. In M. G. Durham & D. M. Kellner (Eds.), *Media and cultural studies: Key works* (pp. 177-197). Walden, MA: Blackwell.

Bing-Canar, J., & Zerkel, M. (1998). Reading the media and myself: Experiences in critical media literacy with young Arab-American women. *Signs, 23*(3), 735-743.

Bristor, J., Lee, R. G., & Hunt, M. (1995). Race and ideology: African-American images in television advertising. *Journal of Public Policy and Marketing, 14*(1), 48-59.

Brown, J. D., & Schulze, L. (1990). The effects of race, gender, and fandom on audience interpretation of Madonna's music videos. *Journal of Communication, 40*(2), 88-102.

Brown, J. D., Steele, J. R., & Walsh-Childers, K. (2002). *Sexual teens, Sexual media.* Mahwah, NJ: Lawrence Erlbaum.

Comstock, G., & Strasberger, V. C. (1990). Deceptive appearances: Television violence and aggressive behavior—An introduction. *Journal of Adolescent Health Care, 11,* 31-44.

Considine, D. (1997). Media literacy: A compelling component of school reform. In R. Kubey (Ed.), *Media literacy in the information age.* New Brunswick, NJ: Transaction Publishers.

Corsaro, W. A. (1992). Interpretive reproduction in children's peer cultures. *Social Psychology Quarterly, 55,* 160-177.

Cross, B. (1993). *It's not about a salary: Rap, race, and resistance in Los Angeles.* London: Verso.

Durham, M. G. (1999). Girls, media and the negotiation of sexuality: A study of race, class and gender in adolescent peer groups. *Journalism & Mass Communication Quarterly, 76*(2), 193-216.

Freire, P. (1973). *Education for critical consciousness.* New York: Continuum.

Freire, P. (1999). *Pedagogy of the oppressed.* New York: Continuum.

Friedrich-Cofer, L., & Huston, A. C. (1986). Television violence and aggression: The debate continues. *Psychological Bulletin, 100*(3), 364-371.

Gaines, D. (1991). *Teenage wasteland: Suburbia's dead end kids.* New York: HarperCollins.

Gilligan, C. (1982). *In a different voice: Psychological theory and women's development.* Cambridge, MA: Harvard University Press.

Giroux, H. (1998). *Channel surfing: Racism, the media, and the destruction of today's youth.* New York: St. Martin's Griffin.

Giroux, H. A. (2000). Disposable youth/disposable futures: The crisis of politics and public life. In N. Campbell (Ed.), *The radiant hour: Versions of youth in American culture* (pp. 71-87). Exeter, Devon, UK: University of Exeter Press.

Goodman, E. (1986, September 20). Commercial for teenage pregnancy. *Washington Post,* p. A-23.

Hall, S. (1986). Cultural studies: Two paradigms. In R. Collins et al. (Eds.), *Media, culture and society: A critical reader* (pp. 33-48). London: Sage.

Heins, M., & Cho, C. (2002). *Media literacy: An alternative to censorship.* New York: Free Expression Project.

Hobbs, R. (1998). The seven great debates in the media literacy movement. *Journal of Communication, 48*(2), 9-29.

Hobbs, R. (2000). Improving reading comprehension by using media literacy activities. *Voices from the Middle, 8*(4), 44-50.

Huston, A., Wartella, E., & Donnerstein, E. (1998). *Measuring the effects of sexual content in the media: A report to the Kaiser Family Foundation.* Menlo Park, CA: Henry J. Kaiser Family Foundation.

Kaiser Family Foundation/YM Magazine. (1998). *National survey of teens: Teens talk about dating, intimacy, and their sexual experiences.* Menlo Park, CA: Henry J. Kaiser Family Foundation.

Klein, N. (1999). *No logo: Taking aim at the brand bullies.* New York: Picador.

Livingstone, S. M. (1989). Interpretive viewers and structured programs. *Communication Research, 16*(1), 25-57.

Lewis, J., & Jhally S. (1998). The struggle over media literacy. *Journal of Communication, 48*(1), 109-120.

Lull, J. (1990). *Inside family viewing: Ethnographic research on television's audiences.* London: Routledge.

Males, M. (1999). *Framing youth: Ten myths about the next generation.* Monroe, ME: Common Courage.

Mazarella, S. R., & Pecora, N. O. (Eds.). (1999). *Growing up girls: Popular culture and the construction of identity.* New York: Peter Lang.

Mediascope. (2000). *Media use in America* (Issue brief). Studio City, CA: Author.

Morley, D. (1986). *Family television: Cultural power and domestic leisure.* London: Comedia.

New Mexico Media Literacy Project. (1999). *The New Mexico media literacy project—Vital statistics.* Albuquerque: Author.

New Mexico Media Literacy Project. (2000). Retrieved April 2000 from: http://www.nmmlp.org/.

Pipher, M. (1994). *Reviving Ophelia: Saving the selves of adolescent girls.* New York: Ballantine.

Roberts, D. F. (2000). Media and youth: Access, exposure, and privatization. *Journal of Adolescent Health, 27*(2, Suppl.), 8-14.

Roberts, D. F., Foehr, U. G., Rideout, V. J., & Brodie, M. (1999). *Kids and media @ the new millennium.* Menlo Park, CA: Henry J. Kaiser Family Foundation.

Robinson, T. (1999). Reducing children's television viewing to prevent obesity: A randomized control trial. *Journal of the American Medical Association, 282*(16), 1561-1567.

Roe, K. (1995). Adolescents' use of socially disvalued media: Towards a theory of media delinquency. *Journal of Youth and Adolescence, 24*(5), 617-632.

Rose, T. (1995). Fear of a black planet. In G. Dines and J. Humez (Eds.), *Gender, race and class in media* (pp. 531-539). Thousand Oaks, CA: Sage.

Seiter, E. (1995). Different children, different dreams. In G. Dines & J. Humez (Eds.), *Gender, race and class in media* (pp. 99-108). Thousand Oaks, CA: Sage.

Skill, T., Robinson, J., & Kinsella, C. (1994, November). *Sexual harassment in network television situation comedies: An empirical content analysis of fictional programming one year prior to the Clarence Thomas Senate confirmation hearings for the U.S. Supreme Court.* Paper presented at the annual meeting of the Speech Communication Association, New Orleans, LA.

Smith, S. L., Wilson, B. J., Kunkel, D., Linz, D., Potter, W. J., Colvin, C., & Donnerstein, E. (1998). Violence in television programming overall: University of California, Santa Barbara, study. In *National television violence study: Vol. 3* (pp. 5-220). Newbury Park, CA: Sage.

Steele, J. R. (1999). Teenage sexuality and media practice: Factoring in the influences of family, friends, and school. *Journal of Sex Research, 36*(4), 331-341.

Steele, J. R., & Brown, J. D. (1995). Adolescent room culture: Studying media in the context of everyday life. *Journal of Youth and Adolescence, 24*(5), 551-557.

Stern, S. R. (2002). Sexual selves on the WWW: Adolescent girls' home pages as sites for sexual expression. In J. D. Brown, J. R. Steele, & K. Walsh-Childers (Eds.), *Sexual teens, sexual media* (pp. 265-286). Mahwah, NJ: Lawrence Erlbaum.

Valsiner, J. (1991). Building theoretical bridges over a lagoon of everyday events. *Human Development, 34,* 307-315.

Wray, J., & Steele, J. R. (2002). What it means to be a girl: Teen girl magazines. In J. D. Brown, J. R. Steele, & K. Walsh-Childers (Eds.), *Sexual teens, sexual media* (pp. 191-210). Hillsdale, NJ: Lawrence Erlbaum.

Yosso, T. J. (2002). Critical race media theory: Challenging deficit discourse about Chicanas/os. *Journal of Popular Film and Television, 30*(1), 52-63.

Zillmann, D., & Bryant, J. (1985). Selective exposure to communication. Hillsdale, NJ: Lawrence Erlbaum.

Part II

ACTION STEPS

12

Success Factors in Community-Wide Initiatives for Youth Development

Kathleen A. Dorgan and Ronald F. Ferguson[1]

This chapter analyzes community-wide initiatives for youth development and factors that help them succeed or cause them to falter. It compares two of the most prominent initiatives of the past 20 years: the New York City (NYC) Beacons and the New Futures Initiative of the Annie E. Casey Foundation (AECF).[2] Both Beacons and New Futures aimed to increase funding and expand the intellectual, social, and physical assets available to youth-serving agencies. In addition to serving youth, both intended to strengthen families and communities. This chapter explores why the NYC Beacons (or simply, "Beacons") appear to be more successful than New Futures, not only at expanding and improving frontline service delivery but also at the types of "system change" that New Futures in particular intended to foster.

The Beacons are community centers that operate in school buildings. The initiative began in New York City, with 10 sites, in 1991. There are currently 80 sites, with one or more in each of the city's 32 school districts. Open 10 to 12 hours a day, Beacons provide social services, recreation, education, vocational training, family support, and health services for children, youth, and families. These programs served over 150,000 children and 50,000 adults in New York City in 2002. Several cities have now adopted the Beacons model, but the discussion in this chapter is for New York City only.[3]

New Futures was a five-city demonstration project of the Annie E. Casey Foundation (AECF) spanning the late 1980s and early 1990s. New Futures began at least partly in response to frustration that the foundation experienced in its work with local service delivery systems. It was the first of several major initiatives that AECF has sponsored and documented to help the field improve.[4] Through New Futures, AECF aimed to change the formal and informal rules affecting how local resources were applied toward reducing the incidence of developmentally unhealthy outcomes that youth experience in high-risk neighborhoods. Cities competed for the opportunity to participate in the New Futures Initiative. The five winners were Little Rock, Arkansas; Dayton, Ohio; Lawrence, Massachusetts; Savannah, Georgia; and Pittsburgh, Pennsylvania. Lawrence was later replaced by Bridgeport, Connecticut. Assisted by the AECF, each city created a new organization called a "collaborative" and made it responsible for reforming local youth-serving arrangements, in other words, for achieving *systems reform*.

Aided by a strong technical assistance intermediary (the Youth Development Institute) and oversight from a sophisticated city agency (the New York City Department of Youth Services), the Beacons mobilized quickly to provide valued services to local youth and families. Although quality varied among the sites, the generally high quality attracted grass-roots political supporters who organized and then advocated to politicians to protect and expand the program. Politicians and others who control resources have responded supportively over the years, fostering improvements to the overall youth development system. Key elements of the story for Beacons are the use of public school facilities under the direction of community-based organizations, organized advocacy by grassroots groups, a very effective technical assistance intermediary, an evaluation structured to measure (and induce) adherence to youth development principles, and core funding from a city government agency that also monitors performance and enforces quality control. New Futures had none of these features, which helped make the Beacons initiative successful.

This chapter has two purposes. The first is to identify some factors that our analysis indicates contribute to the success of community-wide initiatives[5] for youth development. The second is to introduce the schematic framework that we use to organize the analysis. The framework helps highlight the division of roles and responsibilities among levels within what we term "the youth development system" and provides convenient semantics for strategic analysis and planning.

The Youth Development System

Local youth development activities are embedded in a national youth development system, albeit much of it loosely arranged and informal. Our analysis of that system calls attention to the roles assigned to actors in four levels. We describe how arrangements governing these roles affected the ability of actors to be effective.[6] Two key ideas here are that roles are enacted within levels and that levels exist within a hierarchy of power and authority.[7] (Although most actors hold one role, it is possible for the same person to hold more than one role and operate on multiple levels.)

Level Zero is the social location of grassroots activities. Its defining feature is that actors at Level Zero receive no financial compensation for their efforts. (See Table 12.1, "Levels of the Youth Development System.") Some Level Zero activities are relatively formal, such as local scout troops and voluntary sports leagues; others are informal, such as the child care services that neighbors provide for one another's children. A parent advocating for his or her child is performing another Level Zero function, that is, grassroots action. In this framework, families, even wealthy families, are grassroots actors. In their roles as neighborhood residents, people—children, youth, and adults—are all involved in grassroots work.

Level 1 is the location of "frontline" actors. They receive financial compensation for providing services. They work in frontline organizations. In the youth development system, frontline organizations and their staff provide direct services to children, youth, and families. Level 1 organizations exist in the public sector (e.g., public schools, parks and recreation departments, libraries, justice system, health clinics); the private nonprofit sector (e.g., YMCA, Boys and Girls Clubs, faith-based organizations); as well as the for-profit sector (e.g., private music schools, karate studios).

Level 2 of the system is called the "local support" level. It consists of people and organizations that support Level 1 with funding, various forms of technical assistance, and authorization. Level 2 organizations in the youth development system include the headquarters of local public service systems, such as the central offices of the school system or the local school board; philanthropic organizations of various types; and technical assistance providers. The Beacons initiative, for example, was conceived at Level 2 in New York City, by a city-sponsored commission.

Finally, some of the actors that affect local youth development are nonlocal. They operate on Level 3 of the system, which we label "nonlocal support." Level 3 is the nonlocal counterpart to Level 2. It includes national foundations, departments of state and national government, national

Table 12.1   Levels of the Youth Development System

	Examples	Functions of Levels in Youth Development	New Futures	NYC Beacons
Level Zero: Voluntary entities without paid staff At grassroots level, people act without compensation in their positions as members of communities, families, and informal associations.	Voluntary sports leagues Church youth groups Scout troops Neighborhood associations Youth councils Families	Voluntary groups work alone or as partners with Level 1 organizations in mentoring, tutoring, clean-ups, housing rehabilitation, organizing, planning, and other activities. Level Zero organizations contain the informal helping networks that often support individual young people. Within these networks of family, friends, sports teams, prayer groups, and neighbors, most successful young people find their support, guidance, and inspiration. Every functioning person is represented in one or more Level Zero organizations. The sheer numbers of activities on this level make it a vital "location" for community and youth development. Level Zero also plays a primary role in advocating for resources from Levels 1, 2 and 3.	Families Youth as clients for services	Community advisory councils Youth councils Youth as clients for Beacons activities and services Informal social networks
Level 1: Frontline organization	Local branches of national youth-serving organizations	Level 1 includes counselors, coaches, teachers, and probation officers	Case Managers Host schools	Beacons centers Host schools

	Examples	Functions of Levels in Youth Development	New Futures	NYC Beacons
Level 1 providers are people working in paid positions to offer services to individuals and neighborhoods.	Job Corps and YouthBuild centers Community-based organizations (CBOs) Private dance schools Employers Community and youth centers Health clinics Juvenile courts	working in paid jobs. Level 1 works directly to increase the assets of young people and their communities. Paid staff members enable these organizations to undertake complicated long-term efforts. Innovative practices often originate at Levels 1 and Zero. Many Level 1 organizations such as CDCs and other CBOs also actively scour the city, region, and nation for resources and opportunities that might help neighborhood residents. They often transform these resources to fit community needs.	Other service providers	Community-based organizations
Level 2: **Local support organizations** Level 2 includes people in their local positions as officials, policymakers, funders, and technical assistance providers.	Local United Way groups Community foundations Municipal youth bureaus & community development departments School boards Local intermediaries Local officials Local philanthropies	Level 2 makes local laws and regulations. They assemble and control local (and some state, national, and international) resources that fund most youth development programs. Level 2 has a primary role in determining the type of youth development programs that will be provided within a community, as well as the performance measures by which	Local collaboratives	Youth Development Institute (YDI) New York City Board of Education Administration for Children's Services

(Continued)

Table 12.1 (Continued)

	Examples	Functions of Levels in Youth Development	New Futures	NYC Beacons
		programs will be judged. Level 2 may invite participation in decision making from Levels 1 and Zero as well as solicit and administer resources from Level 3.		NYC Department of Youth and Community Development
Level 3: State, regional, national, and international support entities Level 3 is the regional and national counterpart to Level 2. Its functions span more than a single locality.	Federal agencies (e.g., U.S. Department of Health and Human Services) Private foundations researchers, technical assistance providers, and intermediaries (e.g., Public/Private Ventures, Search Institute, Chapin Hall Center for Children, Local Initiatives Support Corporation (LISC), & Development Training Institute) National Headquarters of national youth serving organizations	Level 3 determines policy, collects resources, and promulgates rules and regulations on the regional, state, national, and international levels. Funds and other resources from Level 3 help support all levels of the system. National researchers, foundations, and technical assistance providers fund new initiatives in the field as well as supporting ongoing programs. Level 3 also develops training programs, identifies best practices, and is largely responsible for establishing prevailing practices, policy, and theory in youth development. Sources of support for young people are national youth-serving organizations, such as the Girl Scouts, 4-H Clubs, Job Corps, Girls Inc, and Big Brothers/Big Sisters	Annie E. Casey Foundation Center for the Study of Social Policy	Academy for Educational Development Chapin Hall Center for Children at UIC Annie E. Casey Foundation Ford Foundation Open Society Institute Hunter College Center on AIDS, Drugs, and Community Health Girls Inc.

headquarters of youth-serving organizations, and various organizations that supply research and technical assistance for youth development across areas larger than localities. The New Futures initiative was conceived at Level 3 by AECF. It aimed to foster changes in systems at Levels 1 and 2.

Below, we argue that the New Futures approach was naïve concerning the politics that operate within and across the levels defined above. In contrast, the NYC Beacons initiative was better structured to handle the political challenges to serving more youth more effectively. We argue that the NYC Beacons model would probably have better served the New Futures goals, in part because the Beacons model was more effective than New Futures at generating a grassroots political constituency. An actively supportive grassroots (Level Zero) political constituency is among the most important assets that the field of youth development can have to ensure the sustainability of a Level 2 commitment to support youth development services at Level 1. Because it engages communities in ways that generate a grassroots constituency, the Beacons model may hold more promise for systemic reform than initiatives such as New Futures that specifically target Level 2 for change. In addition to a political constituency, organizational and procedural factors mattered as well, and we explore several of them below.

Origins and Theories of Change

New Futures and Beacons sprang from similar concerns. Each was a response to youth violence, substance abuse, academic failure, and unemployment among young people in disadvantaged communities. Originators of both programs believed they could best address these challenges with programs that were neighborhood based, responsive to young people's developmental needs, and culturally appropriate. Designers of each initiative reviewed literature and consulted with practitioners. Despite these similarities in concerns, diagnoses, and initial direction setting, the New Futures and Beacons initiatives diverged from one another as their theories of change and implementation strategies came into focus.

Conception of New Futures

The AECF conceived the New Futures initiative in response to disappointing experiences with public sector systems for serving youth, especially youth in foster care. AECF observed that young people were "falling through the cracks" of fragmented local systems and not receiving the help they needed. Working with the Center for the Study of Social Policy (1987a), officials at AECF envisioned restructuring youth services to be comprehensive and integrated. The goal was strategic reform, not simply technical improvement. The executives who led the AECF believed that if counselors, parole officers, teachers, and health care providers could work together, reinforcing one another's efforts, young people could find the supports they needed to be resilient and avoid negative outcomes.

The AECF and its consultants began from the premise that local systems could meet young people's needs more effectively than they had in the past. The problem, AECF believed, was that Level 2 leaders had too little accurate information about youth and families (Level Zero) and about conditions affecting the success of frontline agencies (Level 1, using our terms for their analysis). AECF theorized that with more and better information and a way to work together, leaders would design and implement new ways of using resources that would foster healthier life styles and reduce negative outcomes.

The AECF board authorized a 5-year demonstration to test their theory in the five mid-sized cities identified above. They believed that a significant investment by the foundation, advice from national experts, and collaboration among local leaders could raise academic achievement, lower rates of teen parenthood, and raise rates of productive engagement (i.e., school, work, college). They were hoping that substantial 5-year grants for restructuring in communities committed to change would provide sufficient incentive for Level 2 decision makers to set aside territorial concerns and work for a system in which actors at all levels would adjust their practices to serve young people more effectively. Part of the plan was to channel information from frontline service providers (Level 1) to decision makers who controlled both rules and resources at Level 2. AECF expected members of Level 2 collaboratives to use such information as the basis for changing rules and reallocating resources—in other words, reforming systems. They believed this change could be implemented quickly enough to show measurable outcomes for youth within the 5-year period.

Stated succinctly, the New Futures "theory of change" was that *organizing Level 2 decision makers and giving them better information would lead to needed reforms at all levels and improved service delivery at Level 1, which in turn would reduce the incidence of negative outcomes for youth and families at Level Zero.*

Conception of New York City Beacons

The NYC Beacons trace their existence to the recommendation of a committee exploring an integrated approach to antidrug efforts. Beacons began with the idea that creating "safe havens" for young people in neighborhoods would be an effective antidrug policy. Program designers believed that placing more resources and decision-making authority in the neighborhood would enable local leaders to respond to local conditions. In addition, they theorized that youth, families, and neighborhood-based service providers could best design day-to-day services by following the principles of youth development. They were convinced that with support, young people could be partners in improving conditions in their neighborhoods. They believed that strong community-based programs could attract the resources necessary to build a comprehensive initiative. It was postulated that the financial incentive of operating support would attract established neighborhood-based nonprofit organizations to compete to manage the Beacons sites in neighborhood schools. Designers believed they could build support even though the initiative might be seen as intruding on the territory of schools and existing providers.

In brief, the NYC Beacons theory of change was that *colocating services for young people in school buildings would increase neighborhood level access to youth development opportunities and supports and improve outcomes for youth, families, and communities.*

The public emphasis in the Beacons was on the appropriateness and importance of creating safe havens for all young people in the city's most disadvantaged neighborhoods. This narrative frame provided a compelling focus for the initiative.[8] It was easy to understand. It generated visceral narratives about young people with potential who deserved places where they could safely flourish during nonschool hours. It allowed sites to start simply, with small achievements, in route to meeting the needs of youth and communities on a larger scale. As the president of a local community development corporation described it, the idea was "politically glamorous."[9]

A community-based not-for-profit organization at Level 1 manages each NYC Beacons site. These organizations have track records of accomplishment predating the Beacons program in their respective neighborhoods. The city involves neighborhood level stakeholders in selecting these providers to take advantage of local knowledge and maintain local faith in the process. Each site has a community advisory council (Levels 1 and Zero) that includes the school principal, parents, youth, area residents, teachers, neighborhood service providers, community police officers, the district's council member, and others important to the program, such as custodians. Although participation is sometimes less than ideal, these councils assist with evaluation planning, outreach to participants, political advocacy, public relations, and other aspects of program support and development.

Comparison of Initial Conceptions

In contrast to creating safe havens for otherwise good kids, New Futures generated narratives about troubled youth, ineffective service providers, and bureaucratic systems. It aimed to replace these with positive stories of systems change in which innovative people work together across boundaries for the common good. Systems change, however, is an abstract idea and is unlikely to be interpreted consistently at any level of the system. Furthermore, organizing for systems change puts established interests on notice that their own institutions may come under scrutiny and be targeted for reform. It can provoke defensive preparations instead of openness to cooperate. In contrast, the idea that young people should have safe havens seems quite unthreatening.

Initial Implementation

Implementation of Beacons and New Futures began in distinct ways. The Beacons initiative set about selecting neighborhood-based organizations to develop program sites and begin providing services. In contrast, New Futures set out to organize key Level 2 decision makers to collaborate on reforming local systems.

New York City Beacons

The effort that became known as the NYC Beacons began in 1991 with a mayor's budget proposal, which included $10 million to establish 10 school-based community centers in the city's poorest, most "at-risk" neighborhoods. The Department of Youth and Community Development (DYCD), the city department with the most experience in the field, was chosen to administer the program. (DYCD was initially the Department of Youth Services, or DYS, but its name was later changed.) During budget negotiations, DYCD issued a request for proposals (RFP) from community-based organizations to offer activities 16 hours per day, 365 days per year, in designated neighborhoods.

Due to budget cuts before the program began, funding was reduced to $500,000 per year per site, and the required hours of operation were reduced. Each Beacons Center received $450,000 in direct funding, and $50,000 was administered by the city to compensate schools for the use of space. A sophisticated intermediary organization, the Youth Development Institute (YDI) of the Fund for the City of New York was formed under the leadership of DYCD consultant Michele Cahill. It provided (and continues to provide) technical assistance and other support to the initiative.

As an experienced city agency with control of project funding, DCYD had the credibility, organizational infrastructure, and knowledge base necessary to establish funding and selection criteria as well as to conduct ongoing monitoring of performance. Their RFP invited community-based nonprofit organizations to propose the manner in which they would provide "safe, structured, supervised activities for children, youth and families"[10] in neighborhood schools during afternoon and evening hours. The proposals were reviewed in a two-tiered process. Officials at DYCD made the initial cut, selecting the finalists. Then, each member agency of the New York City Interagency Coordinating Council on Youth (ICCY) helped score the finalists' proposals in selecting which Level 1 agencies won the contracts. Involving ICCY agencies in the final selection was a way of initiating their sense of affiliation with the program without imposing any real costs on them.

The Beacons program designers, guided by research and consensus on best practices, sought to increase the following:

1. Opportunities for caring relationships

2. High expectations and clear standards

3. Opportunities to engage in high-quality activities

4. Opportunities to make a contribution

5. Continuity of supports

Over three quarters of the community-based organizations that won contracts to manage first-round Beacons Centers had at least 20 years of experience in their communities delivering services to youth and families. They had established management systems, contacts with funders, and relationships in the community. Some were members of the Neighborhood Family Services Coalition (NFSC), an advocacy organization formed in the late 1970s by Level 1 community-based service providers.[11] The organizations that won contracts to operate Beacons hired experienced youth workers as Beacons directors, staff, and consultants. They used their expertise to build alliances with school principals and other local leaders, to manage programs effectively (most of the time), and to attract additional funding and partners to colocate at the centers. These community-based organizations that managed Beacons centers received term contracts. RFPs are reissued periodically to maintain competition (Department of Youth and Community Development, 2003).

Although much smaller than today, the original scale of the Beacons was large enough to make it visible and to produce valued impacts quickly in the neighborhoods served. Because there were 10 sites, problems at 1 or 2 sites would not be fatal to the initiative. The initial 10 were manageable for the DCYD as the supervising agency and for YDI as the intermediary and technical assistance provider. The location in schools provided space, the aura of legitimacy, and firm connections to communities. These connections and the quality of activities and services provided benefits that led parents and others to advocate for the expansion of the Beacons program to other sites. (These points are emphasized in Pittman, Irby, & Ferber, 2000.)

Initially, the city selected school locations without consulting school officials or local community school boards, and this caused political tensions. In subsequent rounds, schools have been included in multiple ways, helping to set local program objectives and to select program operators. Each Beacons site in New York is required to have a "collaborative framework agreement" with the school in which it locates.

Initiating New Futures

New Futures began by identifying medium-sized cities with substantial numbers of at-risk youth. Each interested city had to prove its commitment and capacity to participate by submitting a detailed application describing an approach to systems reform and pledging to provide matching funds to AECF's contribution. Each city was free to design its own approach to the reform effort. However, the proposals that AECF actually funded followed suggestions outlined in a manual (Center for the Study of Social Policy, 1987a) distributed around the time of the RFP. Five communities were selected for the demonstration. Each was expected to make measurable changes in specifically targeted youth outcomes within 5 years.

After their selection, communities started by creating new organizations and systems for collecting data for tracking youth outcomes. In accordance with the recommendations of the AECF, each city also formed a new local governance body, called a *collaborative*. Members represented government, business, and social service agencies. Each collaborative hired an executive director and staff as well as case managers. Generally, the managers worked in schools with 25 to 30 adolescent students, helping those students to connect with various services and opportunities.[12] Each program created a citywide, school-based information system capable of providing detailed information about student activities and outcomes. Based on their analyses of area needs, collaboratives began organizing academic support programs, health centers, career education centers, and programs to support reforms in the school system. In addition to direct financial support ranging from $5 to $10 million for the 5-year demonstration, each city received technical assistance and an AECF employee as the site manager. Collaborative members and staff participated in multisite conferences. The Center for the Study of Social Policy led a major evaluation of the initiative. Each city matched AECF funds with local contributions.

Reaching Youth and Families

The early decisions by New York City regarding the form of the Beacons initiative allowed it to move from concept to implementation within about a year (Cahill, Perry, Wright, & Rice, 1993). Sites were successful in expeditiously delivering high-quality services that communities valued and supported. Flexible funding allowed each site to hire the individuals or organizations from the neighborhood that they determined could provide the best experiences for young people and facilitate the community development mission. It appears that most of the funds expended directly benefited young people and their communities. This was due in large measure to the use of preexisting assets: well-established organizations, not new start-ups. The Beacons program enabled them to deliver services that were more accessible, more extensive, and more firmly based in a youth development paradigm. Most of the action was at Level 1. Use of school buildings substantially reduced the need to purchase equipment, secure permits, or renovate facilities. Directors were able to concentrate on programming. Even today, Beacons are providing services at more than 80 sites without having created any new organizations.

In contrast, as described above, New Futures began by creating Level 2 organizations called *collaboratives*. New organizations were created even in the communities where similar structures already existed.[13] Each collaborative was a governance body that decided within the structure of the AECF initiative where and how it would expend its funds. Maintaining members' involvement and reaching agreement was difficult. As a result, Lawrence, Massachusetts, withdrew from the program during the second year. At the end of the third year, the entire board of the Pittsburgh collaborative resigned in frustration and was replaced with new members. Dayton and Savannah experienced reoccurring tensions with school leaders, and Little Rock faced challenges engaging the business community. The democratic approach that the collaboratives took may have some long-term benefits, such as stronger bonds and better working relationships among Level 2 decision makers. However, it delayed implementation, frustrating grassroots constituencies impatient to receive benefits and Level 1 agencies hoping to share in new funding.

The collaboratives with strong executive director/chair partnerships were the most successful at overcoming the initial lack of local credibility and influence, and demonstrated some effectiveness.[14] The Savannah collaborative used data, such as the shocking statistic that 13% of black first graders were suspended, to build consensus around the need for school reform. In Little Rock, information that case managers provided to the collaborative was instrumental in crafting a response to a drive-by gang shooting, successfully ending a cycle of retaliation. The Georgia State Legislature also formally authorized Savannah's collaborative. This designation gave the Savannah collaborative a formal role in reviewing some types of state spending in the community as well as a half-million-dollar annual contribution.

The Beacons goal was to create a physical place where young people could thrive. Their early successes generated support among local residents and news reporters and persuaded politicians to expand the program eventually to 80 sites (Cahill et al., 1993; Warren, Feist, & Nevarez, 2002). The simple administrative structure of the Beacons program not only allowed quick implementation of the concept but also continues to be effective (even under new mayors!) as the community level Beacons centers mature.

In contrast to the Beacons, New Futures took time to create new coordinating and information-sharing systems to organize and track efforts to better serve youth. Even after case managers were in place to support young people and help them connect to services, the collaboratives remained unwieldy. They had difficulty responding to the challenges that case managers identified, and they mostly lacked the will or the influence to make real systems change within the initial 5-year grant period.

Matching Responsibility With Capacity

The capacity to serve youth effectively in frontline organizations depends on rules that Level 2 and Level 3 decision makers set and the resources that they control. Frontline workers in the Beacons and New Futures initiatives succeeded, or failed, due in part to the availability, or lack, of important supports from these higher levels. For example, the rules that the AECF set for New Futures gave frontline case managers three types of responsibility: (a) to act as mentors to the students in their caseloads, (b) to help students and their families gain access to community services, and (c) to provide information to the collaborative to inform Level 2 and Level 3 decisions about systems reform. Success or failure depended on the availability of resources and authority sufficient to perform these functions.

Establishing Relationships

New Futures case managers had resources to be most effective at meeting their first responsibility, that of establishing relationships with students and providing appropriate advice. Despite having large caseloads and limited opportunities to meet with students during the school day (due mostly to time conflicts), case managers did connect with students and build relationships. When necessary, they met with students at lunchtime and in hallways between classes and took students to movies and other activities. They used personal funds to pay for small expenses. Anecdotal reports indicate that students valued these relationships. For example, Dave, a 10th-grade African American student in Little Rock, whose mother supported the family with Social Security benefits, was assigned to New Futures in ninth grade. He says of his case manager, "Teresa was somebody to talk to. School counselors are busy all of the time. New Futures got more involved. School counselors wouldn't call my home to talk about problems I had, but Teresa did" (Center for Social Policy, 1995a, p. 29). Teresa, an African American and recent political science graduate, said that she wanted to "provide unconditional, consistent support for kids" (p. 29). Case managers also built relationships with teachers and administrators by helping around the school.

Although it appears that New Futures case managers were usually successful in establishing relationships with students, they were severely constrained when working a conventional workday. Trying to meet between classes or pulling students out of classes necessarily limited student contacts. Many of the meetings that case managers reported were as short as 5 minutes, and much of their time was spent scheduling meetings and trying to reach providers.

Connecting Youth and Families to Services

Case managers enjoyed some degree of success as well in their efforts to make referrals and secure services for students and families. Evaluators estimate that roughly half of referrals actually led to services. For example, Teresa connected Dave with tutoring services, and his grades improved. On one occasion, Dave turned to Teresa because a science teacher refused to give him makeup work for an absence. Teresa was able to secure the assignments by explaining Dave's home situation.

Nonetheless, connecting students and families to services was difficult because of the lack of sufficient services to meet community needs, an inability to ensure that students followed up on referrals (although some caseworkers solved this problem by driving students to appointments), and the lack of adequate directories to help case managers identify what services were available. Case managers lacked resources to overcome these challenges on their own, and mechanisms for referring such problems to the collaborative were often ineffective.

Informing the Collaborative for Systems Change

Case managers were least effective at performing their third responsibility, which was to inform the collaborative in ways leading to systems change. Mechanisms for feedback from case managers to collaboratives (from Level 1 to Level 2) were largely ineffective, in part because collaborative members were unreceptive (Hahn & Lanspery, 2001; White & Wehlage, 1995). For example, a case manager named Leveta Hale reported that initially case managers documented,

> All the barriers to services that people faced, and all the barriers to interagency cooperation. And we sent this information to the board of New Futures, and . . . they actually said, "Don't send us this stuff anymore because we can't do anything with it. It's too big. It's too much." (Hahn & Lanspery, 2001, p. 9)[15]

Still, on some occasions, information that case managers provided to collaboratives was a catalyst for change. In Little Rock, a case manager's persistent concern about gang activity led to the formation of a community-wide task force on violence. In Bridgeport, a student reported to case managers that he was dealing drugs because legitimate employment would cause his mother to lose welfare benefits. A report to the collaborative led to revised income eligibility standards and sparked a successful lobbying effort to exclude all youth earnings from benefit calculations.

Generally, however, institutional impediments inhibited the types of systemic changes that AECF had hoped would occur. The 1987 AECF manual for New Futures states,

> Local government leaders, the school board, state human service officials, and private agency directors will have to agree to delegate some measure of influence over their respective systems to the case management function and to set aside resources to meet its needs. (p. 129)

To the contrary, none of the collaboratives created a "powerful case management role" with effective mechanisms for identifying policy issues, performing analysis, and producing recommendations. Most staff and consultants lacked the professional backgrounds to perform this work. Moreover, even if they had such backgrounds, it may not have mattered, because collaborative members were hesitant to press for change in colleagues' institutions. It seems the spirit at Level 2 was, "You don't tell me how to change my organization, and I won't tell you how to change yours."[16] Even when a reform was launched successfully, opposition from leaders could crash it. For example, in year 3 of New Futures in Dayton, a year-old program to reduce absenteeism was abandoned when the school superintendent refused to cooperate (Center for the Study of Social Policy, 1995a, p. 15).

Like New Futures case managers, Level 1 workers in Beacons are sometimes frustrated by conditions beyond their control. However, there are communication channels linking frontline workers to Beacons site directors, and site directors to DYCD, YDI, and NFSC at Level 2. DYCD, YDI, and NFSC are effective at getting Level 2 organizations and policymakers to pay attention (and sometimes respond) to what Level 1 organizations in New York City, especially Beacons, desire.

Problems With New Futures Technical Assistance

The AECF hired national (Level 3) technical assistance providers to transfer state-of-the-art ideas and practices to the local (Level 2) collaboratives. However, collaboratives were sometimes frustrated by inconsistent direction from AECF staff and their technical assistance providers, some of whom lacked adequate knowledge and experience in politics or policy. Midway through the initiative, the providers that AECF had appointed were replaced by local technical assistance providers selected by each collaborative. This happened for a number of reasons. The AECF providers were experts in the categorical approaches of the existing system, but not in the systems reforms envisioned by the AECF. They also lacked expertise required by collaboratives that were developing new organizations and required help with board development, accounting, and personnel practices. Furthermore, because they were not based in the cities they served and visits were short, they were unable to develop local knowledge, provide the sustained support required by the collaboratives, or gain the locals' trust. Their capacities did not match their responsibilities.

Comparison With Technical Assistance for Beacons

For the NYC Beacons, the YDI served as an effective technical assistance intermediary. Ninety-five percent of the directors of Beacons Centers in New York describe the services of the YDI as "essential" or "very helpful" to the success of the Beacons initiative (57% "essential" and 38% "very helpful"; Warren, 1999b, p. 16). YDI facilitates monthly Beacons directors' meetings, professional development activities, and a small grant program for developing activities. In addition, YDI vouches to Level 2 agencies on behalf of Beacons sites, builds collaborative relationships among sites, and helps identify additional sources of funding. As a self-identified agent of the centers, YDI works with DYCD and the centers to advance the Beacons program and develop evaluation criteria to inform program improvement. However, program evaluation and monitoring for purposes of accountability are conducted by DYCD, not YDI.[17] This avoids role conflict for YDI. If YDI monitored or evaluated sites for accountability purposes, sites might not be as open in seeking its assistance.[18]

YDI's success stems from its sophisticated knowledge of youth development as well as familiarity with the organizations, politics, and communities of New York City. The centers trust YDI and value its support.[19] YDI does a small amount of grant making, limited to small-scale capacity-building activities. Its primary roles are building capacity at Level 1 of the system and facilitating the flow of information between Levels 1, 2, and sometimes 3. YDI builds capacity at Level 1 by focusing primarily on social and intellectual capital. This is accomplished through training, technical assistance, forums, and building alliances.

The problems that intermediaries face assisting Level 1 organizations can include being regarded by clients as competitors for funds and attention or access to Level 2 decision makers. To avoid such problems, YDI does not receive municipal funds for the work it does with NYC Beacons. Separate foundation funding allows it to maintain an independent voice and avoid competition with Beacons centers. In addition, YDI works to make sure that DYCD, the centers, funders, and cooperating organizations receive the attention and credit they deserve. When describing their work, they pay attention to the subtlety of wording so that their role is represented appropriately. Finally, they try to avoid being placed in a position in which they are allocating resources among competing Beacons centers.

We should note here that the New Futures programs in Savannah, Dayton, and Little Rock have evolved in recent years after the 5-year demonstration. Efforts in these communities are starting to generate some of the types of change originally envisioned. The organizations in Savannah and Little Rock have begun to look more like intermediaries. In Savannah, this includes adding community representatives to the collaborative and undertaking capacity building with community organizations. The Little Rock collaborative has a contract with that city to support a minigrant program similar to a model pioneered as part of New Futures. They are working with Level 1 organizations to build capacity through technical assistance and training in grant writing, board development, hiring, data collection, and evaluation. Little Rock approved a 0.5% sales tax that is supporting 32 youth-serving organizations. Ohio adopted a statewide system inspired by the New Futures model (Hahn & Lanspery, 2001, p. 19).

YDI and other effective intermediaries foster an "ongoing culture of inquiry, assessment and reflection" (Wynn, 2000, p. 15) in the organizations and communities they serve. They facilitate exchange horizontally, among people in similar jobs, and vertically, from the grass roots to national leaders. They provide expertise and clout. They have the ability to attract resources, help solve problems, and build support. Their work is fundamentally important to the field of community youth development (Pittman, 1998, p. 55; Schorr, 1997; Wynn, 2000). The success of NYC Beacons and its promise as an engine of change is due in a major way to the expertise and commitment of YDI. Indeed, it is not misleading to say that YDI is an essential part of the Beacons model. Intermediaries in cities that adopt the Beacons model should develop similar capacities and provide similar services.[20]

Evaluation Can Help or Hinder

Beacons and New Futures developed different approaches to evaluation. The New Futures evaluation (Center for the Study of Social Policy, 1995a) set out to answer three questions: (a) Did sites develop their collaboratives into powerful vehicles for change on behalf of at-risk children? (b) Did sites make lasting institutional changes in the way services were financed, administered, and delivered to youth? and (c) Was there improvement in youth outcomes, either in the pilot schools or citywide? The youth outcomes that the evaluation measured were attendance, scores on standardized tests, course failure, over-age for grade, retention in grade, suspensions, dropout rates, graduation rates, pregnancy rates, and postgraduate plans for school or work. Other information collected included qualitative data on the development of the collaboratives, aggregate data on student outcomes, and narrative profiles of students and families.

Collaborative directors felt pressure to achieve on many of the above measures, which set standards too ambitious to achieve in only 5 years. Tensions arose between those focusing on individual student outcomes through extensive support for the work of case managers versus those concentrating on systems change among Level 2 organizations. In response, sites tried to affect both individual and systems level outcomes by reforming schools. However, they generally lacked the political, financial, and analytic resources to do so effectively. Confusion was compounded by shifting interpretations of New Futures program goals due to leadership changes at the AECF. (A more recent study of the most successful New Futures sites documents progress beyond that measured in the initial evaluation period; Hahn & Lanspery, 2001, p. 17.)

Assessment of the NYC Beacons has taken two major forms: One is formal evaluation, and the other is ongoing monitoring as part of program management (Warren, 1999a). First, to gather insights for improving the program and to generate judgments concerning program impacts, YDI commissioned a formal evaluation by the Academy for Educational Development (AED) in collaboration with the Chapin Hall Center for Children and the Hunter College Center on AIDS, Drugs, and Community Health. Phase I of the evaluation was an implementation study of 40 sites, begun in 1997. The Phase I Report released in 1999 (Warren, 1999b) concluded that although the degree of implementation varied, "All sites [were] successful in serving as a 'safe haven,' offering a range of activities for youth and adults, as well as some community improvement activities" (Warren et al., 2002, pp. 1-2). The report for Phase II appeared in 2002 (Warren et al., 2002). It focused on six representative sites. It found problems at some sites and offered a number of recommendations for improvement. The generally positive evaluation concluded, "In summary, the New York City Beacons clearly play a pivotal role in the education and development of their young participants, as well as the lives of their families and communities" (Warren et al., 2002, p. 128). The evaluation reported that the majority of youth were "taking advantage of . . . challenging activities and believed they were developing new competencies (Warren et al., 2002, p. v). Again, this evaluation was to inform YDI efforts at helping programs to improve, not for determining rewards or penalties or for providing definitive measures of impacts.

Monitoring Beacons program performance for accountability purposes is the responsibility of the DCYD. From time to time, community-based organizations have lost their contracts to manage Beacons because of these performance assessments. DCYD evaluates Beacons on the basis of stakeholder satisfaction, adherence to established principles of youth development, and outcomes for young people, but precisely which outcomes are targeted and how they are tracked vary from site to site. DCYD makes both scheduled and unannounced site visits to monitor that staff are in place and adequate numbers of youth are actually being served. There is oversight on financial management. Monthly site reports are required as part of the monitoring process, and there is a financial penalty for late submission. Grants managers at DCYD also receive plenty of feedback from community advisory councils, schools, and parents about issues at sites. The monitoring process allows each Beacons center to measure changes, to benchmark achievements against those of other centers, and to collect specific feedback for use in program design, management, advocacy, and public relations. DCYD provides each center with feedback for improving its performance.

In contrast to New Futures, evaluation and monitoring of the Beacons program appear to be well calibrated to what sites can actually accomplish, and they probably help rather than hinder program performance. The AED evaluation of Beacons measures participant satisfaction and compliance with youth development principles and thereby maintains a focus on the Beacons's mission. Monitoring by the DCYD focuses on performance objectives described in the Beacons Program Manual (Soler-McIntosh, 1999) and contracts. DCYD takes pride in the quality of contract managers who perform monitoring duties.[21]

The Challenge of Sharing Facilities

Sharing school facilities presents challenges that no discussion of Beacons should go without mentioning. There is no blueprint from Level 2 in New York City to govern how the community-based organizations that operate Beacons work with the schools in which they locate. Hence, each center represents a unique set of agreements and understandings worked out at Level 1 among the organizations involved. Initially, some teachers objected to having their classrooms used after school, especially when classrooms were not returned to their original condition. Centers responded by developing systems for returning classrooms to their original condition, including cleaning and immediate replacement of broken equipment.

Trust and reciprocity that penetrate the school organization are quite important, especially when there is turnover among school principals. Therefore, some Beacons build relationships with school staff by providing positions for them on advisory councils, hiring school staff for Beacons jobs, and communicating regularly about what the Beacons are doing. In addition, some share their computers with teachers, improve playgrounds and other facilities, and respond to requests for particular types of programming.[22] However, the most recent evaluation report says that building relationships with school staff continues to be challenging, and some Beacons are more successful than others (Warren et al., 2002).

Systems Change

As indicated above, the system changes achieved during the New Futures initiative were quite limited compared with what AECF had envisioned. They included changes in income eligibility requirements for receipt of welfare in Bridgeport, Connecticut, and a line item for the Savannah collaborative (and similar organizations) in the State of Georgia.[23] These are not trivial. However, they are more limited than what AECF expected. In contrast, Beacons and the organizations that support them are succeeding not only in the announced mission of providing safe havens but also in achieving the types of systemic changes at Levels 1 and 2 that AECF envisioned for New Futures.

In contrast to the central-planning approach that New Futures attempted using the collaboratives, most system level changes in the Beacons case have been negotiated one at a time, each involving a limited number of agencies and decision makers. Unlike New Futures, the Beacons program originated inside city government. Base funding was a line item in the municipal budget from the very beginning in 1991, and for the past decade, it has been sustained and even expanded.[24] Although the New York City Interagency Coordinating Council on Youth (ICCY) was consulted and helped with selecting Beacons operators, Beacons was neither envisioned nor presented as an attempt at Level 2 reforms. Instead, it was conceived and presented, first and foremost, as an effort to create safe havens at Level 1 for children in high-risk communities, a goal that was easy to understand and support.

Admittedly, we are not privy to all of the behind-the-scenes politics that may be involved. However, it appears that resulting changes at Level 2 have been products of the confidence that agencies have in the capacity of DYCD, neighborhood service providers, and Beacons to help them fulfill their missions. For example, foster care prevention is the responsibility of another Level 2 agency, not DYCD. However, that agency has delegated responsibility to DYCD to oversee foster care prevention contracts at 16 Beacons sites, where foster care prevention is now integrated with other Beacons services. This almost surely results in better-coordinated services for targeted youth. Another example is that DYCD now administers funds of the After School Corporation (ASC), a nonprofit grant-making corporation initiated by the Open Society Institute. ASC gives grants of $40 million annually, to which the city adds another $10 million per year. Placing some foster care and ASC resources under DYCD control represents substantive, systemic reforms that reduce service fragmentation and cut the number of Level 2 agencies with which Beacons must interact.

The Beacons program offers a variety of agencies a mechanism through which to deliver their services more effectively by encouraging some of their Level 1 providers to locate at Beacons sites. YDI, ICCY, Beacons site leaders, and others have been effective at promoting partnerships between the Beacons and other community and youth-serving organizations. An array of social and educational service agencies have now colocated their programs at Beacons centers and sponsored activities with Beacons.

Health care is another example. From the very beginning, school principals, Beacons directors, and community members identified health care as a priority. Accordingly, Beacons began in 1991 to develop partnerships with health care providers to deliver services at their sites. By 1993, 90% of Beacons provided health workshops; 10 had on-site clinics, and 3 were developing comprehensive family health services (Cahill et al., 1993). Beacons are now aligned with service providers and embedded in local neighborhoods in ways that sometimes produce impressive results quite expeditiously. For example, the youth of the El Puente de Williamsburg Beacons organized a door-to-door campaign of outreach using local seniors and young people that resulted in the immunization of 1,000 children.

Under the Beacons umbrella, DYCD funds have been used successfully as matching funds for a variety of programs. Sites have secured money from the New York State Department of Social Services, Health, and Alcohol, and Substance Abuse Services; the New York City Child Welfare Administration; the Board of Education; the Department of Employment and Health; and the Community Development Agency. Some (though not all) Beacons Centers and the Level 2 agencies that support them are moving toward becoming the comprehensive but flexible system that New Futures aspired to create.

Lessons

No program, including Beacons, is perfect. Nonetheless, in our view, the Beacons initiative is relatively more successful than the New Futures because it has more of the following characteristics:[25]

- *Flexibility* enables Beacons to respond to opportunities, fix problems, fill gaps, cooperate with partners, and allow individuals to make distinct contributions. Flexibility is achieved by decentralizing management and operations. To the extent possible, decision makers are placed in physical proximity to the point of implementation. Each level of the system has simple governance structures. Actions require limited sign-offs. Programming responds to the needs of users in scheduling, location, and format, and there is a greater capacity to change as needs change than there would be if more decisions were centralized.

• *Transparency* is critical for building trust, creating community, sharing knowledge, and creating social ties. Information flows easily within and among levels of the system. Clients, workers, and allies understand the system. The public can understand the programs and their importance. Agencies are selected to operate Beacons according to clear criteria, and the participation of diverse reviewers shields the process from political manipulation. Community advisory councils, DYCD, community-based organizations, NFSC, and evaluators all work to share information and to clarify the bases on which decisions are made—holding one another accountable for serving youth well.[26]

• *Capacity* is adequate to undertake the required work. Service providers are generally credible, respectful, and supportive of those they serve, and are dependable. Skilled leadership, management, and intermediary support are available, along with reliable core operating support. Programs are located in accessible, safe, and visible areas. The best sites and programs are continually building knowledge and alliances. They employ reflection and evaluation to improve their capacities.

• *Accountability* is maintained to the community, youth, families, managers, and funders. The best programs communicate regularly with participants and routinely test their satisfaction with programs. Sites have community advisory councils, establish performance goals, conduct regular evaluations, and measure their work against that of their peers.

In contrast to the Beacons program, "The Path of Most Resistance" encapsulates why New Futures failed to achieve its aspirations (Nelson, 1996). The theory of systems change proved much more difficult to implement than envisioned.

Conclusion

New Futures was conceived at Level 3, intended to foster systems reform at Level 2 and to reduce fragmentation and improve service delivery at Level 1 in order to reduce the incidence of negative outcomes for youth at Level Zero, in high-risk neighborhoods. It was not a total failure. Despite many disappointments and frustrations during the 5-year demonstration, interagency collaboratives continue in all host communities of New Futures, including those that no longer receive financial support from the AECF. The collaboratives established under New Futures and the individuals trained and supported by the initiative have continued to work for youth development. Furthermore, New Futures did improve some youth outcomes. Narratives describe ways in which case managers performed valuable services that made a real difference for some young people in each community. In addition, there have been positive reports from Savannah, where the collaborative has been effective as an intermediary. In the 5 years preceding 1996, the birthrate for black teens fell 12%, mortality of black infants declined by 45%, and foster care placements were reduced by 25% (Walsh, 1998, p. 24).

Nonetheless, the NYC Beacons seem clearly to be the more effective model. The Department of Youth and Community Development (DYCD), a Level 2 agency, allocates core funding to lead agencies at Level 1, and the latter attract other Level 1 agencies to colocate services in school buildings. The colocation agreements are among Level 1 agencies and entail minimal Level 2 involvement. When the model works as intended, youth and families (Level Zero) help plan and implement programming. There is variability among sites in whether they approximate this ideal.[27] However, those that come closest tend to take most advantage of training and technical assistance services from the Youth Development Institute (YDI). In addition to providing training and advice, YDI organizes formative assessments to document practices and gather lessons. The Neighborhood Family Services Coalition (NFSC) advocates for children and families and looks for continuing opportunities to improve services and increase resources. Due to NFSC vigilance and activism, Level 2 agencies that fail to adequately support youth development risk public scrutiny. Finally, for accountability, the DYCD monitors sites and requires monthly reports on their operation. Lead agencies that fail to perform adequately risk losing their contracts to operate Beacons. This system of checks, balances, and supports is a promising model that other cities are attempting to emulate.

The field of community youth development is active and growing as part of a national youth development system, with a growing number of Level 3 organizations that offer tools and advice to Levels Zero, 1, and 2.[28] As the system develops, the division of roles and responsibilities among levels in the system will differ among communities. In high-income communities, Level Zero performs some of the funding and monitoring functions that

Level 2 often handles in low-income communities. Even some typical Level 1 functions, such as coaching in youth sports leagues, are largely Level Zero functions in communities where residents have more time and resources. In any case, no matter what the income levels, wherever there are children and youth, there are needs for developmental supports and systems to provide them. This chapter compares two of the most prominent attempts of the past 20 years to improve local systems in communities where youth encounter too many risks and too few supports to reach their full potential.[29]

Notes

1. The authors thank Sarah McCann, Carlos Santos, and the editors of this volume for helpful comments.

2. Resources for the analysis of New Futures include Center for the Study of Social Policy (1987a, 1987b, 1995a, 1995b); Annie E. Casey Foundation (1995); Hahn and Lanspery (2001); Nelson (1996); Walsh (1998); and White and Wehlage (1995). Resources for analysis of the NYC Beacons include Cahill, Perry, Wright, and Rice (1993); Forum for Youth Investment (1997); Pittman (1998); Warren (1999b, 2002), as well as interviews with Luis Garden Acosta, Mario Bruno, Steven Goodman, Jim Marly, and Peter Kleinbard.

3. The San Francisco Beacons (Walker & Arbreton, 2001) as well as programs in Minneapolis, Oakland, Savannah, and Denver have adopted the Beacons model.

4. In fact, AECF has been an ongoing provider of core support for the Youth Development Institute, which provides technical assistance to the NYC Beacons.

5. Valuable analyses of community-wide initiatives consulted for this chapter include Chaskin and Joseph (1995); Connell, Gambone, and Smith (2000); Forum for Youth Investment (2001, 2002); Hartmann, Watson, and Kantorek (2001); Kotloff, Roaf, and Gambone (1995); McLaughlin (2000); National Research Council and Institute of Medicine (2002); Stone (1996).

6. Our analysis is limited to the structure of the initiatives. Other factors, including the quality of individual leadership and resistance, are critical to the success of community-wide (and all) initiatives. Interesting stories of individuals committed to youth development at all levels of the systems studied and their successes remain largely to be told.

7. See Ferguson and Stoutland (1999) for a discussion of levels applied to the community development system.

8. See Briggs (2001) for a discussion of stories "that make sense of complex ideas and influence diverse interests to act in common cause" (p. 30).

9. Luis Garden Acosta, in an interview for this chapter (January 2003).

10. First Request for Proposals to Operate School-Based Community Centers, New York City Department of Youth Services, 1991, as quoted in Warren (1999b, p. 8.).

11. The NFSC won a political struggle against the School Janitor's Union in the early 1980s in order to reduce the fee charged to community-based organizations for using school facilities after regular school hours. Resulting activities were precursors of the Beacons program.

12. There is some variation among the sites in the structure of case management that is not reflected in this description.

13. Some collaboratives combined efforts with these preexisting groups following the 5-year demonstration period.

14. The discussion in this section draws on analysis and evaluations of New Futures cited in Note #2.

15. Leveta Hale credits New Futures with providing the training and social network connections that enabled her and several colleagues to find future positions in which they more effectively pursued the changes they envisioned as case managers (Hahn & Lanspery, 2001, p. 12).

16. For example, a case manager in Little Rock was working with a student who was being used as a decoy in a drug operation. The adults who placed her in this position were relatives designated to be foster parents while the mother was incarcerated. Despite the case manager's persistent efforts to have her removed from the home, the collaborative failed to challenge the foster care system to act (Center for the Study of Social Policy, 1995a, p. 31).

17. DYCD has a staff of 11 people, including seven contract managers. New York's financial division conducts financial reviews using a contract auditor.

18. The issue here is simply that there are incentives not to reveal damaging evidence to the entity that will stand in judgment.

19. Foundations fund YDI separately from the municipal funding for the Beacons. YDI's parent organization, the Fund for the City of New York, functions on a university model. It provides managerial and operating support to YDI as well as access to professional colleagues and a support for organizational continuity. The Fund for the City of New York provides space, equipment, financial, and personnel management services. This frees the YDI staff to concentrate on professional responsibilities. The Fund charges YDI an administrative overhead for the services provided. The Fund receives core operating support from the Ford Foundation.

20. This is taking place with the assistance of YDI in some of the Beacons replication projects.

21. The assistant commissioner we interviewed told us that because there is very little turnover in government positions, selection of high-quality people is critical.

22. Hiring school staff to work after school is not simply for the purpose of improving relationships. Finding qualified staff to work evenings and weekends is often difficult. Appointing codirectors has been one solution for covering the many hours the programs are open. Half the sites supplement their regular staff with student interns and volunteers. The City Volunteer Corps has provided trained volunteers to work full-time for 12-week shifts. YDI helps train staff to work with youth and to do community organizing and outreach. However, directors would like more on-site training to expand the number of staff members receiving instruction.

23. The Savannah model is being replicated throughout the State of Georgia.

24. Although funding for the program has expanded, support for each center has actually declined, from $450,000 to $400,000 during the past 12 years. It remains to be seen whether the systems described will be able to secure the resources necessary to continue the program at existing or increased levels of service. Although NFSC has campaigned to increase funding for individual sites, their efforts have been unsuccessful.

25. Hahn and Lanspery (2001) analyze five programs, including three New Futures sites, and propose an alternate yet overlapping collection of success factors.

26. In an interview for this chapter, Jim Marly of NFSC suggested that the conversation should be "public and prominent; legitimacy will stand the light of day."

27. In an interview for this chapter, Luis Garden Acosta, founding director and CEO/President of El Puente and one of the acknowledged leaders of the community youth development movement, cautioned that "with certain very notable exceptions, the Beacons program has deteriorated into a service program for individuals."

28. These include, for example, the Academy for Educational Development; Public/Private Ventures; the Search Institute; the National Institute on Out of School Time (NOIST); the Forum for Youth Development; the Institution for Educational Leadership; national offices of name-brand organizations such as the YMCA, Boys and Girls Clubs of America, Big-Brothers/Big Sisters; and a number of others.

29. It is important to note that these two initiatives do not totally characterize their sponsors. New York City has many other ways of serving youth and families aside from Beacons, and the Annie E. Casey Foundation has supported many other initiatives aimed at helping youth (including core operating funds for YDI's capacity building work with Beacons).

References

Annie E. Casey Foundation. (1995). *The path of most resistance: Reflections on lessons learned from New Futures*. Baltimore, MD: Author.

Briggs, X. de. Souza. (2001). *The will and the way: Local partnerships, political strategy, and the well-being of America's children and youth*. Cambridge, MA: Harvard University, John F. Kennedy School of Government.

Cahill, M., Perry, J., Wright, M., & Rice, A. (1993). *A documentation report on the New York City Beacons initiative*. New York: Youth Development Institute, Fund for the City of New York.

Center for the Study of Social Policy. (1987a). *The Annie E. Casey Foundation's New Futures initiative: Strategic planning guide*. Washington, DC: Author.

Center for the Study of Social Policy. (1987b). *A framework for child welfare reform*. Washington, DC: Author.

Center for the Study of Social Policy. (1995a). *Building New Futures for at-risk youth: Findings from a five year, multi-site evaluation.* Washington, DC: Author.

Center for the Study of Social Policy. (1995b). *Changing governance to achieve better results for children and families.* Washington, DC: Child Protective Clearinghouse, Center for the Study of Social Policy.

Chaskin, R., & Joseph, M. L. (1995). *The Neighborhood and Family Initiative, moving toward implementation: An interim report.* Chicago: Chapin Hall Center for Children, University of Chicago.

Connell, J. P., Gambone, M. A., & Smith, T. J. (2000). Youth development in community settings: Challenges to our field and our approach. In *Youth development: Issues, challenges and directions* (pp. 281-299). Philadelphia: Public/Private Ventures.

Department of Youth and Community Development. (2003). *Request for proposals (RFP): Beacon Community Centers.* New York: City of New York.

Ferguson, R. F., & Stoutland, S. E. (1999). Reconceiving the community development field. In R. F. Ferguson & W. T. Dickens (Eds.), *Urban problems and community development* (pp. 33-77). Washington, DC: Brookings Institution.

Forum for Youth Investment. (1997). *Beacons: A union of youth and community development: Case study review* (Community & Youth Development Series). Takoma Park, MD: Author.

Forum for Youth Investment. (2001). *Youth development and community change: A guide to documents and tools developed through the Forum's Ford Foundation-funded projects 1997-2001.* Takoma Park, MD: Author.

Forum for Youth Investment. (2002). Helping cities help their young people: An update on multi-site initiatives. *FYI Newsletter, 2,* 16-20.

Hahn, A., & Lanspery, S. (2001). *Change that abides: A retrospective look at five community and family strengthening projects, and their enduring results.* Waltham, MA: Brandeis University Center for Human Resources/Institute for Sustainable Development.

Hartmann, T., Watson, B. H., & Kantorek, B. (2001). *Community change for youth development in Kansas City. A case study of how a traditional youth-serving organization (YMCA) becomes a community builder.* Philadelphia: Public/Private Ventures.

Kotloff, L. J., Roaf, P. A., & Gambone, M. A. (1995). *The plain talk planning year: Mobilizing communities to change.* Philadelphia: Public/Private Ventures.

McLaughlin, M. W. (2000). *Community counts: How youth organizations matter for youth development.* Washington, DC: Public Education Network.

National Research Council and Institute of Medicine. (2002). *Community programs to promote youth development.* J. Eccles & J. A. Gootman (Eds.). Board on Children, Youth, and Families, Division of Behavioral and Social Sciences and Education. Washington, DC: National Academy Press.

Nelson, D. W. (1996). The path of most resistance: Lessons learned from "New Futures." In A. J. Kahn & S. B. Kamerman (Eds.), *Children and their families in big cities* (pp. 163-184). New York: Columbia University School of Social Work, Cross-National Studies Research Program.

Pittman, K. (1998, June). A strategic success. *Youth Today*, p. 55.

Pittman, K., Irby, M., & Ferber, T. (2000). Unfinished business: Further reflections on a decade of promoting youth development. In *Youth development: Issues, challenges and directions* (pp. 18-64). Philadelphia: Public/Private Ventures.

Schorr, L. B. (1997). *Common purpose: Strengthening families and neighborhoods to rebuild America.* New York: Doubleday.

Soler-McIntosh, J. (1999). *Beacon program manual.* New York: City of New York, Department of Youth and Community Development.

Stone, R. (Ed.). (1996). *Core issues in comprehensive community-building initiatives.* Chicago: University of Chicago, Chapin Hall Center for Children.

Walker, K. E., & Arbreton, A. J. A. (2001). *Working together to build Beacon Centers in San Francisco: Evaluation findings from 1998-2000.* Philadelphia: Public/Private Ventures.

Walsh, J. (1998). *The eye of the storm: Ten years on the front lines of new futures.* Baltimore, MD: Annie E. Casey Foundation.

Warren, C. (1999a). *Evaluating the New York City Beacons initiative: Using a theory-driven mixed-method approach to study a complex community strategy.* Orlando, FL: Academy for Educational Development.

Warren, C. (1999b). *Evaluation of the New York City Beacons: Summary of Phase I findings.* New York: Academy for Educational Development.

Warren, C., Feist, M., & Nevarez, N. (2002). *A place to grow: Evaluation of the New York City Beacons.* New York: Academy for Educational Development.

White, J. A., & Wehlage, G. (1995). Community collaboration: If it is such a good idea, why is it so hard to do? *Educational Evaluation and Policy Analysis, 17,* 23-38.

Wynn, J. R. (2000). *The role of local intermediary organization in the youth development field.* Chicago: University of Chicago, Chapin Hall Center for Children.

13

Understanding and Improving Youth Development Initiatives Through Evaluation

Charles V. Izzo, James P. Connell,
Michelle A. Gambone, and Catherine P. Bradshaw

W ith the rapid growth of youth development initiatives in recent years has come an increased demand for evidence about their effectiveness. This has posed a particular challenge for community organizations that lack resources and expertise to employ conventional evaluation approaches but nevertheless find that their funding is contingent on demonstrating positive results. Evaluation approaches are clearly needed that can adequately meet the information needs of both program funders and operators.

In this chapter, we first describe the underlying logic of program evaluation and highlight some general principles and strategies used in evaluating program effectiveness. We then present an approach to evaluation, termed the *theory of change approach,* that we believe can help to improve the quality and utility of evaluations of youth development initiatives (Connell & Kubisch, 1998). Finally, we provide an example of how the theory of change approach can be applied to the evaluation of a specific youth development initiative.

The growing emphasis on program evaluation has the potential to greatly improve the quality of youth development services in the community. Experience has shown that well-designed evaluations can serve at least two valuable functions: (a) to help judge *program effectiveness* (i.e., identify programs that are most likely to improve developmental outcomes for youth) and (b) inform *program improvement* efforts. Most that are conducted locally by practitioners, however, do not serve either of these two functions well. That is, they typically use methods that make it impossible to accurately assess program effectiveness, and they rarely provide information that offers guidance regarding how to improve program effectiveness (National Research Council and Institute of Medicine, 2002). Therefore, after significant resources have been expended collecting data and writing reports, the findings rarely make their way back into the program improvement and planning processes.

One reason for the disconnect between organizations' data collection efforts and their planning is that the program operators themselves (i.e., program developers, managers, and practitioners) rarely play active roles in determining their own *evaluation questions* (i.e., statements about what they ultimately want to learn from the evaluation) (Weiss, 1983). For most organizations, evaluations primarily involve collecting data that funders have mandated, which typically focus on answering questions about overall program effectiveness, such as "Did the program lead to decreased rates of teen smoking?" or "Did the initiative lead to greater numbers of youth who are prepared for the workforce?" Although program operators are undoubtedly interested in questions about long-term program effectiveness, they also need more timely information that can help them make midcourse corrections to improve their practice (e.g., "What changes can we make to reduce early dropout from the program?"). We believe that if evaluations follow a different kind of framework that makes program improvement a more prominent goal and gives program operators a greater role in defining evaluation questions, it is likely that data from those evaluations will provide more meaningful and useful results (Greene, 1987).

The Logic of Evaluation

Let us begin by defining three key terms that will be used throughout the chapter. First, *evaluation* will be defined as the systematic gathering of evidence to determine whether a program was effective in producing its intended effects and to understand the factors contributing to its success (or lack of success) (Struening & Brewer, 1983). Second, *program* will be defined broadly as any strategy or initiative designed to promote positive developmental outcomes for youth. Third, *outcomes* will be defined as the benefits youth experience as a result of being exposed to the program.

In program evaluation, we must start with the premise that it is virtually impossible to *prove* that a program was effective (i.e., that it produced its intended outcomes). Even in the most expensive and rigorous evaluations, there remains some degree of uncertainty about whether positive outcomes actually did occur and could be attributed to the program (Campbell, 1984). Instead, we must be satisfied gathering whatever evidence we can to help reduce our uncertainty about whether the program resulted in positive outcomes. Specifically, the evaluation must provide evidence that (a) positive outcomes did occur among those exposed to the program and (b) those outcomes can be causally attributed, at least partly, to the program (i.e., exposure to the program *caused* the outcomes). This leaves the evaluator with two essential tasks: *measuring outcomes* and *attributing outcomes*. Each task is described in detail below.

Measuring Outcomes

One important aspect of measurement is the decision about what needs to be measured. Specifically, one must ask, "If this program is successful, what positive outcomes do I expect to see among the youth who are targeted?" In youth development, program effectiveness is often determined by whether the program succeeded in building basic competencies among youth and positively influencing their behavior (National Research Council and Institute of Medicine, 2002; Roth, Brooks-Gunn, Murray, & Foster, 1998). These can be thought of as the *ultimate outcomes* that programs are aiming for. But unfortunately, these are the only outcomes measured in most evaluations, and other important outcomes are neglected. For example, many youth development programs try to achieve their ultimate outcomes by influencing aspects such as knowledge and attitudes of youth, their social and physical environment, and organizational structures in their community. The challenge for evaluation is that changes need to occur in all of these before we can expect to see improved outcomes for youth (Gambone, Klem, & Connell, 2002; National Research Council and Institute of Medicine, 2002). By failing to examine these more immediate and intermediate outcomes, one may learn about a program's effectiveness but gain no clues about how to improve its effectiveness. (We will revisit this issue later in the chapter.)

Evaluators must also make some important decisions about the timing of measurement. A classic mistake in the evaluation of youth development programs occurs when the ultimate outcomes are measured immediately following the program and the evaluator, failing to see the expected results, concludes that the program was not effective. In many cases, however, the program may have led to substantial improvements in the lives of youth, but those improvements did not manifest themselves until long after the evaluation was ended. Thus, positive program outcomes often go undetected due to lack of adequate follow-up assessment. Moreover, other intermediate outcomes that youth do experience in the short-term are usually not assessed at all, resulting in the loss of valuable program information. In still other cases, the measured outcomes are inappropriate because the program did not last long enough or was not comprehensive enough to realistically achieve a meaningful effect on the ultimate outcome (e.g., a three-session career awareness program is unlikely to produce substantial changes in delinquency on a community-wide scale but may affect applications to college or job-seeking behavior). Our discussion of the theory of change approach below will explain how measurement problems such as these can be avoided by using a detailed framework to guide major measurement decisions. Other measurement-related issues are described in Box 13.1.

Attributing Outcomes to the Program

For an evaluation to reflect anything about program effectiveness, it must show that the positive outcomes one observes can be attributed at least partly to the program and are not solely due to other factors (e.g., new resources for youth in the school or community, normal developmental processes of youth). The approaches used for demonstrating attribution, known collectively as *evaluation design,* typically work by comparing people who were exposed to the program (the program group or treatment group) to an equivalent group of people who were not exposed (a comparison or control group). If the expected outcomes occurred in the program group and not in the comparison group (or to a smaller degree), one takes that as evidence that the outcomes were attributable to the program. This approach falls into the general category of *experimental* evaluation designs. Alternatively, participants can be used as their own comparison groups in situations in which one can conduct several outcome measurements both before and after the program begins. This is referred to as the *interrupted time-series* design. It is beyond the scope of this chapter to thoroughly address these two approaches, although a brief discussion is presented in Box 13.2.

Box 13.1 Measuring Outcomes Well

Some major considerations related to the measurement of outcomes include the following.

Sampling (Who Gets Included in the Assessments)

Evaluation results are most useful when they represent the entire population that the program aims to reach. Simply including everyone is safest, but if that is not possible, a representative sample must be carefully constructed. If important segments of this *target population* are consistently excluded from data collection, evaluation results cannot be applied to them. For example, suppose an evaluator measures outcomes in the final weeks of a summer mentoring program. If only 60% of youth remained in contact with the program by the end, the evaluation will describe only that unique group of youth who decide to remain. It will provide no information about the "hard-to-retain" group that is missed in the data collection.

Depth vs. Breadth

Surveys have the advantage of making it easy to gather data from large numbers of people and are relatively easy to summarize into a few key conclusions. One of the drawbacks is that they typically do not allow for in-depth examinations of how the program has influenced its participants. Less structured methods such as in-depth interviews and focus groups can provide a more complete understanding about how respondents experienced the program and how it influenced their lives. This is because participants are given an opportunity to respond in their own words and are not constrained to a set of predetermined response choices. In addition, evaluators have the opportunity to adapt the delivery of questions to ensure that respondents understand what is being asked. The extra effort involved, however, often leads evaluators to sample fewer respondents, in some cases making it more difficult to generalize findings to the entire population of interest (Frechtling & Sharp, 1997).

Accurately Measuring the Outcome of Interest

Some outcomes can be measured with a single question or indicator. For example, if one is interested in knowing the rate of teen auto

(Continued)

Box 13.1   (Continued)

---

fatalities, those data are usually available and their interpretation is rather straightforward. However, many outcomes are much more elusive and require greater effort to measure accurately. For example, to assess the quality of collaboration between home and school, simply surveying school officials will tell only a small part of the story. By including surveys and focus groups with parents, observations of parent-teacher interactions, and reviews of policies, one will get a richer and presumably more accurate description of home-school collaboration. This multimethod approach has the advantage that each measurement strategy provides some information that the other strategies do not, so that together, they allow one to gain a more complete understanding of the phenomenon being measured (Frechtling & Sharp, 1997). Although it requires more effort to collect data from multiple sources and to blend qualitative with quantitative data, the quality of the information it generates often makes it a worthwhile endeavor.

These more conventional evaluation designs are not feasible in many evaluations, either because of the resources and expertise required or because they interfere with optimal program practice. Therefore, one must use other approaches to look for evidence of program effectiveness. The following section describes one such approach.

Theory of Change Approach

For the remainder of the chapter, we shall describe an increasingly prevalent approach to evaluation, referred to as the theory of change (TOC) approach (Fulbright-Anderson, Kubisch, & Connell, 1998; Weiss, 1995), which offers a pragmatic alternative to conventional approaches for examining program effectiveness while still tackling the critical measurement and attribution issues described above. Most evaluations are designed to examine a program's ultimate outcomes but not to reveal anything about what factors led to a program's success or failure. These evaluations are sometimes called "black box" evaluations (Patton, 1997), because they do not

---

Box 13.2   Two Common Evaluation Designs

Evaluation designs commonly used in the social sciences attempt to demonstrate that outcomes may be attributed to a program by showing what outcomes would have naturally occurred to participants had they not been exposed to the program and then comparing those to the outcomes that were actually observed after participants were exposed to the program. One way to do this is to conduct an *experiment,* in which one observes two groups of people over time[1] (Campbell, 1984). The *program group* is exposed to the program and the *comparison* or *control group* is not. If there are more positive outcomes in the program group than in the comparison group (assuming accurate measurement and equivalence between groups), then one has some evidence that the program was effective. The practical difficulties of recruiting and tracking a comparison group, plus the reluctance of most organizations to withhold services from them, makes this option unattractive for most community evaluators. But even when comparison groups are used, results are usually biased (i.e., program effects are either overestimated or underestimated) because of preexisting differences between the two groups before the program began (Hollister & Hill, 1995). Despite the many problems with using experimental designs in community research, there are some circumstances in which they can be used without significant practical or ethical barriers (e.g., Roth et al., 1998).

A second method, known as the *interrupted time-series design,* involves letting the program group serve as its own comparison group (Cook & Campbell, 1979; Granger, 1998). With this method, one first examines outcomes over several consecutive time periods to determine whether they are changing naturally before the program begins. Then, after the program begins, one examines outcomes over several more time periods to determine whether the program has affected the *pattern of change* in outcomes over time. For example, one may review several years of attendance data and observe that attendance rates have declined steadily for 3 consecutive years but stopped their decline (remained constant) after the program began. Assuming that the outcome was measured accurately, this pattern of findings would provide credible evidence that the program was responsible (at least in part) for stopping the decline in attendance.

(continued)

Box 13.2 (Continued)

This method is often more appropriate than experimental designs, given the difficulty of finding equivalent comparison groups. However, it is often only practical when one has access to data that are routinely measured at regular intervals (e.g., annual surveys of student behavior, school records indicating the percent of seniors applying to college) and the program begins at a distinct time period (e.g., new evening activity center, career-planning program). Bloom (1999) describes an effective use of this approach in evaluating a school-restructuring program. For further information about these and other evaluation design options, the reader may consult the sources listed in the "Additional Evaluation Resources" section at the end of the chapter.

examine what happens in the program and therefore provide little guidance for making program improvements (see Figure 13.1).

In contrast, the explicit purpose of the TOC approach is to understand what happens to participants during and after the program that leads to its ultimate success. The TOC approach essentially involves laying out one's ideas (one's theory) about *how* the program is expected to produce its effects (i.e., the key pathways the program initiates that facilitate positive outcomes). The evaluation is then designed to ask "Did the expected outcomes occur?" and "Did they occur through the pathways proposed by the theory?" (Chen & Rossi, 1987). Although it first emerged as a tool for evaluation planning, the TOC approach has quickly become popular as a program planning tool as well (see Connell & Klem, 2000; Connell & Kubisch, 1998).

Some Conceptual Foundations

In constructing a TOC approach for youth development initiatives, one starts with two important premises. First, rather than producing positive outcomes directly, youth development programs work indirectly by initiating or nurturing a sequence of positive developmental processes in the lives of youth that ultimately place them on a healthy trajectory (Connell, Gambone, & Smith, 2000; MacDonald & Valdivieso, 2000; National Research Council and Institute of Medicine, 2002). This makes it important to start out by clarifying, even at a general level, what causal pathways a program is trying to initiate in the lives of youth and how program strategies will initiate those

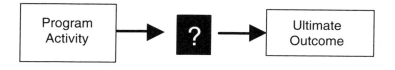

Figure 13.1   Black Box Evaluation

pathways. This essentially amounts to a working theory about how the program brings about positive changes (thus, "theory of change") and provides a map for both designing the program and planning its evaluation (Fishman, Farrell, Allen, & Eiseman, 2000).

The second premise of the TOC approach is that any program is based on a set of assumptions about how its activities will be carried out, how they will be received by participants, and what kinds of outcomes will and will not result from those activities (Patton, 1997; Rossi & Freeman, 1985; Weiss, 1995). Many who develop or implement programs are not even aware of these assumptions, despite the fact that they may have critical implications for program effectiveness (see Case 13.1). One important purpose of developing a TOC is to surface assumptions that are critical to program success. Then, once they are made explicit, the evaluation can focus at least partly on testing those assumptions empirically. Hence, evaluating from a TOC approach fosters program improvement by helping program operators learn what aspects of their theory can be safely assumed (e.g., that promoting supportive relationships with adults will foster healthy social and emotional development) and what parts cannot (e.g., that providing information about drugs will prevent drug use). The use of evaluation to test assumptions and refine program strategies is discussed more in the "Using Theory to Help Interpret Results" section that follows.

How It Works

The process of developing the TOC is best viewed as being *collaborative,* in that the best theory emerges when the perspectives of all relevant stakeholders are incorporated (e.g., administrators, frontline staff, teachers, parents, youth, etc.) (Greene, 1987), and *iterative,* in that the theory is continually reevaluated and modified as new data and new perspectives are considered (Philliber, 1998). Initially, a planning group comprising program administrators, their staff, evaluators, and others work collaboratively, preferably with some technical assistance, to articulate each component of the TOC that guides the program. This involves spelling out

Case 13.1 Surfacing and Examining Assumptions

A very small percentage of students from a rural school had historically enrolled in college. A team of students, teachers, guidance counselors, and administrative staff convened to develop and carry out a yearlong program for seniors designed to increase the number of students applying to and enrolling in college. Their program strategy involved the following:

- A series of education fairs designed to inform seniors about available options for continuing their education
- College student mentors who met monthly with seniors to answer questions and discuss relevant issues
- A career resource room including guidance staff, materials, and computer software designed to help students explore career options

It appears quite plausible that this approach would motivate more students to seek a college education. However, the program's likelihood of success is contingent on several assumptions. Specifically, it assumes the following:

College Student Mentors

- Mentors meet regularly with seniors.
- Mentors have enough information and experience to answer students' questions.
- There are enough mentors available to meet the demand.
- The information students receive actually increases their enthusiasm and confidence about college, rather than simply increasing anxiety.

Career Resource Room

- The school is willing to invest space and staff.
- Students know about the room and understand what is available there.

Student-Teacher-Staff Coalition

- Student ideas are seriously discussed and incorporated into final strategies.
- The teachers and staff know how to work effectively with students in a collaborative arrangement.

General

- Students are interested enough to participate.
- The students who actually participate in the activities are the ones who need the program most (i.e., those who are eligible for college but do not apply).
- Family members will support student efforts to attend college.
- The goal of going to college does not strongly conflict with students' existing family roles and responsibilities.
- Students are able to pay for college if accepted.
- Students are able to write effective letters and complete applications properly.
- The most important time to engage students in college planning is during senior year (rather than in earlier grades).

Examining these assumptions can provide valuable insight for improving one's TOC (and thus for improving the program). For example, if indeed most students could not pay for college, this would suggest the need for an added component to help students acquire financial aid. If not enough students found the mentoring visits valuable, this might suggest the need for better matching between mentors and seniors or mentor training. If families fail to support students' enrollment efforts, the program may need to consider engaging family members in some constructive way.

with explicit operational statements (a) the ultimate outcomes they hope to achieve, (b) the immediate and intermediate outcomes resulting from the program that effectively serve as the mechanisms through which it produces the ultimate outcomes, (c) the expected causal linkages between these elements, (d) the program activities and aspects of program implementation that will influence program success (sometimes referred to as *process factors*), and (e) the resources and conditions that need to be present to carry out the program effectively (United Way of America, 1996). The resulting TOC is essentially a sequence of "if-then" statements that give a plausible explanation for how the program will achieve the ultimate outcomes it is aiming for. The organization then works with an evaluator to develop a detailed evaluation plan guided by the TOC. Optimally, the process begins before the program is already under way, so that the TOC can guide both program development and evaluation. More typically, however, the TOC is developed after the program is already under way, with the primary aim of guiding the evaluation plan.

The TOC is often depicted in a diagram, referred to as a *logic model*, that shows the causal pathways between program implementation and its ultimate outcomes. Although not essential, logic models can be a user-friendly way for a planning group to communicate their ideas about how a program's activities will produce the outcomes they are aiming for. Such a diagram also provides a focal point for discussion and brainstorming as a group attempts to reach consensus about their own TOC.

A Sample Application of Theory of Change

We will illustrate the TOC approach in the context of a sample program designed to foster better educational outcomes for youth. The overall example is hypothetical, although the program we describe is based on the School Transitional Environment Project (Felner & Adan, 1988; modified here for illustrative purposes). To help incoming freshmen adapt better to high school, the program changed the school structure by (a) grouping students into cohorts that share most classes together throughout the year and (b) localizing all freshman classes in close proximity. The program also changed the structure of the classroom environment by (a) reducing class size and (b) extending the homeroom period and expanding the role of homeroom teachers to include that of guidance counselor and mentor.

In this section, we will describe the program's TOC to explain how it is expected to produce positive outcomes. Then, we will describe how this TOC can be used to guide evaluation decisions and the interpretation of evaluation findings.

Our logic model is divided into four steps (see Figure 13.2). *Ultimate outcomes* are the criteria on which the program's effectiveness will ultimately be judged. *Intermediate outcomes* are expected to play a direct causal role in bringing about the ultimate outcomes, whereas *immediate outcomes* result immediately from the program and are seen as initiating the change process. Last, *activities* refer to the content of the program and aspects of its implementation that affect its ability to produce positive outcomes. It is important to emphasize that activities are not outcomes of the program. Rather, they reflect what the program does in practice to achieve its intended outcomes.

We start with the ultimate outcomes of the program (on the far-right side of the model) and "work backward" to specific program activities.

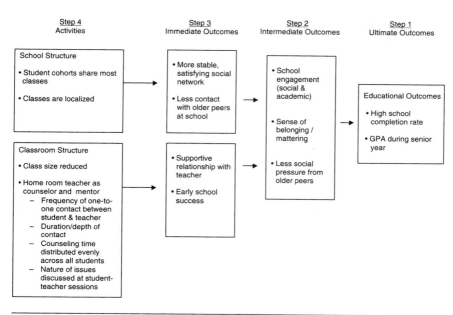

Figure 13.2   Sample Logic Model

Working backward is a technique that is particularly useful at the program development stage, because it keeps the group's thinking focused on outcomes and helps them zero in on critical pathways that must occur for activities to eventually produce those outcomes. Although working backward is often recommended as a planning technique (e.g., United Way, 1996), some find it easier to work in a forward direction, especially in the more typical case when the evaluation is being planned after the program is already in operation.

Step 1: Ultimate Outcomes

This step first requires establishing the time frame and scope of the evaluation. In this case, due to practical considerations and our desire to remain focused on the teenage years, we define the ultimate outcome as *high school completion* and *grade point average (GPA) during senior year*. Another evaluation might use a longer time frame, given that the larger purpose of the program is to help teens become healthy, educated, responsible citizens capable of economic self-sufficiency. This decision must be determined partly by whether the organization has sufficient resources to track students into adulthood.

Step 2: Intermediate Outcomes

The next step involves determining some early-stage program outcomes that should facilitate students completing school with a higher GPA. In this case, evaluators and program operators drew from existing research showing that to achieve success in school, students need to (a) be fully engaged in the school (both socially and academically) (Finn, 1989), (b) feel a sense of belonging and mattering while at school (McNeely, Nonnemaker, & Blum, 2002), and (c) experience fewer social pressures from older peers to behave in ways that jeopardize their chances for school success (Thornberry & Krohn, 1997).

Step 3: Immediate Outcomes

The immediate outcomes expected from this program were that students (a) have a more stable and satisfying social network as a result of sharing the same classes, (b) have less contact with older peers as a result of classes being localized, (c) experience a supportive ongoing relationship with their teachers due to the teachers' expanded roles, and (d) experience early school success as a result of smaller class size. Together, these immediate outcomes were expected to start youth on a positive social and academic trajectory in high school and thus facilitate the intermediate and ultimate outcomes described above.[2]

Step 4: Activities

This step involves describing the specific program strategies that are expected to produce the outcomes of interest. The activities listed in Figure 13.2 are those specified by the program design. When one is constructing a TOC to use as a guide for program development, this step becomes a brainstorming activity to identify what strategies will most effectively achieve the program's immediate outcome goals. Regardless of whether the program is already established or not, this step provides an opportunity for innovative thinking about how the program can best achieve the desired outcomes for youth. In this example, the activities involved grouping students into cohorts, localizing freshmen classes, reducing class size, and expanding the role of the homeroom teacher.

Process Factors

During Step 4, planners should also identify indicators that the activities were implemented at sufficient levels and with sufficient quality to have a substantial impact on any outcomes already identified. This process data typically includes information about who was engaged in or was exposed to the program, what was provided to them, and how much exposure they received. In this example, it was believed that for students to develop meaningful relationships with teachers, they needed to have regular one-to-one contact that lasted a sufficient amount of time. It was also important that teachers' time was distributed evenly across all students and was not dominated by a few students with excessive needs. Finally, it was important that a substantial portion of teacher-student discussions focused on student needs rather than being dominated by issues on the teachers' or school's agenda.

Resources (Not Shown in Figure 13.2)

In addition to the four steps, the planning group must describe or map (and evaluators should document) the human, economic, and political supports that the organization will require to carry out the program successfully. Obviously, this may require a considerable amount of planning, depending on the complexity of the program and a range of organizational factors. Resources typically pertain to tangible items such as money, equipment, and staff. Some key resources in the current example included funds and space for extra classrooms, given the reduction in class size, and training for teachers in counseling techniques and in how to capitalize on smaller class size. Less tangible resources must also be considered, such as a history of effective collaboration between school administrators and staff and the support of parents for the initiative, both of which should greatly ease the restructuring effort.

In sum, the theory proposes that this program strategy works through several key pathways. A more stable social network (including peers and teachers) increases students' sense of belonging and strengthens their school engagement socially. Students also experience fewer negative social pressures from older peers due to reduced contact with them. Finally, early school success and supportive relationships with teachers increase students' school engagement academically. These factors are proposed to work in combination to place youth on a positive developmental trajectory that increases their chances for school success. The purpose of the evaluation, then, is not only to look for improvements in high school completion and GPA but also to test the overall theory.

Using Theory to Guide
the Measurement Strategy

Generally speaking, a TOC provides evaluators with a road map for many of the critical measurement decisions they must make. Considering our previous discussion about the limitations of measuring only ultimate outcomes and the need to understand why a program was or was not effective, evaluators face numerous decisions, such as "What additional outcome variables should we measure that would provide insight regarding the program's success or failure?" "What process factors should we document?" "If we can't measure everything of interest, how should we prioritize?" and "When should measurements be made?" The TOC provides a general framework that helps to inform these decisions.

Deciding What to Measure

The logic model in the example above provides some explicit suggestions about selecting the outcomes and process factors on which one should collect data. First, it suggests that we need to document how the program was implemented (e.g., frequency, duration, and depth of student-teacher contacts) because these factors will affect its likelihood of producing any of the proposed outcomes (Patton, 1997). It also suggests that rather than simply measuring school success in the senior year, other key outcomes should be measured as well, such as student relationships with peers and homeroom teachers, early school performance, and school engagement. The program's success at producing those immediate and intermediate outcomes will determine its likelihood of affecting the ultimate educational outcomes.

We also need "measures" of the resources and supports being put in place to get the program's activities off the ground and to threshold levels of implementation deemed sufficient to produce outcomes. In this example, these measures might come in the form of interviews with administrators and teachers, as well as tracking budgets, levels of effort, and qualifications of staff hired. This information will be more useful to guide program planning if done early in the process, rather than after evaluation has already shown that the program was not implemented sufficiently to affect outcomes.

Timing of Measurement

Decisions about when to measure each variable are less straightforward, although the sequential layout of the logic model provides at least a rough template. Program implementation data need to be gathered as the program is under way (in the sample case, during freshman year). Optimally, we would gather data on all outcomes both before and after the program begins. We would likely measure our immediate outcomes during or shortly after freshman year, the ultimate outcomes at the end of senior year, and intermediate outcomes somewhere in between. The specific timing of the intermediate outcome assessments depends on more careful consideration of the change process we are trying to facilitate. This is where a well-thought-out TOC can be helpful. For example, suppose that the research literature suggests that improved social networks in the freshman year are not sufficient and that teens must have healthy relationships throughout high school to have lasting effects on school performance. That would suggest that the measurement plan also needs to include yearly assessments of students' social networks.

Prioritizing Outcomes

Typically, one cannot measure every outcome of interest, especially in more complex models with dozens of variables (Patton, 1997). The logic model helps identify the most critical pathways and filter out the less critical ones. These choices may be informed by previous research, past experience, the collective wisdom of the planning group, or some other credible source of insight. In our example, one might decide that the most important outcomes to measure are early school success and school engagement, because the research literature indicates that those factors consistently predict higher rates of school completion (Finn, 1989; Stipek, 2001). The decision about where to focus the evaluation also depends partly on the stage of the program's development (Jacobs, 1988). It is often inappropriate to focus on ultimate outcomes unless the program has been operating long enough to be running at full capacity. At earlier stages, the program will benefit most from information about the quality of implementation or whether immediate outcomes are being achieved. Such information can reveal a program's progress toward achieving its intended ultimate outcomes and can inform program operators about midcourse corrections that need to be made.

Using Theory to Help Interpret Results

When the TOC approach is used, evaluation findings are easier to interpret because they can be viewed within the context of the TOC and they have more direct relevance to specific questions posed by the evaluation's planners. To the extent that findings confirm the theory guiding the program, even nonexperimental data can support the claim that the program caused whatever changes were measured.

Making a Case for Attribution

As mentioned above, most evaluations have great difficulty showing that positive outcomes can be attributed to the program, because conventional evaluation designs are not feasible. If, however, a program has a clear TOC and the evaluation shows a pattern of results consistent with the theory (i.e., the program was delivered as intended; achievement of ultimate outcomes was preceded by achievement of immediate and intermediate outcomes), those findings can strengthen the scientific case that the program is at least partly responsible for those changes (Chen & Rossi, 1987; Connell & Kubisch, 1998). For example, suppose that in our example, the evaluation found a dramatic increase in graduation rate among students who were involved in the program during freshman year. The TOC would direct us to look at whether the students who graduated also experienced better social networks and early school success, followed by stronger school engagement, compared with students in the same class who did not graduate and compared with previous classes of students. If indeed that were the case, it would provide evidence that the positive outcomes observed in those students were related to their involvement in the program. This is not to suggest that using a TOC approach eliminates the need for conventional evaluation designs (Granger, 1998). One will never be able to make a definitive case for attribution without somehow estimating what outcomes would have naturally occurred without the program (e.g., using a control group). However, given the difficulty of finding *equivalent* control groups, the TOC approach offers a practical alternative that can significantly add to the credibility of evaluation findings.

Making Use of Negative Findings

As discussed earlier, an important advantage of a TOC approach to evaluation is that it helps to uncover the reasons why a program *fails* to achieve its intended outcomes. If even one or two key assumptions built into the program model are faulty, the program can appear to be a complete failure.

In our example, an important assumption was that small class size would lead to early academic success. Suppose the evaluation found that the program failed to increase the graduation rate or GPA in senior year. Suppose further that although the program had a strong effect on students' support networks (peers and teachers), social pressure from older peers, and sense of belonging, it had no effect on freshman grades or on school engagement. Those findings would suggest two important conclusions that have great implications for the future direction of the program. First, reduced class size was not sufficient to produce either early academic success or school engagement; the program must take additional steps to influence those outcomes. Second, many components of the program did have their intended effects and should probably be continued. Therefore, the program was far from being a complete failure.

As another example, suppose that after finding no overall program effects, data analysis indicated that girls tended to use the sessions with homeroom teachers much more frequently and effectively than did boys, whereas boys were more likely than girls to benefit academically from reduced class size. This would challenge another unstated assumption: namely, that one can use the same strategies for boys as for girls. It would also suggest the need to modify the program so that both genders benefit more from each of those program components.

These examples illustrate that when data collection is guided by a theoretical framework, evaluators are better able to identify and test critical program assumptions and thus to better understand what factors contribute to a program's success or failure (Patton, 1997). Such insights are far more valuable than a simple judgment that a program has succeeded or failed.

Conclusions

In this chapter, we have argued that program evaluation should ideally begin with a careful examination of the theory describing how the program strategy is expected to produce its ultimate intended outcomes. Such a theory provides concrete guidance about a range of key evaluation decisions pertaining to both the collection and interpretation of data. As a result, evaluation findings will have more direct relevance to practice decisions because they not only indicate whether a program succeeded or failed but also suggest likely reasons for those results and how one might enhance future program success. This evaluation approach does not eliminate the need for careful decisions regarding evaluation design or measurement, but it boosts the credibility and meaning of evaluation findings by placing them in the context of a coherent, a priori program theory. Beyond its value for guiding the evaluation, the TOC approach improves the program development process by stimulating careful and critical thinking about promising program strategies.

What most funders want from evaluations is some indication about whether the program is likely to contribute to better outcomes for youth and communities. Because evaluation results are usually not sufficient for the reasons outlined above (e.g., inadequate methodology, faulty interpretation of results), additional information is needed from which to judge a program's future likelihood of success. How can TOC evaluations help funders make sound judgments about programs? First, the fact that program operators are able to articulate a plausible theory of change must engender some confidence in their ability to succeed, particularly if parts of the theory have foundations in the research literature. Second, even if an evaluation cannot provide definitive evidence that a program has produced its ultimate intended outcomes, it may be able to provide fairly strong evidence of producing valuable shorter-term outcomes. High-quality evidence about immediate or intermediate outcomes should be weighted at least as heavily as questionable evidence about ultimate outcomes. Finally, it is probably safe to assume that programs that demonstrate a pattern of continually gathering and using data to guide future practice are more likely to succeed in the long run. Such a pattern is a hallmark of good practice and should not be overlooked in the effort to identify the most promising programs.

The TOC approach holds great promise for making evaluation a vital tool in the community effort to promote positive youth development. It seeks to engage program planners in a sustained process of program analysis and adaptation in which key practice decisions are based on empirical evidence. However, to realize this potential, evaluators and funders alike must be willing to expand the scope of evaluation so that greater emphasis is placed on generating information relevant to program improvement. Thus, organizations must (a) be given the latitude to direct the focus of their own evaluations and (b) receive sustained support for this type of evaluation approach. Because resources are finite, this will require shifting away from a sole focus on "showing results." This is not only a technical matter but also requires a shift in the priorities of funders and others who establish standards for program evaluations. We believe that such a shift is warranted because it will likely result in funders gaining a richer base of information about the programs they support and, ultimately, more effective programs.

Additional Evaluation Resources

Print Resources on Program Evaluation

Applied Social Research Methods Series (Sage). Series contains several useful resources on various aspects of program evaluation, including *Volume 5: Case Study Research: Design and Methods* (Yin, 1994); *Volume 20: Focus Groups* (Stewart & Shamdasani, 1990); *Volume 32: Applied Research Design*

(Hendrick, Bickman, & Rog, 1993); *Volume 44: Randomized Experiments for Planning and Evaluation* (Boruch, 1997); *Volume 45: Measuring Community Indicators* (Gruenewald, Treno, Taff, & Klitzner, 1997).

Measuring Program Outcomes: A Practical Approach. (1996). United Way of America. Alexandria, VA: United Way of America.

New Approaches to Evaluating Community Initiatives: Volume 1. Concepts, Methods, and Contexts. (1995). Connell, J. P., Kubisch, A., Schorr, L. B., & Weiss, C. H. (Eds.), Washington, DC: Aspen Institute.

New Approaches to Evaluating Community Initiatives: Volume 2. Theory, Measurement, and Analysis. (1998). Fulbright-Anderson, K., Kubisch, A., & Connell, J. P. (Eds.). Washington, DC: Aspen Institute.

Utilization-Focused Evaluation (3rd ed.). (1997). Patton, M.Q. Thousand Oaks: Sage.

Internet Resources on Program Evaluation

General Evaluation

Evaluation Primer: An Overview of Evaluation. Provides an overview of process, outcome, and impact evaluations and suggestions for interpreting and reporting evaluation findings. Prepared for the U.S. Department of Education by Westat, Inc. Available at: http://www.ed.gov/offices/OUS/PES/primer1.html.

Taking Stock: A Practical Guide to Evaluating Your Own Program. Report summarizes several evaluation approaches. Describes how to document and use program implementation data and gives suggestions for identifying indicators of change. Describes the effective use of both quantitative and qualitative data, including tips for organizing, interpreting, and reporting evaluation findings. Prepared by the Horizon Research, Inc. Available at: http//www.horizon-research.com/publications/stock.pdf.

Community Tool Box: Evaluating Community Programs and Initiatives. A comprehensive "How-to" Web resource providing plain-language guidance on the planning and evaluation of programs and comprehensive community evaluations. Designed to help community organizations produce information that will inform their community change efforts. Sponsored by the University of Kansas. Available at: http://ctb.lsi.ukans.edu/tools/EN/part_1010.htm.

Community-Based Project Evaluation Guide. Follows five-tiered evaluation approach (Jacobs, 1988). This Web resource takes program managers through several stages of evaluation, from describing the program's vision, mission, goals, objectives, and characteristics to distributing the evaluation findings. It also provides links to several resources, including evaluation templates and report forms that program managers and evaluation teams might find useful. Sponsored by the Institute for Children, Youth, and Families at the University of Arizona. Available at: http://ag.arizona.edu/fcr/fs/cyfar/evalgde.htm.

Project STAR: Support and Training for Assessing Results. Web-based resource to help program managers with evaluation planning and the use of evaluation findings. Developed by Project STAR, an organization that provides technical assistance in conducting program evaluations. Available at: http://www. projectstar.org/star/Library/toolkit.html.

Electronic Resources for Evaluators. Provides links to information and resources regarding all aspects of program evaluation, including educational resources, training, workshops, funding sources, computer software, statistics, and instruments. Available at: http://www.be-webbed.com/evalResources.html.

Collaborative, Participatory, and Empowerment Evaluation. Provides an introduction to empowerment evaluation. Gives several links to other Internet resources, including software, evaluation guides, downloadable papers and newsletters, suggested readings, related organizations, and so on. Sponsored by American Evaluation Association. Available at: http://www.stanford.edu/~davidf/empowermentevaluation.html.

User-Friendly Handbook for Mixed-Method Evaluations. Provides a guide for conducting mixed-method evaluations, suggestions for evaluation design, data analysis, and reporting findings. Sponsored by the National Science Foundation. Available at: http://www.ehr.nsf.gov/EHR/REC/pubs/NSF97-153/start.htm.

Getting to Outcomes: Methods and Tools for Planning, Self-Evaluation, and Accountability. This manual guides readers through an empowerment evaluation model by addressing 10 questions that incorporate the basic elements of program planning, implementation, evaluation, and sustainability. Sponsored by Center for Substance Abuse Prevention. Available at: http://www.stanford.edu/~davidf/GTO_Volume_I.pdf.

Design, Methods, and Measures

Community Tool Box: Methods for Evaluating Comprehensive Community Initiatives. Provides suggestions for monitoring progress, developing surveys, identifying existing surveys, conducting interviews, and gathering community-level indicators. Sponsored by the University of Kansas. Available at: http://ctb.lsi.ukans.edu/tools/EN/chapter_1039.htm.

Survey Development at Surveykey.com. Provides guide to developing professional-looking on-line surveys, polls, tests, questionnaires, and surveys. Provides summary results and graphs and puts data into a spreadsheet to allow users to analyze data. Available at: http://www.surveykey.com/.

Evaluation Tool Kit: Quasi-Experimental Evaluation. Provides information on quasi-experimental evaluations, interrupted time-series designs, selection bias, selecting outcome measures, choosing a comparison group, and determining an appropriate sample size. Sponsored by Human Resources Development Canada. Available at: http://www11.hrdc-drhc.gc.ca/pls/edd/v_report.a?p_site=EDD&sub=QEE.

Trochim's Center for Social Research Methods. Provides information on measurement and evaluation design, plus relatively basic descriptions of several statistical issues related to evaluation. Also includes information on "concept mapping," a collaborative method that can be used to incorporate the ideas and priorities of large groups of individuals as they develop their TOCs. Sponsored by Professor William Trochim at Cornell University. Available at: http://trochim.human. cornell.edu/index.html.

Evaluation Tool Kit: Focus Groups. Suggestions for designing and conducting focus groups, and using the information collected. Sponsored by Human Resources Development Canada. Available at: http://www11.hrdc-drhc.gc.ca/pls/edd/v_report.a?p_site=EDD&sub=ETKFG.

Theory of Change and Logic Model

Program Evaluation Tool Kit. Guide to evaluation and logic models. Sponsored by the Community Health Research Unit at the University of Ottawa. Available at: http://www.uottawa.ca/academic/med/epid/excerpt.htm.

United Way of America's Outcome Measurement Resource Network. Information on evaluation, logic models, measuring program outcomes, and links to other resources. Sponsored by the United Way of America. Available at: http://national.unitedway.org/outcomes/resources/.

Notes

1. When people are randomly assigned to groups to minimize the preexisting differences between groups, it is referred to as a *true experiment;* when random assignment is not used, it is referred to as a *quasi-experiment.*

2. There are usually many potential levels of intermediate outcomes one might include. For example, one may argue that the most immediate outcome of the smaller class size is greater opportunity for individualized instruction and easier classroom management. One may also argue that reduced social pressure must translate into less truancy and fewer problem behaviors to influence the rate of school completion. The level of detail in the TOC varies depending on what is appropriate for the project. Also, the labels applied to the outcomes (*immediate, intermediate*) are less important than ensuring that the theory has sound logic and is informed by the research literature.

References

Bloom, H. S. (1999, August). *Estimating program impacts on student achievement using "short" interrupted time series.* New York: MDRC. Retrieved February 21, 2003, from: www.mdrc.org/Reports99/EstimatingImpacts/Interrupted TimePaper.html.

Campbell, D. T. (1984). Can we be scientific in applied social science? In R. F. Conner, D. G. Altman, & C. Jackson (Eds.), *Evaluation studies review annual* (Vol. 9, pp. 26-48). Beverly Hills, CA: Sage.

Chen, H., & Rossi, P. H. (1987). The theory-driven approach to validity. *Evaluation and Program Planning, 10,* 95-103.

Connell, J. P., Gambone, M. A., & Smith, T. J. (2000). Youth development in community settings: Challenges to our field and our approach. In P. J. Benson & K. J. Pittman (Eds.), *Trends in youth development.* Boston: Kluwer. Also in Public/Private Ventures (Ed.), *Youth development: Issues, challenges and directions.* Philadelphia: Author.

Connell, J. P., & Klem, A. M. (2000). You can get there from here: Using a theory of change approach to plan urban education reform. *Journal of Educational and Psychological Consulting, 11*(1), 93-120.

Connell, J., & Kubisch, A. (1998). Applying a theory of change approach to the evaluation of comprehensive community initiatives: Progress, prospects, and problems. In K. Fulbright-Anderson, A. Kubisch, & J. Connell (Eds.), *New approaches to evaluating community initiatives: Vol. 2. Theory, measurement, and analysis.* Washington, DC: Aspen Institute. Retrieved April 29, 2003, from: http://www.aspeninstitute.org/?bid=1264.

Cook, T. D., & Campbell, D. T. (1979). *Quasi-experimentation: Design and analysis issues for field settings.* Chicago: Rand-McNally.

Felner, R. D., & Adan, A. M. (1988). The School Transitional Environment Project: An ecological intervention and evaluation. In R. Price (Ed.), *Fourteen ounces of prevention.* Washington, DC: American Psychological Association.

Finn, J. D. (1989). Withdrawing from school. *Review of Educational Research, 59,* 117-142.

Fishman, M., Farrell, M., Allen, V., & Eiseman, E. (2000). *Evaluating community collaborations: A research synthesis* (Rep. No. 194123). Washington, DC: Department of Health and Human Services.

Frechtling, J., & Sharp, L. (1997). *User-friendly handbook for mixed-method evaluations.* Washington, DC: National Science Foundation.

Fulbright-Anderson, K., Kubisch, A. C., & Connell, J. P. (1998). *New approaches to evaluating community initiatives: Vol. 2. Theory, measurement, and analysis.* Washington, DC: Aspen Institute.

Gambone, M. A., Klem, A. M., & Connell, J. P. (2002). *Finding out what matters for youth: Testing key links in a community action framework for youth development.* Philadelphia: Youth Development Strategies, Inc., and Institute for Research and Reform in Education.

Granger, R. C. (1998). Establishing causality in evaluations of comprehensive community initiatives. In K. Fulbright-Anderson, A. Kubisch, & J. Connell (Eds.), *New approaches to evaluating community initiatives: Vol. 2. Theory, measurement, and analysis.* Washington, DC: Aspen Institute. Retrieved April 29, 2003, from: http://www.aspeninstitute.org/?bid=1264.

Greene, J. C. (1987). Stakeholder participation in evaluation design: Is it worth the effort? *Evaluation and Program Planning 19*(4), 379-394.

Hamilton, S. (1980). Evaluating your own program. *Educational Leadership, 37*(7), 545-552.

Hollister, R., & Hill, J. (1995). Problems in the evaluation of community-wide initiatives. In J. P. Connell, A. Kubisch, L. B. Schorr, & C. H. Weiss (Eds.), *New approaches to evaluating community initiatives: Vol. 1. Concepts, methods, and contexts.* Washington, DC: Aspen Institute. Retrieved April 29, 2003, from http://www.aspeninstitute.org/?bid=1263.

Jacobs, F. H. (1988). The five-tiered approach to evaluation: Context and implementation. In H. B. Weiss & F. H. Jacobs (Eds.), *Evaluating family programs* (pp. 37-68). New York: Aldine de Gruyter.

MacDonald, G. B., & Valdivieso, R. (2000). Measuring deficits and assets: How we track youth development now, and how we should track it. In Public/Private Ventures (Ed.), *Youth development: Issues, challenges and directions* (pp. 149-184). Philadelphia: Public/Private Ventures.

McNeely, C. A., Nonnemaker, J. M., & Blum, R. W. (2002). Promoting school connectedness: Evidence from the National Longitudinal Study of Adolescent Health. *Journal of School Health, 72*(4), 138-146.

National Research Council and Institute of Medicine. (2002). *Community programs to promote youth development.* In J. Eccles & J. A. Gootman (Eds.). Board on Children, Youth, and Families, Division of Behavioral and Social Sciences and Education. Washington, DC: National Academy Press.

Patton, M. Q. (1997). *Utilization-focused evaluation* (3rd ed.). Thousand Oaks, CA: Sage.

Philliber, S. (1998). The virtue of specificity in theory of change evaluations: Practitioner reflections. In A.K. Fulbright-Anderson, C. Kubisch, & J. P. Connell (Eds.), *New approaches to evaluating community initiatives: Vol. 2. Theory, measurement, and analysis.* Washington, DC: Aspen Institute. Retrieved April 29, 2003, from: http://www.aspeninstitute.org/?bid=1264.

Rossi, P. H., & Freeman, H. E. (1985). *Evaluation: A systematic approach* (3rd ed.). Beverly Hills, CA: Sage.

Roth, J., Brooks-Gunn, J., Murray, L., & Foster, W. (1998). Promoting healthy adolescents: Synthesis of youth development program evaluations. *Journal of Research on Adolescence, 8,* 423-459.

Stipek, D. J. (2001). Pathways to constructive lives: The importance of early school success. In A. C. Bohart & D. J. Stipek (Eds.), *Constructive and destructive behavior: Implications for family, school, and society* (pp. 291-315). Washington, DC: American Psychological Association.

Struening, E. L., & Brewer, M. B. (1983). *Handbook of evaluation research.* Beverly Hills, CA: Sage.

Thornberry, T. P., & Krohn, M. D. (1997). Peers, drug use, and delinquency. In D. M. Stoff, J. Breiling, & J. D. Maser (Eds.), *Handbook of antisocial behavior* (pp. 218-233). New York: John Wiley.

United Way of America. (1996). *Measuring program outcomes: A practical approach*. Alexandria, VA: Author.

Weiss, C. H. (1983). Toward the future of stakeholder approaches in evaluation. In A. S. Bryk (Ed.), *Stakeholder-based evaluation* (pp. 83-96). San Francisco: Jossey-Bass.

Weiss, C. H. (1995). Nothing as practical as good theory: Exploring theory-based evaluation for comprehensive community initiatives for children and families. In J. P. Connell, A. Kubisch, L. B. Schorr, & C. H. Weiss (Eds.), *New approaches to evaluating community initiatives: Vol. 1. Concepts, methods, and contexts*. Washington, DC: Aspen Institute.

14

Understanding the Lay of the Land

Strategies for Funding Youth Development Programs

Glenda L. Partee

A scan of funding sources—federal, state, local, and private philanthropy—indicates a great deal of funding potentially available for youth development activities and their infrastructure. The problem is that these funds often are not conveniently labeled "Youth Development," tend to be categorical in nature or narrowly defined to a specific activity or category of youth, are time limited, do not support sustainable efforts, and are not always packaged in ways that are easily accessible to local program providers. Funding for youth development represents a complicated puzzle, and parts of the picture remain incomplete.

This chapter is designed to help professionals working with youth acquire a better understanding of the landscape of funding opportunities for youth development. References are provided to a number of guides, organizations, and Web sites to access sources of support. The following sections provide a cursory map of diverse sources, including the roles of the public and private sectors, strategies for supporting youth development, and trends that may bear on the future of the field.

While embracing the definition of youth development as a process designed to promote assets and inclusive of all youth, this chapter cites a number of funding sources that do not fit totally with this definition. Many categorical funding sources are beginning to integrate a youth development philosophy into their work. Thus, they may become an important part of a more comprehensive approach that tailors services and activities to the needs of particular young people to ensure their healthy development.

Hacking Through the Maze

Newman, Smith, and Murphy (2000) established an initial framework and formula for assessing the financial resources necessary to reach what they call the "ideal" funding for youth development: "Adequate and secure funding for the developmental supports and opportunities that *all* youth need on the road to a productive, healthy and economically viable adulthood" (p. 84). Using cost figures from programs that fill the nonschool hours with positive supports such as those related to after-school programs, mentoring, prevention, recreation, Scouts, and service opportunities, they arrived at a figure of $3,060 per U.S. school-aged youth (6 to 17 years old) for 1,200 unsupervised/unstructured hours per year (about $144 billion). They concluded that current sources to support this ideal were fragmented across an array of disparate government entities, lacked a comprehensive strategy for youth, focused on crisis intervention rather than development, and targeted at-risk youth as opposed to all youth.

These observations reflect those of the General Accounting Office (GAO; 1997), which found not only fragmentation of approach and delivery but also duplication and inefficiency among federally funded efforts focused on targeted youth populations. According to the GAO, multiple federal departments and agencies spend billions of dollars on a wide variety of programs serving at-risk and delinquent youth (a 1996 report documented 131 federally funded programs in 16 agencies focused on delinquent youth). Many of the programs are potentially duplicative, providing services that seem to overlap those of programs in the same agency and other agencies. This system of multiple federal programs across several agencies appears to be quite inefficient.

A patchwork of funding sources exists as well for more universally accessible initiatives, such as after-school programming. Halpern, Deich, and Cohen (2002) identify a range of funding sources and revenues supporting after-school programs and systems, including parent fees, public funding, private funding, and in-kind contributions, as well as sources for funding infrastructure (facilities improvement, professional development, and technical assistance). They describe a fragmented, categorical, unpredictable system that places programs that should complement each other in competition for scare resources. Typically, funding for after-school programs may be patched together with portions of child care, compensatory or remedial education, parks and recreation funding, and some funding from federal, state, or local agencies that seek to prevent violence, delinquency, drug use, school dropouts, or other problems. These public funds are then combined in innovative ways and/or supplemented by local private foundations, corporate funding, and in-kind contributions from businesses or individuals.

In response to a lack of clarity over who funds what and how, a number of efforts have been mounted to help grant seekers understand the maze of funding options. Meanwhile, funders, both public and private, working within their respective sectors and occasionally across sectors, are trying to channel their efforts in less duplicative and conflicting ways. In some cases, they are working to make their efforts complementary.

Probably the most definitive compilation of federal funding sources for out-of-school time and community school initiatives to date has been developed by The Finance Project. A 2003 revised and updated version of an earlier guide provides information on 116 funding sources, as well as strategies for accessing and using federal funds (Padgette, 2003). A companion piece identifies resources to support rural out-of-school time programs and strategies that state and local leaders can use to support and sustain programs in rural communities (The Finance Project, 2003).

The Finance Project has continued to build technical assistance capability on financing and sustainability supports by developing resources to assist state and community leaders in devising short- and long-term financing strategies and by providing targeted support and assistance to national and/or regional out-of-school time and community school initiatives.[1] A Finance Project publication by Hayes (2002), *Thinking Broadly: Financing Strategies for Comprehensive Child and Family Initiatives,* provides a conceptual framework for understanding a range of financing options and how they can be aligned with various investments. It is the first in a series of products focused on strategies (not just sources) for financing children and family services and community development, including options for generating and using resources to fund specific programmatic needs. Though focused on the larger issue of creating comprehensive community support systems, *Thinking Broadly* provides generic guidance to professionals working with youth. Specific guidance is provided on the following:

- Aligning financing strategies with the program services they are intended to support
- Changing fiscal needs over the life cycle of the initiative
- Incorporating multiple funding sources that cut across traditionally separate services and programs
- Maximizing the use of resources already in the system
- Using new funding to leverage other public and private sector resources
- Contributing to a positive return on investment

See the "Additional Resources on Funding" section at the end of this chapter for a list of sources of information on funding youth development activities.

Before developing a funding strategy, grant seekers should get an understanding of the potential sources of funding and their applications. This requires a basic knowledge of the role of private philanthropy as well as public sector support for youth development.

Private Philanthropy

Private philanthropy includes private foundations and charities, community foundations, and corporate grant makers, such as employee-giving programs and cause-related marketing (i.e., creating good will by providing a service or a percentage of sales to the customers corporations are trying to reach).

Private Foundations

Private foundations include both large national and international foundations such as Ford and Rockefeller and smaller family foundations with a local, state, or regional focus. Private philanthropy supports research, demonstrations, and advocacy. It has pioneered and sustained many new ideas and organizations to illustrate their efficacy and pave the way for larger, sustained government support. In addition to infusing youth development into many traditional institutions, it has helped localities build a variety of youth development programs and partnered with community sites to promote positive youth development outcomes.

Foundations may offer a number of strategies and opportunities for support to different sectors of the community, or they may be more focused in their support. The Wallace–Reader's Digest Funds exemplify the diversified approach. They have helped public institutions such as libraries, children's museums, and science-technology centers build their capacity to better serve school-aged youth and create high-quality programs that incorporate the principles of positive youth development. Wallace Funds have provided supports for training and resources for local YMCAs to develop programs in the literary, performing, and visual arts and helped the adaptation of promising extended-service school models to be more effective educational resources for young people. Wallace Funds have also funded promising school-age care in selected cities to improve service quality, to exchange information and programming ideas, and to link providers to new funding opportunities.

The Edna McConnell Clark Foundation is much more narrowly focused on strengthening the field of youth development through support to selected individual youth development organizations. The foundation hopes that "efforts to strengthen already promising youth-serving organizations will result in new knowledge about effective youth development practices and standards of success" (The Edna McConnell Clark Foundation, 2002, p. 5). Another example of a focused approach is the Charles Stewart Mott Foundation, which has built on its more than six decades of support for community education to partner with the U.S. Department of Education in a multiyear public-private partnership in support of 21st Century Community Learning Centers (21st CCLC) and other after-school initiatives. Grant making supports research and evaluation, identification and dissemination of promising practices, professional development for practitioners, policy development, and public awareness and advocacy, while infusing issues of access and equity to ensure program quality and availability among low-income and hard-to-reach populations (Charles Stewart Mott Foundation, 2002).

Community Foundations

Added to the mosaic of funding sources are community foundations that fill a particular niche. They are better positioned than many national foundations to understand the local political and resource landscape. Many have experience in building alliances across the public, private, and independent sectors and increasingly venture into public policy. All have strong ties to traditional business and civic leaders through their donor base and boards of directors—groups whose support is essential to sustaining progress in building the field of youth development. Community foundations may serve as intermediaries and play pivotal roles in helping to expand and replicate models of youth development locally. They provide leadership in helping communities build an infrastructure that provides all youth with quality supports and opportunities (Coalition of Community Foundations for Youth, 1999).

Collaboratives

Increasingly, "collaboratives" of funders organize efforts around specific areas of youth development to address perceived gaps. One group of grant makers, the Funder's Collaborative on Youth Organizing, works to strengthen the capacities of groups involved in youth organizing and is committed to raising funds to support such efforts (Funder's Collaborative on Youth Organizing, 2002). The Youth Transition Funders Group operates across boundaries to reduce barriers and create opportunities for vulnerable youth by expanding high-quality educational opportunities and integrating youth development principles into the systems with which these youth interact (e.g., juvenile justice, welfare, foster care, and workforce development). The group has no structured funding mechanism, but through improved communications across funding sources (public and private) seeks to include the interests of vulnerable youth on the agendas of policymakers and foundations. Finally, foundations not only inform themselves of changes in the youth development field but also inform the public about philanthropy in various regions of the country (see for example, the Forum of Regional Associations of Grantmakers, 2002).

Community-Based Fund Raising

Community-based organizations such as the United Way raise funds locally and invest them in affiliated agencies and nonprofit organizations to address community needs, including programming for youth. Community foundations are an increasingly prominent form of community-based fund raising.

Corporate Grant Making

Another area of private philanthropy is corporate grant making. Corporations may donate to charity by means of a company-sponsored foundation, through a separate corporate giving program, or both. A company's public or community relations department generally manages corporate giving programs and usually limits benefits to employees, their families, or residents of specific locations where the company conducts business. Employee matching gifts programs are increasingly common vehicles for giving.

Youth Philanthropy

Rounding out the private funding sector is a rising area of interest, the field of youth philanthropy. This new area brings a youth perspective to issues, decision making, and priority setting while helping to incorporate youth development theory and practices. Youth philanthropy "engages young people in grant making that is intentional in its social change outcomes and, by funding projects conceived, planned and carried out by young people, influences how institutions and the community view the role of youth" (Coalition of Community Foundations for Youth, 1999, para. 1). Community-Based Youth as Resources (YAR) programs provide grants to young people to design and carry out service projects. Local YAR programs raise funds from many sources, including community-based foundations, civic and faith-based organizations, individual donors, fundraising events, and government grants for substance abuse prevention, schools, juvenile justice, and other programs (Center for Youth as Resources, 2001).

Whereas private philanthropies represent a major source of direct service grants to youth development programs, most do so only in limited local areas and with targeted focuses/populations of youth. Their support may not be dependable over the long haul because of fluctuating priorities and time limits (see Case 14.1). Still, their strategic role in the development and sustainability of youth development programs is important. They represent sources of noncategorical "glue-money" for functions such as collaboration, administrative coordination, and program components (Hayes, 2002).

Case 14.1 Private Philanthropy: "Start-Up Funds"
for "Long-Term Undertakings"

For the past several years, many school-based community centers in the United States have been funded primarily through time-limited grants. The federal government's 21st Century Community Learning Centers initiative, which is designed to provide expanded learning opportunities for children in a safe environment, grants funds to school districts for 3 years. In the philanthropic community, the Wallace–Reader's Digest Funds currently support a 5-year adaptation of four different models for extended-service schools. In California, the Healthy Start initiative, designed to use schools as localized places for providing traditional social services, also provides funds for 3 years. Most funders who provide short-term grants view them as start-up funds for what they hope will be long-term undertakings. They expect that the grantees will be able to identify and acquire funding that will allow the work to continue into the future.

SOURCE: Quoted in Walker & Arbreton (2001, p. 61).

Federal Funding

Public agencies have increasingly stepped up to initiate, support, and enhance the capacity of young people, as well as organizations, institutions, and individuals that work with youth at the community level. For example, federal funds from diverse agencies support the following:

- Healthy and safe environments for school-aged children and youth; provision of a range of services that benefit the community[2]
- Community-based programs for at-risk children and their families[3]
- Mentoring for youth at risk of failing in school, dropping out of school, or becoming involved in delinquent behavior[4]
- Service-learning in schools and community-based programs[5]
- Shelter, skills training, and support services for homeless youth[6] and unemployed and undereducated youth[7]
- High school education completion, on-site training experiences, and activities to promote self-sufficiency for disadvantaged young people in distressed communities[8]
- Efforts to reduce substance abuse[9]

In an effort to better align myriad funding streams that support these and other initiatives, federal policymakers have developed strategies, such as block grants, to combine funding streams and to provide states and localities with greater flexibility to adjust programming to local needs and priorities. The devolution of federal power is designed to place decision-making authority in the hands of governors and mayors and increase program responsiveness to local needs. Some advocates feel that this trend can reduce support for youth programming as different needs are forced to compete for the same funds.

Federal funds may come with other strings attached. Matching provisional grants require private-public partnerships (see Case 14.2). A typical requirement is that grant recipients match the federal amount (e.g., the Transitional Living for Homeless Youth Program requires a 10% match of the federal share, which can be either in cash or in-kind contributions). Some awards are made on a 1-year basis, whereas others may be for multiyear periods, dependent on satisfactory performance and availability of funds. Eligible grantees may vary depending on the specific program and may require that collaborative efforts exist (e.g., between local education agencies and public agencies, land grant university extension services, private for-profit or nonprofit organizations, including faith-based organizations or tribal nations, etc.).

One of the biggest drawbacks to federal funding is the frequent lack of forward funding. Many federal grants are not available in advance of the immediate year of their use. Too often, funds are appropriated and dispensed too close to the time of implementation, forestalling time for appropriate planning. One-year funding cycles can be difficult for any program but can be a destabilizing force for small, developing programs.

To secure a steady flow of funds, program administrators need to acquaint themselves with requirements and provisions of multiple funding sources. Although some requirements may be considered burdensome, requirements may also add value, for example, by bringing partners together from different sectors and infusing standards of accountability that strengthen the organization (through mandated reports).

Case 14.2 AmeriCorps: A Federal Private-Public Partnership

Among the federal private-public partnership programs is the Corporation for National and Community Service's Office of AmeriCorps. This "domestic Peace Corps," is dedicated to strengthening and improving communities through the services of its more than 25,000 members. Corps members serve in projects that protect and conserve national resources, promote public safety, and meet the educational needs of young people. Implementation costs are shared by local community organizations and the federal government. In addition, the corporation pays education awards for members who successfully complete service. In this balanced arrangement, youth are employed as resources to support community priorities, they learn and develop, and they are supported in turn by community institutions and with educational awards for their continuing education and development (National Clearinghouse on Families and Youth, 2002).

State Government

The state's role in youth development appears to be growing, fueled by recognition of the needs for statewide youth development programming, information about the benefits of youth development, and the devolution of federal responsibilities to the states.

Findings from a review (Langford, 2001) of state statutes enacted in legislative sessions ending June 30, 2000, indicated a growing interest in community school supports and services (especially out-of-school time programs but also school-based and/or school-linked health and social services for school-aged children and their families) and efforts to build infrastructure or provide supports for local programs (such as licensure systems; coordination, planning and evaluation; and training and technical assistance). A scan of enacted legislation in 2000 to 2001 showed at least 20 states passing legislation pertaining to after-school policies ranging from the creation of new programs to financing and regulating existing ones (National Conference of State Legislatures, 2002). In addition, many states are examining innovative financing approaches for after-school programming, including funding with federal TANF (Temporary Assistance for Needy Families) dollars or establishing different tax incentives. A number of states are using tobacco settlement revenues for youth services (e.g., school health, school-based youth services, education trust funds, children services endowment funds, youth development; Dixon, Johnson, Kendell, Cohen, & May, 1999).

Federal policies are increasingly linking opportunities for extended learning to improve student achievement and greater accountability for student achievement. The transfer in administration of the federal 21st CCLCs program to states has the potential to promote a more cohesive agenda for extended-learning opportunities at the state level. It also creates new opportunities for local and community youth service providers to compete directly for funds[10] and to provide supplemental services (e.g., tutoring, remediation, and academic intervention) to help students increase their academic achievement in activities outside the school day.

State governments are beginning to recognize the cross-jurisdictional nature of youth programming that is more comprehensive and less categorical. Youth programming includes education, human services, recreation, workforce development, and juvenile justice, as well as changes in the field of youth services. A few states are beginning to grapple with the implications of this change on the structure of state agencies and funding streams. The Family and Youth Services Bureau of the U.S. Department of Health and Human Services seeks to strengthen innovative youth development strategies through grants for State Youth Development Collaboration Programs (Family and Youth Services Bureau, 2002). States are working to develop more comprehensive approaches to youth services and ways of infusing a youth development approach in state and local agency services (e.g., for runaway and homeless youth, those leaving the foster care system, abused and neglected youth, and those served by the child welfare and juvenile justice systems) and community programming. These initiatives focus primarily on awareness and infrastructure building to create a more rational system in which youth-serving agencies embrace a youth development approach; youth development opportunities are recognized and expanded statewide; and there is improved coordination and collaboration of various funding streams (see Case 14.3).

Case 14.3 Comprehensive Approaches to Youth
Development Funding in New York State

New York's Youth Development and Delinquency Prevention program, implemented through county and municipal Youth Bureaus, encourages collaboration between Youth Bureaus and libraries, museums, and religious organizations so that these facilities can be used for youth development activities in the out-of-school hours. Similarly, the state education department funding initiative for parent and child library services encourages libraries to provide innovative services during out-of-school hours for both parents and children (up to age 18) to support child/youth readiness to learn and assist parents to become teachers and nurturers. Partners for Children is a collaboration of several state agencies, a number of youth-related professional associations, and the United Way of New York State. The initiative's Adolescent Project, focusing on youth ages 10 to 18 years old, pools funds to create school-linked services to provide structured use of young people's leisure/discretionary time, promote school-community planning to help young people gain important development assets, and create training and technical assistance centers to enhance youth-related programming (Family and Youth Services Bureau, 1998).

Municipal Funding

Cities and counties have long supported youth development through general fund revenues and the mandates of city agencies (such as parks and recreation or children and youth services). The jury is still out with respect to the degree to which municipal funding represents a source of reliable, long-term funding for youth development programs.

In some cities, funds are used for start-up or expansion efforts with the expectation that over time, programs will be weaned from these sources of support. Also, the legislation for dedicated tax schemes is time limited and tied to voter approval and political priorities. Some municipalities, such as Denver, have faced difficult uphill battles to approve dedicated sales tax ballot initiatives for children and youth services, and have not succeeded. San Francisco has transformed the power of children's issues via the ballot box and replicated the successful 1991 ballot initiative in 2001, approving a requirement that a fixed percentage of city tax revenues go to the Children's Fund to support youth activities. The measure in San Francisco generated broad-based community support because citizens value the services provided (Slambrouck, 2000).

Among the well-known examples of sustained municipal commitment to youth programming are the Beacons of New York City (see Chapter 12, by Dorgan & Ferguson, in this volume), now replicated in other parts of the country. In San Francisco, local funders of Beacons initiatives made long-term commitments to sustain and expand them. As a result, each Beacons center receives core support, the bulk of it from the Department of Children, Youth, and Their Families, and additional funds from a collaborative of local funders. Each center leverages additional funds in grants and in-kind services provided by other youth-serving agencies. Private funders provide support for capacity building, intermediary activities, evaluation, and public support campaigns (see also Case 14.4).

Case 14.4 Municipal Funding for Youth Development

Farmington Hills, Michigan. The first youth center in Farmington Hills opened in March 1996. Today, there are four youth centers, with a fifth center in the planning stages. Initial funding came from several sources including Title V (Juvenile Justice and Delinquency Prevention Act of 1974, Incentive Grants for Local Delinquency Prevention Programs), the school district, and city matching funds. Eight years after the first youth center opened, almost 50% of youth center funding comes from private sources. The other 50% of funding comes from the city, primarily through a special parks and recreation millage reauthorized in 1996: $100,000 per year for after-school programming for a 10-year period. The city also contributes approximately $25,000 annually to assist with center operations.

Jacksonville, Florida. The Jacksonville Children's Commission was created by City Council Ordinance in April 1994. The ordinance specifies that commission funding will increase by $1 million annually until its budget is equal to ½ mil of the ad valorem tax base. The commission and its staff of 90 administer a budget of $51 million, funding services that affect nearly 50,000 children and their families. This budget includes almost $14 million of local funds combined with $37 million of federal, state, and other funds. Local funds are provided for early learning services ($3.7 million) and youth development ($9 million), with an emphasis on after-school services. Other funds are used for administrative services, youth worker training, minigrants distributed by citizen groups, scholarships, and other initiatives.

Oakland, California. The Oakland Fund for Children and Youth (OFCY) was established in November 1996. The fund was created with the public's approval of the Kids First! (Measure K) initiative, an amendment to the city charter that set aside 2.5% of the city's unrestricted General Purpose Fund to support direct services for children and youth less than 21 years of age. An overwhelming 75% of voters supported this initiative. OFCY is administered jointly by East Bay Community Foundation and the City of Oakland. The OFCY represents a long-term commitment to support the development of a network of integrated services for children and youth in Oakland. The fund amounts to $6.8 million to $7.2 million annually for children's services.

Santa Fe, New Mexico. The Santa Fe Children and Youth Commission and the Santa Fe Youth Fund were established by city resolution in 1989. The youth fund is fed by 3% of the city's gross receipts tax. In 2001, the youth commission distributed almost $1 million from the children's fund to youth-serving programs. Their decisions are subject to the approval of the city finance committee and the city council. Recently, the commission and fund were further institutionalized as part of Santa Fe government through the passage of a city ordinance (Private correspondence, Institute for Youth, Education, and Families, National League of Cities; and Jacksonville Children's Commission, June 2001).

Trends, Strategies, and Lessons in Fundraising

Though it is hazardous to guess about the future of funding for youth development, a number of trends bear noting. The devolution of federal responsibilities to the states is likely to continue, along with a move toward community-based programs and services, coupled with greater use of public facilities (such as schools, libraries, and museums) and more efforts to build local autonomy and flexibility into grant initiatives. As noted earlier, states and localities will play greater roles in determining how federal funds will be spent, heretofore the province of the federal categorical programs. State and local needs, priorities, and capacities will help to shape the use of these funds at the local level. As successful youth development programs gain greater visibility and become more integral to school and community activities, state and local governments will view them more inclusively among other public services. Emphasis will continue on improving student academic achievement and providing the necessary supports, focused on extended learning time and complementary activities.

Research documents the benefits of extended-learning programs on academic achievement and other outcomes, for example, better grades and conduct in school; improved school attendance and study skills; better peer relations and emotional adjustment; lower incidences of drug use, violence, and pregnancy; and more likelihood to continue education beyond high school (National Institute on Out-of-School Time, 2003). This evidence has made policymakers and the public take notice and increase funding. However, it will be up to youth development practitioners to continue to make the case and champion their cause.

School-age child care and after-school programming will remain a federal and state priority. Increasingly, federal agencies attempt to align resources to support improved youth outcomes. The Child Care and Development Block Grant (CCDBG) of 1990 is up for reauthorization, and Congress seeks to extend the authorization of appropriations to improve families' access to high-quality school-age child care, as well as various provisions related to TANF and child care. Funding support will continue for CCDBG, Title I (compensatory education measures aimed at improving achievement), and 21st CCLSs (with increasing leadership and responsibility at the state and local levels).

Federal agencies are increasingly focused on promoting a continuum of care in communities to respond to the needs of youth at critical stages in their development through prevention, intervention, and treatment services (e.g., Office of Juvenile Justice and Delinquency Prevention). Some agencies incorporate a youth development focus into their traditional missions (e.g., Department of Labor youth employment programs) and encourage partnerships among youth-serving organizations and agencies (e.g., Division of Adolescent and School Health of the Centers for Disease Control and Prevention).

On the downside, the vagaries of political change, reflecting the policies and positions of newly elected leaders as well as a downturn in the economy, can have a major impact on the funding of youth programs. As executive administrations change, so do their priorities. The priorities and policies of the previous administration are often sacrificed. Also, when times are booming and unemployment is low, funding is more plentiful for youth initiatives. Downturns in state revenues coupled with increased needs for critical state services, such as welfare and Medicaid, and unprecedented homeland security responsibilities since September 11, 2001, have created shortfalls in most state budgets. The National Governors Association reports that in fiscal 2002, 39 states were forced to reduce their enacted budgets by about $15 billion, tap "rainy-day funds," or make transfers from other reserves. Inasmuch as youth are not major political players and their advocates are typically nonprofit agencies, leveraging support for youth causes in times of tight economies will be difficult, but not hopeless. In this dynamic environment, the following responses are recommended.

Think Creatively. Program providers, researchers, and communities must think creatively about ways to take youth development principles and processes, wrap them with appropriate services, seek enrichments and other opportunities for young people to develop a range of competencies, and build on the knowledge, additional resources, and service bases of other community-based organizations and agencies, including those funded through federal sources (e.g., Boys & Girls Clubs from the Department of Justice, 4-H Clubs from the Department of Agriculture, YouthBuild from the Department of Housing and Urban Development).

Find the Hidden Youth Development Focus. Don't be put off by the name: Youth development can easily be a part of efforts to create smaller learning environments; support compensatory education and improve academic achievement through extended-learning opportunities; develop service-learning and community service activities; and improve career options for youth. What is important is to first consider the youth development principles, capacities, and processes your program seeks to support (e.g., mentoring, leadership development, civic responsibility) and then look for sources of support that match your needs. As we have seen, these sources may take many forms (see Case 14.5).

Think Entrepreneurial. Grassroots fundraising and fees for service users provide sources of funds for programs, and various forms of youth entrepreneurship provide potential for youth to earn and learn. Service and conservation corps illustrate how entrepreneurial sources of support can become sustaining resources while providing mechanisms for young people to develop a range of competencies, such as work readiness, occupational skills, leadership, and community service. Fee-for service contracts with

---

Case 14.5 Support for Youth Development Comes in Many Forms

The youth provisions of the Workforce Investment Act (WIA) of 1998 codify much of what has been learned in recent years about how to prepare young people for adulthood and provide opportunities for states and communities to combine traditional youth employment and training services with activities based on principles of youth development. WIA offers youth-serving agencies opportunities to fold in a number of formative experiences and opportunities for young people to make them ready for work and college, for example, tutoring, employment linked to academic and occupational learning, internships and job shadowing, leadership development activities, peer-centered activities encouraging responsibility and other positive social behaviors during nonschool hours, adult mentoring, guidance and counseling, and follow-up services for not less than 12 months after completion of participation (Brown, 1998).

Another potential source of youth development funding not readily apparent is Temporary Assistance for Needy Families (TANF). TANF funds are available for job preparation and employment, preventing out-of-wedlock births, and promoting marriage (for needy and nonneedy families). TANF funds can also support out-of-school time and community school initiatives directly under both of these purposes and also by transferring a portion of federal TANF block grant monies into the Child Care and Development Fund (CCDF) (Cohen, 1999; Flynn, 1999).

---

local governments represent approximately 20% of the budgets of service and conservation corps.

Learn to Work in Collaboration With Other Providers and Sectors. Acquiring and sustaining funding for youth development activities can make strange bedfellows. As indicated earlier, federal grant requirements often call for various types of cross-sector collaborations, and the trend in federal, state, and local policies is to better integrate funding streams that have traditionally served only single functions. Youth-serving programs will increasingly be required to participate in various forms of partnerships and collaboratives to maximize and access available resources, as well as to leverage their contributions with those of other sectors (education, health, social services) to ensure that young people have access to a range of opportunities and experiences.

WIA youth provisions require a field once distinguished by discrete programs focused on short-term outcomes to develop a *comprehensive system* to help young people make effective transitions to higher education and living-wage careers. It requires the creation of youth councils representative of a range of youth-serving interests to develop local plans for youth services, recommend youth service providers, and coordinate local youth programs and initiatives (Case 14.6). To be effective in helping to shape these more rational systems for youth development, representatives of youth development programs must learn to work in collaboration with other stakeholders and become conversant with the possibilities and complementary functions of other, often better-entrenched funding streams in order to maximize and leverage these funds in support of their own program goals.

Case 14.6 Youth Council Collaboration

Youth Council members, who may have little history of working together, must develop a shared understanding of their new role, as well as a vision for a youth system that effectively provides services to all young people. They must work to identify and align funding streams tied to multiple state and federal agencies—and often directed at distinct age groups or geographical areas. Institutions that may not have collaborated effectively in the past—for example, K-12 schools and "second chance" alternative schools or employers and youth service providers—must develop linkages that improve services for youth.

SOURCE: Jobs for the Future and John J. Heldrich Center for Workforce (Development, 2002, p. 1).

Know the Strengths and Weaknesses of Funding Sources. Administrators of youth development programs may need to solicit targeted funds and supplement them with more general-use funds to serve a broader population of youth in a wider range of activities. This requires knowledge about a range of funding sources and the ability to identify the best source for the job at hand. For example, although interest in support from private funders remains high, the leadership of the San Francisco Beacons initiative determined that these funds are better suited for short-term start-up needs than for long-term core funds. This allows them to tailor their needs to the private funders' giving strengths: funds with fewer restrictions, for new or experimental activities, for technical-assistance efforts to build local capacity, and for quick response to emergency needs (Walker & Arbreton, 2001).

Develop a Comprehensive Funding Plan for Comprehensive Approaches. Youth-serving professionals must align youth and program needs with the requirements of funding sources. This requires a working knowledge of the vocabulary of grants and contracts and, in some cases, special bookkeeping systems required of various funding streams. They must become conversant in the eligibility requirements of various programs and develop strategies for addressing these parameters. Packaging many strategies to support different aspects of youth development is most effective. Hence, a comprehensive funding strategy—one that ultimately taps into multiple funding sources—requires a thoughtful, more sophisticated approach.

Advocate, Inform, Document, and Illustrate the Efficacy of Youth Development. Using what we know about the efficacy of youth development programming, now is the time to make the case for youth development as a category of effective investment. Now is the time to make the case to citizens, communities, and policymakers about the potential inherent in youth development efforts for community development and youth asset building. Also, to the extent that corporate giving programs are usually aligned with the self-interests of the funder, it is incumbent upon the potential grantee to educate local funders about the need for youth development opportunities and services.

Strive for Long-Term, Sustainable Funding. The Finance Project (2002) has developed a sustainability framework containing eight critical elements for achieving a stable base of fiscal and nonfiscal resources. The framework is designed to help program developers, policymakers, and other stakeholders at the community and state levels identify the basic resources needed and address the critical decisions necessary to sustain comprehensive initiatives. These elements include (a) vision, a clear-cut objective that describes how the program or activities will improve the lives of individuals; (b) results orientation; (c) strategic financing orientation; (d) adaptability to changing conditions; (e) broad base of community support; (f) key champions; (g) strong internal systems; and (h) a sustainability plan.

Seeking to move away from the time-limited sources of support, more and more practitioners and communities are looking to long-term, sustained sources of support. Municipal funding may be the most obvious sustaining source of support for youth development and is growing as youth programming becomes a more common expectation of city services. Also, as we have seen in the case of Beacons, principal reliance on city funds provides leverage for supports from a variety of city agencies as well as private funds.

Another strategy becoming increasingly popular is the development of CBO (community-based organization) schools. CBOs, with a history of providing services to youth that package their youth development curriculum and approach into diploma-granting academic programs, can tap into public education dollars (Smith & Thomases, 2001). These schools receive state and local education funds through various means, including contracts and agreements with local school districts and most recently, charter designation. In so doing, they have tapped into a sustained funding stream shared with public schools to continue and expand their youth development work.

Conclusion

The most definitive statement about funding for youth development is that it is dynamic, constantly changing to (a) influence trends in public policy, (b) respond to the needs of localities and the values and concerns they have for their youth, and (c) conform to particular perceptions of youth at a given time and period and to the organization and configuration of agencies and funding streams. Although many examples of successful funding sources and strategies have been provided in this chapter and many others can be found, we are still far from the goal of establishing enduring, comprehensive approaches to promote the development of all youth. It is therefore incumbent upon practitioners to continue to make the case for enduring and comprehensive policy by implementing responsible, accountable, high-quality youth programs and especially, by documenting their positive impact on youth and their communities.

Additional Resources on Funding

The following is a listing of additional sources of information on funding youth development.

National Youth Development Information Center identifies funding alternatives for youth development programs, including a searchable database of funding opportunities and resources of national and community/family foundations, corporate giving programs, federally funded programs, and sources of staffing assistance. The information center also provides basic facts on funding youth development programs and basic links to other funding sources and information (see http://www.nydic.org).

The Institute for Youth Development (IYD) is a resource for parents, youth workers, teachers, coaches, policymakers, and media professionals who are interested in learning how adults can effectively help youth make healthy lifestyle choices. IYD publishes comprehensive lists of federal grants available from the Department of Health and Human Services and other cabinet level departments and agencies to states, organizations, and individuals to help youth avoid unhealthy risk behaviors (see http://www.youthdevelopment.org.).

The National Endowment for the Arts lists sources of cultural funding and federal opportunities for programs focused on positive youth development on its Web site. The site also provides descriptions of how youth programs use funds in creative ways to support this goal (see http://www.artsendow.gov:591).

The National Governors Association Extra Learning Opportunities (ELO) Database includes more than 170 ELO programs from 44 states, territories, and commonwealths. Programs that receive funding from a variety of sources are included: state, federal, and local; foundations and parent fees (see http://www.nga.org/eodata).

States Guides to Funding for Youth. Among the goals of the Iowa Collaboration for Youth Development (ICYD), a partnership of state and local entities concerned with youth and youth policies, is to identify or develop resources for use at the community level to promote youth development and facilitate planning and implementation of effective youth development programs. On its Web site (see http://www.icyd.org), ICYD provides examples of initiatives and activities that support youth development policies and practices in state government as well as state, federal, and private (state, regional, and national) grants and funding sources. Similarly, Connecticut for Community Youth Development (CCYD), a statewide project that stimulates state and local commitment to positive youth development as an essential prerequisite for healthy communities, provides useful information to Connecticut direct service providers, supervisors, planners, advocates, youth funders, and program managers who work with youth aged 12 to 18. The Web site provides information on youth development, training programs, Web links, resources, and funding opportunities from state departments, family and independent foundations, corporate giving programs, other grant providers in Connecticut, and federal sources (see http://www.opm.state.ct.us).

Notices of Funding Availability (NOFAs) are announcements that appear in the *Federal Register,* which is printed each business day by the United States government, inviting applications for federal grant programs (see http://ocd.usda.gov/nofa.htm).

The National Conference of State Legislatures has developed the School Health Finance Project to gather information about how states and territories fund coordinated school health programs. The data collected is designed to identify sources of school health funding and the procedures required to access funds that vary from state to state. The project has developed two data bases: (a) the block grant data base providing information about how states use six specific federal block grants to fund school health programs, and (b) the state revenue database providing information about which states appropriate state general revenue for coordinated school health programs.

The National Clearinghouse on Families & Youth (NCFY) provides reference tools for those who work with young people or youth policy. Each tool is designed to help youth service professionals and others save time and resources in their efforts to support young people, families, and communities (see http://www.ncfy.com).

The Foundation Center provides information on private foundations, corporate grant makers, grant-making public charities, and community foundations. The center collects, organizes, and communicates information on U.S. philanthropy; conducts and facilitates research on trends in the field; provides education and training; and ensures public access to information and services through its Web site (see www.fdncenter.org).

The Chronicle of Philanthropy is a periodical providing information on grants, fundraising ideas and resources, information on trends in the philanthropic field, products, and available services (see www.philanthropy.com).

Notes

1. The reader should visit The Finance Project's Web site (http://www.finance-project.org) for additional tools for short- and long-term financing strategies.

2. Examples of funding sources include (a) Child-Care and Development Fund, an aggregate of several funding sources distributed in block grants by the U.S. Department of Health and Human Services (DHHS) to the states and territories and (b) 21st CCLCs, providing tutorial and academic enrichment activities designed to help students meet local and state academic standards, and youth development activities to enhance the academic component of the program.

3. For example, U.S. Department of Agriculture Research Extension and Education Services, Children, Youth, and Families at Risk (CYFAR) program.

4. For example, Department of Justice, Juvenile Mentoring Program (JUMP).

5. For example, Learn and Serve, Corporation for National Service.

6. For example, Transitional Living for Homeless Youth Grant, DHHS.

7. For example, Job Corps, U.S. Department of Labor; Civilian Conservation Centers, U.S. Department of Agriculture and U.S. Department of the Interior.

8. For example, YouthBuild, Department of Housing and Urban Development.

9. For example, Drug-Free Communities Support Program, Department of Justice.

10. Probably one of the most well-known sources and a recent anchor for out-of-school time activities, the 21st CCLC has been converted to a state formula grant. This is in keeping with the trend toward devolution of responsibility and decision making from the federal to the state level and in-line with the requirements of the new Elementary and Secondary Education Act (No Child Left Behind, 2001) to assist states in helping students in low-performing schools meet local and state academic standards. Funds will flow to states based on their share of compensatory education funds to make competitive awards to local educational agencies, community-based organizations, other public or private entities, or consortia of these groups. According to the provisions of the No Child Left Behind Act of 2001, Title I Supplemental Service Providers may include nonprofit organizations, for-profit entities, institutions of higher education, local education agencies, 21st CCLCs, and youth-serving and other community- and faith-based organizations that have high-quality after-school programs.

References

Brown, D. E. (1998). Advancing youth development under the workforce investment act. Adapted from an article by the same name published in *Workforce Investment Quarterly, V,* 4. Washington, DC: National Governors Association Center for Best Practices. Retrieved June 26, 2002, from: http://www.nyec.org/yd&wia.htm.

Center for Youth as Resources. (2001). Retrieved March 6, 2003, from: http://www.cyar.org.

Charles Stewart Mott Foundation. (2002). Retrieved May 6, 2002, from: http://www.mott.org/programs/p-ice.asp.

Coalition of Community Foundations for Youth. (1999). Retrieved June 24, 2002, from: http://www.ccfy.org/aboutus/index.htm and http://www.ccfy.org/yp/why.htm.

Cohen, D. (1999). *TANF funds: A new resource for youth programs.* Washington, DC: Center for Law and Social Policy.

Dixon, L., Johnson, P., Kendell, N., Cohen, C., & May, R. (1999). *Using tobacco settlement revenues for children's services: State opportunities and actions.* Washington, DC: The Finance Project. Retrieved May 26, 2002, from: http://www.financeproject.org/tobaccoattach.htm.

Edna McConnell Clark Foundation. (2002). *An explanation of institution and field building.* Retrieved May 6, 2002, from: http://www.emcf.org/programs/youth/ifb/index.htm.

Family and Youth Services Bureau. (1998, October). *State youth development collaboration projects' proposed plans.* Retrieved July 15, 2002, from: www.acf.dhhs.gov/programs/fysb/merge01.htm.

Family and Youth Services Bureau. (2002). *State youth development collaboration projects.* Retrieved August 8, 2002, from: http://www.acf.dhhs.gov/programs/fysb/State-YD-Collb.htm.

The Finance Project. (2002, April). *Sustaining comprehensive community initiatives: Key elements for success* (Financing strategy brief). Washington, DC: Author.

The Finance Project. (2003). *Finding resources to support rural out-of-school time programs.* Retrieved March 6, 2003, from: http://www.financeprojectinfo.org/Publications/ruralost.pdf.

Flynn, J. (October 1999). *Using TANF to finance out-of-school time and community school initiatives, 1(2)* (Strategy brief). Washington, DC: The Finance Project.

Forum of Regional Associations of Grantmakers. (2002). Retrieved June 24, 2002, from: http://www.rag.org/about/index.html.

Funder's Collaborative on Youth Organizing. (2002). Retrieved May 16, 2002, from: http://www.fcyo.org.

General Accounting Office. (1997). *At-risk and delinquent youth: Multiple programs lack coordinated federal effort* (GAO/T-HEHS-96–34). Retrieved June 10, 2002, from: http://frwebgate5.access.gpo.gov/cgi-bin/waisgate.cgi?WAISdocID=72885111011+2+2+0.

Halpern, R., Deich, S., & Cohen, C. (2002). *Financing after-school programs.* Washington, DC: The Finance Project.

Hayes, C. D. (2002). *Thinking broadly: Financing strategies for comprehensive child and family initiatives.* Washington, DC: The Finance Project.

James, D. W. (Ed.), with Jurich, S. (1999). *MORE things that DO make a difference for youth: A compendium of evaluations of youth programs and practices, Volume II.* Washington, DC: American Youth Policy Forum.

Jobs for the Future and John J. Heldrich Center for Workforce Development. (2002). *Evaluation of the transition to comprehensive youth services under the Workforce Investment Act.* Boston: Jobs for the Future.

Langford, B. H. (2001). *State legislative investments in school-age children and youth.* Washington, DC: The Finance Project.

National Clearinghouse on Families and Youth. (2002). *Federal support for youth and family planning.* Retrieved June 14, 2002, from: http://www.ncfy.com/thefeds.htm.

National Conference of State Legislatures. (2002). *Before and after-school legislative enactments 2000-2001.* Retrieved June 6, 2002, from: http://www.ncsl.org/programs/cyf/aftertrends01.htm.

National Governors Association. (2002, May 16). *State fiscal woes continue.* Retrieved June 6, 2002, from: http://www.nga.org/nga/newsRoom/1,1169,C_PRESS_RELEAS^D_3751.00.html.

National Institute on Out-of-School Time. (2003, January). *Making the case: A fact sheet on children and youth in out-of-school time.* Retrieved March 6, 2003, from: http://www.niost.org/Factsheet_2003.PDF.

Newman, R. P., Smith, S. M., & Murphy, R. (2000). A matter of money: The cost and financing of youth development. In *Youth development: Issues, challenges and directions* (pp. 82-124). Philadelphia: Public/Private Ventures.

Padgette, H. C. (2003, January). *Finding funding: A guide to federal sources for out-of-school time and community school initiatives, revised and updated.* Washington, DC: The Finance Project.

Slambrouck, P. V. (2000, November 6). San Francisco's bold experiment in children's issues. *The Christian Science Monitor.* Retrieved June 6, 2002, from: http://csmweb2.emcweb.com/durable/2000/1106/p3s1.htm.

Smith, S. M., & Thomases, J. G. (2001). *CBO schools: Profiles in transformational education.* Washington, DC: AED Center for Youth Development & Policy Research.

Walker, K. E., & Arbreton, A. J. A. (2001). *Working together to build Beacon Centers in San Francisco* (p. 61). Philadelphia: Public/Private Ventures.

15

Implications for Youth Development Practices

Stephen F. Hamilton and
Mary Agnes Hamilton

Each of the foregoing chapters provides a brief introduction to a large topic. Trying to summarize all of the chapters here would be a futile exercise. Instead, we shall draw from them some key themes and insights that cut across those topics. Our treatment is far from exhaustive. We invite readers to conduct their own cross-cutting analyses, seeking points of convergence or divergence that result from the treatments of youth development in different settings. We discuss seven themes: the ecological perspective; mentoring; insights into race, ethnicity, class, and gender; tensions between a positive, universal approach and a focus on problems; building community-wide systems; evidence-based practice; and youth participation.

The Ecology of Youth Development

The chapters on youth development in different contexts substantiate the ecological conception of development by portraying how influences emanating from those contexts interact. Simply comparing research findings

351

on the influences of neighborhoods, families, peer groups, schools, media culture, and the other chapter topics strongly supports the conception that no single influence (genetics, the brain, parental style) is decisive. Studies cited in each chapter have traced the influences of each context and the ways in which differences such as race and gender interact with those influences.

The chapter on health care provides a good example of an ecological ("biopsychosocial") approach to dealing with drug addiction. The practitioner must understand and take into account the nature of the addictive substance, the individual's predisposition to addiction, developmental stage and previous experience, personality factors such as depression, cognitive factors such as learning problems, and risk and protective factors in the person's family and community. Taking only one or a few of these influences into account reduces the treatment's likelihood of success.

But the influence of multiple contexts is not merely additive; it is interactive. As research on the effects of peers illustrates, their power depends crucially on adolescents' relationships with their parents. Moreover, peers do not come out of nowhere. They are found in schools and neighborhoods that parents have chosen based on their income and education level (i.e., social class). Therefore, a young person's friends are likely to have parents who share many of the same aspirations and values as her or his parents. As a result, it is misleading to imagine peers as an autonomous influence on youth development. Their influence depends crucially on the influence of parents and on the influence of other contexts such as schools, youth-serving organizations, and workplaces. The same interaction or interdependence applies to all contexts.

A related ecological principle, which is especially critical to the development of the human species, in which thinking (cognition) is highly developed, is that although we think of contexts or settings as physical spaces, it is more accurate to think of them as centers of influence spreading beyond a physical location. Certainly parents hope that their moral teachings constrain their children's behavior outside the home and when they are out of sight. What one learns in school opens up a range of possibilities in other locations, including reading the instructions for repairing an antilock braking system, raising sheep as youth entrepreneurs, and interviewing patients about their hospital stay. The influences of these various settings overlap; each affects the other and is affected in return.

As these different contexts interact, the various influences on youth development may be mutually reinforcing, they may cancel each other out, or those from one context may compensate for something that is missing in another. Reinforcement occurs in cases such as peer influence, as described above. Though their tastes in music and clothing may diverge from their parents', most peer groups reinforce parents' expectations about education. Youth who hope for admission to selective colleges tend to hang around together. But it can also be the case that influences conflict. Youth who have been brought up to value honesty might find themselves in jobs in which petty theft is normal and, as a result, acquire behavior patterns and rationalizations for them that are inconsistent from one setting or influence to another.

Compensation is an especially important possibility for youth who have been poorly served by most of the contexts they inhabit. Schools and youth-serving organizations often strive to compensate for the failings of distressed families and socially toxic neighborhoods. Research on "resilient" children (cited in the chapter on juvenile justice) affirms that an enduring relationship with a caring adult can help a youth overcome enormous disadvantages. One way to think of youth development is as creating a web of positive influences to counteract or compensate for all the negative influences.

Another implication of this conception, however, is that the most powerful interventions to promote youth development affect more than one context in the same way. A good example is aftercare following incarceration in the juvenile justice system. A good detention facility can give a youth who has been convicted of a crime both the motivation and the opportunity to change her life, using individual and group counseling, positive peer interactions, education, and vocational training. However, recidivism is the most likely prospect if she simply returns to her former neighborhood and family, where her new aspirations seem unreal and her new behavior patterns seem out of place. If her site-based rehabilitation is accompanied by aftercare that maintains the positive influence and guides her toward further schooling and employment as she returns to her community, her chances of making a new start are much greater.

Thinking about the overlapping influences described and implied in the chapters suggests many other possibilities for more comprehensive interventions. Youth who learn to be more critical of mass media are more likely to invoke their critical faculties if they learned them with the same peers with whom they listen to music and watch movies and go shopping. Youth can take greater advantage of the learning opportunities afforded by work and service if they can make direct connections between what they are doing at work and what they are learning in school. But the adults in these contexts need to encourage youth to reflect on those opportunities, and who they are and want to be, so they can make choices about how to realize their dreams after high school, as in the case of the hospital intern who planned to continue his education because of his positive experience with the program: "And when I joined the program, my whole life changed. I started seeing the point of my education" (work and service chapter). Youth who serve on the boards of community organizations not only gain skill and confidence in communication and decision making but also make contacts (build bridging social capital) that can link them to opportunities for employment, provide letters of recommendation to college, and otherwise open doors for them.

Mentoring

Matching a youth with a caring adult companion, advisor, and role model is one of the most prominent current youth development strategies (Walker, 2001), and it has unusually strong empirical support (DuBois, Holloway, Valentine, & Cooper, 2002; Grossman & Tierney, 1998). In the work and service chapter, we introduced a broader conception of mentoring, using the term not only for the kind of relationship designated in mentoring programs but also for any adult-youth relationship that includes a combination of teaching, advising, and caring over an extended period of time. Although the term is not used in most of the other chapters, the role is frequently described or at least implied.

Mentoring, using this broader definition, captures the nature of supportive adult-youth relationships identified in the principles of youth development in the introductory chapter, in which it is paired with challenging activities. The authors of the chapter on youth-serving organizations use the term *embedded curriculum* to describe the way in which such organizations plan and implement activities that foster development. It is "embedded" in the sense that it is not made explicit in the manner of a school curriculum, but rather built in to the activities as they are carried out. In a parallel manner, we might refer to *embedded mentoring* as the teaching and advising behavior of adults in all the contexts in which youth and adults interact. Although all of those adults would not identify themselves or be identified by the youth as mentors, what they do often fits our definition of mentoring. Calling attention to this helps to make that an intentional practice, just as the term *embedded curriculum* highlights the need to plan for and actively promote learning outside classrooms.

Professional and volunteer adult leaders in youth-serving organizations often become mentors for youth without necessarily assuming that title. The authors of the chapter on youth-serving organizations referred to the adults in HOME as "coaches," a useful term that emphasizes their teaching role but places it in the context of learning to participate in a valued activity, such as organizing and then reflecting on the annual youth conference. The lessons taught in this manner are not only about technical issues involved in organizing an event but also about how to be constructively critical and how to build on both successes and failures. Coaches are different from classroom teachers not only for what they teach but also in their less didactic manner of teaching, often involving repeated cycles of performance and improvement. Coaches usually work with teams, in contrast with one-to-one mentoring, yet youth often develop much closer emotional relationships with coaches than with classroom teachers. (Nettles, 1992, has also used the term *coaching* in tracing the kinds of relationships we include in our definition of mentoring.)

Organizations serving all ages are excellent examples of what Freedman (1993) called "mentor-rich environments," that is, places where youth and adults have opportunities to get to know each other without the intervention of a program and naturally form mentoring relationships. This may happen in programs designed for youth. For example, youth ministers, volunteers, and youth workers in parks and recreation departments have the same opportunities as adults in youth-serving organizations to perform the role of mentor; or it may happen in activities that mix ages, such as a church choir or social service project. As long as young people interact regularly with adults in such organizations, they also have opportunities to find mentors. When health care providers act in the manner prescribed by Bright Futures (see chapter on health care), they engage in a kind of mentoring, especially if they see the same youth regularly over a period of years.

Schoolteachers in conventional classrooms seldom become mentors simply because of the numbers of youth they deal with and the relative formality of the setting. However, one of the reasons for creating small learning communities in high schools, as advocated in the chapter on schools, is precisely to break down those barriers. When teachers have smaller classes, when they see the same students over several years, when teachers and students jointly make plans and decisions, and when teachers are also advisors, then they become mentors, too. School-sponsored work and service also give teachers a better chance of becoming mentors, with the added benefit that adults in the work and service settings are also potential mentors.

Emphasis on social capital in the chapter on neighborhoods illustrates another benefit from mentoring. Bonding social ties between youth and adults contribute to making youth feel they are part of their neighborhoods. Bridging social ties give youth access to resources beyond those available in their neighborhoods, such as internships, jobs, and advising about further education. Mentoring builds both types of social capital, not only through the adult-youth relationship directly but also through additional relationships that adults can arrange for their mentees.

Peer mentoring is one of the major forms taken by programs that engage youth in fostering each other's development, as described in the chapter on peers. The notion of peers as mentors stretches the term farther than we would prefer (because the term implies a quasi-parental relationship), but certainly it makes sense for youth to advise one another, especially when the advisors have special knowledge, training, and support for their role.

Intentionally creating mentor-rich environments and fostering mentoring relationships is a major way of putting into practice the youth development principle that all youth need challenging activities and caring relationships. Whether the caring adults are labeled as mentors is not as important as having programs and adults intentionally embed mentoring practices into their relationships with youth.

Race, Ethnicity, Class, and Gender

Research is reported throughout the book that finds important differences associated with race, ethnicity, class, and gender. But that is hardly novel. The social science literature is filled with correlations between these characteristics and all manner of important phenomena. These chapters add something more. They examine the locations in which young people experience what it means to be disadvantaged and how to identify with their groups, for good or ill. Even the popular media culture, which might be assumed to have a unifying effect, is filtered through these differences. People use and respond to media differentially along lines of race, class, language, and gender. The finer-grained analysis of such differences begins to tell us more about how these characteristics have their effects on development. They help us begin to answer questions, for example: What is it about family income that affects school performance? In what ways and by what mechanisms does Latino heritage shape a young person's emerging sense of identity? Exploring such issues moves us well beyond the fact that race, ethnicity, gender, and class are important.

Poverty means not only being born into poor families but also growing up surrounded by neighbors who are also poor. Poor youth attend schools that are substandard, as are most of the other public services that are accessible to them. When they move into the larger world outside their neighborhoods, as applicants to college or for jobs or as citizens seeking to improve their communities, they must make a place for themselves among people who have enjoyed far more advantages. If they also suffer discrimination because of their race, ethnicity, gender, sexual preference, disability status, and other such markers, these disadvantages multiply. These disadvantages are not decisive; many chapters provide illustrations of youth overcoming them. But the struggle is great, and the odds are long.

Youth development must support this struggle not only by fostering the development of individuals but also by actively confronting and enabling others to confront the barriers that keep our society stratified. Those who wish to foster youth development must recognize that bias based on race, ethnicity, class, and gender influences how young people are treated and how they think of themselves. But they also need to be able to examine this bias and understand how it works in all the settings in which youth live and grow. Although the differences usually line up to reinforce disadvantage, that is not always the case. For example, it appears that a broad definition of *family* among African Americans aids youth in single-parent families (see families chapter). Girls and boys both benefit from work experience, but it seems especially valuable for improving girls' self-efficacy when their jobs pay well and involve helping others (see chapter on work and service). Faith-based communities provide refuge and support for youth seeking asylum from chaos in their lives resulting from substance abuse or poverty (see chapter on organizations for all ages). The chapters are rich with insights into distinctions like this, which youth development professionals can use to build on strengths.

Such findings must be applied with caution. Research findings are always generalizations. A difference between boys and girls, African Americans and European Americans, and youth from working-class and middle-class neighborhoods can never be assumed to apply to every member of the group. Some African American youth will suffer from being in single-parent families, and some European American youth will thrive in spite of that experience, going against the general trend. It is also important to recognize that many of the trends reported in research are small in scale. The probability of the overall difference being reflected in any individual is rather small. Research findings are not a basis for stereotyping. Youth must be treated as individuals rather than as representatives of a class (including the class of *youth*).

Universal Versus Targeted Approaches

The place of youth development in overcoming social stratification is related to the tension between universal approaches and those that target specific youth as being "at risk" or "in need." As described in Chapter 1, the youth development movement arose in part in reaction against what advocates perceived as an overemphasis in youth programs and policy on preventing or correcting negative behavior and on identifying youth who are either at risk of that behavior or have already demonstrated it. The Committee on Community-Level Programs for Youth (National Research Council and Institute of Medicine, 2002, pp. 35-36) rather summarily dismissed this tension, observing that prevention and treatment programs are often difficult to distinguish in practice from those calling themselves positive youth development. They essentially urge youth development practitioners to set aside the tension and get on with the work at hand.

Consistent with this sentiment, we organized this volume to demonstrate how settings such as the juvenile justice system and health care, which are often associated with prevention and treatment ("the medical model"), can promote youth development and contribute to a community-wide youth development system. Nonetheless, we find the tension more challenging than the Committee on Community-Level Programs for Youth acknowledges. The following are some serious conflicts between universal and targeted approaches that the previous chapters identify or imply. We believe that coping with this tension requires hard work among all parties, not merely agreement in principle that everyone favors youth development.

Funding

Perhaps the most obvious and most troublesome source of tension is that funding for youth programs, especially federal funding, is nearly all tied to problem behavior (see funding chapter). As noted in the juvenile justice chapter, youth workers and advocates who are committed to specific populations fear that a universal approach will simply dilute their targeted programs to the point where they no longer meet the pressing, even life-threatening needs, for example, of drug users. Some handle this tension by arguing that because drug use is common, nearly all youth are at risk of abuse and that youth development is an effective form of primary prevention. But this argument does not lessen the reality that youth who are already addicted require specialized services (secondary and tertiary prevention) that are more expensive. It may be true that greater investment in primary prevention now will reduce those costs in the future, but what is to be done with youth who need those services now? In an ideal world, every community would offer the full range of services, supports, and opportunities that promote youth development. In reality, policymakers and practitioners must make choices, both about which youth should benefit and what initiatives to put in place. The choice between universal and targeted approaches arises repeatedly; no formula allows easy comparison of the costs and benefits of each approach.

Outcomes

A central distinction between the youth development approach and more conventional prevention and treatment approaches is that youth development outcomes are stated in terms of positive developmental achievements, whereas prevention aims to keep youth from destructive behaviors and their consequences and the goal of treatment is to bring them out of those behaviors and the states that result. Sometimes, this is merely a matter of emphasis or even just semantics. Everyone in the juvenile justice system wishes that youth released from detention facilities would return to their communities and avoid criminal behavior, but they understand that such avoidance is dependent on youth availing themselves of supports and opportunities to engage in positive behavior, notably, pursing an education, finding employment, and forming relationships with prosocial peers. Although the juvenile justice system may measure success in terms of avoiding recidivism, that outcome implies the attainment of other more positive outcomes as well. With her typical incisiveness, Pittman captured a real difference in her slogan, "Problem free isn't fully prepared" (Pittman & Irby, 1996, p. 3). A youth with a criminal record who avoids further criminal behavior and re-arrest is unlikely to assume a constructive place in society without attaining additional education, finding gainful employment, and achieving other positive markers of youth development. Prevention and treatment outcomes are undoubtedly important, but the youth development approach demands that we set our sights higher and achieve positive developmental outcomes. The cases featured in the chapter on youth-serving organizations are exemplary in this regard.

Collaboration

Tension between universal and targeted approaches complicates collaboration among youth programs and organizations. One example we have experienced is that staff working in federally subsidized employment training programs often view schools as part of the problem rather than as partners. This reflects their perception that the schools have failed "their" youth, the ones they are helping to develop work-related skills and behaviors. On the other side, overburdened teachers and principals who are asked to provide special attention to students who have not performed well in school or to give one more chance to students who have behaved disruptively may take the position that they should use their limited resources to work with students who are not so demanding. From the perspective of people in the schools, out-of-school employment-training programs may be seen as welcome destinations for their dropouts rather than partners in preventing or retrieving dropouts.

Peer Interventions

As noted in the chapter on peers, engaging peers to promote each other's development can be a powerful strategy. However, putting together youth who have in common some serious problem behavior can result in *deviancy training,* meaning that they reinforce each other's negative behaviors. To prevent that from happening, peer interventions should ideally incorporate youth with different levels of risk and problematic behavior. This ideal can prove difficult to implement because youth who have not demonstrated such behavior may find little to attract them to a program in which they will be engaged with troubled youth. Their parents might also object precisely because of the danger of deviancy training. Peer interventions that expect troubled youth to help younger peers as tutors (as in the Time Dollar and Coca-Cola Valued Youth examples described in the peers chapter) or coaches (as in the Unity Soccer Clinic in the juvenile justice chapter) are ways to cope with this problem. If same-age youth are put together, research and theory on intergroup relations makes clear that all youth should have contributions to make and should be placed on an equal plane.

Work and Service

The growing popularity of the term *service-learning* is one manifestation of the tension between universal and targeted approaches. The positive reason for using the term is to emphasize that service and learning are equally important. Another reason is to distinguish a universal form of community service from the community service sometimes mandated by the juvenile justice system as a form of punishment and restitution. Members of a youth organization who volunteer to clean up a river do not wish to be confused with youth who are picking up trash under the supervision of their probation officers. One of the challenges facing staff in subsidized youth employment programs is that membership in the program can be stigmatizing. Because admission is restricted to youth from low-income families, some potential employers assume they are seriously troubled and resist hiring them even if their wages will be subsidized or if they claim to have learned work skills in a program. Vocational education can have such perverse effects when employers view it as the pathway of choice for unsuccessful students.

School staff whose responsibility is to find and arrange work-based learning opportunities struggle to find sufficient places for all the students who would like and could benefit from the experience. They are justified in reserving such places for students who need both the experience and the money. If work and service are considered parallel opportunities for acquiring some of the same competencies, then family financial need seems even more relevant as a criterion for placing some students in paid employment and others in volunteer positions. However, in view of the possibility, noted in the chapter on work and service, that some volunteer opportunities may be richer developmental opportunities than paid work, it is critical that a two-tiered system be avoided in which youth from poor families do routine work for pay while those from middle-class families engage in stimulating and satisfying volunteer work. One way to achieve this ideal is to work collaboratively with employers and providers of subsidized employment training to enrich those experiences with opportunities for growth similar to those found in the best internships.

Community-Wide Initiatives and System Building

Although we have taken care to define youth development as an approach that can be taken in individual programs and organizations and the preceding chapters describe some of those well, youth development as a community-wide initiative is far more powerful. The ecological perspective encourages the approach of trying to make the community a good place for all youth to grow up in rather than just putting programs in place to promote the development of youth one at a time. Because the community is so important, two chapters bear on the topic, one on neighborhoods as settings for youth development and the other on community-wide initiatives. The former chapter highlighted new research and theory that are exceptionally useful to youth development professionals. The latter examined in detail two youth development initiatives aimed at entire cities. The difference in scale represented in the two chapters reflects the ambiguous definition of the term *community,* which can legitimately apply to neighborhoods, to entire cities, and to units in between, including some that are not geographically defined (e.g., a faith community, a collection of Internet game players from around the world).

Thinking about whole communities entails thinking in systems terms. As the preceding chapters make abundantly clear, it is impossible and unwise for the different organizations and other entities that influence youth development to try to do the job alone. The chapter on community-wide initiatives suggests how difficult it is to act on this widely accepted principle.

Applying the criteria we developed for school-to-work systems (inclusive, coherent, connected, and enduring; introductory chapter) to community-wide youth development systems, we would want such systems to be *inclusive* in the sense that they provide for all youth.

An internally *coherent* system is one that makes sense to those who are in it. A coherent system provides a logical progression of opportunities so that, for example, youth who have demonstrated their capacity for leadership in one context are able to assume leadership positions in another. For example, a member of Youth in Charge at the Jamestown Community Center (described in the chapter on youth organizations) would be well prepared to serve on a community development board.

In a *connected* youth development system, schools that require service-learning would recognize service-learning that is sponsored by other organizations and give credit for it. The diverse subsystems treated in previous chapters, including education, juvenile justice, health care, and organizations serving all ages, would work together to ensure that all youth have access to needed services, supports, and opportunities and that resources are allocated rationally. Thus, for example, creating the system of care for a juvenile offender as described in the juvenile justice chapter requires contributions from all contexts in which the youth participates and coordination among them to ensure that those contributions add up to a connected whole. Some of the challenges to and opportunities for such collaboration are revealed by chapters on different contexts, such as youth-serving organizations and schools.

Endurance may be the greatest challenge. It requires funding, of course, which is often available only in the form of competitive categorical grants— the absolute least enduring form of financial support! Yet various chapters contain a wealth of suggestions for moving toward a more enduring system. The funding chapter makes a case for strategic thinking about grant seeking that can enable an organization to put together a diverse portfolio of funding sources that all contribute to a central mission. The chapter on youth-serving organizations provides an excellent example of an organization, the East Oakland Youth Development Center, that has struggled with the dangers of this approach and settled on a core set of activities, making a commitment to "doing chicken right" rather than following the money wherever it leads. The fact that they acquired an endowment that provides substantial dependable support every year that remains in their control surely makes it easier for them to adhere to this principle. Tax-supported organizations such as parks and recreation departments and schools can achieve some of this stability. Although their budgets may rise and fall with the economy, they need not annually fear for their continued existence. Leaders of organizations that depend on tax money must cultivate relationships with the elected officials who allocate that money to ensure that they know what those officials want and to keep them informed about how tax money is being used responsibly.

But an enduring system requires stability for all its component parts, not just some of them, and this remains an enormous challenge. The description in the chapter on community-wide initiatives of the Annie E. Casey Foundation's New Futures initiative demonstrates that the problem is deeper than lack of money. Even with a substantial infusion of new funding tied to a mandate to take a more systemic approach to youth development, most participating cities encountered daunting obstacles. One of the secrets of New York City's (NYC) Beacons initiative was that it incorporated a politically feasible growth plan. Another was that it promised changes that were understandable, desirable, and visible and then delivered on that promise. A third secret, according to the chapter authors, was that the NYC Beacons initiative focused most of its effort and resources on what they call "Level 1," the daily work of youth development professionals with youth, whereas much of the activity in New Futures cities was at Level 2, which supports Level 1 youth development work but does not do it directly. It makes sense to try to maximize the resources at Level 1 and rely on Level 2 for support, not as the driver of change.

Evidence-Based Practice

Communities That Care represents in the field of youth development an approach that is increasingly prevalent in many fields: evidence-based practice (see especially Catalano, Berglund, Ryan, Lonczak, & Hawkins, 1998; Developmental Research and Programs, Inc., 2000). The basic idea is that professional practice should be guided by more than tradition and the judgment of practitioners. It should be guided by empirical research that has rigorously tested alternative practices and identified those that work best. The movement arose in medicine, which seems unexpected because, for more than a century, medicine has been the exemplar of professional practice based in scientific research. The elimination or control of many diseases and the extension of human life have resulted quite directly from steady progress in understanding basic science and applications of that understanding to health care. However, advocates of evidence-based practice in medicine have pointed out that physicians retain considerable latitude in prescribing treatments for various conditions. Although most of the treatments have been validated scientifically, questions arise about which of them should be applied in which cases. The goal of evidence-based practice is to give physicians specific empirical guidance that will improve outcomes. This entails producing enough data to establish which treatments have the greatest likelihood of success in which cases and to make the results readily available so that physicians can easily draw on those results in making treatment recommendations.

However, some limitations should be acknowledged about how far this approach can go. Using medical research as a point of comparison helps establish some of those limitations. The magnitude of research conducted in medicine dwarfs what is done in youth development or in all of education and the human services combined. Medical research is not only conducted in medical schools but also in academic departments outside medical schools (e.g., physiology, neurology) and even in schools of veterinary medicine. In addition, the federal government supports a formidable research enterprise in the National Institutes of Health. Medical foundations also conduct research independently, and the pharmaceutical industry and makers of medical equipment and supplies also conduct research to develop and refine products. The total investment comes to more than $50 billion annually in the United States alone, yet many important medical questions remain unanswered and even unexplored (Research America, 2003).

Comparing the amount of research generated around health issues with that done on youth development makes clear why youth development professionals should not expect to receive the quality of practical guidance from research that physicians enjoy. There is and will remain for the foreseeable future simply not enough research to provide the level of information we would like to have. This inescapable fact should not become an excuse for ignoring research. Quite the opposite. It is a compelling reason to work toward generating more and to make the best possible use of what we have. But we must also avoid accepting inadequate research as definitive or not acting because the research has not yet been done to guide what we believe must be done.

Youth development professionals and advocates must continue to make a host of decisions in the absence of definitive empirical guidance. They should, however, make the fullest use possible of the research that is available. The purpose of this volume is to provide ready access to some of that research and to refer readers to additional sources. In addition to the CTC compendia of research-based programs cited above, we also recommend the Search Institute volume (Scales & Leffert, 1999); the report of the Committee on Community-Level Programs for Youth (National Research Council and Institute of Medicine, 2002); and the volume edited by Benson and Pittman (2001). Practitioners who are conversant with these sources and able to apply their findings will be able to claim legitimately that they are using the best evidence available to guide their practice.

By far the most important reason to draw on the research is to improve the quality of services, supports, and opportunities for youth. However, another reason is to build the profession of youth development. Historically, occupations have been counted as professions as they have generated a body of knowledge and then codified it in professional training programs, for example, for physicians, lawyers, engineers, teachers, and nurses. We emphasize again that the primary purpose of building a youth development profession is not occupational prestige and compensation for practitioners, but effectiveness in promoting youth development. But it is also unlikely that youth development will flourish so long as its practitioners are poorly paid, sketchily trained, and viewed by taxpayers and other professionals as people doing jobs that anyone could do.

Evaluation research is essential to building an evidence base for practice. But for that purpose, it must be sound in its design and methods, and its results must be made widely available. A critical step for most programs is to engage youth workers on the front line as part of a planning team with youth, parents, and boards to collaborate together to design evaluations. The theory of change approach described in the chapter on evaluation is ideally suited to such a collaborative process. One of its strengths is leading planners to break down broad, long-term goals into short-term and intermediate goals whose attainment can be monitored regularly to guide program improvement. In the case of programs that have been thoroughly tested and validated, a different kind of evaluation is called for, one that is not so concerned about measuring outcomes—which has already been done—as about ensuring that the program has been implemented as it was designed and tested.

Youth Participation

Parallel to the principle that all youth thrive is the principle that youth themselves should play a major role in their own development. We chose not to devote a separate chapter to youth participation, but rather to encourage all authors to address it in relation to their topics. This approach carries the risk that the topic loses visibility. The advantage, however, is that it is treated concretely in relation to a range of contexts and activities. To capitalize on that advantage, we shall extract some of the illustrations and practices from several chapters, not to replace what is in the chapters, but to call readers' attention to what they might find by looking for this theme in different chapters.

That exercise reveals that youth participation is multidimensional, which is one of the reasons for multiple terms related to the topic. Youth participation implies activity, but it could be relatively passive activity, for example, simply showing up to be part of an activity that is planned and directed by others. Youth participation in decision making clarifies that ambiguity, but it narrows the field to decision-making processes. The term *youth voice* emphasizes giving youth a chance to express their views. It alludes to Carol Gilligan's book *In a Different Voice* (1982), which brought attention to girls' and young women's distinctive ways of thinking about ethical issues, amplifying the voices of people who had not been heard before. *Youth empowerment* is also used to capture what we mean by participation, but it suffers from the baggage accumulated by that term, which can be criticized for implying that someone must "give" power to youth rather than youth possessing power by right.

At the very least, youth should be able to make choices about their own participation. Beyond that, they should have opportunities to shape their activities, to take leadership, and to participate in decisions that affect them, formally as members of boards and committees and informally as they are asked their opinions and preferences. When youth become leaders, the balance shifts even further, including not just their ideas but also placing them in positions in which they wield considerable power and assume serious responsibility. If we think of youth participation as applying to all youth, it is clear that simply having a youth in charge with all the other youth subservient is not sufficient. Youth participation entails open, democratic processes.

Youth-serving organizations would seem to be the most accommodating to youth participation. They exist for youth. Engaging youth in their direction fits with their missions, at least in principle. Consistent with this assumption, the chapter on youth-serving organizations contains some of the most compelling accounts of youth participation, which the authors include as part of a larger characteristic they call *youth-centeredness*. They describe how HOME gives youth opportunities to share their perspectives, both one-to-one with adults and in groups, and how adults consistently seek and respond to young people's advice. After youth participants called for a rethinking of HOME's organizational structure, they participated in a daylong retreat organized for that purpose. Through projects such as the Cityview Skate Park, youth invented and directed the organization's activities. The Jamestown Community Center formed Youth in Charge, a group of teenagers who represent the Center to the community and provide feedback to staff on programs and activities. Participants perform important and visible roles both publicly (security at a block party) and privately (internal assessment of effectiveness). In another illustration of youth voice, the Youth Power group identified some members' late returns from breaks as a problem for the group. They then discussed various alternatives and chose by vote a way of addressing members who violated the rules they adopted.

The authors noted that tension can occur between a youth-centered approach and the goal of involving the whole community. Whose voice prevails when youth and adult community members disagree? They also point out that youth participation entails mutual respect between staff and youth and among youth and that it is central to creating caring communities. Youth participation is especially critical to involving adolescents, who quickly lose patience with being told what to do.

Service-learning provides multiple opportunities for cultivating youth participation. Practitioners agree that the best service activities are designed and guided by youth participants. As noted in the chapter, youth who plan and carry out their own service projects have far more authority over what happens and how than those who participate in adult-directed projects or volunteer in adult organizations. Projects such as R.I.V.E.R. Team and Growing Up in Cities (work and service chapter) and YouthBuild (neighborhoods chapter) are ideal opportunities for contributing to one's own neighborhood. The chapter on community-wide initiatives also touches on youth participation, noting the presence of youth as members of the community advisory boards that guide each Beacons site. Dorgan and Ferguson's levels can be used to identify different bodies in which youth can be incorporated. What youth do as decision makers varies by the level of the group in which they participate.

Another type of service is noted in the chapter on funding; in some communities, youth themselves control philanthropic funds, making decisions about how to invest in their communities. They can also serve on boards and committees and take other leadership positions in organizations that serve all ages. Some faith-based organizations, especially those with congregational forms of governance, incorporate youth in their governing bodies as a matter of course. Although the evaluation chapter does not explicitly deal with youth voice, the *theory of change* approach it describes is best implemented by a planning group that can and should include youth. Good examples can be found of youth engagement in data collection and analysis (Camino, 2001; Chawla, 2002; Driskell, 2002; Hart, 1997, especially chap. 5).

The chapter on peers introduces a neglected dimension of youth participation: the engagement of youth in actively promoting their peers' development. As the research cited in that chapter demonstrates, such involvement typically promotes the development of both parties, those being helped and those doing the helping. This is certainly one reason for supporting youth participation: It promotes development. However, as capable and responsible human beings, youth have a right to be heard, regardless of whether participation can be shown to be good for them.

If youth-serving organizations are the most natural settings for youth participation, schools may be among the least natural. But as the chapter on schools makes clear, students are not alone in being excluded from power in schools. Administrators typically keep teachers and parents at arm's length, too. Ensuring that youth exercise real choices and real power in schools requires serious restructuring. Excellent models can be found in many small alternative schools that have found effective ways to do both and have maintained youth involvement over time (see cases in chapter on schools). The author's advice that schools look to youth-serving organizations to learn how to share power with students is provocative and sensible.

Introducing youth participation into health care is even more of a stretch. Schools, at least, are designed for youth, whereas health care is not only a service for all ages but also the epitome of an expert-driven service. Adults often find their voices ignored in the health care system. But in the chapter on health, the authors, all health care practitioners themselves, set out a very different approach to health care that does not fit "the medical model" introduced in the juvenile justice chapter. Rather, the approach is informed by public health, a field that is more concerned with environmental influences and broad trends than with individual diagnosis and treatment. Several aspects of youth participation are reflected in this approach. One is that the health care provider following the Bright Futures protocol for individual medical treatment questions a youth patient not only about physical symptoms and obviously health-related practices, such as alcohol use, but also about school experiences, social relations, and participation in activities. Such questions help the practitioner to place strictly health-related issues in a broader context and also open that broader context for discussion in relation to improving well-being, broadly defined. Another aspect of youth participation addressed by the authors is taking youth *agency* seriously, that is, the principle that youth are active and responsible human beings who are not merely shaped by developmental influences, but are capable of selecting among those influences and guiding their own development. The *readiness to change model* and the idea of *autonomy alignment* recognize this agency. They tailor the health care provider's intervention to match the youth's definition of the situation and preferences, rather than assuming the paternalistic position of knowing what is best and taking the same approach to all youth.

Youth who enter the juvenile justice system lose most of their autonomy. The system is designed to control young people, not to build their sense of agency. However, some of the examples given in the chapter on juvenile justice illustrate how youth participation fits into even such an inhospitable context. The Unity Soccer Clinic was created with significant input from young probationers and gives them responsible roles as coaches and leaders for younger youth. The Mural Project engages young offenders and others in planning and executing large-scale works of public art and encourages experienced youth to return as leaders and mentors. The restorative justice approach, illustrated by Denver's Community Accountability Board, enables juvenile offenders to do something positive for their community, partly as a means of demonstrating their willingness to accept responsibility for the consequences of their actions.

Families are seldom thought of as settings for youth participation; they are, after all, the locus of paternalism. Yet the research on authoritative parenting clearly demonstrates the value to youth development of parents listening to their children, allowing them to contribute to family decisions, and, increasingly as they become older, to make decisions for themselves.

Perhaps the chapter on mass media and popular culture takes the strongest position on youth participation, without using that term. The vision it portrays of critical media literacy is one in which youth gain the analytical tools to understand how the media culture functions, build confidence in their ability to use those tools, become aware of the possibility of acting collectively to change others' understanding and the messages conveyed, and learn to use media for their own purposes rather than being manipulated by media for commercial purposes. This perspective should serve as a reminder that the idea of youth participation is, when carried to its logical conclusion, radically democratic. Applications of the idea that do not go so far should not be belittled, but those who accept this principle should be prepared to deal with the potentially unsettling consequences of participating in the liberation of youth.

What's Next?

The principles and practices for promoting youth development change in response to changes in the contexts in which development occurs, not just the physical locations, but the values, ideas, and assumptions that permeate them. The principles stated and illustrated in this volume reflect a view of youth as responsible, engaged, and capable in the present, as well as preparing for the future. Today, we believe all youth should thrive; historically, many have not been afforded that right. The principles interact reciprocally with reality: The more we can put them into practice, the more they hold true for more youth. Acting on the principles helps to create a world in which they are self-evident.

Acting in a manner that is consistent with a set of principles is difficult not only because we may sometimes lack the courage of our convictions but also because sometimes we simply do not know what to do to be consistent or how to apply principles to a particular situation. A major reason for including examples throughout this book has been to portray, as a colleague used to say, "What good looks like."

The current practice of youth development has been guided and inspired by adults who know what it takes and by youth who have the courage to articulate and act on their views. In recent years, a body of scientific knowledge has grown that validates what those leaders know and provides a sound basis for continuing to improve and to disseminate good practice. That knowledge is represented in this book, and many additional sources are identified. We hope that readers will consider all sources carefully but critically, comparing them with each other, with other sources, and with their personal and professional experience and judgment. The field of youth development will advance if practitioners can engage in continuing dialogue with each other and with researchers. We hope this book contributes to that dialogue.

References

Benson, P. L., & Pittman, K. J. (Eds.). (2001). *Trends in youth development: Visions, realities and challenges.* Boston: Kluwer.

Camino, L. (2001). *Evaluation as a tool in community building: Perspectives on the role of youth.* Paper presented at the annual meeting of the American Evaluation Association, St. Louis, MO. Madison, WI: University of Wisconsin-Madison, School of Human Ecology, and Camino & Associates.

Catalano, R. F., Berglund, M. L., Ryan, J. A. M, Lonczak, H. S., & Hawkins, J. D. (1998). *Positive youth development in the United States: Research findings on evaluations of positive youth development programs.* Seattle: University of Washington School of Social Work, Social Development Research Group. Available at: http://aspe.os.dhhs.gov/hsp/positiveyouthdev99/.

Chawla, L. (Ed.). (2002). *Growing up in an urbanising world.* London: UNESCO & Earthscan.

Developmental Research and Programs, Inc. (2000). *Communities That Care: Prevention strategies: A research guide to what works.* Seattle, WA: Author.

Driskell, D. (2002). *Creating better cities with children and youth: A manual for participation.* London: UNESCO & Earthscan.

DuBois D. L., Holloway B. E., Valentine J. C., & Cooper H. (2002). Effectiveness of mentoring programs for youth: A meta-analytic review. *American Journal of Community Psychology, 30,* 157-197.

Freedman, M. (1993). *The kindness of strangers: Adult mentors, urban youth, and the new volunteerism.* San Francisco: Jossey-Bass.

Gilligan, C. (1982). *In a different voice: Psychological theory and women's development.* Cambridge, MA: Harvard University Press.

Grossman, J. B., & Tierney, J. P. (1998). Does mentoring work? An impact study of the Big Brothers/Big Sisters. *Evaluation Review, 22,* 403-426.

Hart, R. A. (1997). *Children's participation: The theory and practice of involving youth citizens in community development and environmental care.* London: Earthscan.

National Research Council and Institute of Medicine. (2002). *Community programs to promote youth development.* J. Eccles & J. A. Gootman (Eds.). Board on Children, Youth, and Families, Division of Behavioral and Social Sciences and Education. Washington, DC: National Academy Press.

Nettles, S. M. (1992, April). *Coaching in community settings: A review* (Report No. 9). Baltimore, MD: The Johns Hopkins University, Center on Families, Communities, Schools and Children's Learning.

Pittman, K., & Irby, M. (1996). *Preventing problems or promoting development: Competing priorities or inseparable goals?* Baltimore, MD: International Youth Foundation.

Research America. (2003). Retrieved on March 23, 2003, from: http://www.researchamerica.org/media/briefs/spent.html.

Scales, P. C., & Leffert, N. (1999). *Developmental assets: A synthesis of the scientific research on adolescent development.* Minneapolis, MN: Search Institute.

Walker, G. (2001). The policy climate for early adolescent initiatives. In P. L. Benson & K. J. Pittman (Eds.), *Trends in youth development: Visions, realities and challenges* (chap. 3, pp. 77-90). Boston: Kluwer.

Name Index

LeBailly, S., 203
Lee, R. G., 244
Leffert, N., 9, 58, 61, 177, 181, 365
Leicester, N., 202
Lein, L., 225
Leiter, V., 92
Lerner, R. M., 193, 199
Leventhal, T., 218
Levins, L., 92
Levy, F., 152
Lewin Group, 122, 124
Lewis, J., 250
Lewis, S. S., 201
Li, S. D., 64, 65
Liau, A. K., 195
Liccio, B., 163
Lieberman, S. N., 201
Linder, G. F., 199
Lindwall, J., 194, 203
Linz, D., 242
Livingstone, S. M., 248
Lochman, J. E., 204
Lonczak, H. S., 12, 112, 194, 200, 204, 363
Lull, J., 245
Lykken, D. T., 175

Maccoby, E. E., 170, 171
MacDonald, G. B., 308
MacKenzie, D. L., 83
MacLeod, J., 228
MacMillan, R., 228
Males, M., 244
Males, M. A., 57
Mangual, F., 163
Marhall, S. K., 60
Markstrom, C. A., 60
Martens, R., 61
Martin, M., 166
Maslovaty, N., 63
Maslow, A. H., 16
Massey, D. S., 222
Mathews, T. J., 112
Matute-Bianchi, M. E., 197
May, R., 336
Mayer, R., 5
Mayer, S. E., 222, 232
Mazarella, S. R., 243
McCord, J., 193, 195, 198, 206
McDaniel, A. K., 15, 141, 142
McDonald, M., 28, 50
McGinnis, M., 85
McGue, M., 175
McGuigan, K., 182

McKenry, P. C., 173
McLanahan, S. S., 176
McLaughlin, M., 26, 28, 50
McLaughlin, M. W., 272, 296
McLellan, J., 158
McLellan, J. A., 60, 63
McMahon, P. M., 199
McMahon, R. J., 172
McMullin, I., 196
McNamara, K., 203
McNeely, C. A., 314
Mead, M., x, xi
Mediascope, 242
Meier, D., 129
Meier, K. S., 115
Melchior, A., 159
Metz, E., 158
Miller, J. Y., 84, 86
Minuchin, S., 177
Montecel, M. R., 197, 203
Moody, E. E., 201
Morenoff, J. D., 225, 230
Morest, V. S., 156
Morley, D., 248
Morris, P., 13
Mortimer, J. T., 154, 155
Motika, S., 88, 96
Mulhall, P. F., 204
Mural and Cultural Arts Program, 228–229
Murname, R. J., 152
Murphy, R., 328
Murray, L., 204, 303, 307

Nakkula, M. J., 201
National Center on Education and the Economy, 152
National Clearinghouse on Families and Youth, 335, 347
National Conference of State Legislatures, 336, 346–347
National Governors Association, 341
National Institute of Mental Health, 113
National Institute on Drug Abuse, 113
National Institute on Out-of-School Time, 340
National Research Council and Institute of Medicine, 6–7, 8, 9, 15, 25, 26, 49, 52, 154, 158, 272, 296, 302, 303, 308, 358, 365
Neighborhood Academy, 226–227
Nelson, D. W., 271, 294, 296
Nelson, S., 205, 206

U.S. Department of Education, 128,
    186, 326
U.S. Department of Health and Human
    Services, Office of Disease Prevention,
    106, 108, 109
U.S. Department of Labor, Bureau of Labor
    Statistics, 148, 153
U.S. General Accounting Office, 112, 328
United Way of America, 111, 275, 311,
    313, 332
Upchurch, D. M., 232
Urquiola, M., 156

Valdivieso, R., 308
Valentine, J. C., 203, 354
Valsiner, J., 246
Vandell, D. L., 173
VanDenBerg, J. E., 90
VanDyke, D. J., 184
Van Ingen, W. B., 62
Vazsonyi, A. T., 204
Veblen-Mortenson, S., 192, 205
Velicer, W. F., 115
Ventura, S. J., 112
Verma, S., 194, 197
Villarruel, F. A., 16
Vitaro, F., 170
Vuori, H., 105

W. K. Kellogg Foundation and the Robert
    Wood Johnson Foundation, 119
Walgrave, L., 88
Walker, G., 354
Walker, J., 68
Walker, K. E., 48, 50, 272, 296, 333, 344
Wallerstein, J. S., 175
Walsh, A. S., 63
Walsh, J., 271, 295, 296
Walsh-Childers, K., 243
Wang, C. H., 203
Wang, G., 63
Warner, K. E., 114
Warren, C., 271, 281, 284, 288,
    290, 292, 296
Warren, M. R., 226, 234
Wartella, E., 243
Washington-Steward, E., 197, 203
Wasley, P. A., 130, 135
Wasserman, J., 114
Watanabe, S., 148
Watson, B. H., 272, 296
Watts, C. L., 193, 196, 201

Waul, M., 82
Way, N., 199
Weber, M., 63
Wehlage, G., 271, 286, 296
Weir, L. H., 62
Weiss, C. H., 302, 306, 309
Wentworth, D., 92
Werner, E. E., 85
West, E., 112
White, J. A., 271, 286, 296
White, L., 68
Whiteley, M., 199, 202
Whitlock J. L., 12
Wiebush, R. G., 92
Wilcox, S., 92
Williams, C. L., 192, 205
Wilson, B. J., 242
Wilson, J. J., 82, 87
Wilson, J. Q., 228
Wilson, S., 194, 197
Wilson, W. J., 217, 218, 219, 229, 230,
    231, 232
Winner, L., 83
Wirt, J., 148
Witt, P. A., 54, 56, 62, 66, 67, 69
Worland, J., 85
World Health Organization, 103
Wray, J., 249
Wright, M., 271, 283, 284, 293, 296
Wright-Buckley, C, 200
Wynn, J. R., 289

Yates, M., 60, 63, 194
Yinger, J., 222
Yoerger, K., 198
Yogev, A., 199, 203
Yohalem, N., 6, 11
Yosso, T. J., 254
Young, A., 228, 229
Young Life Service Center, 57–58, 275
Youniss, J., 60, 63, 158, 191, 193, 194
YouthBuild, 156, 215–217, 232, 234,
    341, 367

Zamberlan, C., 83
Zeldin, R. S., 15, 141, 142
Zerkel, M., 251
Zill, N., 171
Zillmann, D., 248
Zimbardo, P., 92
Zinger, I., 82
Zuckerman, A., 156

Subject Index

social expectations, 158
social responsibility/citizenship, 159
understanding self, 158
understanding the world, 158
value expression, 158
Services for all, 12
  targeted, 12
Settlement house, 53
Sex in media, 243, 261
  girls and, 243
Small learning communities (SLCs), 134
  Philadelphia (PA), 134
Social capital, 221, 225, 229, 231, 355
  building bridges, 354
  building varieties of neighborhood,
    232–233
  definition, 221
  mentoring and, 355–356
  resources from, 221
Social capital development, linking
  economic development with, 232
Social cause service, 158
Social class, youth development and, 13
Social competence, 152, 153, 157, 159,
  160, 161
Social Development Research Group,
  University of Washington, 12, 18
Social toxicity, 173, 185
  parents combating, 175–176
Social toxicity education, 181, 187
Soft skills, 152
Special education, 83
St. Ann's Episcopal Church (NYC),
  67–68
State Youth Development Collaboration
  Programs, 334
Status offense, 76–77
STEP program, 204
Stereotyping minority youth, media,
  244–245, 261
Strong families, six attributes of, 180
Substance use. See Adolescent substance
  use, youth development and
Supports for all, 11–12
System:
  endurance, 17
  externally connected, 17
  inclusive, 17
  internally coherent, 17
System of care, 89–90
  Child and Adolescent Service System
    Program (CASSP), 91, 96
  culturally competent, 89

multiagency collaborative
  environment, 89
strength-based services, 89
See also Wraparound services

Talking With Your Kids About Tough
  Issues, 189
Teaching behaviors, "challenging," 162
Technical competence, 152, 157, 161
Teenage mothers, peer support
  interventions and, 1101
Teen Outreach Program, 113, 204
Television violence, youth and,
  242–243, 261
Temporary Assistance for Needy Families
  (TANF), 334, 338, 342
Ten Point Coalition (Boston, MA), 68
Theory of change (TOC) approach, 301,
  302, 304, 306–310, 363, 367
  as iterative, 307
  as logic model, 310
  collaborative development, 307
  conceptual foundations, 306–307
  explicit purpose, 306
  for evaluation planning, 306
  for program planning, 306
  sample application, 310–313
  surfacing/examining assumptions, 307,
    308–309
  See also Theory of change (TOC)
    approach, guiding measurement
    strategy with; Theory of change
    (TOC) approach, interpreting
    results with
Theory of change (TOC) approach, guiding
  measurement strategy with, 314–317
  prioritizing outcomes, 315
  timing of measurement, 314–315
  what to measure, 314
Theory of change (TOC) approach,
  interpreting results with, 315–317
  making case for attribution, 316
  making use of negative findings,
    316–317
Tilden High School (NYC), 139
Time Dollar Cross-Age Peer Tutoring
  program, 197, 1101, 197,
    198, 203, 360
Title I, 338
Title V, 336
Transitional Living for Homeless Youth
  Program, 332
Turning Point, 119–122

About the Editors

Stephen F. Hamilton is Professor of Human Development and Co-Director of the Family Life Development Center at Cornell University. His research and outreach support youth development, especially through 4-H, the youth component of Cooperative Extension. As a Fulbright Senior Research Fellow, he studied Germany's apprenticeship system as an institution supporting the transition to adulthood of youth without college degrees. His book, *Apprenticeship for Adulthood,* and the youth apprenticeship demonstration project he designed and led with Mary Agnes Hamilton helped to guide the School-to-Work Opportunities Act of 1994. He has also conducted research and contributed to program development related to service-learning and mentoring. He received his M.A.T. and Ed.D. from the Harvard Graduate School of Education and taught for 3 years in a Washington, D.C., vocational high school.

Mary Agnes Hamilton is a Senior Research Associate in Human Development at Cornell and Director of the Cornell Youth and Work Program in the Family Life Development Center. Hamilton taught for 4 years in public schools in Richmond, Virginia, and Montgomery County, Maryland. Her primary interests are education and adolescent development. Her research and program development focus on the quality of learning environments in the community, mentoring relationships between nonrelated adults and youth, and the transition to adulthood. She seeks to advance educational opportunities and challenges for all youth to gain character and competence. She is especially interested in those young people who do not graduate from 4-year colleges. She has an M.A.T. from Duke, C.A.S. from Harvard, and Ph.D. from Cornell.

About the Contributors

William H. Barton is Professor and Director of the Office of Research Services at the Indiana University School of Social Work, Indiana University–Purdue University in Indianapolis. He received an M.A. from Swarthmore College and his M.S.W. and Ph.D. from the University of Michigan, where he also did postdoctoral research at the Institute for Social Research and the Center for the Study of Youth Policy. Barton teaches courses in juvenile justice policy, program evaluation research methods, and the philosophy of science. His interests include juvenile justice, delinquency prevention and youth development issues, program evaluation, and needs assessment.

Catherine P. Bradshaw holds a master's degree in Counseling Psychology from the University of Georgia and is a candidate for a doctorate in Developmental Psychology at Cornell University. She is a graduate research assistant in the Family Life Development Center at Cornell and a predoctoral fellow of the National Consortium on Violence Research. Her research focuses on the development of aggressive and problem behavior in childhood and adolescence and the design and evaluation of youth development programs.

B. Bradford Brown is Professor of Human Development and former Chair of the Department of Educational Psychology at the University of Wisconsin–Madison. He received a Ph.D. in human development from the University of Chicago before joining the faculty of the University of Wisconsin in 1979. Brown's research has focused on adolescent peer relations. He is currently the Editor of the *Journal of Research on Adolescence,* and coeditor of two recent books, *The Development of Romantic Relationships in Adolescence* (with Wyndol Furman and Candice Feiring), and *The World's Youth: Adolescence in 8 Regions of the Globe* (with Reed Larson and T.S. Saraswathi).

Jane D. Brown is the James L. Knight Professor at the School of Journalism and Mass Communication at the University of North Carolina at Chapel Hill. She received her Ph.D. from the University of Wisconsin–Madison in 1978. She studies how adolescents use and are influenced by the mass media. Her current focus is on the role the media play in shaping adolescents' sexual lives. She is coeditor of *Sexual Teens, Sexual Media* (2002).

James P. Connell is the President of the Institute for Research and Reform in Education. Connell received his Ph.D. in developmental psychology from the University of Denver. He has published numerous articles on youth development and community and school influences on urban youth. He is coeditor of *New Approaches to Evaluating Community Initiatives: Concepts, Methods and Contexts* (1995) and *New Approaches to Evaluating Community Initiatives: Theory, Measurement and Analysis* (1998). Connell is developing new approaches to planning, implementing, and evaluating complex, multifaceted initiatives involving children and youth.

Sarah Deschenes is a postdoctoral fellow at the John W. Gardner Center for Youth and Their Communities at Stanford University. Her research has focused on the learning environments of youth development organizations and nonprofit organizations' roles in supporting community change for youth; her dissertation is *Lessons from the Middle: Neighborhood Reform for Youth in San Francisco*. She holds an M.A. in American history from New York University and a Ph.D. in Administration and Policy Analysis from the Stanford University School of Education.

Kathleen A. Dorgan is a practitioner of comprehensive community development. As a registered architect and planner (M.S., Pratt), she contributes to incremental strategies for neighborhood renewal and community building. Her projects are featured in *Good Neighbors, The Design Advisor,* and *Design Matters.* During her tenure as Executive Director, Capital Hill Improvement renovated 1,563 buildings and developed a rich variety of programs with residents and merchants. A Loeb, HUD, and Brown-Hazen Fellow, she is past president of the Association for Community Design, as well as a frequent speaker, university instructor, and writer on issues of design and community.

Peter Edelman served in all three branches of government before joining the faculty at Georgetown University's Law Center in 1982. A native of Minnesota, he went to Harvard College and Harvard Law School. He clerked on the Supreme Court for Justice Arthur Goldberg, worked at the Justice Department, and was a Legislative Assistant to Senator Robert Kennedy. In the 1970s he was Vice President of the University of

Massachusetts and Director of the New York State Division for Youth. After a stint in private practice, he served as Issues Director for Senator Edward Kennedy's 1980 Presidential campaign.

At Georgetown, Edelman has taught constitutional law and courses about American poverty. He served as Associate Dean and then took leave to be Counselor to HHS Secretary Donna Shalala and then Assistant Secretary for Planning and Evaluation. He is the author of *Searching for America's Heart; RFK and the Renewal of Hope*, which was recently released in paperback.

Douglas W. Elliott is a doctoral candidate in his final year of the Cornell University graduate program in Human Development. His research interests are focused on adolescent social support networks, with particular reference to the development and use of extra-familial sources of support. He is currently investigating the differences and similarities between heterosexual and sexual-minority adolescent support networks. His work is concerned with the overall structure of the support networks, as well as the process through which the youths from these two populations utilize the support offered from different members of their network.

Ronald F. Ferguson is on the faculty at Harvard University's John F. Kennedy School of Government, where he has taught since 1983, and he is Senior Research Associate at the Wiener Center for Social Policy Research. His publications cover issues in education policy, youth development programming, community development, economic consequences of skill disparities, and state and local economic development. He was a member of the National Research Council Committee on Community-Level Youth Programming that produced the volume, *Community Programs to Promote Youth Development*. He earned a Ph.D. from MIT in economics.

Michelle A. Gambone holds a Ph.D. in sociology from Princeton University. She conducts research and has published numerous reports on youth development, community mobilization, and youth policy and program effectiveness. She has contributed articles to the Aspen Roundtable series on evaluating comprehensive community initiatives and has conducted research on several community-youth development initiatives. She is currently the president of Youth Development Strategies, Inc., a not-for-profit organization that conducts and disseminates research, evaluates programs, and provides evaluation tools to youth development organizations. Gambone also continues the work of Gambone & Associates, assisting organizations in developing planning, management, and evaluation tools.

James Garbarino is Professor at the Boston College Graduate School of Social Work. Previously, he was Co-Director of the Family Life Development Center and Elizabeth Lee Vincent Professor of Human Development at Cornell, where he earned his Ph.D. His books include *And Words Can Hurt Forever: How To Protect Adolescents from Bullying, Harassment and Emotional Violence* (2003) (with Ellen deLara); *Parents Under Siege: Why You Are the Solution Not The Problem in Your Child's Life* (2001) (with Claire Bedard); *Lost Boys: Why Our Sons Turn Violent and How We Can Save Them* (1999); and *Raising Children in a Socially Toxic Environment* (1995).

Charles V. Izzo is a community psychologist, currently working as a senior research analyst with the New York State Office of Children and Family Services, Bureau of Evaluation and Research. His research focuses on understanding the factors that contribute to effective parenting practices and the pathways through which early childhood interventions produce benefits for mothers and children. He also develops and conducts trainings on program evaluation and on incorporating data into policy and program planning. He received his Ph.D. in clinical psychology from the University of Illinois at Chicago.

Michael J. Karcher is an Assistant Professor of Education and Human Development at the University of Texas–San Antonio. He earned a Ph.D. in Counseling Psychology at the University of Texas at Austin and an Ed.D. in Human Development and Psychology from Harvard University. He has trained school counselors in Wisconsin, Massachusetts, and Texas, and conducts research on developmental interventions, such as pair counseling and developmental mentoring, that promote youths' connectedness.

Richard E. Kreipe completed graduate, residency, and fellowship training at Temple University School of Medicine, St. Christopher's Hospital for Children, and the University of Rochester, respectively. He is Professor of Pediatrics and Chief of the Division of Adolescent Medicine at the University of Rochester. Dr. Kreipe directs the Rochester Leadership Education in Adolescent Health (LEAH) interdisciplinary training program. He was on the Board of Directors of the Society for Adolescent Medicine and recently completed serving as the Chair of the Adolescent Medicine Committee of the American Board of Pediatrics. His professional focus is on healthy adolescent growth and development.

Morva McDonald received her master's degree in Curriculum and Teacher Education in June 1998, and her PhD in Administration and Policy Analysis in June 2003 from Stanford University. Her dissertation, *The Integration of Social Justice: Reshaping Teacher Education,* focused on the integration of social justice and equity in teacher education and the preparation of preservice teachers to work with an increasingly diverse student population. In addition to this research focus, her professional interests include urban education, in particular students' opportunities to learn in and out of school, sociocultural theory, and the sociology of race and culture.

Milbrey McLaughlin is the David Jacks Professor of Education and Public Policy at Stanford University. Professor McLaughlin is Co-Director of the Center for Research on the Context of Teaching, an interdisciplinary research center engaged in analyses of how teaching and learning are shaped by teachers' organizational, institutional, and social cultural contexts. She is also Executive Director of the John W. Gardner Center for Youth and Their Communities, a partnership between Stanford University and Bay Area communities to build new practices, knowledge, and capacity for youth development and learning both in communities and at Stanford. Her Ph.D. is from Harvard.

Glenda L. Partee, is Codirector and President of the American Youth Policy Forum, a Washington, D.C., nonprofit, nonpartisan organization that informs policymakers and practitioners about effective interventions for youth. She has extensive policy and program experience in youth development, preparation for careers, public K-12, and higher education. She received a master's degree from the City University of New York and a Ph.D. from The Pennsylvania State University. She serves on the board of a public charter high school, the D.C. Youth Investment Council, and the executive committee of D.C. VOICE, a citizens' collaborative for reform of D.C. public education.

Karen Pittman is Executive Director of the Forum for Youth Investment and President of Impact Strategies, Inc. As the executive director of the Forum for Youth Investment, which she founded with Merita Irby in 1999, she has dedicated much of her professional career to promoting positive youth development. A sociologist, published author, and nationally recognized leader in the youth development field, Pittman's contributions range from her earliest efforts at the Urban Institute to her 1995 appointment as the director of the unfortunately short-lived President's Crime Prevention Council.

Geoffrey L. Ream is a Ph.D. Candidate in the Department of Human Development, Cornell University. He is a student Affiliate of the American Psychological Association, divisions 44 (sexual minority issues) and 36 (psychology of religion). His current work is on the role of religion in positive youth development; neighborhood influences on parenting and child outcomes; religion and sexual-minority youth; gay youth suicide; family, religion, and romantic relationships as protective factors for adolescence; and variation in youth resiliency processes based on race, sex, and sexual orientation.

LaHoma S. Romocki is a Research Associate at North Carolina Central University in Durham, North Carolina, with joint appointments at the JLC Biomedical and Biotechnology Research Institute and the Department of Health Education. She was named a 1999 Park Foundation Fellow at the School of Journalism and Mass Communication at the University of North Carolina at Chapel Hill and is currently completing dissertation research that examines black adolescent girls and their interpretations of sexual health messages on the Internet.

Sheryl A. Ryan is Associate Professor of Pediatrics at the University of Rochester, Director of Adolescent Services at Rochester General Hospital, and Training Director for the Leadership Education in Adolescent Health (LEAH) interdisciplinary training program. She received her M.D. from Yale University and completed a fellowship in Adolescent Medicine at the University of California at San Francisco and a health services research fellowship at the Johns Hopkins School of Public Health. Her current activities focus on child health services research, interpersonal violence prevention, and positive youth development, and assisting community agencies to develop programs that use models of youth development.

Rebecca Schaffer is an independent evaluation consultant with experience in the fields of early childhood education, arts-based youth development, media literacy, and multicultural education. She is currently assisting with an evaluation of the Animating Democracy Initiative, a national arts-based civic dialogue project, and is pursuing a Ph.D. in cultural anthropology at the University of North Carolina–Chapel Hill. As a research assistant at the FPG Child Development Institute, she is conducting research on children's perceptions of and negotiations around human differences. Her dissertation will focus on children's political worlds. She coauthored *The YouthARTS Handbook: Arts Programs for Youth at Risk*.

Susan M. Seibold-Simpson received her M.S. from Binghamton University in New York and a master's degree in Public Health from the State University of New York at Albany. She is currently a full-time doctoral student at the University of Rochester School of Nursing. Her area of interest is adolescent sexual risk-taking behaviors and community level interventions. She is a family nurse practitioner who maintains a part-time practice in reproductive health care. Her professional background includes serving as the Deputy Public Health Director of the Broome County Health Department in New York for 3 years.

Ray Swisher is Assistant Professor of Policy Analysis and Management at Cornell University. He earned a Ph.D. in sociology from the University of North Carolina at Chapel Hill and a master's degree in City and Regional Planning from Ohio State University. He worked as a Social Policy Analyst with the Metropolitan Human Services Commission in Columbus, Ohio. His current research focuses on neighborhood poverty, with an emphasis on adolescence and the transition to adulthood. He is particularly interested in the effects of exposure to violence on adolescent perceptions of future life chances, their own violence, and other indicators of well-being.

Lucila Vargas is a Chapman Fellow and an associate professor in the School of Journalism and Mass Communication, University of North Carolina at Chapel Hill. She received her M.A. in Latin American Studies and her Ph.D. in International Communication from the University of Texas at Austin. She edited *Women Faculty of Color in the White Classroom* and wrote *Social Uses and Radio Practices: The Use of Radio by Ethnic Minorities in Mexico*. Her current research focuses on critical media literacy and the media use of Latina immigrant young women.

Janis Whitlock is currently a doctoral candidate in Human Development at Cornell University. There, she studies adolescent development in the context of school and community environments. She is particularly interested in understanding the environmental conditions most likely to encourage healthy development, connectedness, the formation of social capital, and civic engagement. She earned a master's degree in public health from the University of North Carolina at Chapel Hill and has 15 years of experience designing, administering, and evaluating public heath initiatives for youth and their families related to the areas of sexuality, HIV, and dating violence.

Peter A. Witt is the Bradberry Professor of Recreation and Youth Development in the Department of Recreation, Park, and Tourism Sciences, Texas A&M University. He received his Ph.D. from the University of Illinois and master's degree from the University of California at Los Angeles. Witt is the author of a number of articles and books on youth development, including *Best Practices in Youth Development in Public Park and Recreation Settings* (with John Crompton). His awards and honors include the Research Excellence award from the National Recreation and Park Association. He currently edits the *Journal of Park and Recreation Administration*.

Jerome M. Ziegler is Professor and Dean Emeritus, College of Human Ecology, Cornell University. Previous to Cornell, he served as Vice President of the State University of New York, College of Old Westbury; Commissioner of Higher Education in Pennsylvania; and Chair of the Department of Urban Affairs and Policy Analysis at the New School for Social Research. He was Director of an urban Job Corps Center in New Bedford, Massachusetts and has written and consulted widely on problems of urban youth. He holds an M.A. in political science and anthropology from the University of Chicago.